FIX-IT and FORGET-IT®
5-Ingredient Favorites

More than 750 Comforting
Slow-Cooker Recipes

Phyllis Pellman Good

RODALE.

Exclusive direct mail edition published by Rodale Inc. in June 2011.

Portions of *Fix-It and Forget-It Recipes for Entertaining,*
Fix-It and Forget-It 5-Ingredient Favorites, and *Fix-It and Forget-It*
Christmas Cookbook reprinted by permission from Good Books, Intercourse, PA.

Printed in the United States of America
Rodale Inc. makes every effort to use acid-free ♾, recycled paper ♻.

Illustrations by Cheryl Benner

Book design by Christina Gaugler

Library of Congress Cataloging-in-Publication Data is on file with publisher.

ISBN 13: 978–1–60961–057–9

4 6 8 10 9 7 5 3   hardcover

For more of our products visit **rodalestore.com**
or call 800–848–4735

Contents

About *Fix-It and Forget-It 5-Ingredient Favorites*

Too little time to cook?

Worried about your skills in the kitchen?

The exclusive, expanded edition of *Fix-It and Forget-It 5-Ingredient Favorites* can be your steady kitchen companion.

This packed-full collection has more than 750 recipes, each with 5 or fewer ingredients.

And each recipe's instructions spell out every step so you won't get stranded along the way. This book makes cooking manageable.

Think of *Fix-it and Forget-It 5-Ingredient Favorites* as your inspiration and encourager. All of its recipes come from home cooks. These are their favorite dishes, loved by families and households across the country. So get out your slow cooker—or cookers—and choose from these flexible, forgiving, and absolutely scrumptious recipes.

What Qualifies as a 5-Ingredient Recipe?

Any recipe with 5—or fewer—ingredients.

1. Water does *not* count.

2. Salt and pepper count as *one* ingredient.

3. Ingredients listed as *optional* do *not* count.

4. Nonstick cooking spray does *not* count.

5. The "base" over which the recipe is to be served (for example, crackers or chips, rice, pasta, or potatoes) does *not* count.

A Word about Slow Cookers

These great little appliances can vary considerably in their heat intensity and speed of cooking. Older models often require more cooking time than newer ones. That's why we give a range of cooking times for many of the recipes. Experiment by using the shorter cooking time first. Then make a note right on the recipe page itself about what you discovered works best for your cooker. Personalize this cookbook!

Variables to Keep in Mind

Ideally, you should fill your slow cooker about two-thirds full. You may need to increase the cooking time if you've exceeded that amount, or reduce the time if you have put in less than that.

- The fuller your slow cooker, the longer it will take its contents to cook.
- The more densely packed the cooker's contents are, the longer they will take to cook.
- The larger the chunks of meat or vegetables, the longer they will take to cook.

If you put ingredients into the cooker straight out of the refrigerator, you may need to add 20–30 minutes to the cooking time.

If you put frozen meat into the cooker, you should add 4–6 hours of cooking time on Low, or 2 hours on High.

If you're using a slow cooker at an altitude over 3,500 feet, you will need to cook its contents somewhat longer than the recipe states. Allow time to experiment, and then write what worked next to the recipe.

If you want to check that the meat in your slow cooker is fully cooked, use a food thermometer:

- Beef should reach an internal temperature of 170°F.
- Pork should reach an internal temperature of 180°F.
- Poultry should reach an internal temperature of 190°F.

Don't Miss the Quickie Go-Alongs at the Back of the Book

If you want to round out a meal that has a slow-cooker main dish, turn to the Quickie Go-Alongs chapter beginning on page 363. Most of these recipes have more than 5 ingredients, but

I added them because they meet two important tests: (1) They're quick to prepare. (2) They are irresistibly delicious. Don't miss them.

Look for the Entertaining Chapter

When a special occasion dish is in order, impress your family and friends with the recipes in this exclusive Entertaining chapter on page 377. So delicious, people will think you've spent the day in the kitchen. So simple, you will want to entertain more often.

The Pass-It-On Tradition

Good cooks love to share their recipes. They don't possess them; they pass them on. This collection is rich because of all the home cooks who generously offered their favorite recipes, so that all of us could fix satisfyingly delicious food at home. Thank you to each of you who has shared your gems. This book holds your precious food traditions, and we are all grateful.

So relax and let this collection of 5-ingredient recipes be your friendly kitchen companion. Mark your favorites—but don't hesitate to keep trying new ones.

This exclusive edition of *Fix-It and Forget-It 5-Ingredient Favorites* makes it possible for you to sit at the dinner table *together*, with your family and friends, around absolutely tasty food, no matter how wild and crazy your day.

—Phyllis Pellman Good

SOUPS, STEWS, AND CHILIS

Bean and Bacon Soup

JEANETTE OBERHOLTZER • MANHEIM, PA

Prep Time: 25 minutes • Cooking Time: 11–13½ hours • Ideal slow cooker size: 4-qt.

1 ¼ cups dried bean soup mix, or any combination of mixed dried beans

5 cups water

1 onion, chopped

3 cups water

4 slices fried bacon (pre-cooked bacon works well), crumbled

1 envelope taco seasoning

2 14-oz. cans diced tomatoes, undrained

1. Place dried beans in a large stockpot. Cover with 5 cups water. Cover pot and bring to a boil. Cook 2 minutes over high heat.

2. Remove pot from heat and allow to stand, covered, 1 hour. Return pot to stovetop and cook, covered, 2½–3 hours, or until beans are tender. Drain.

3. Combine cooked beans, onion, 3 cups water, bacon, and taco seasoning in slow cooker. Mix well.

4. Cook on Low 8–10 hours.

5. Add tomatoes. Stir well. Cook another 30 minutes.

Makes 6 servings

Note: If you like a thickened soup, mash some of the beans before adding the tomatoes.

Black Bean Soup

DOROTHY VAN DEEST • MEMPHIS, TN

Prep Time: 10 minutes to precook beans • Cooking Time: 6½–8½ hours ▪ Ideal slow cooker size: 4-qt.

1 lb. dried black beans

9 cups water

3 cups water

¼ lb. bacon, fried crisp and crumbled, or ½ lb. smoked ham, chopped

2 medium-sized onions, chopped

1 tsp. garlic salt

¼ tsp. coarsely ground pepper

1. Place dried beans in large stockpot. Cover with 9 cups water. Cover pot and bring to a boil.

2. Boil 10 minutes. Reduce heat and simmer, covered, 1½ hours, or until beans are tender. Discard cooking water.

3. Combine cooked beans, 3 cups water, bacon, onions, garlic salt, and pepper in slow cooker, stirring well.

4. Cover and cook on High 4–6 hours.

Makes 8 servings

Note: To serve beans as a side dish, add a 4-oz. can of chopped green chilies, 1 tsp. powdered cumin, and ¼ tsp. dried oregano to 5–6 cups of fully cooked beans. Simmer for 25 minutes to blend flavors.

—Bonita Ensenberger, Albuquerque, NM

Holiday Soup

RUTH RETTER • MANHEIM, PA

Prep Time: 10 minutes to precook beans • Cooking Time: 6½–9 hours ▪ Ideal slow cooker size: 4-qt.

1 lb. holiday soup mix of dried beans, or your choice of 1 lb. of mixed dried beans

9 cups water

6 cups water

1 large onion, chopped

14-oz. can stewed or whole tomatoes

juice of 1 lemon

2 ham hocks

1. Place dried beans in a large stockpot and cover with 9 cups water. Cover and bring to a boil. Continue boiling 10 minutes.

2. Remove beans from heat, keeping covered. Allow to stand 1 hour.

3. Return covered pot of beans to stove and bring to a boil. Then turn to simmer and continue cooking, covered, 2½–3 hours, or until beans are soft. Drain.

4. Place drained beans in slow cooker. Add 6 cups water, onion, tomatoes, lemon juice, and ham hocks. Mix together well.

5. Cover and cook on High 3 hours, or on Low 5 hours.

6. Remove ham from bone. Cut meat into small pieces and stir into soup before serving.

Makes 12–16 servings

Beans with Tomatoes and Ham

KRISTIN TICE • SHIPSHEWANA, IN

Prep Time: 10–20 minutes • Cooking Time: 7½–9½ hours • Ideal slow cooker size: 5- to 6-qt.

3 cups dried beans (northern, navy, black, or pinto, or a combination of any of them)

12 cups water

4 cups fresh tomatoes, chopped, or 28-oz. can stewed or diced tomatoes

½ cup chopped onion

1 tsp. salt

4 cups water

2 cups ham

1. Place beans and 12 cups water in a large stockpot. Cover and bring to a boil.

2. Uncover and boil 2 minutes.

3. Cover, remove from heat, and set aside 1 hour. Drain beans.

4. Place beans in slow cooker. Add tomatoes, onion, salt, and 4 cups water.

5. Cover and cook on High 6–8 hours, or until beans are tender.

6. After beans are tender, stir in ham and cook an additional 30 minutes on Low.

Makes 10 servings

Old-Fashioned Bean Soup

SHIRLEY SEARS • SARASOTA, FL

Prep Time: 10 minutes • Cooking Time: 13–20 hours • Ideal slow cooker size: 4- to 5-qt.

1 lb. dried navy beans, soaked overnight

16 cups water, divided

1 lb. meaty ham bones, or ham pieces

1 tsp. salt

½ tsp. pepper

½ cup chopped celery leaves

1 medium-sized onion, chopped

1 bay leaf, optional

1. Place dried beans and 8 cups water in a large stockpot. Cover and allow to soak 8 hours or overnight. Drain.

2. Place soaked beans and 8 cups fresh water in slow cooker.

3. Add all remaining ingredients.

4. Cover and cook on Low 10–12 hours, or on High 5–6 hours, or until meat is falling off the bone and beans are tender but not mushy.

Makes 8-10 servings

Sauerkraut-Sausage Bean Soup

BONNIE GOERING • BRIDGEWATER, VA

Prep Time: 10 minutes • **Cooking Time:** 2–3 hours • **Ideal slow cooker size:** 3- to 4-qt.

3 15-oz. cans white beans, undrained

16-oz. can sauerkraut, drained and rinsed

1 lb. link sausage, sliced

¼ cup brown sugar

½ cup ketchup

1. Combine all ingredients in slow cooker.

2. Cover. Cook on High 2–3 hours.

3. Serve with cornbread, applesauce, or coleslaw.

Makes 8–10 servings

Note: You may add tomato juice or water if you prefer a thinner soup. Also, be aware that adding salt to dry beans before they are cooked soft will prevent them from getting soft.

Split Pea Soup with Ham

ELENA YODER • CARLSBAD, NM

Prep Time: 15 minutes • **Cooking Time:** 4 hours • **Ideal slow cooker size:** 4-qt.

2½ qts. water

1 ham hock, or pieces of cut-up ham

2½ cups split peas, dried

1 medium-sized onion, chopped

3 medium-sized carrots, cut in small pieces

salt and pepper to taste

1. Bring water to a boil in a saucepan on stovetop.

2. Place all other ingredients into slow cooker. Add boiling water and stir together well.

3. Cover and cook on High 4 hours, or until vegetables are tender.

4. If you've cooked a ham hock, remove it from soup and debone the meat. Stir cut-up chunks of meat back into soup before serving.

Makes 8 servings

Italian Bean Soup

EYLENE EGAN • BABYLON, NY

Prep Time: 10 minutes • Cooking Time: 8–10 hours • Ideal slow cooker size: 4-qt.

1 lb. dried baby lima beans

9 cups water

2 8-oz. cans tomato sauce

3–4 cloves garlic, minced

6 cups water

salt and pepper to taste

1. Place dried beans in a large stockpot. Cover with 9 cups water. Cover pot and bring to a boil.

2. Boil 10 minutes. Remove from heat and allow beans to stand 1 hour, covered.

3. Return to stovetop, keep covered, and bring to a boil. Reduce heat to a simmer, and continue cooking 2½–3 hours, or until beans are tender. Drain.

4. Place drained, cooked beans in slow cooker. Add remaining ingredients and stir together well.

5. Cover and cook on High 1 hour, and then cook on Low 4–5 hours.

Makes 8 servings

Mountain Bike Soup

JONATHAN GEHMAN • HARRISONBURG, VA

Prep Time: 10 minutes • Cooking Time: 2–6 hours • Ideal slow cooker size: 2- or 3-qt.

12-oz. can chicken broth

12-oz. can V8 juice, regular or spicy

⅓ cup uncooked barley, rice, or broken spaghetti noodles

⅓ cup chopped pepperoni, ham, or bacon

15-oz. can cut green beans with liquid

1. Dump all ingredients into slow cooker. Put on lid. Turn cooker on Low.

2. Go for a long ride on your bike, from 2–6 hours.

Makes 4 servings

Note: This soup seems to accept whatever vegetables you throw in: a little corn, okra, diced potatoes, shredded zucchini, whatever. . . . I often add more liquid before serving if it seems to be getting more like stew and less like soup.

Smoked Sausage Stew

CAROL SHERWOOD • BATAVIA, NY

Prep Time: 35–40 minutes ▪ Cooking Time: 4–5 hours ▪ Ideal slow cooker size: 5-qt.

4-5 potatoes, peeled and
   cubed

2 15-oz. cans green beans

1 lb. smoked sausage, sliced

1 onion, chopped

2 Tbsp. butter

1. Layer potatoes, green beans, sausage, and onion in slow cooker in the order listed.

2. Dot top with butter.

3. Cook on Low 4–5 hours, or until potatoes are tender but not mushy.

Makes 4–5 servings

Toscano Soup

SHEILA SOLDNER • LITITZ, PA

Prep Time: 20–25 minutes ▪ Cooking Time: 6–8 hours ▪ Ideal slow cooker size: 4-qt.

2 medium-sized russet
   potatoes

1 lb. spicy Italian sausage

5$\frac{1}{2}$ cups chicken stock, or
   low-sodium chicken broth

2 cups chopped kale

$\frac{1}{2}$ tsp. crushed red pepper
   flakes, optional

$\frac{1}{2}$ cup cream, or evaporated
   milk

1. Cut potatoes into $\frac{1}{2}$" cubes. Place in slow cooker.

2. Grill, broil, or brown sausage in a nonstick skillet. When cool enough to handle, cut into $\frac{1}{2}$"-thick slices.

3. Add sliced sausage to slow cooker. Stir in all remaining ingredients, except cream.

4. Cover and cook on Low 6–8 hours.

5. Fifteen to 20 minutes before serving, add cream or evaporated milk, and cook until soup is heated through.

Makes 4–6 servings

Note: If you don't want the soup to be too spicy, use $\frac{1}{2}$ lb. sweet sausage and $\frac{1}{2}$ lb. spicy sausage.

Hearty Lentil and Sausage Stew

CINDY KRESTYNICK • GLEN LYON, PA

Prep Time: 5–10 minutes • Cooking Time: 4–6 hours • Ideal slow cooker size: 6-qt.

2 cups dry lentils, picked over
and rinsed

14½-oz. can diced tomatoes

8 cups canned chicken broth,
or water

1 Tbsp. salt

½–1 lb. pork or beef sausage,
cut into 2" pieces

1. Place lentils, tomatoes, chicken broth, and salt in slow cooker. Stir to combine. Place sausage pieces on top.

2. Cover and cook on Low 4–6 hours, or until lentils are tender but not dry or mushy.

Makes 6 servings

Sauerkraut Soup

NORMA GRIESER • CLARKSVILLE, MI

Prep Time: 10 minutes • Cooking Time: 4–6 hours • Ideal slow cooker size: 3- to 4-qt.

2 14½-oz. cans stewed
tomatoes

2 cups sauerkraut

1 cup diced potatoes

1 lb. fresh or smoked sausage,
sliced

OPTIONAL INGREDIENTS:

1 medium-sized onion,
chopped

⅓ cup brown sugar

1. Combine all ingredients in slow cooker.

2. Cover and cook on Low 4–6 hours, or until flavors have blended and soup is thoroughly heated.

Makes 4 servings

Pork-Veggie Stew

RUTH E. MARTIN • LOYSVILLE, PA

Prep Time: 15 minutes • Cooking Time: 6 hours • Ideal slow cooker size: 4-qt.

2 lbs. boneless pork loin, cut into 1" cubes

8 medium-sized potatoes, peeled and cut into 2" pieces

6 large carrots, peeled and cut into 2" pieces

1 cup ketchup

2¼ cups water, divided

1. Brown pork cubes in a large nonstick skillet.

2. Lightly spray slow cooker with nonstick cooking spray.

3. Place all ingredients except ketchup and ¼ cup water in slow cooker.

4. Cover and cook on High 5 hours. One hour before serving, combine ketchup with ¼ cup water. Pour over stew. Cook 1 more hour.

Makes 8 servings

Notes:

• To prevent potatoes from turning black or discoloring, toss in water with a small amount of cream of tartar (6 cups water to 1 tsp. cream of tartar).

• Try to have vegetable and meat pieces all cut about the same size and thickness. Pieces of uniform size tend to finish cooking at the same time.

—Mary Puskar, Forest Hill, MD

Pork Potato Stew

KRISTIN TICE • SHIPSHEWANA, IN

Prep Time: 20 minutes • Cooking Time: 4 hours • Ideal slow cooker size: 3-qt.

1 lb. ground pork

½ cup onion, chopped

1 sweet potato, cubed and peeled, approximately 3 cups

2 beef bouillon cubes

½ tsp. dried rosemary

3 cups water

1. Place meat and onion in a nonstick skillet. Brown on stovetop.

2. Place drained meat, along with onion, into slow cooker. Add remaining ingredients.

3. Cover and cook on Low 4 hours.

Makes 4 servings

Note: Add a bit of hot sauce to make the soup spicy, or serve on the side to accommodate those who don't like hot food.

Chili-Taco Soup

FRANCES L. KRUBA • DUNDALK, MD

Prep Time: 25–30 minutes • Cooking Time: 5–7 hours • Ideal slow cooker size: 1- to 2-qt.

2 lbs. lean stew meat

2 15-oz. cans stewed tomatoes, Mexican or regular

1 envelope dry taco seasoning mix

2 15-oz. cans pinto beans

15-oz. can whole-kernel corn

¾ cup water

1. Cut large pieces of stew meat in half and brown in a large nonstick skillet.

2. Combine all ingredients in slow cooker.

3. Cover and cook on Low 5–7 hours.

   Makes 8 servings

Beef and Black-Eyed Pea Soup

JEANETTE OBERHOLTZER • MANHEIM, PA

Prep Time: 25 minutes • Cooking Time: 8–10 hours • Ideal slow cooker size: 6 qt.

16-oz. pkg. dried black-eyed peas

10-oz. can condensed bean and bacon soup

3–4 cups water

4 large carrots, peeled and sliced

3-lb. beef chuck roast, cut into 2″ cubes

½ tsp. each salt and pepper

1. Rinse and drain peas.

2. Combine all ingredients in slow cooker.

3. Cook on Low 8–10 hours, or until peas and beef are tender.

   Makes 6 servings

Variation: For added flavor, add chopped onion and minced garlic, or a 14½-oz. can chopped tomatoes, to Step 2.

Busy Cook's Stew

DENISE NICKEL • GOESSEL, KS

Prep Time: 30–40 minutes • Cooking Time: 6–8 hours • Ideal slow cooker size: 3-qt.

1 lb. boneless stew meat, cut up

10¾-oz. can cream of
   mushroom soup

2 cups water

3 potatoes, cubed

3 carrots, diced

1 onion, chopped

1. Brown meat in a large nonstick skillet. Don't crowd skillet; be sure meat browns on all sides. (If your skillet is 10" or smaller, brown beef in 2 batches.)

2. Place meat in slow cooker. Add remaining ingredients in the order listed. Stir well after each addition.

3. Cover and cook on Low 6–8 hours, or until meat and vegetables are tender but not mushy. Stir occasionally.

Makes 4–6 servings

Note: If you wish, add salt and pepper to taste.

Beef Barley Soup

STACIE SKELLY • MILLERSVILLE, PA

Prep Time: 15 minutes • Cooking Time: 9¼–11½ hours • Ideal slow cooker size: 6-qt.

3-4-lb. chuck roast

2 cups carrots, chopped

6 cups vegetable, or tomato,
   juice, divided

2 cups quick-cook barley

water, to desired consistency

salt and pepper to taste,
   optional

1. Place roast, carrots, and 4 cups juice in slow cooker.

2. Cover and cook on Low 8–10 hours.

3. Remove roast. Place on a platter and cover with foil to keep warm.

4. Meanwhile, add barley to slow cooker. Stir well. Turn heat to High and cook 45 minutes to 1 hour, or until barley is tender.

5. While barley is cooking, cut meat into bite-sized pieces.

6. When barley is tender, return chopped beef to slow cooker. Add 2 cups juice, water if you wish, and salt and pepper, if you want. Cook 30 minutes on High, or until soup is heated through.

Makes 8–10 servings

Easy Slow-Cooker Vegetable Soup

BETH PEACHEY • BELLEVILLE, PA

Prep Time: 10 minutes • Cooking Time: 6–8 hours • Ideal slow cooker size: 3-qt.

1 cup carrots, chopped or
sliced

1 cup green beans, fresh,
frozen, or canned

1 cup corn, fresh, frozen, or
canned, and drained

1 qt. canned tomatoes

1 cup cooked beef, cut in
bite-sized pieces

1. Combine all ingredients in slow cooker.

2. Cover and cook on Low 6–8 hours, or until vegetables are
tender.

   Makes 8–10 servings

Beef Vegetable Soup

MARGARET MOFFITT • BARTLETT, TN

Prep Time: 15 minutes • Cooking Time: 6–8 hours • Ideal slow cooker size: 4-qt.

1 lb. stewing beef, cut into
chunks

28-oz. can stewed tomatoes,
undrained

1 tomato can water

16-oz. pkg. of your favorite
frozen vegetable

half a 10-oz. pkg. frozen
chopped onions

$1\frac{1}{2}$ tsp. salt and $\frac{1}{4}$–$\frac{1}{2}$ tsp.
pepper

2 Tbsp. chopped fresh parsley,
optional

1. Combine all ingredients in slow cooker.

2. Cover and cook on High 6–8 hours.

   Makes 12 servings

Note: Double this recipe (using a 7- to 8-qt. slow cooker). Freeze
any leftovers for a quick second meal.

Homemade Beef Soup

ELEANOR LARSON • GLEN LYON, PA

Prep Time: 10 minutes • **Cooking Time:** 3 hours • **Ideal slow cooker size:** 12-qt., or 2 6-qt. cookers

2 lbs. beef cubes

2 onions, chopped or sliced

2 16-oz. bags frozen
   vegetables

6 potatoes, cubed

6 beef bouillon cubes

5 cups water

1. Heat slow cooker to High. Brown beef cubes and onions in slow cooker, stirring frequently.

2. Stir in frozen vegetables and potatoes. Stir in bouillon cubes and water.

3. Cover and cook on Low 3 hours, or until meat is tender and vegetables are cooked to your liking. (Cooking it longer makes it even more tasty!)

Makes 6–8 servings

Note: Add more flavor by stirring in salt and pepper to taste, and/or fresh parsley, basil, and thyme.

Ground Beef Bean Soup

DALE PETERSON • RAPID CITY, SD

Prep Time: 25 minutes • **Cooking Time:** 3–4 hours • **Ideal slow cooker size:** 6-qt.

2 lbs. ground beef

3 15-oz. cans pinto beans,
   drained

2 10¾-oz. cans tomato soup

10¾-oz. can cheddar cheese
   soup

salt and pepper to taste

1. Brown beef in a large nonstick skillet. Drain.

2. Place browned beef in slow cooker. Add remaining ingredients and mix well.

3. Cover and cook on Low 3–4 hours, or until soup is hot and flavors have blended.

Makes 8 servings

Chili with Two Beans

PATRICIA FLEISCHER • CARLISLE, PA

Prep Time: 15 minutes • Cooking Time: 4½–5 hours • Ideal slow cooker size: 6-qt.

1 lb. ground beef

6-oz. can tomato paste

40½-oz. can kidney beans, undrained

2 15½-oz. cans pinto beans, undrained

2 Tbsp. chili powder

1. Brown beef in a large nonstick skillet. Drain.

2. Combine all ingredients in slow cooker.

3. Cover and cook on Low 4½–5 hours.

   Makes 6–8 servings

Extra Easy Chili

JENNIFER GEHMAN • HARRISBURG, PA

Prep Time: 10 minutes • Cooking Time: 4–8 hours • Ideal slow cooker size: 4-qt.

1 lb. ground beef or turkey, uncooked

1 envelope dry chili seasoning mix

16-oz. can chili beans in sauce

2 28-oz. cans crushed or diced tomatoes seasoned with garlic and onion

1. Crumble meat in bottom of slow cooker.

2. Add remaining ingredients. Stir.

3. Cover. Cook on High 4–6 hours, or on Low 6–8 hours. Stir halfway through cooking time.

4. Serve over white rice, topped with shredded cheddar cheese and chopped raw onions.

   Makes 4–6 servings

Note: I decided to make this chili recipe one year for Christmas. Our family was hosting other family members—and we had had guests for about a week prior to Christmas. Needless to say, I was tired of cooking, so this seemed easy enough. It was so nice to put the ingredients in the slow cooker and let the dish cook all day long. Not only did the chili warm us up on a cold day, but it was a welcome change from the traditional Christmas meal. It has been my tradition ever since!

Mexican Chili Mix and Fritos

MELANIE THROWER • MCPHERSON, KS

Prep Time: 10–15 minutes • Cooking Time: 4 hours • Ideal slow cooker size: 2- to 3-qt.

1 lb. ground beef

14 3/4-16-oz. can cream-style
corn, drained

1/2 cup chunky picante sauce

16-oz. can pinto or black
beans, drained

half an envelope dry taco
seasoning

1. Brown ground beef in a large nonstick skillet. Drain.

2. Mix beef, corn, picante sauce, beans, and taco seasoning
in slow cooker.

3. Cover and cook on Low 4 hours.

4. Serve over corn chips with optional garnishes of shredded
cheese, chopped olives, sour cream, and salsa.

Makes 4–6 servings

Note: I like to substitute ground elk or venison for the beef in
this recipe.

Easy Spicy Chili

BECKY GEHMAN • BERGTON, VA

Prep Time: 15 minutes • Cooking Time: 4–10 hours • Ideal slow cooker size: 4- to 5-qt.

2 lbs. lean ground beef

3 15 1/2-oz. cans red kidney
beans, drained

2-3 14 1/2-oz. cans diced
tomatoes, undrained

2 onions, chopped

1 green pepper, chopped,
optional

2-3 Tbsp. chili powder

1. Brown ground beef in a large nonstick skillet. Drain.

2. Place beef in slow cooker. Add kidney beans, tomatoes,
onions, and green pepper, if you wish, to cooker. Fold
together well.

3. Cover and cook on Low 8–10 hours, or on High 4–6 hours.

4. Add chili powder 2 hours before end of cooking time.

Makes 9–12 servings

Note: This can be successfully frozen and reheated later. You may
want to pass salt and pepper as you serve the chili. You may add
about 2 Tbsp. of flour along with the chili powder in Step 4 if you
want to thicken the chili.

Versatile Slow-Cooker Chili

MARGARET MOFFITT • BARTLETT, TN

Prep Time: 25 minutes ▪ Cooking Time: 6 hours ▪ Ideal slow cooker size: 3-qt.

1 lb. ground beef, or turkey

2 15-oz. cans tomato sauce

2 15-oz. cans kidney beans or black beans, drained

1 envelope dry chili seasoning

15-oz. can water, or more or less

1. Brown ground beef or turkey in a nonstick skillet. Drain.

2. Combine all ingredients in slow cooker.

3. Cover and cook on Low 6 hours.

Makes 6–8 servings

Notes:
▪ If you do not have time to brown your ground beef or turkey, just put it in your slow cooker without browning it. It will cook sufficiently during the 6 hours.

Flavorful Chili

SHARON HANNABY • FREDERICK, MD

Prep Time: 15–20 minutes ▪ Cooking Time: 6–8 hours ▪ Ideal slow cooker size: 5- to 6-qt.

2 lbs. ground beef

52-oz. can kidney beans, rinsed and drained

2 28-oz. cans diced tomatoes with garlic, basil, and oregano

2–3 Tbsp. chili powder, or 2–3 tsp. Tabasco sauce, according to your preference for heat

10½-oz. can tomato soup

1. Brown beef in a large nonstick skillet, breaking up chunks of meat. Drain.

2. Place in slow cooker. Mix in all other ingredients.

3. Cover and cook on Low 6–8 hours.

Makes 10–12 servings

Note: Serve over baked potatoes or rice. Or serve with chopped scallions or onions, shredded cheese, and sour cream as toppings.

Cooking Tip

Keep hot dishwater in the sink so you can clean up the kitchen as you go and while the food is baking or cooking.

Chunky Chili

ELEANOR LARSON • GLEN LYON, PA

Prep Time: 10 minutes • Cooking Time: 4–5 hours • Ideal slow cooker size: 3-qt.

1½ lbs. cubed beef stew meat, or venison

1 medium-sized onion, chopped

1 or 2 8-oz. cans tomato sauce, depending upon how thick or thin you prefer chili to be

1½–3 tsp. chili powder, depending upon your taste preference

16-oz. can kidney beans, drained

1. Place all ingredients in slow cooker. Mix well.

2. Cover and cook on High 4–5 hours, or until meat is tender but not over-cooked.

Makes 4–5 servings

Beef and Beans

MARGARET H. MOFFITT • BARTLET, TN

Prep Time: 20–25 minutes • Cooking Time: 4–6 hours • Ideal slow cooker size: 3-qt.

1½ lbs. ground beef

15-oz. can tomato sauce with garlic and onion

2 15-oz. cans kidney beans, undrained

salt and pepper to taste

1. Brown beef in a nonstick skillet, just until the pink is gone. Drain.

2. Place beef in bottom of slow cooker.

3. Add tomato sauce, beans, and salt and pepper.

4. Cover and cook on Low 4–6 hours.

Makes 4–6 servings

Variation: For a juicier dish to serve over rice, use two cans of tomato sauce.

Cooking Tip

Put your cooker meal together the night before you want to cook it. The following morning, put the mixture in the slow cooker, cover, and cook.

—*Sara Wilson, Blairstown, MO*

Green Chili Stew

COLLEEN KONETZNI • RIO RANCHO, NM

Prep Time: 30 minutes • Cooking Time: 6–8 hours • Ideal slow cooker size: 4-qt.

1 lb. ground beef

6 potatoes, peeled and cubed

1 onion, sliced

salt and pepper to taste

¾ cup chopped green chilies

OPTIONAL INGREDIENTS:

1 tsp. garlic powder

1 bouillon cube

1. Brown ground beef in a nonstick skillet. Drain. Place in slow cooker.

2. Add remaining ingredients to slow cooker. Stir together thoroughly.

3. Cover and cook on Low 6–8 hours, or until vegetables are tender.

Makes 4 servings

Chili Pie

ANDREA CUNNINGHAM • ARLINGTON, KS

Prep Time: 15 minutes • Cooking Time: 6–8 hours • Ideal slow cooker size: 4- to 6-qt.

1 lb. ground beef

2 12-oz. cans chili beans, drained

4 large tomatoes, diced

salt and pepper to taste

OPTIONAL INGREDIENTS:

1 Tbsp. chili powder

small onion, chopped

corn chips

1½ cups shredded cheese of your choice

1. Brown ground beef in a nonstick skillet. Drain.

2. Spray slow cooker with nonstick cooking spray. Combine ground beef, chili beans, tomatoes, and any optional ingredients you want in cooker.

3. Cover and cook on Low 6–8 hours.

4. Serve over corn chips and top with cheddar cheese, if you wish.

Makes 6 servings

Taco Soup

NORMA GRIESER • CLARKSVILLE, MI

Prep Time: 10–12 minutes • Cooking Time: 4–6 hours • Ideal slow cooker size: 3-qt.

1 lb. ground beef

1 qt. tomato juice

15-oz. can kidney beans

1 envelope dry taco seasoning

10½-oz. can tomato soup

1 medium-sized onion,
    chopped, optional

1. Brown beef in a nonstick skillet. Drain. Place in slow cooker.

2. Add remaining ingredients to slow cooker and stir until well combined.

3. Cover and cook on Low 4–6 hours.

Makes 4–6 servings

Note: Serve with Doritos, sour cream, and shredded cheddar cheese as toppings, if you wish.

Taco Pizza-Sauce Soup

MARY E. SHROCK • SUGARCREEK, OH

Prep Time: 30 minutes • Cooking Time: 30 minutes • Ideal slow cooker size: 4-qt.

2 lbs. ground beef

1 small onion, chopped

1 Tbsp. taco seasoning

16-oz. can refried beans, or
    chili beans

3 qts. pizza sauce

salt and pepper to taste,
    optional

1. Brown meat with onion in a large nonstick skillet. Drain.

2. Place browned beef and onions in slow cooker. Add taco seasoning, and then beans. Stir in pizza sauce and additional seasonings, if you wish.

3. Simmer on High 30 minutes. Turn to Low and keep warm until ready to serve.

Makes 8 servings

Note: If the soup is too thick, add water or more pizza sauce. Serve with sour cream, shredded cheese, and tortilla chips.

Veggie-Beef Soup

CHAR HAGNER • MONTAGUE, MI

Prep Time: 10 minutes • Cooking Time: 3–8 hours • Ideal slow cooker size: 4- to 5-qt.

1 lb. ground beef

14½-oz. can beef broth

1½ cups water

10-oz. pkg. frozen mixed
   vegetables

14½-oz. can diced tomatoes

1 Tbsp. dried minced onion

1. Brown meat in a nonstick skillet. Drain.

2. Place all ingredients in slow cooker.

3. Cover and cook on Low 6–8 hours, or on High 3–4 hours.

Makes 6 servings

Variation: Stir in 1 cup dry macaroni 1 hour before the end of the cooking time.

Ground Beef Vegetable Soup

RENEE BAUM • CHAMBERSBURG, PA / JANET OBERHOLTZER • EPHRATA, PA

Prep Time: 15 minutes • Cooking Time: 8–9 hours • Ideal slow cooker size: 5-qt.

1 lb. ground beef

46-oz. can tomato, or V8, juice

16-oz. pkg. frozen mixed
   vegetables, thawed

2 cups frozen cubed hash
   browns, thawed

1 envelope dry onion soup mix

1. Brown beef in a nonstick skillet. Drain.

2. Place beef in slow cooker. Stir in remaining ingredients.

3. Cover and cook on Low 8–9 hours, or until vegetables are cooked through.

Makes 10 servings

Tomato Pea Soup

RUTH ANN PENNER • HILLSBORO, KS

Prep Time: 10–12 minutes • Cooking Time: 2 hours • Ideal slow cooker size: 3-qt.

1 lb. ground beef

¼ cup dried onions

5- or 10-oz. can diced
   tomatoes, depending upon
   how much you like
   tomatoes

15-oz. can peas

half a tomato can water

2 beef bouillon cubes

1. Brown beef in a nonstick skillet. Drain.

2. Combine all ingredients in slow cooker.

3. Cover and cook on High 2 hours, stirring occasionally.

   Makes 4 servings

Campfire Stew

SHARON WANTLAND • MENOMONEE FALLS, WI

Prep Time: 15 minutes • Cooking Time: 2–3 hours • Ideal slow cooker size: 2-qt.

1 lb. ground beef

1 medium-sized onion,
   chopped

half a green pepper, chopped

salt and pepper to taste

2 cans vegetable soup, your
   favorite variety

1. Brown ground beef with onion and green pepper in a
   nonstick skillet, stirring until crumbly. Drain.

2. Combine all ingredients in slow cooker.

3. Cover and cook on Low 2–3 hours.

   Makes 4 servings

Quick Taco Chicken Soup

KAREN WAGGONER • JOPLIN, MO

Prep Time: 5 minutes ▪ Cooking Time: 1 hour ▪ Ideal slow cooker size: 4-qt.

12-oz. can cooked chicken, undrained

14-oz. can chicken broth

16-oz. jar mild thick-and-chunky salsa

15-oz. can ranch-style beans

15-oz. can whole-kernel corn

1. Mix all ingredients in slow cooker.

2. Cover and cook on High 1 hour. Keep warm on Low until ready to serve.

Makes 4–6 servings

Buffalo Chicken Wing Soup

MARY LYNN MILLER • REINHOLDS, PA / DONNA NEITER • WAUSAU, WI
JOETTE DROZ • KALONA, IA

Prep Time: 10 minutes ▪ Cooking Time: 4–5 hours ▪ Ideal slow cooker size: 3-qt.

6 cups milk

3 10¾-oz. cans condensed cream of chicken soup, undiluted

3 cups (about 1 lb.) shredded or cubed cooked chicken

1 cup (8 ozs.) sour cream

1–8 Tbsp. hot pepper sauce, according to your preference for heat!

1. Combine milk and soups in slow cooker until smooth.

2. Stir in chicken.

3. Cover and cook on Low 3¾–4¾ hours.

4. Fifteen minutes before serving, stir in sour cream and hot sauce.

5. Cover and continue cooking just until bubbly.

Makes 8 servings

Note: Start with a small amount of hot sauce, and then add more to suit your—and your diners'—tastes!

Split Pea with Chicken Soup

MARY E. WHEATLEY • MASHPEE, MA

Prep Time: 20 minutes • Cooking Time: 4–10 hours • Ideal slow cooker size: 5-qt.

16-oz. pkg. dried split peas

¾ cup finely diced carrots

3 cups cubed raw potatoes

8 cups chicken broth

1 cup diced cooked chicken

1. Combine peas, carrots, potatoes, and chicken broth in slow cooker.

2. Cook on High 4–5 hours, or on Low 8–10 hours, or until all vegetables are tender. Stir after soup begins to slowly boil.

3. Ten minutes before serving, stir in cooked chicken.

Makes 6–8 servings

Chunky Chicken Vegetable Soup

JANICE MULLER • DERWOOD, MD

Prep Time: 20 minutes • Cooking Time: 2–6 hours • Ideal slow cooker size: 3½- to 4-qt.

2½ cups water

8-oz. can tomato sauce

10-oz. pkg. frozen mixed vegetables, partially thawed

1½ tsp. Italian seasoning

1 envelope dry chicken noodle soup mix

2 cups cut-up cooked chicken or turkey

1. Combine all ingredients in slow cooker.

2. Cook on Low 2–6 hours, depending upon how crunchy you like your vegetables.

Makes 6 servings

Mary's Chicken and Rice Soup

BECKY FREY • LEBANON, PA

Prep Time: 10–20 minutes • Cooking Time: 3–4 hours • Ideal slow cooker size: 3½-qt.

4.4-oz. pkg. chicken-flavored
rice and sauce

2 cups diced, cooked chicken

15-oz. can diced tomatoes and
green chilies

49½-oz. can chicken broth

1. Prepare rice and sauce according to package directions.

2. Place all ingredients in slow cooker. Stir until well mixed.

3. Cover and cook on Low 3–4 hours.

Makes 8–10 servings

Note: If you can't find tomatoes with chilies, add a 4-oz. can of diced green chilies. Or add them anyway for extra heat. Also, you can add the rice and sauce without preparing them according to their package directions. Just stir them in uncooked, and simmer the soup an hour longer in the slow cooker, or until the rice is thoroughly cooked. Serve the soup over corn chips and sprinkle with shredded cheese, if you wish.

Chicken Noodle Soup

JEAN BUTZER • BATAVIA, NY

Prep Time: 15 minutes • Cooking Time: 3½–8½ hours • Ideal slow cooker size: 4-qt.

2 10¾-oz. cans creamy
chicken mushroom soup

5 cups water

2 cups chopped cooked
chicken

10-oz. pkg. frozen mixed
vegetables

½–1 tsp. pepper

1½ cups dried egg noodles

1. Place soup in slow cooker. Blend in water. Stir in chicken, vegetables, and pepper.

2. Cover and cook on Low 6–8 hours, or on High 3–4 hours.

3. Turn to High if using Low setting. Stir in noodles.

4. Cover and cook another 20–30 minutes, or until noodles are just tender.

Makes 6–8 servings

Note: You may substitute other flavors of cream soups; and/or you may use chicken broth in place of all, or part of, the water.

Chicken Rice Soup

NORMA GRIESER • CLARKSVILLE, MI

Prep Time: 30 minutes • Cooking Time: 4–8 hours • Ideal slow cooker size: 4- to 6-qt.

4 cups chicken broth

4 cups cut-up chicken, cooked

1⅓ cups cut-up celery

1⅓ cups diced carrots

1 qt. water

1 cup uncooked long-grain rice

1. Put all ingredients in slow cooker.

2. Cover and cook on Low 4–8 hours, or until vegetables are cooked to your liking.

Makes 8 servings

Tasty Chicken Soup

RHONDA FREED • LOWVILLE, NY

Prep Time: 10–15 minutes • Cooking Time: 6–7 hours • Ideal slow cooker size: 4-qt.

12 cups chicken broth

2 cups chicken, cooked and
cut into small pieces

1 cup shredded carrots

small onion

3 whole cloves

16-oz. bag dry noodles,
cooked, optional

1. Place broth, chicken, and carrots in slow cooker.

2. Peel onion. Using a toothpick, poke 3 holes on the cut ends. Carefully press cloves into the holes until only their round part shows. Add to slow cooker.

3. Cover and cook on High 6–7 hours.

4. If you'd like a thicker soup, add a bag of cooked fine egg noodles before serving.

Makes 12 servings

Note: You can make the broth and cook the chicken in your slow cooker, too. Just put 2–3 lbs. cut-up chicken pieces into the slow cooker. Add 12 cups water. Cook on High 4–5 hours, or until chicken is tender and falling off the bone. Remove the chicken with a slotted spoon. Debone when cooled enough to handle. Measure 2 cups chicken meat and return to slow cooker. Completely cool the remaining chicken and freeze or refrigerate for future use. Continue with the recipe above to make the soup.

Vegetable Chicken Soup

ANNABELLE UNTERNAHRER • SHIPSHEWANA, IN

Prep Time: 10 minutes • Cooking Time: 4–8 hours • Ideal slow cooker size: 5-qt.

2 14½-oz. cans chicken broth

1 Tbsp. dried, minced onion

16-oz. pkg. frozen mixed
    vegetables

2 cups precooked chicken
    breast, cubed

2 10¾-oz. cans cream of
    chicken soup

1. Combine broth, onion, vegetables, and chicken in slow cooker.

2. Cover and cook on Low 3–7 hours, depending upon how crunchy you like your vegetables.

3. Add chicken soup and continue cooking 1 more hour.

4. Stir and serve.

Makes 6 servings

Note: Don't allow the mixture to boil after adding the cream of chicken soup. For a heartier meal, serve over steamed rice, allowing about ½ cup cooked rice for each serving.

Chinese Chicken Soup

KAREN WAGGONER • JOPLIN, MO

Prep Time: 5 minutes • Cooking Time: 1–2 hours • Ideal slow cooker size: 4-qt.

3 14½-oz. cans chicken broth

16-oz. pkg. frozen stir-fry
    vegetable blend

2 cups cooked cubed chicken

1 tsp. minced fresh ginger

1 tsp. soy sauce

1. Mix all ingredients in slow cooker.

2. Cover and cook on High 1–2 hours, depending upon how crunchy or soft you like your vegetables.

Makes 6 servings

Creamy Corn and Turkey Soup

JANESSA HOCHSTEDLER • EAST EARL, PA

Prep Time: 15 minutes ▪ Cooking Time: 3–8 hours ▪ Ideal slow cooker size: 3-qt.

2 cups shredded cooked
    turkey

1 cup milk

2 cups chicken broth

15-oz. can Mexican-style corn

4 ozs. (half an 8-oz. pkg.)
    cream cheese, cubed

1 red bell pepper, chopped,
    optional

1. Place all ingredients in slow cooker.

2. Cover and cook on Low 7–8 hours, or on High 3 hours.

   Makes 5–6 servings

Easy Turkey Chili

DEE SNYDER • LINDENWOLD, NJ

Prep Time: 10–15 minutes ▪ Cooking Time: 6–8 hours ▪ Ideal slow cooker size: 5-qt.

2 1-lb. rolls ground turkey
    (found in freezer case of
    grocery store), thawed

2 15½-oz. cans red kidney
    beans, drained

2 envelopes dry chili
    seasoning mix

24-oz. jar salsa

OPTIONAL INGREDIENTS:

1 large onion, chopped

1 large bell pepper, chopped

1. Place turkey in slow cooker. Break it up with a spoon into small chunks.

2. Add remaining ingredients to slow cooker. Stir together until thoroughly mixed.

3. Cover and cook on Low 6–8 hours.

   Makes 6 servings

Note: Do not add water. This versatile dish can be served over baked potatoes, spaghetti, noodles, rice, hot dogs, or tortilla chips. If you wish, you can top individual servings with grated sharp cheese.

Quick Clam and Corn Chowder

CAROL L. STROH • AKRON, NY

Prep Time: 5–10 minutes ▪ Cooking Time: 3–4 hours ▪ Ideal slow cooker size: 1½- to 2-qt.

2 10½-oz. cans cream of
  potato soup

1 pint frozen corn

6½-oz. can minced clams,
  drained

2 soup cans milk

1. Place all ingredients in slow cooker. Stir to mix.

2. Cook on Low 3–4 hours, or until hot.

   Makes 4–6 servings

Clam Chowder

MARILYN MOWRY • IRVING, TX

Prep Time: 10 minutes ▪ Cooking Time: 2–3 hours ▪ Ideal slow cooker size: 1- to 2-qt.

15-oz. can New England–style
  clam chowder

1½ cups milk, or half-and-half

6½-oz. can minced clams,
  undrained

half a stick (¼ cup) butter

¼ cup cooking sherry

1. Mix all ingredients together in slow cooker.

2. Heat on Low 2–3 hours, or until good and hot.

   Makes 3 servings

Crabmeat Soup

CAROL L. STROH • AKRON, NY

Prep Time: 5–10 minutes • Cooking Time: 5–6 hours • Ideal slow cooker size: 3½-qt.

2 10¾-oz. cans cream of tomato soup

2 10½-oz. cans split pea soup

3 soup cans milk

1 cup heavy cream

1-2 6-oz. cans crabmeat, drained

¼ cup sherry, optional

1. Pour soups into slow cooker. Add milk and stir to mix.

2. Cover and cook on Low 4 hours, or until hot.

3. Stir in cream and crabmeat. Continue to cook on Low 1 hour, or until heated through.

Makes 8 servings

Shrimp Soup/Chowder

JOANNE GOOD • WHEATON, IL

Prep Time: 25 minutes • Cooking Time: 7–8 hours • Ideal slow cooker size: 4-qt.

1 medium-sized onion, chopped

5 medium-sized russet potatoes, peeled and cubed

1½ cups diced, precooked ham

4–6 cups water

salt and pepper to taste

2 lbs. shrimp, peeled, deveined, and cooked

CHOWDER OPTION:

4 Tbsp. flour

1 cup heavy (whipping) cream

1. Place chopped onion in a microwave-safe bowl and cook in microwave 2 minutes on High.

2. Place onion, cubed potatoes, diced ham, and 4 cups water in slow cooker. (If you're making the Chowder option, whisk 4 Tbsp. flour into 4 cups water in bowl before adding to slow cooker.)

3. Cover and cook on Low 7 hours, or until potatoes are softened. If soup base is thicker than you like, add up to 2 cups more water.

4. About 15–20 minutes before serving, turn heat to High and add shrimp. If making chowder, also add heavy cream. Cook until shrimp are hot, about 15 minutes.

Makes 12 servings

Note: If you wish, you can add these optional ingredients in Step 2: ½ tsp. thyme, 1 bay leaf (remove leaf before serving).

Oyster Stew

LINDA OVERHOLT ▪ ABBEVILLE, SC

Prep Time: 15–20 minutes ▪ Cooking Time: 2 hours ▪ Ideal slow cooker size: 3½- to 4-qt.

1 pt. oysters with liquor

half a stick (¼ cup) butter

1 pt. milk

1 pt. half-and-half

salt and pepper to taste

1. In a large nonstick skillet, heat oysters slowly in their own juice until edges begin to curl (do not boil).

2. Place oysters and their liquor in slow cooker.

3. Add butter, milk, and half-and-half. Season with salt and pepper to taste.

4. Cook on Low about 2 hours, or until heated through.

Makes 4 servings

Sunday Night Soup

SARA HARTER FREDETTE ▪ GOSHEN, MA

Prep Time: 10–15 minutes ▪ Cooking Time: 4–5 hours ▪ Ideal slow cooker size: 4-qt.

1.8-oz. pkg. dry Knorr tomato basil soup mix

4 cups water

2 cups diced potatoes

3 cups chopped vegetables (celery, carrots, peppers, onions), or 1-lb. pkg. frozen mixed vegetables

2 cups cooked chicken or cooked beef cubes, or browned ground beef, optional

1. In slow cooker, blend powdered soup mix into water. Add vegetables.

2. Cover and cook on High 1 hour, and then on Low 3 hours, or until vegetables are tender.

3. One-half hour before end of cooking time, stir in meat, if you choose to include it.

Makes 4–6 servings

Emergency Soup

ELAINE SUE GOOD • TISKILWA, IL

Prep Time: 10–15 minutes • Cooking Time: 6–12 hours • Ideal slow cooker size: 5-qt.

32-oz. pkg. frozen mixed
  vegetables

16-oz. pkg. cocktail wieners, or
  hot dogs cut into bite-sized
  pieces

46-oz. can tomato juice

1 Tbsp. dried basil or parsley

1. Combine all ingredients in slow cooker.

2. Cover and cook on Low 6–12 hours.

   Makes 8 servings

Note: This is one of those emergency recipes that I like to use if I suddenly get called away for the day at the last minute. I know everyone will be hungry when I get home. You can use almost whatever is available in your pantry and refrigerator in this recipe. You can also adjust the seasonings to your own preference.

Cheesy Broccoli Soup

DEDE PETERSON • RAPID CITY, SD

Prep Time: 15 minutes • Cooking Time: 5–6 hours • Ideal slow cooker size: 3-qt.

1 lb. frozen chopped broccoli,
  thawed

1 lb. Velveeta cheese, cubed

10¾-oz. can cream of celery
  soup

14½-oz. can chicken, or
  vegetable, broth

dash of pepper

dash of salt

1. Combine ingredients in slow cooker.

2. Cover. Cook on Low 5–6 hours.

   Makes 4 servings

Broccoli Soup

LINDA OVERHOLT • ABBEVILLE, SC

Prep Time: 5–10 minutes • Cooking Time: 1–1½ hours • Ideal slow cooker size: 3½- to 4-qt.

1 lb. fresh broccoli, chopped

2 12-oz. cans evaporated milk

2 10½-oz. cans cheddar cheese soup

2 10½-oz. cans cream of potato soup

1–2 cups cubed Velveeta cheese, optional

1. Place chopped broccoli in a medium-sized saucepan. Add ¼ cup water, cover, and steam briefly. Remove from heat while broccoli is still a bit crunchy. Set aside.

2. Mix milk and soups together in slow cooker.

3. Add broccoli and cooking water and cover. Cook on High 1 hour, or on Low 1½ hours.

4. Twenty minutes before serving, stir in cubed Velveeta cheese, if you wish.

Makes 8 servings

Note: For a little more zest, stir in ¼ tsp. black pepper in Step 3.

Creamy Tomato Soup

SARA KINSINGER • STUARTS DRAFT, VA

Prep Time: 20 minutes • Cooking Time: 1½ hours • Ideal slow cooker size: 4-qt.

26-oz. can condensed tomato soup, plus 6 ozs. water to equal 1 qt.

½ tsp. salt, optional

half a stick (4 Tbsp.) butter

8 Tbsp. flour

1 qt. milk (whole, or reduced-fat)

1. Put tomato soup, salt if you wish, and butter in slow cooker. Blend well.

2. Cover and cook on High 1 hour.

3. Meanwhile, place flour and 1 cup milk in 2-qt. microwave-safe container. Whisk together until big lumps disappear. Then whisk in remaining milk until only small lumps remain.

4. Place flour-milk mixture in microwave and cook on High 3 minutes. Remove and stir until smooth. Return to microwave and cook on High another 3 minutes.

5. Add thickened milk slowly to hot soup in slow cooker.

6. Heat thoroughly 10 to 15 minutes.

Makes 6 servings

Note: Serve with freshly ground pepper, dried chives or your choice of green herbs, and oyster crackers or croutons.

Easy Potato Soup

YVONNE KAUFFMAN BOETTGER • HARRISONBURG, VA

Prep Time: 10 minutes • Cooking Time: 5 hours • Ideal slow cooker size: 4- to 6-qt.

3 cups chicken broth

2-lb. bag frozen hash brown potatoes

1½ tsp. salt

¾ tsp. pepper

3 cups milk

3 cups shredded Monterey Jack, or cheddar, cheese

1. Place chicken broth, potatoes, salt, and pepper in slow cooker.

2. Cover and cook on High 4 hours, or until potatoes are soft.

3. Leaving broth and potatoes in slow cooker, mash potatoes lightly, leaving some larger chunks.

4. Add milk and cheese. Blend in thoroughly.

5. Cover and cook on High until cheese melts and soup is hot.

Makes 8 servings

Potato Chowder

SUSAN WENGER • LEBANON, PA

Prep Time: 15 minutes • Cooking Time: 8½–10½ hours • Ideal slow cooker size: 5-qt.

8 cups peeled, diced potatoes

3 14½-oz. cans chicken broth

10¾-oz. can cream of chicken soup

¼ tsp. pepper

8-oz. pkg. cream cheese, cubed

OPTIONAL INGREDIENTS:

⅓ cup chopped onion

½ lb. sliced bacon, cooked and crumbled

snipped chives

1. In slow cooker, combine potatoes, chicken broth, chicken soup, and pepper. Added chopped onion, if you wish.

2. Cover and cook on Low 8–10 hours, or until potatoes are tender.

3. Add cream cheese, stirring until well blended.

4. Heat until cheese melts and soup is hot throughout.

5. Garnish individual servings of soup with bacon and chives, if you like.

Makes 12 servings

Potato Soup with Possibilities

JANIE STEELE • MOORE, OK

Prep Time: 20–30 minutes • Cooking Time: 5–6 hours • Ideal slow cooker size: 4- to 6-qt.

6-8 cups homemade chicken broth, or 2 14-oz. cans chicken broth, plus ½ soup can water

1 large onion, chopped

3 celery stalks, chopped, including leaves, if you like

6 large white potatoes, peeled, chopped, cubed, or sliced

salt and pepper to taste

OPTIONAL INGREDIENTS:

shredded sharp cheddar cheese

2-3 cups chopped clams

10- or 16-oz. pkg. frozen corn

1. Place all ingredients in slow cooker.

2. Cover and cook on High 5 hours, or on Low 6 hours, or until vegetables are soft but not mushy.

Makes 6 servings

Potato Soup with Ground Beef

SHARON TIMPE • JACKSON, WI

Prep Time: 15–20 minutes • Cooking Time: 3½–4 hours • Ideal slow cooker size: 4- to 5-qt.

1 lb. ground beef

4 cups potatoes, peeled and cut into ½" cubes

1 small onion, chopped

3 8-oz. cans tomato sauce

2 tsp. salt

½ tsp. pepper

4 cups water

½ tsp. hot pepper sauce, optional

1. Brown ground beef in a nonstick skillet. Drain well. Place meat in slow cooker.

2. Add cubed potatoes, chopped onion, and tomato sauce.

3. Stir in salt, pepper, water, and hot pepper sauce, if you wish.

4. Cover and cook on High until mixture starts to simmer, about 1 hour.

5. Turn to Low and continue cooking until potatoes are tender, about 2½–3 hours.

Makes 6-8 servings

Note: I like to use red potatoes, because they stay more firm. Also, you can garnish each bowl of soup with chopped parsley.

Curried Limas and Potato Soup

BARBARA GAUTCHER • HARRISONBURG, VA

Prep Time: 15 minutes • Cooking Time: 4–10 hours • Ideal slow cooker size: 3-qt.

1½ cups dried large lima
    beans

4 cups water, divided

5–6 medium-sized potatoes,
    finely chopped

½ head cauliflower, optional

2 cups (16 ozs.) sour cream

2 Tbsp. curry

1–2 tsp. salt and pepper to
    taste

For faster cooking:

1. In a medium-sized saucepan, bring dried limas to a boil in 2 cups water. Boil, uncovered, 2 minutes. Cover, turn off heat, and wait 2 hours.

2. Drain water. Place beans in slow cooker.

3. Add 2 cups fresh water. Cover and cook 2 hours on High.

4. During the last hour of cooking, add diced potatoes and florets of cauliflower. Cook longer if vegetables are not as tender as you like after 1 hour.

5. Ten minutes before serving, add sour cream, curry, and salt and pepper to taste.

For slower cooking:

1. Soak limas in 2 cups water overnight. In the morning, drain water. Put limas in slow cooker and follow directions above, beginning with Step 3.

Makes 6 servings

Note: Sprinkle grated cheese on top of each serving. And/or serve with chopped fresh fennel as a topping.

Cheese Soup

DARLENE G. MARTIN • RICHFIELD, PA / KAYE TAYLOR • FLORISSANT, MO
ESTHER HARTZLER • CARLSBAD, NM

Prep Time: 15 minutes • Cooking Time: 2–6 hours • Ideal slow cooker size: 3-qt.

2 10¾-oz. cans cream soup
    (celery, mushroom, or
    chicken)

1 cup milk

1 lb. cheddar cheese, cubed

1 tsp. Worcestershire sauce

¼ tsp. paprika

1. Put all ingredients in slow cooker.

2. Cover and cook on Low 4–6 hours, or on High 2 hours.

Makes 4 servings

Note: Top each serving with croutons.

Vegetable Cheese Soup

ROSALIE D. MILLER • MIFFLINTOWN, PA

Prep Time: 15–20 minutes • Cooking Time: 4–10 hours • Ideal slow cooker size: 3-qt.

2 cups cream-style corn

1 cup potatoes, peeled and chopped

1 cup carrots, peeled and chopped

2 14½-oz. cans vegetable, or chicken, broth

16-oz. jar processed cheese

OPTIONAL INGREDIENTS:

1 tsp. celery seed

½ tsp. black pepper

½ cup chopped onion

1. Combine all ingredients except cheese in slow cooker.

2. Cover and cook on Low 8–10 hours, or on High 4–5 hours.

3. Thirty to 60 minutes before serving, stir in cheese. Then cook on High 30–60 minutes to melt and blend cheese.

4. If you choose to use any or all optional ingredients, add them in Step 1.

Makes 5 servings

Super Cheese Soup

KATE JOHNSON • ROLFE, IA

Prep Time: 15 minutes • Cooking Time: 4 hours • Ideal slow cooker size: 4- to 5-qt.

4 or 5 potatoes, diced

16-oz. pkg. frozen vegetables

2–3 tsp. chicken bouillon granules

2–3 cups water

¾ lb. Velveeta cheese, cubed

1. Place potatoes, frozen vegetables, chicken bouillon, and water (use 1 tsp. bouillon to 1 cup water) in a large saucepan on stovetop and cook until tender.

2. Add Velveeta cheese and mix well.

3. Place soup in slow cooker and keep warm on Low up to 4 hours.

Makes 6 servings

Note: If you've made the soup ahead of time and had it refrigerated, you may need to heat it longer on Low. If you're nearby, stir the soup after 2 hours in order to move the colder soup out of the center and along the edges of the cooker.

Cheddar Cheese Chowder

RUTH ZENDT • MIFFLINTOWN, PA

Prep Time: 15 minutes • Cooking Time: 3½–4½ hours • Ideal slow cooker size: 3- to 4-qt.

10-oz. pkg. frozen mixed
   vegetables

10¾-oz. can cream of chicken
   soup

1 soup can milk

1 cup shredded cheddar
   cheese

1. In a saucepan, cook and drain frozen vegetables according to package directions. Combine vegetables, soup, and milk in slow cooker.

2. Cover and cook on Low 3–4 hours, or until vegetables are done to your liking. Stir occasionally if you're nearby.

3. Sprinkle individual servings with cheese.

Makes 4 servings

Onion Soup with Cheese

JEAN H. ROBINSON • CINNAMINSON, NJ

Prep Time: 25 minutes • Cooking Time: 4 hours • Ideal slow cooker size: 6-qt.

4 large sweet white onions,
   sliced very thin

1 stick (½ cup) butter

8-oz. loaf French bread, sliced
   very thin

2 48-oz. cans beef, chicken,
   or vegetable broth

1 lb. Swiss cheese, shredded

1. Sauté onion rings in butter in a large nonstick skillet or saucepan until soft and golden, about 15 minutes.

2. Put one-third of onions in bottom of slow cooker. Layer one-third of bread slices over top. Repeat layering 2 more times.

3. Pour broth over all.

4. Cover and cook on High 4 hours.

5. Stir in cheese 10 minutes before serving.

Makes 10 servings

Onion Soup

PATRICIA HOWARD • GREEN VALLEY, AZ

Prep Time: 15–20 minutes • Cooking Time: 6–8 hours • Ideal slow cooker size: 4-qt.

3 cups thinly sliced onions

half a stick (¼ cup) butter

3 Tbsp. sugar

2 Tbsp. flour

1 qt. beef broth

1. Cook onions in butter in a large nonstick skillet or saucepan. Cover and sauté 15 minutes, stirring frequently. Then add sugar and flour, mixing well.

2. While onions are cooking, place broth in slow cooker on High. Add onion mixture to broth.

3. Cover and cook on Low 6–8 hours.

Makes 6-7 servings

Note: Serve topped with toasted bread and grated Parmesan cheese, if you like.

Butternut Squash Soup

ELAINE VIGODA • ROCHESTER, NY

Prep Time: 5 minutes • Cooking Time: 4–8 hours • Ideal slow cooker size: 4- to 5-qt.

45-oz. can chicken broth

1 medium-sized butternut squash, peeled and cubed

1 small onion, chopped

1 tsp. ginger

1 tsp. garlic, minced, optional

¼ tsp. nutmeg, optional

1. Place chicken broth and squash in slow cooker. Add remaining ingredients.

2. Cover and cook on High 4 hours, or on Low 6–8 hours, or until squash is tender.

Makes 4-6 servings

Cooking Tip

Some new slow cookers cook hotter and faster than older models. So get to know your slow cooker. We suggest a range of cooking times for many of the recipes, since cookers vary. When you've found the right length of time for a recipe done in your cooker, note that in your cookbook.

Creamy Vegetable Soup

LAUREN M. EBERHARD • SENECA, IL

Prep Time: 5 minutes • Cooking Time: 3 hours • Ideal slow cooker size: 7-qt., or 2 4-qt. cookers, soup divided equally between them

3 14-oz. cans chicken stock

3 15-oz. cans creamed corn

3 cups fat-free milk

48-oz. pkg. frozen mixed
    vegetables, or other
    vegetables of your choice

1 onion, chopped

1. Mix all ingredients in slow cooker.

2. Cover and cook on Low 3 hours.

   Makes 12–15 servings

Variations: Add 2 potatoes, cubed, to Step 1. And/or add seasonings of your choice—salt, pepper, fresh herbs—to Step 1.

Harry's Vegetable Soup

BETTY B. DENNISON • GROVE CITY, PA

Prep Time: 4–5 minutes • Cooking Time: 2–4 hours • Ideal slow cooker size: 4-qt.

4 15¼-oz. cans mixed
    vegetables, drained

46-oz. can vegetable juice

4 cups beef broth

1 tsp. Mrs. Dash

1. Mix all ingredients in greased slow cooker.

2. Cover and cook on Low 4 hours, or on High 2 hours.

   Makes 16 servings

Variation: If you have a beef roast, you may want to add a pound of cut-up pieces in Step 1. Also, leftover vegetables may be used instead of canned vegetables.

Tomato Vegetable Soup
(Clean-the-Fridge-Monday-Night Soup)

ELAINE SUE GOOD • TISKILWA, IL

Prep Time: 10 minutes • Cooking Time: 4–10 hours • Ideal slow cooker size: 3½-qt.

2 cloves garlic, pressed and chopped

8- or 16-oz. pkg. frozen peppers and onions

3 Tbsp. Italian seasoning mix, or basil, oregano, etc.

32-oz. pkg. frozen mixed vegetables, or leftover vegetables from your refrigerator, chopped

46-oz. can vegetable juice, or V8, or Bloody Mary mix, or beef broth

1. Place garlic into bottom of slow cooker. Add peppers and onions.

2. Sprinkle seasonings over top.

3. Add vegetables. Then pour juice over all ingredients.

4. Cover and cook on High 4 hours, or on Low 8–10 hours.

Makes 8 servings

Notes:

• Being flexible is the key to this recipe. You can add whatever you have on hand. Add water if you like a thinner consistency. You may add leftover meat—and/or cooked pasta or rice or barley—to bowls when serving. Sometimes I add leftover or canned lentils or beans to each bowl before serving the soup.

• This recipe came about when our family was given 3 cases of Bloody Mary mix!

Chicken and Turkey Main Dishes

Poached Chicken

MARY E. WHEATLEY • MASHPEE, MA

Prep Time: 15 minutes • Cooking Time: 7–8 hours • Ideal slow cooker size: 4½-qt.

1 whole broiler-fryer chicken, about 3 lbs.

1 celery rib, cut into chunks

1 carrot, sliced

1 medium-sized onion, sliced

1 cup chicken broth, seasoned, or water, or dry white wine

1. Wash chicken. Pat dry with paper towels and place in slow cooker.

2. Place celery, carrot, and onion around chicken. Pour broth over all.

3. Cover and cook on Low 7–8 hours, or until chicken is tender.

4. Remove chicken from pot and place on a platter. When cool enough to handle, debone.

5. Strain broth into a container and chill.

6. Place chunks of meat in fridge or freezer until ready to use in salads or main dishes.

Makes 6 servings

Herby Chicken

JOYCE BOWMAN • LADY LAKE, FL

Prep Time: 10 minutes • Cooking Time: 5–7 hours • Ideal slow cooker size: 5-qt.

2½–3½-lb. whole roasting chicken

1 lemon, cut into wedges

1 bay leaf

2–4 sprigs fresh thyme, or ¾ tsp. dried thyme

salt and pepper to taste

1. Remove giblets from chicken.

2. Put lemon wedges and bay leaf in cavity.

3. Place whole chicken in slow cooker.

4. Scatter sprigs of thyme over chicken. Sprinkle with salt and pepper.

5. Cover and cook on Low 5–7 hours, or until chicken is tender.

6. Serve hot with pasta or rice, or debone and freeze for your favorite casseroles or salads.

Makes 4–6 servings

Roast Chicken or Hen

BETTY DRESCHER • QUAKERTOWN, PA

Prep Time: 30 minutes • Cooking Time: 9–11 hours • Ideal slow cooker size: 4- to 5-qt.

3–4-lb. roasting chicken, or hen

1½ tsp. salt

¼ tsp. pepper

1 tsp. parsley flakes, divided

1 Tbsp. butter

½–1 cup water

1. Thoroughly wash chicken and pat dry.

2. Sprinkle cavity with salt, pepper, and ½ tsp. parsley flakes. Place in slow cooker, breast side up.

3. Dot with butter or brush with melted butter.

4. Sprinkle with remaining parsley flakes. Add water around chicken.

5. Cover and cook on High 1 hour. Turn to Low and cook 8–10 hours.

Makes 6 servings

Note: Sprinkle the chicken with basil or tarragon in Step 4, if you wish. To make this dish a more complete meal, put carrots, onions, and celery in the bottom of the slow cooker.

Easy Mushroom Chicken

TRISH DICK • LADYSMITH, WI / JANICE BURKHOLDER • RICHFIELD, PA
CAROL SHIRK • LEOLA, PA / CARRIE DARBY • WAYLAND, IA
SARA KINSINGER • STUARTS DRAFT, VA / CLARA NEWSWANGER • GORDONVILLE, PA

Prep Time: 5–10 minutes ▪ Cooking Time: 3–8 hours ▪ Ideal slow cooker size: 4-qt.

4–6 chicken legs and thighs (joined), skinned

salt and pepper to taste

1/2 cup chicken broth, or dry white wine

10 3/4-oz. can cream of mushroom, or celery, soup

4-oz. can sliced mushrooms, drained

1. Sprinkle salt and pepper on each piece of chicken. Place chicken in slow cooker.

2. In a small bowl, mix broth and soup together. Pour over chicken.

3. Spoon mushrooms over top.

4. Cover and cook on Low 6–8 hours, or on High 3–4 hours, or until chicken is tender but not dry.

Makes 4–6 servings

Yummy Slow-Cooker Chicken

TERESA KENNEDY • MT. PLEASANT, IA

Prep Time: 10–15 minutes ▪ Cooking Time: 8 hours ▪ Ideal slow cooker size: 4-qt.

3 lbs. chicken pieces

1 onion, cut up

7-oz. can mushroom pieces, drained

10 3/4-oz. can condensed cream soup, your choice of flavor

your choice of fresh herbs

OPTIONAL INGREDIENTS:

6 carrots, sliced or cut into chunks

rib celery, sliced or cut into chunks

1. Place chicken in slow cooker.

2. Mix all remaining ingredients except fresh herbs in a mixing bowl. Pour over chicken.

3. Cover and cook on Low 8 hours, or until chicken is tender.

4. Fifteen minutes before serving, toss in your choice of fresh herbs. Blend in well.

5. Serve over cooked rice, potatoes, or noodles.

Makes 6 servings

Slow-Cooker Chicken and Gravy

BETTY MOORE • PLANO, IL

Prep Time: 5 minutes • Cooking Time: 6 hours • Ideal slow cooker size: 4-qt.

6–8 bone-in chicken breast halves

salt and pepper to taste

$10\,^3/_4$-oz. can cream of mushroom soup

1 Tbsp. flour

$1/_2$ cup water

paprika to taste

1. Season chicken breasts with salt and pepper. Place in slow cooker.

2. Pour soup over chicken.

3. Cover and cook on Low 6 hours.

4. Remove chicken to a serving dish or platter. Cover to keep warm.

5. Turn slow cooker to High. In a small mixing bowl, blend flour into water until smooth. Stir into hot gravy in slow cooker.

6. Cook until thickened. Pour over chicken to serve.

7. Sprinkle with paprika just before serving.

Makes 6–8 servings

Honey Baked Chicken

MARY KENNELL • ROANOKE, IL

Prep Time: 15 minutes • Cooking Time: 3–6 hours • Ideal slow cooker size: 5-qt.

4 skinless, bone-in chicken breast halves

2 Tbsp. butter, melted

2 Tbsp. honey

2 tsp. prepared mustard

2 tsp. curry powder

salt and pepper, optional

1. Spray slow cooker with nonstick cooking spray and add chicken.

2. Mix butter, honey, mustard, and curry powder together in a small bowl. Pour sauce over chicken.

3. Cover and cook on High 3 hours, or on Low 5–6 hours.

Makes 4 servings

Honey Mustard Chicken

JEAN HALLORAN • GREEN BAY, WI

Prep Time: 15 minutes • Cooking Time: 3–7 hours • Ideal slow cooker size: 5-qt.

8 boneless, skinless chicken breast halves

1½ cups honey mustard dressing

½ cup water

1. Spray slow cooker with nonstick cooking spray.

2. Cut chicken into approximately 2" pieces. Place in slow cooker.

3. In a bowl, mix together dressing and water. Pour over chicken pieces.

4. Cover and cook on High 3–4 hours, or on Low 6–7 hours.

Makes 8 servings

Note: If you prefer a slightly milder flavor, add another ¼ cup water to Step 3.

Chicken in Piquant Sauce

BETH SHANK • WELLMAN, IA / KAREN WAGGONER • JOPLIN, MO / CAROL ARMSTRONG • WINSTON, OR
LOIS NIEBAUER • PEDRICKTOWN, NJ / JEAN BUTZER • BATAVIA, NY / VERONICA SABO • SHELTON, CT
CHARLOTTE SHAFFER • EAST EARL, PA

Prep Time: 10–15 minutes • Cooking Time: 3–4 hours • Ideal slow cooker size: 3- to 4-qt.

16-oz. jar Russian, or Creamy French, salad dressing

12-oz. jar apricot preserves

1 envelope dry onion soup mix

4-6 boneless, skinless chicken breast halves

1. In a bowl, mix together dressing, preserves, and soup mix.

2. Place chicken breasts in slow cooker.

3. Pour sauce over top of chicken.

4. Cover and cook on High 3 hours, or on Low 4 hours, or until chicken is tender but not dry.

Makes 4–6 servings

Chicken, Sweet Chicken

ANNE TOWNSEND • ALBUQUERQUE, NM

Prep Time: 15 minutes • Cooking Time: 5–6 hours • Ideal slow cooker size: 3-qt.

2 medium-sized raw sweet potatoes, peeled and cut into $\frac{1}{4}$"-thick slices

8 boneless, skinless chicken thighs

8-oz. jar orange marmalade

$\frac{1}{4}$ cup water

$\frac{1}{4}$-$\frac{1}{2}$ tsp. salt

$\frac{1}{2}$ tsp. pepper

1. Place sweet potato slices in slow cooker.

2. Rinse and dry chicken pieces. Arrange on top of potatoes.

3. Spoon marmalade over chicken and potatoes.

4. Pour water over all. Season with salt and pepper.

5. Cover and cook on High 1 hour, and then turn to Low and cook 4–5 hours, or until potatoes and chicken are both tender.

Makes 6–8 servings

Chicken a la Orange

CARLENE HORNE • BEDFORD, NH

Prep Time: 7 minutes • Cooking Time: 4–6 hours • Ideal slow cooker size: 4-qt.

8 boneless, skinless chicken breast halves

$\frac{1}{2}$ cup chopped onion

12-oz. jar orange marmalade

$\frac{1}{2}$ cup Russian dressing

1 Tbsp. dried parsley, or to taste

1. Place chicken and onion in slow cooker.

2. Combine marmalade and dressing. Pour over chicken.

3. Sprinkle with parsley.

4. Cover. Cook on Low 4–6 hours.

5. Serve with rice.

Makes 8 servings

Orange Glazed Chicken Breasts

CORINNA HERR • STEVENS, PA / KAREN CENEVIVA • NEW HAVEN, CT

Prep Time: 15 minutes • Cooking Time: 4–9 hours • Ideal slow cooker size: 4-qt.

12 ozs. orange juice concentrate, undiluted and thawed

$\frac{1}{2}$ tsp. dried marjoram leaves

6 boneless, skinless chicken breast halves

salt and pepper to taste

$\frac{1}{4}$ cup water

2 Tbsp. cornstarch

1. Combine thawed orange juice and marjoram in a shallow dish. Dip each breast in orange juice mixture.

2. Sprinkle each breast with salt and pepper; then place in slow cooker. Pour remaining orange sauce over breasts.

3. Cover and cook on Low $6\frac{1}{2}$–$8\frac{1}{2}$ hours, or on High $3\frac{1}{2}$–$4\frac{1}{2}$ hours, or until chicken is tender but not dry.

4. Half an hour before serving, remove chicken breasts from slow cooker and keep warm on a platter.

5. Mix water and cornstarch together in a small bowl until smooth. Turn slow cooker to High. Stir cornstarch water into liquid in slow cooker.

6. Place cover slightly ajar on slow cooker. Cook until sauce is thickened and bubbly, about 15–30 minutes. Serve sauce over chicken.

Makes 6 servings

Picnic Chicken

ANNE TOWNSEND • ALBUQUERQUE, NM

Prep Time: 5 minutes • Cooking Time: 6~7 hours • Ideal slow cooker size: 3-qt.

2 lbs., or 4 large, chicken thighs

$\frac{1}{4}$ cup dill pickle relish

$\frac{1}{4}$ cup Dijon mustard

$\frac{1}{4}$ cup mayonnaise

$\frac{1}{2}$ cup chicken broth

1. Rinse chicken well. Pat dry. Place in slow cooker skin side up.

2. In a mixing bowl, stir together relish, mustard, and mayonnaise. When well blended, stir in chicken broth. Mix well.

3. Pour sauce over chicken.

4. Cover and cook on Low 6–7 hours, or until chicken is tender but not dry or mushy.

Makes 4 servings

Orange Garlic Chicken

SUSAN KASTING • JENKS, OK

Prep Time: 15 minutes • Cooking Time: 2½–6 hours • Ideal slow cooker size: 4-qt.

1½ tsp. dry thyme

6 cloves garlic, minced

6 skinless, bone-in chicken breast halves

1 cup orange juice concentrate

2 Tbsp. balsamic vinegar

1. Rub thyme and garlic over chicken. (Reserve any leftover thyme and garlic.) Place chicken in slow cooker.

2. Mix orange juice concentrate and vinegar together in a small bowl. Stir in reserved thyme and garlic. Spoon over chicken.

3. Cover and cook on Low 5–6 hours, or on High 2½–3 hours, or until chicken is tender but not dry.

Makes 6 servings

Note: Remove chicken from slow cooker and keep warm on a platter. Skim fat from sauce. Bring remaining sauce to a boil in a saucepan to reduce. Serve sauce over chicken and cooked rice.

Oregano Chicken

TINA GOSS • DUENWEG, MO

Prep Time: 5 minutes • Cooking Time: 4–6 hours • Ideal slow cooker size: 4- to 5-qt.

3½–4 lbs. chicken, cut up

half a stick (¼ cup) butter, or margarine, melted

1 envelope dry Italian salad dressing mix

2 Tbsp. lemon juice

1–2 Tbsp. dried oregano

1. Place chicken in bottom of slow cooker. Mix butter, dressing mix, and lemon juice together and pour over top.

2. Cover and cook on High 4–6 hours, or until chicken is tender but not dry.

3. Baste occasionally with sauce mixture and sprinkle with oregano 1 hour or just before serving.

Makes 6 servings

Cooking Tip

Liquids don't boil down in a slow cooker. At the end of the cooking time, remove the cover, set dial on High, and allow the liquid to evaporate, if the dish is soupier than you want.

—*John D. Allen, Rye, CO*

Greek Chicken Pita Filling

JUDI MANOS • WEST ISLIP, NY / JEANETTE OBERHOLTZER • MANHEIM, PA

Prep Time: 10 minutes • Cooking Time: 6–8 hours • Ideal slow cooker size: 2- to 3-qt.

1 onion, chopped

1 lb. boneless, skinless chicken thighs

1 tsp. lemon pepper

½ tsp. dried oregano

½ cup plain yogurt

1. Combine first 3 ingredients in slow cooker. Cover and cook on Low 6–8 hours, or until chicken is tender.

2. Just before serving, remove chicken and shred with 2 forks.

3. Add shredded chicken back into slow cooker and stir in oregano and yogurt.

4. Serve as a filling for pita bread.

Makes 4 servings

Pacific Chicken

COLLEEN KONETZNI • RIO RANCHO, NM

Prep Time: 10 minutes • Cooking Time: 7–8 hours • Ideal slow cooker size: 3- to 4-qt.

6-8 skinless chicken thighs

½ cup soy sauce

2 Tbsp. brown sugar

2 Tbsp. grated fresh ginger

2 garlic cloves, minced

1. Wash and dry chicken. Place in slow cooker.

2. Combine remaining ingredients. Pour over chicken.

3. Cover. Cook on High 1 hour. Reduce heat to Low and cook 6–7 hours.

4. Serve over rice with a fresh salad.

Makes 6 servings

Tangy Chicken Legs

FRANCES L. KRUBA • DUNDALK, MD

Prep Time: 10–15 minutes • Cooking Time: 4–5 hours ▪ Ideal slow cooker size: 5- to 6-qt. (oblong is best)

8 chicken drumsticks

$\frac{1}{3}$ cup soy sauce

$\frac{2}{3}$ cup packed brown sugar

scant $\frac{1}{8}$ tsp. ginger

$\frac{1}{4}$ cup water

1. Place chicken in slow cooker.

2. Combine remaining ingredients in a bowl and spoon over chicken.

3. Cover and cook on Low 4–5 hours, or until chicken is tender but not dry.

Makes 4–6 servings

Simple Chicken

NORMA GRIESER • CLARKSVILLE, MI

Prep Time: 10 minutes ▪ Cooking Time: 4–8 hours ▪ Ideal slow cooker size: 5- to 6-qt.

$\frac{1}{2}$ cup water

4 lbs. boneless, skinless chicken breasts

garlic salt

$1\frac{3}{4}$ cups (14 ozs.) barbecue sauce

1. Put water in bottom of slow cooker. Layer in chicken pieces, sprinkling each layer with garlic salt.

2. Pour barbecue sauce over all.

3. Cover and cook on Low 8 hours, or on High 4 hours, or until chicken is tender but not dry or mushy.

Makes 8–10 servings

Note: You can add slices of onion to each layer, if you wish. And/or you can use legs and thighs in place of breasts, if you wish.

Tender Barbecued Chicken

MARY LYNN MILLER • REINHOLDS, PA

Prep Time: 10–15 minutes • Cooking Time: 8–10 hours • Ideal slow cooker size: 5-qt.

3-4-lb. broiler/fryer chicken, cut up

1 medium-sized onion, thinly sliced

1 medium-sized lemon, thinly sliced

18-oz. bottle barbecue sauce

¾ cup cola

1. Place chicken in slow cooker. Top with onion and lemon slices.

2. Combine barbecue sauce and cola. Pour over all.

3. Cover and cook on Low 8–10 hours, or until chicken is tender but not dry.

Makes 4–6 servings

Herby Barbecued Chicken

LAUREN M. EBERHARD • SENECA, IL

Prep Time: 10 minutes • Cooking Time: 6–8 hours • Ideal slow cooker size: 4- to 5-qt.

1 whole chicken, cut up, or 8 of your favorite pieces

1 onion, thinly sliced

1 bottle Sweet Baby Ray's Barbecue Sauce

1 tsp. dried oregano

1 tsp. dried basil

1. Place chicken in slow cooker.

2. Mix onion slices, sauce, oregano, and basil together in a bowl. Pour over chicken, covering as well as possible.

3. Cover and cook on Low 6–8 hours, or until chicken is tender but not dry.

Makes 4–6 servings

Come-Back-for-More Barbecued Chicken

LEESA DEMARTYN • ENOLA, PA

Prep Time: 10 minutes • Cooking Time: 6–8 hours • Ideal slow cooker size: 5-qt.

6–8 chicken breast halves

1 cup ketchup

⅓ cup Worcestershire sauce

½ cup brown sugar

1 tsp. chili powder

½ cup water

1. Place chicken in slow cooker.

2. Whisk remaining ingredients in a large bowl. Pour sauce mixture over chicken.

3. Cover and cook on Low 6–8 hours, or until chicken is tender but not overcooked.

Makes 6–8 servings

Note: If the sauce begins to dry out as the dish cooks, stir in another ½ cup water.

Quickie Barbecued Chicken

CAROL SHERWOOD • BATAVIA, NY / SHARON SHANK • BRIDGEWATER, VA

Prep Time: 20 minutes • Cooking Time: 3–7 hours • Ideal slow cooker size: 4-qt.

4 boneless, skinless chicken breast halves

¾ cup chicken broth

1 cup barbecue sauce

1 medium-sized onion, sliced

salt to taste

pepper to taste

1. Place all ingredients in slow cooker. Stir gently.

2. Cook on High 3 hours, or on Low 6–7 hours, or until chicken is tender but not dry.

3. Serve breast pieces whole, or cut up and stir through the sauce.

Makes 4 servings

Chicken and Potatoes Barbecue

BETTY B. DENNISON • GROVE CITY, PA

Prep Time: 5–10 minutes • Cooking Time: 4–9 hours • Ideal slow cooker size: 4- to 5-qt.

8 boneless, skinless chicken breast halves, divided

8 small or medium-sized potatoes, quartered, divided

1 cup honey barbecue sauce

16-oz. can jellied cranberry sauce

1. Spray slow cooker with nonstick cooking spray. Place 4 chicken breasts in slow cooker.

2. Top with 4 cut-up potatoes.

3. Mix barbecue sauce and cranberry sauce together in a bowl. Spoon half of sauce over chicken and potatoes in cooker.

4. Place remaining breasts in cooker, followed by remaining potato chunks. Pour rest of sauce over all.

5. Cover and cook on Low 8–9 hours, or on High 4 hours, or until chicken and potatoes are tender but not dry.

Makes 8 servings

Note: You may peel the potatoes or leave the skins on. Red potatoes are especially appealing when they retain their skins.

Cranberry Chicken Barbecue

GLADYS M. HIGH • EPHRATA, PA

Prep Time: 10 minutes • Cooking Time: 4–8 hours • Ideal slow cooker size: 4- to 5-qt.

4 lbs. chicken pieces, divided

½ tsp. salt

¼ tsp. pepper

16-oz. can whole-berry cranberry sauce

1 cup barbecue sauce

OPTIONAL INGREDIENTS:

½ cup diced celery

½ cup diced onion

1. Place one-third of chicken pieces in slow cooker.

2. Combine all sauce ingredients in a mixing bowl. Spoon one-third of sauce over chicken in cooker.

3. Repeat Steps 1 and 2 twice.

4. Cover and bake on High 4 hours, or on Low 6–8 hours, or until chicken is tender but not dry.

Makes 6-8 servings

Cranberry Chicken

JANIE STEELE • MOORE, OK / SHEILA SOLDNER • LITITZ, PA

Prep Time: 10 minutes • Cooking Time: 6–8 hours • Ideal slow cooker size: 4- to 5-qt.

6 chicken breast halves, divided

8-oz. bottle Catalina, or creamy French, salad dressing

1 envelope dry onion soup mix

16-oz. can whole-berry cranberry sauce

1. Place 3 chicken breasts in slow cooker.

2. Mix other ingredients together in a mixing bowl. Pour half of sauce over chicken in cooker.

3. Repeat Steps 1 and 2.

4. Cover and cook on Low 6–8 hours, or until chicken is tender but not dry.

Makes 6 servings

Bacon-Feta Stuffed Chicken

TINA GOSS • DUENWEG, MO

Prep Time: 10 minutes • Cooking Time: 1½–3 hours • Ideal slow cooker size: 3-qt.

¼ cup crumbled cooked bacon

¼ cup crumbled feta cheese

4 boneless, skinless chicken breast halves

2 14½-oz. cans diced tomatoes

1 Tbsp. dried basil

1. In a small bowl, mix bacon and cheese together lightly.

2. Cut a pocket in the thicker side of each chicken breast. Fill each with one-quarter of bacon and cheese mixture. Pinch shut and secure with toothpicks.

3. Place chicken in slow cooker. Top with tomatoes and sprinkle with basil.

4. Cover and cook on High 1½–3 hours, or until chicken is tender but not dry or mushy.

Makes 4 servings

Cooking Tip

Keep a supply of cream of mushroom soup in your pantry. It is a quick and convenient staple for beef, veal, and pork roasts and for casseroles. It makes a good sauce or gravy, with just a few additional seasonings or some sour cream.

Chicken Supreme

JEANETTE OBERHOLTZER • MANHEIM, PA

Prep Time: 15–20 minutes • Cooking Time: 4–5 hours • Ideal slow cooker size: 4- to 6-qt.

3 slices bacon

6 boneless, skinless chicken breast halves

4-oz. jar sliced mushrooms, drained

10¾-oz. can cream of chicken soup

½ cup shredded Swiss cheese

1. In a large nonstick skillet, cook bacon until crisp. Drain bacon well on paper towels, but reserve drippings. Crumble bacon. Set aside.

2. In bacon drippings, cook 3 chicken breasts over medium heat 3–5 minutes, or until light brown, turning once. Place chicken in slow cooker. Repeat with remaining 3 breasts.

3. Top with mushrooms.

4. Heat soup in skillet until creamy. Pour over mushrooms and chicken.

5. Cover and cook on Low 4 hours, or until chicken is tender but not dry.

6. Top chicken with shredded cheese. Sprinkle with bacon.

7. Cover and cook on High 10–15 minutes, or until cheese melts.

Makes 6 servings

Chicken in Mushroom Sauce

CAROL EBERLY • HARRISONBURG, VA / RUTHIE SCHIEFER • VASSAR, MI

Prep Time: 10–15 minutes • Cooking Time: 4–5 hours • Ideal slow cooker size: 4- to 5-qt.

4 boneless, skinless chicken breast halves

10¾-oz. can cream of mushroom soup

1 cup (8 ozs.) sour cream

7-oz. can mushroom stems and pieces, drained, optional

4 bacon strips, cooked and crumbled, or ¼ cup precooked bacon crumbles

1. Place chicken in slow cooker.

2. In a mixing bowl, combine soup and sour cream, and mushroom pieces, if you wish. Pour over chicken.

3. Cover and cook on Low 4–5 hours, or until chicken is tender but not dry.

4. Sprinkle with bacon before serving.

5. Serve over cooked rice or pasta.

Makes 4 servings

Simply Delicious Chicken Breasts

DONNA TRELOAR • HARTFORD CITY, IN

Prep Time: 3 minutes • Cooking Time: 4–6 hours • Ideal slow cooker size: 3-qt.

4 bone-in chicken breast
   halves, or chicken legs and
   thighs

10¾-oz. can golden
   mushroom soup

1 envelope dry onion soup mix

1. Place chicken in slow cooker.

2. Pour soup over chicken. Sprinkle with dry soup mix.

3. Cover and cook on Low 4–6 hours, or until chicken is tender but not dry.

Makes 4 servings

Quilters' Chicken

SARA HARTER FREDETTE • GOSHEN, MA

Prep Time: 5 minutes • Cooking Time: 4–8 hours • Ideal slow cooker size: 4-qt.

6 boneless, skinless chicken
   breast halves

10¾-oz. can cream of
   mushroom soup

1 envelope dry onion soup mix

¼-½ cup sour cream

4-oz. can mushrooms,
   drained, optional

1. Place chicken in slow cooker.

2. Blend mushroom soup and onion soup mix together in a small bowl. Pour over chicken.

3. Cover and cook on Low 4–8 hours, or until chicken is tender but not dry.

4. Fifteen minutes before serving, stir in sour cream and mushrooms. Cover and continue cooking. Serve over rice or noodles.

Makes 6 servings

Creamy Cheddary Chicken

NORMA GRIESER • CLARKSVILLE, MI

Prep Time: 10 minutes • Cooking Time: 4–6 hours • Ideal slow cooker size: 5- to 6-qt.

8-10 chicken breast halves, divided

10¾-oz. can cream of chicken soup

10¾-oz. can cream of celery, or mushroom, soup

½ cup cooking wine or sherry

¾ cup shredded cheddar cheese

1. Place half of chicken in slow cooker.

2. In a bowl, mix soups and wine together. Pour half of sauce over chicken.

3. Place other half of chicken in slow cooker. Pour remaining sauce over that layer.

4. Cover and cook on Low 4–6 hours, or until chicken is tender.

5. Ten minutes before serving, sprinkle with cheese.

Makes 8-10 servings

Variations: Stir your favorite seasonings into Step 2—parsley, thyme, basil, lemon pepper. And/or add ½ cup toasted almonds to Step 5.

Easy Chicken

JENNIFER KUH • BAY VILLAGE, OH

Prep Time: 5-10 minutes • Cooking Time: 4–8 hours • Ideal slow cooker size: 3- to 4-qt.

4 boneless, skinless chicken breast halves, fresh or frozen

10¾-oz. can low-fat cream of chicken soup

10¾-oz. can low-fat cream of mushroom soup

½ cup low-fat sour cream

1. Place chicken in slow cooker.

2. Mix soups well in a mixing bowl, and then pour over chicken.

3. Cover and cook on Low 4–8 hours, or until chicken is tender but not dry.

4. Stir in sour cream ½ hour before serving.

Makes 4 servings

Cheesy Chicken

SUSAN TJON • AUSTIN, TX / KATRINA EBERLY • STEVENS, PA / BETTY MOORE • PLANO, IL

Prep Time: 10–15 minutes ▪ Cooking Time: 6–8 hours ▪ Ideal slow cooker size: 3½- to 4-qt.

6 boneless, skinless chicken breast halves, divided

salt to taste

freshly ground pepper to taste

garlic powder to taste, or 2 Tbsp. minced garlic

2 10¾-oz. cans cream of chicken soup

10¾-oz. can cheddar cheese soup

1. Rinse chicken, pat dry, and then sprinkle with salt, pepper, and garlic powder or garlic.

2. Place 3 breasts in bottom of slow cooker.

3. Combine undiluted soups in a mixing bowl. Pour half of soup mixture over 3 breasts in cooker.

4. Repeat Steps 2 and 3.

5. Cook on Low 6–8 hours, or until chicken is tender but not dry.

Makes 6 servings

Note: If the sauce looks too thick 30 minutes before serving, add a little water.

Easy Creamy Chicken

KAREN WAGGONER • JOPLIN, MO

Prep Time: 5 minutes ▪ Cooking Time: 2–4 hours ▪ Ideal slow cooker size: 4-qt.

8 boneless, skinless chicken breast halves, divided

lemon pepper to taste

10¾-oz. can cream of chicken soup

3-oz. pkg. cream cheese, softened

8-oz. carton sour cream

1. Place 4 breasts in bottom of slow cooker. Sprinkle with lemon pepper.

2. Mix soup and cream cheese together in a bowl. When blended, fold in sour cream.

3. Pour half of sauce over breasts in cooker.

4. Repeat Steps 1 and 3.

5. Cover and cook on High 2–4 hours, or until chicken is tender but not dry.

Makes 8 servings

Note: This is good served over cooked rice.

Creamy Italian Chicken

KATHY ESH • NEW HOLLAND, PA / MARY ANN BOWMAN • EAST EARL, PA

Prep Time: 5–10 minutes • Cooking Time: 4 hours • Ideal slow cooker size: 5-qt.

4 boneless, skinless chicken breast halves

1 envelope dry Italian salad dressing mix

¼ cup water

8-oz. pkg. cream cheese, softened

10¾-oz. can cream of chicken, or celery, soup

4-oz. can mushroom stems and pieces, drained, optional

1. Place chicken in slow cooker. Combine salad dressing and water. Pour over chicken.

2. Cover and cook on Low 3 hours.

3. In a small bowl, beat cream cheese and soup until blended. Stir in mushrooms, if you wish. Pour over chicken.

4. Cover and cook on Low 1 hour, or until chicken is tender but not dry.

Makes 4 servings

Note: Remove chicken from sauce and serve on a platter. Serve the sauce over cooked noodles. Or shred chicken after cooking, and then stir into the sauce. Serve over cooked noodles.

Creamy Chicken Curry

GLORIA FREY • LEBANON, PA

Prep Time: 20 minutes • Cooking Time: 2–4 hours • Ideal slow cooker size: 3- to 4-qt.

2 10¾-oz. cans cream of mushroom soup

1 soup can water

2 tsp. curry powder

⅓–½ cup chopped almonds, toasted

4 skinless chicken breast halves, cooked and cubed

1. Combine ingredients in slow cooker.

2. Cover and cook on Low 2–4 hours. Stir occasionally.

3. Serve over cooked rice.

Makes 4–6 servings

Chicken Delicious

ORPHA HERR • ANDOVER, NY

Prep Time: 15–20 minutes • Cooking Time: 4–10 hours • Ideal slow cooker size: 5-qt.

10 boneless, skinless chicken breast halves

1 tsp. fresh lemon juice

salt and pepper to taste

2 10¾-oz. cans cream of celery soup

⅓ cup sherry or wine, optional

¼ cup grated Parmesan cheese

1. Rinse chicken breasts and pat dry. Place chicken in slow cooker in layers. Season each layer with a sprinkling of lemon juice, salt, and pepper.

2. In a medium-sized bowl, mix soups with sherry or wine, if you wish. Pour mixture over chicken. Sprinkle with Parmesan cheese.

3. Cover and cook on Low 8–10 hours, or on High 4–5 hours, or until chicken is tender but not dry or mushy.

Makes 10 servings

Savory Chicken, Meal #1

SHARI MAST • HARRISONBURG, VA

Prep Time: 15 minutes • Cooking Time: 4–5 hours • Ideal slow cooker size: 5-qt.

4 boneless, skinless chicken breast halves

4 skinless chicken quarters

10¾-oz. can cream of chicken soup

1 Tbsp. water

¼ cup chopped sweet red peppers

1 Tbsp. chopped fresh parsley, or 1 tsp. dried parsley, optional

1 Tbsp. lemon juice

½ tsp. paprika, optional

1. Layer chicken in slow cooker.

2. Combine remaining ingredients and pour over chicken. Make sure all pieces are covered with sauce.

3. Cover. Cook on High 4–5 hours.

Makes 8 servings

Savory Chicken, Meal #2

SHARI MAST • HARRISONBURG, VA

Prep Time: 20 minutes • Cooking Time: 3¼–4¼ hours • Ideal slow cooker size: 3-qt.

leftover chicken and broth from Savory Chicken Meal #1

2 carrots, thinly sliced

1 rib celery, thinly sliced

2 medium-sized onions, cut in chunks

2 Tbsp. flour or cornstarch

¼ cup cold water

1. For a second Savory Chicken Meal, pick leftover chicken off bone. Set aside.

2. Return remaining broth to slow cooker. Stir in carrots, celery, and onions. Cook 3–4 hours on High.

3. In a separate bowl, mix flour or cornstarch with cold water. When smooth, stir into hot broth.

4. Stir in cut-up chicken. Heat 15–20 minutes, or until broth thickens and chicken is hot.

5. Serve over rice or pasta.

Makes 3–4 servings

Creamy Chicken with a Touch of Broccoli

STACY PETERSHEIM • MECHANICSBURG, PA

Prep Time: 10 minutes • Cooking Time: 6–8 hours • Ideal slow cooker size: 2-qt.

4 bone-in, skinless chicken breast halves

10¾-oz. can cream of broccoli soup

1 Tbsp. minced garlic

¼ cup finely chopped onion

salt and pepper to taste

1. Line slow cooker with aluminum foil. Place chicken on top of foil.

2. In a mixing bowl, stir together remaining ingredients. Pour over chicken. Seal foil shut.

3. Cover and cook on Low 6–8 hours, or until chicken is tender.

Makes 4 servings

Note: Serve over cooked rice or noodles.

Elegant Chicken with Gravy

LEESA LESENSKI • SOUTH DEERFIELD, MA

Prep Time: 10 minutes • Cooking Time: 3–6 hours • Ideal slow cooker size: 3- to 4-qt.

6 boneless chicken breast
  halves

10¾-oz. can cream of
  broccoli, or broccoli
  cheese, soup

10¾-oz. can cream of chicken
  soup

½ cup white wine

4-oz. can sliced mushrooms,
  undrained, optional

1. Place chicken breasts in slow cooker.

2. In a bowl, mix together soups, wine, and mushroom slices, if you wish. Pour over chicken.

3. Cover. Cook on High 3 hours, or on Low 6 hours, or until chicken is tender but not dry.

4. Serve over rice or noodles.

Makes 6 servings

Creamy Baked Chicken with Stuffing

VERA MARTIN • EAST EARL, PA

Prep Time: 10–15 minutes • Cooking Time: 4½ hours • Ideal slow cooker size: 6-qt.

8 boneless chicken breast
  halves, divided

10¾-oz. can cream of chicken
  soup

¼ cup water

1 cup crushed stuffing,
  herb-seasoned

half a stick (4 Tbsp.) butter,
  melted

7 slices white American
  cheese

1. Lightly grease slow cooker. Layer half of chicken in bottom of slow cooker.

2. In a small bowl, mix soup and water together. Spoon half of sauce over chicken in cooker.

3. Layer 4 breasts into cooker. Top with remaining sauce.

4. Sprinkle crumbs over top. Drizzle with melted butter.

5. Cover and cook on High 4 hours, or until chicken is tender.

6. Place cheese slices over crumbs. Cover and cook another 30 minutes.

Makes 8 servings

Chicken and Stuffing

KAREN WAGGONER • JOPLIN, MO

Prep Time: 5 minutes ▪ Cooking Time: 2–2½ hours ▪ Ideal slow cooker size: 4-qt.

4 boneless, skinless chicken breast halves

6-oz. box stuffing mix for chicken

16-oz. pkg. frozen whole-kernel corn

half a stick (4 Tbsp.) butter, melted

2 cups water

1. Place chicken in bottom of slow cooker.

2. Mix remaining ingredients together in a mixing bowl. Spoon over chicken.

3. Cover and cook on High 2–2½ hours, or until chicken is tender and stuffing is dry.

Makes 4 servings

Scalloped Chicken

BRENDA JOY SONNIE • NEWTON, PA

Prep Time: 10 minutes ▪ Cooking Time: 2–3 hours ▪ Ideal slow cooker size: 3-qt.

4 cups cooked chicken

1 box stuffing mix for chicken

2 eggs

1 cup water

1½ cups milk

1 cup frozen peas

1. Combine chicken and dry stuffing mix. Place in slow cooker.

2. Beat eggs, water, and milk together in a bowl. Pour over chicken and stuffing.

3. Cover. Cook on High 2–3 hours.

4. Add frozen peas during last hour of cooking.

Makes 4–6 servings

Note: For more flavor, use chicken broth instead of water.

Apricot Stuffing and Chicken

ELIZABETH COLUCCI • LANCASTER, PA

Prep Time: 10 minutes ▪ Cooking Time: 2–3½ hours ▪ Ideal slow cooker size: 5-qt.

1 stick (8 Tbsp.) butter, divided

1 box cornbread stuffing mix

4 boneless, skinless chicken breast halves

6–8-oz. jar apricot preserves

1. In a mixing bowl, make stuffing, using ½ stick (4 Tbsp.) butter and amount of water called for in instructions on box. Set aside.

2. Cut up chicken into 1" pieces. Place on bottom of slow cooker. Spoon stuffing over top.

3. In a microwave, or on stovetop, melt remaining ½ stick (4 Tbsp.) butter with preserves. Pour over stuffing.

4. Cover and cook on High 2 hours, or on Low 3½ hours, or until chicken is tender but not dry.

Makes 5 servings

Chicken Cordon Bleu

BETH PEACHEY • BELLEVILLE, PA

Prep Time: 10 minutes ▪ Cooking Time: 6–8 hours ▪ Ideal slow cooker size: 4- to 5-qt.

4 boneless, skinless chicken breast halves

½ lb. deli-sliced cooked ham

½ lb. baby Swiss cheese, sliced

10¾-oz. can cream of chicken soup

1 box dry stuffing mix, prepared according to box directions

1. Layer all ingredients in the order listed into slow cooker.

2. Cover and cook on Low 6–8 hours, or until chicken is tender but not dry.

Makes 4 servings

Cooking Tip

A slow cooker is great for taking food to a potluck supper, even if you didn't prepare the food in the cooker.

—*Irma H. Schoen, Windsor, CT*

Slow-Cooker Dried Beef and Chicken

MARTHA BENDER • NEW PARIS, IN

Prep Time: 15-20 minutes • Cooking Time: 3-9 hours • Ideal slow cooker size: 4- to 5-qt.

6-8 ozs. dried beef

6-8 boneless, skinless chicken breasts

10¾-oz. can cream of mushroom soup

1 cup sour cream

¼ cup flour

1. Arrange dried beef on bottom of slow cooker.

2. Layer chicken breasts on top of dried beef.

3. In a medium-sized mixing bowl, blend together soup, sour cream, and flour. Pour over chicken.

4. Cover and cook on Low 7-9 hours, or on High 3-5 hours.

5. To serve, arrange chicken on a platter. Top with the dried beef. Spoon sauce over top. Serve with cooked rice or noodles.

Makes 6-8 servings

Creamy Chicken and Carrots

RUTH ANN BENDER • COCHRANVILLE, PA / AUDREY L. KNEER • WILLIAMSFIELD, IL

Prep Time: 5-10 minutes • Cooking Time: 4-5 hours • Ideal slow cooker size: 1½-qt.

2 boneless, skinless chicken breast halves, about 6 ozs. each

8-oz. pkg. fresh baby carrots, cut in half lengthwise

10¾-oz. can cream of mushroom soup

4-oz. can mushroom stems and pieces, drained

1. Place chicken in slow cooker. Top with remaining ingredients.

2. Cover and cook on High 4-5 hours, or until chicken pieces are tender.

3. Serve over rice, if you wish.

Makes 2 servings

Chicken with Dried Beef and Bacon

RHONDA FREED • LOWVILLE, NY / DARLENE G. MARTIN • RICHFIELD, PA
SHARON MILLER • HOLMESVILLE, OH / JENA HAMMOND • TRAVERSE CITY, MI

Prep Time: 15 minutes ▪ Cooking Time: 3–8 hours ▪ Ideal slow cooker size: 4-qt.

4-6 slices bacon

8-12 slices low-sodium dried beef, divided

4-6 boneless, skinless chicken breasts, divided

10¾-oz. can low-fat, low-sodium cream of mushroom soup

1 cup sour cream

1. Place a paper towel on a paper plate. Top with 4–6 slices bacon. Cover with another paper towel. Microwave on High 2 minutes, until bacon is partially cooked. Lift bacon onto a fresh paper towel and allow towel to absorb fat.

2. Line slow cooker with half of slices of dried beef.

3. Wrap a slice of bacon around each chicken breast and place first layer of chicken into slow cooker. Cover first layer of chicken breasts with remaining slices of dried beef. Add second layer of chicken.

4. In a mixing bowl, combine soup and sour cream well. Pour over chicken and dried beef.

5. Cover and cook on Low 7–8 hours, or on High 3–4 hours.

6. Serve over cooked noodles or rice.

Makes 4–6 servings

Mix-It-and-Run Chicken

SHELIA HEIL • LANCASTER, PA

Prep Time: 10 minutes ▪ Cooking Time: 8–10 hours ▪ Ideal slow cooker size: 4- to 5-qt.

2 15-oz. cans cut green beans, undrained

2 10¾-oz. cans cream of mushroom soup

4-6 boneless, skinless chicken breast halves

½ tsp. salt, divided

1. Drain beans, reserving juice in a medium-sized mixing bowl.

2. Stir soups into bean juice, blending thoroughly. Set aside.

3. Place beans in slow cooker. Sprinkle with salt.

4. Place chicken in cooker. Sprinkle with salt.

5. Top with soup.

6. Cover and cook on Low 8–10 hours, or until chicken is tender but not dry or mushy.

Makes 4 servings

Chicken Pot Roast

CAROL EBERLY • HARRISONBURG, VA / SARAH MILLER • HARRISONBURG, VA

Prep Time: 10–15 minutes ▪ Cooking Time: 3–4 hours ▪ Ideal slow cooker size: 4- to 5-qt.

4 boneless, skinless chicken breast halves

salt, or garlic salt, and pepper to taste

4-6 medium-sized carrots, peeled and sliced

2 cups lima beans, fresh or frozen

1 cup water

1. Salt and pepper chicken breasts. Use garlic salt, if you wish. Place chicken in slow cooker and start cooking on High.

2. Place carrots on top of chicken. Add limas on top. Pour water over all.

3. Cover and cook on Low 3–4 hours, or until chicken and vegetables are tender but not dry or mushy.

4. This is good served over rice.

Makes 4 servings

One-Pot Chicken Dinner

ARIANNE HOCHSTETLER • GOSHEN, IN

Prep Time: 15 minutes ▪ Cooking Time: 3–6 hours ▪ Ideal slow cooker size: 4- to 5-qt.

12 chicken drumsticks or thighs, skin removed

3 medium-sized orange sweet potatoes, cut into 2" pieces

12-oz. jar chicken gravy, or 10¾-oz. can cream of chicken soup

2 Tbsp. unbleached flour, if using chicken gravy

10-oz. pkg. frozen cut green beans

OPTIONAL INGREDIENTS:

1 tsp. dried parsley flakes

½ tsp. dried rosemary leaves, crushed

salt and pepper to taste

1. Place chicken in slow cooker. Top with sweet potato chunks.

2. In a small bowl, combine remaining ingredients, except beans, and mix until smooth. Pour over chicken.

3. Cover and cook on High 1½ hours, or on Low 3½ hours.

4. One-and-one-half hours before serving, stir green beans into chicken mixture. Cover and cook on Low 1–2 hours, or until chicken, sweet potatoes, and green beans are tender but not dry or mushy.

Makes 6 servings

Note: If you want to include the parsley, rosemary, and/or salt and pepper, add to Step 2. And instead of adding the green beans into the slow cooker, you can stir-fry 1 lb. French-cut green beans with 1 chopped onion. Serve alongside chicken and sweet potatoes.

Chicken with Vegetables

JANIE STEELE • MOORE, OK

Prep Time: 10–15 minutes • Cooking Time: 6–8 hours • Ideal slow cooker size: 6-qt.

4 bone-in chicken breast halves

1 small head cabbage, quartered

1-lb. pkg. baby carrots

2 14½-oz. cans Mexican-flavored stewed tomatoes

1. Place all ingredients in slow cooker in the order listed.

2. Cover and cook on Low 6–8 hours, or until chicken and vegetables are tender.

Makes 4 servings

Rachel's Chicken Casserole

MARYANN MARKANO • WILMINGTON, DE

Prep Time: 25–30 minutes • Cooking Time: 4 hours • Ideal slow cooker size: 5-qt.

2 16-oz. cans sauerkraut, rinsed and drained, divided

1 cup Light Russian salad dressing, divided

6 boneless, skinless chicken breast halves, divided

1 Tbsp. prepared mustard, divided

6 slices Swiss cheese

fresh parsley for garnish, optional

1. Place half of sauerkraut in slow cooker. Drizzle with ⅓ cup dressing.

2. Top with 3 chicken breast halves. Spread half of mustard on top of chicken.

3. Top with remaining sauerkraut and chicken breasts. Drizzle with another ⅓ cup dressing. (Save remaining dressing until serving time.)

4. Cover and cook on Low 4 hours, or until chicken is tender but not dry or mushy.

5. To serve, place a breast half on each of 6 plates. Divide sauerkraut over chicken. Top each with a slice of cheese and a drizzle of remaining dressing. Garnish with parsley, if you wish, just before serving.

Makes 6 servings

Uncle Tim's Chicken and Sauerkraut

TIM SMITH • RUTLEDGE, PA

Prep Time: 30 minutes • Cooking Time: 5–8 hours • Ideal slow cooker size: 3½-qt.

4 large boneless, skinless chicken breast halves

1-lb. bag sauerkraut

12-oz. can beer

8 medium-sized red potatoes, washed and quartered

salt and pepper to taste

water

1. Place chicken in slow cooker.

2. Spoon sauerkraut over chicken.

3. Pour beer into slow cooker.

4. Add potatoes. Sprinkle generously with salt and pepper.

5. Pour water over all until everything is just covered.

6. Cover and cook on High 5 hours, or on Low 8 hours, or until chicken and potatoes are tender but not dry.

Makes 4 servings

Sunday Chicken Dinner

BEVERLY FLATT-GETZ • WARRIORS MARK, PA

Prep Time: 15–20 minutes • Cooking Time: 4–8 hours • Ideal slow cooker size: 4- to 5-qt.

1 large onion, sliced

4–5 potatoes, peeled and sliced about ¼" thick

3–4 lbs. chicken, cut up

10¾-oz. can cream of mushroom soup

1 soup can milk

garlic powder to taste, optional

1. Line bottom of slow cooker with onion slices.

2. Spread potatoes over top of onions. Then add chicken.

3. Mix together soup and milk. Pour over chicken.

4. If you wish, sprinkle with garlic powder.

5. Cook on High 4 hours, or on Low 8 hours, or until potatoes and chicken are tender.

Makes 4 servings

Note: Add up to a second can of milk if you'd like to have more sauce.

Lemon Pepper Chicken and Veggies

NADINE MARTINITZ • SALINA, KS

Prep Time: 20 minutes • Cooking Time: 4–10 hours • Ideal slow cooker size: 4-qt.

4 carrots, sliced ½" thick

4 potatoes, cut in 1" chunks

2 cloves garlic, peeled and minced, optional

4 whole chicken legs and thighs, skin removed

2 tsp. lemon pepper seasoning

¼ –½ tsp. poultry seasoning, optional

14½-oz. can chicken broth

1. Layer vegetables and chicken in slow cooker.

2. Sprinkle with lemon pepper seasoning and poultry seasoning, if you wish. Pour broth over all.

3. Cover and cook on Low 8–10 hours, or on High 4–5 hours.

Makes 4 servings

Curried Chicken Dinner

JANESSA HOCHSTEDLER • EAST EARL, PA

Prep Time: 20 minutes • Cooking Time: 5–10 hours • Ideal slow cooker size: 3-qt.

1½ lbs. boneless, skinless chicken thighs, quartered

3 potatoes, peeled and cut into chunks, about 2 cups

1 apple, chopped

2 Tbsp. curry powder

14½-oz. can chicken broth

1 medium-sized onion, chopped, optional

1. Place all ingredients in slow cooker. Mix together gently.

2. Cover and cook on Low 8–10 hours, or on High 5 hours, or until chicken is tender but not dry.

3. Serve over cooked rice.

Makes 6 servings

Chicken Divan

KRISTIN TICE • SHIPSHEWANA, IN

Prep Time: 15 minutes ▪ Cooking Time: 3–4 hours ▪ Ideal slow cooker size: 3-qt.

4 boneless, skinless chicken breast halves

4 cups chopped broccoli, fresh or frozen

2 10¾-oz. cans cream of chicken soup

1 cup mayonnaise

½–1 tsp. curry powder, depending upon your taste preference

1. Place chicken breasts in slow cooker.

2. Top with broccoli.

3. In a small mixing bowl, blend soup, mayonnaise, and curry powder together. Pour over top of chicken and broccoli.

4. Cover and cook on High 3–4 hours, or until chicken and broccoli are tender but not mushy or dry. Serve with rice.

Makes 4 servings

Sweet 'n' Sour Chicken with Veggies

JENNIFER EBERLY • HARRISONBURG, VA

Prep Time: 10 minutes ▪ Cooking Time: 8–10 hours ▪ Ideal slow cooker size: 3½- to 4-qt.

2 lbs. boneless, skinless chicken thighs (about 12), cut into 1½" pieces

25–28-oz. jar sweet-and-sour simmer sauce

1-lb. pkg. San Francisco vegetables (frozen broccoli, carrots, water chestnuts, and red peppers), thawed

1. Combine chicken chunks and cooking sauce in slow cooker.

2. Cover and cook on Low 8–10 hours, or until chicken is tender and no longer pink.

3. Ten minutes before serving, stir in vegetables. Cover and increase heat to High. Cook 10 minutes, or until vegetables are crisp-tender.

4. Serve over hot cooked rice.

Makes 6 servings

Sweet Potato Chicken Casserole

BEVERLY FLATT-GETZ • WARRIORS MARK, PA

Prep Time: 20 minutes • Cooking Time: 3–6 hours • Ideal slow cooker size: 3-qt.

3–4 lbs. chicken, cut up

6 raw sweet potatoes, julienned

20-oz. can pineapple chunks, in juice

14½-oz. can chicken broth

2 Tbsp. cornstarch

2 Tbsp. cold water

1. Place cut-up chicken in slow cooker.

2. Top with sweet potatoes.

3. Pour pineapples and juice over potatoes.

4. Then pour chicken broth over all ingredients.

5. Cover and cook on Low 6 hours, or on High 3 hours, or until chicken and potatoes are tender but not dry or mushy.

6. Just before serving, mix cornstarch and cold water together until smooth. Turn cooker to High. Stir cornstarch paste into cooker and cook for a few minutes, until sauce thickens.

7. Place chicken and potatoes on a serving dish or platter. Top with sauce.

Makes 4–6 servings

Note: I sprinkle chives over the chicken when I serve it.

Sweet and Sour Chicken

KAY KASSINGER • PORT ANGELES, WA

Prep Time: 15 minutes • Cooking Time: 8–10 hours • Ideal slow cooker size: 3-qt.

2–3 lbs. boneless, skinless chicken thighs, approximately 12 pieces

14-oz. can pineapple chunks in juice

1 medium-sized yellow onion, chopped

1¼ cups bottled sweet-and-sour sauce

garlic salt

pepper to taste

¼ cup water, optional

1. Spray slow cooker with nonstick cooking spray.

2. Layer chicken in cooker. Pour pineapple chunks and juice over chicken. Spread onion over pineapple.

3. Pour sweet-and-sour sauce over all. Sprinkle with garlic salt and pepper. If you'd like plenty of sauce, add water.

4. Cover and cook on Low 8–10 hours, or until chicken is tender but not dry.

Makes 6 servings

Note: This is wonderful served over jasmine rice.

Sweet and Sour Chicken Breasts

RUTH FISHER • LEICESTER, NY

Prep Time: 20–65 minutes ▪ Cooking Time: 2½–3 hours ▪ Ideal slow cooker size: 4-qt.

3-4 lbs. boneless, skinless chicken breasts

1¾ cups ketchup

10¾-oz. can tomato soup

¼ cup brown sugar

8-oz. can pineapple chunks with juice

sliced green pepper, optional

1. Place chicken breasts in a large nonstick skillet. Add ¼ cup water. Cover and cook gently until tender, about 15 minutes. Or place in a baking dish, add ¼ cup water, cover, and bake at 350° until chicken is tender, about 40–60 minutes.

2. While chicken is cooking, combine ketchup, soup, sugar, and pineapples. Mix well. Stir in green pepper slices, if you wish.

3. Cut cooked chicken into chunks. Place in slow cooker.

4. Pour sauce over chicken. Stir slightly.

5. Cover and cook on High 2 hours.

Makes 8 servings

Note: This dish is versatile and can be prepared to match your schedule. You can do Step 1 the day before you want to serve the dish. Just refrigerate the cooked meat overnight. Or prepare Step 1 2–4 weeks in advance of serving the chicken and freeze it until you need it. On the day you want to serve Sweet and Sour Chicken Breasts, thaw the chicken if it's been frozen, and then begin with Step 2. When I make this dish, I cook rice, and then arrange the rice in the center of a large platter. I spoon the chicken around the rice for an attractive presentation of the dish.

Chicken a la Fruit

TERESA KENNEDY • MT. PLEASANT, IA

Prep Time: 20 minutes • Cooking Time: 6–8 hours • Ideal slow cooker size: 6-qt.

½ cup crushed pineapple, drained

3 whole peaches, mashed

2 Tbsp. lemon juice

2 Tbsp. soy sauce

½–¾ tsp. salt, optional

¼ tsp. pepper, optional

1 chicken, cut up

1. Spray slow cooker with nonstick cooking spray.

2. Mix pineapple, peaches, lemon juice, and soy sauce in a large bowl. Add salt and pepper, if you wish.

3. Dip chicken pieces in sauce and then place in slow cooker. Pour remaining sauce over all.

4. Cover and cook on Low 6–8 hours, or until chicken is tender but not dry.

Makes 5–6 servings

Hawaii Chicken

SANDY CLUGSTON • ST. THOMAS, PA

Prep Time: 10 minutes • Cooking Time: 3–8 hours • Ideal slow cooker size: 3-qt.

4 boneless, skinless chicken breast halves

10¾-oz. can cream of mushroom soup

½ cup sour cream

10-oz. can pineapple tidbits, drained

large red bell pepper, cut into strips

OPTIONAL INGREDIENTS:

1 small red onion, sliced

salt and pepper to taste

1. Spray slow cooker with nonstick cooking spray. Place chicken in slow cooker.

2. In bowl, mix soup and sour cream and pour over chicken.

3. Place pineapple tidbits and sliced red pepper over mixture. Add onion and a good sprinkling of salt and pepper, if you wish.

4. Cover and cook on Low 7–8 hours, or on High 3–4 hours, or until chicken is tender but not dry.

5. Serve over cooked rice.

Makes 4 servings

Stewed Oriental Chicken

STANLEY KROPF • ELKHART, IN

Prep Time: 15–20 minutes • Cooking Time: 4 hours • Ideal slow cooker size: 4- to 5-qt.

1 whole chicken, cut up

3 Tbsp. hot sweet mustard, or
    2 Tbsp. hot mustard and
    1 Tbsp. honey

2 Tbsp. soy sauce

1 tsp. ginger

1 tsp. cumin

1. Wash chicken and place in slow cooker. Pat dry.

2. Mix remaining ingredients in a bowl. Taste and adjust seasonings, if you want. Pour over chicken.

3. Cover and cook on High at least 4 hours, or until tender. If it's more convenient, you can cook the meat an hour or so longer with no negative effect.

Makes 4–6 servings

Notes:

• This is a folk recipe, so the cook should experiment to taste. I often use a variety of optional ingredients, depending on how I'm feeling. These include teriyaki sauce, oyster sauce, cardamom, sesame and olive oil, dry vermouth, and garlic, in whatever amount and combination seems right.

• If you cook the dish longer than 4 hours, the chicken tends to fall apart. In any event, serve it in a bowl large enough to hold the chicken and broth. I like to serve this with cooked plain or saffron rice.

Chicken Oriental

ANNE TOWNSEND • ALBUQUERQUE, NM

Prep Time: 5 minutes • Cooking Time: 4–8 hours • Ideal slow cooker size: 3-qt.

1 Tbsp. hot chili sesame oil

4 large chicken thighs

3 cloves garlic, sliced

½ cup brown sugar

3 Tbsp. soy sauce

1. Spread oil around bottom of slow cooker.

2. Rinse chicken well and remove excess fat. Pat dry. Place in cooker.

3. Sprinkle garlic slices over top of chicken. Crumble brown sugar over top. Drizzle with soy sauce.

4. Cover and cook on Low 4–8 hours, or until thighs are tender but not dry.

5. Serve over rice, prepared with juice from cooked chicken instead of water.

Makes 4 servings

Chicken Chow Mein

CLARA YODER BYLER • HARTVILLE, OH

Prep Time: 30 minutes • Cooking Time: 4–5 hours • Ideal slow cooker size: 4-qt.

1 lb. boneless, skinless chicken breasts, or thighs, cubed

2 cups diced celery

1 cup diced onion

2 Tbsp. soy sauce

2 cups water

½ tsp. salt, optional

½ tsp. pepper, optional

1 Tbsp. cornstarch

¼ cup water

1. Place chicken in slow cooker. Add celery, onion, soy sauce, 2 cups water, and salt and pepper, if you wish.

2. Cover and cook on High 4 hours.

3. Just before serving, mix cornstarch with ¼ cup water in a small bowl. When smooth, add to slow cooker to thicken sauce a bit. Heat for a few more minutes.

4. I like to serve this over cooked rice, or chow mein noodles, or both.

Makes 5–6 servings

Cooking Tip

When buying bakeware and kitchen tools, spend the extra money for good quality.

Thai Chicken

JOANNE GOOD • WHEATON, IL

Prep Time: 5 minutes • Cooking Time: 8-9 hours • Ideal slow cooker size: 4-qt.

6 skinless chicken thighs

¾ cup salsa, your choice of mild, medium, or hot

¼ cup chunky peanut butter

1 Tbsp. low-sodium soy sauce

2 Tbsp. lime juice

OPTIONAL INGREDIENTS:

1 tsp. grated fresh ginger

2 Tbsp. cilantro, chopped

1 Tbsp. dry-roasted peanuts, chopped

1. Put chicken in slow cooker.

2. In a bowl, mix remaining ingredients together, except cilantro and chopped peanuts.

3. Cover and cook on Low 8-9 hours, or until chicken is cooked through but not dry.

4. Skim off any fat. Remove chicken to a platter and serve topped with sauce. Sprinkle with peanuts and cilantro, if you wish.

5. Serve over cooked rice.

Makes 6 servings

Variation: Vegetarians can substitute 2 15-oz. cans of white beans, and perhaps some tempeh, for the chicken.

Raspberried Chicken Drumsticks

PAT BECHTEL • DILLSBURG, PA

Prep Time: 10 minutes • Cooking Time: 5¼-6¼ hours • Ideal slow cooker size: 3½-qt.

3 Tbsp. soy sauce

⅓ cup red raspberry fruit spread or jam

5 chicken drumsticks or chicken thighs

2 Tbsp. cornstarch

2 Tbsp. cold water

1. Mix soy sauce and raspberry spread or jam together in a small bowl until well blended.

2. Brush chicken with sauce and place in slow cooker. Spoon remainder of sauce over top.

3. Cook on Low 5-6 hours, or until chicken is tender but not dry.

4. Mix together cornstarch and cold water in a small bowl until smooth. Then remove chicken to a serving platter and keep warm. Turn slow cooker to High and stir in cornstarch and water to thicken. When thickened and bubbly, after about 10-15 minutes, spoon sauce over chicken before serving.

Makes 3 servings

Teriyaki Chicken

ELAINE VIGODA • ROCHESTER, NY

Prep Time: 15 minutes • Cooking Time: 5–6 hours • Ideal slow cooker size: 5-qt.

1 lb. boneless, skinless chicken thighs, cut into chunks

1 lb. boneless, skinless chicken breasts, cut into large chunks

10-oz. bottle teriyaki sauce

½ lb. snow peas, optional

8-oz. can water chestnuts, drained, optional

1. Place chicken in slow cooker. Cover with sauce. Stir until sauce is well distributed.

2. Cover and cook on Low 4–5 hours, or until chicken is tender. Add snow peas and water chestnuts, if you wish.

3. Cover and cook another hour on Low.

4. Serve over cooked white rice or Chinese rice noodles.

Makes 6 servings

Tomato-y Chicken

JOYCE SHACKELFORD • GREEN BAY, WI

Prep Time: 5 minutes • Cooking Time: 3–5 hours • Ideal slow cooker size: 4-qt.

8-oz. can tomato sauce

1 envelope dry spaghetti sauce mix

1 cup water

4-oz. can mushrooms, undrained

2–3 lbs. chicken parts

1. Mix tomato sauce, dry spaghetti mix, water, and mushrooms together in a bowl.

2. Place chicken in slow cooker. Pour sauce over.

3. Cover and cook on High 3 hours, or on Low 4–5 hours, or until chicken is tender.

Makes 4 servings

Chicken Marengo

MARCIA PARKER • LANSDALE, PA

Prep Time: 5–10 minutes • Cooking Time: 6–7 hours • Ideal slow cooker size: 6-qt.

2½–3-lb. frying chicken, cut up and skinned

2 envelopes dry spaghetti sauce mix

½ cup dry white wine

2 fresh tomatoes, quartered

¼ lb. fresh mushrooms

1. Place chicken pieces in bottom of slow cooker.

2. In a small bowl, combine dry spaghetti sauce mix with wine. Pour over chicken.

3. Cover and cook on Low 5½–6½ hours.

4. Turn temperature to High. Then add tomatoes and mushrooms.

5. Cover and cook on High 30–40 minutes, or until vegetables are hot.

6. Serve with cooked noodles or your favorite other pasta.

Makes 4–5 servings

Chicken Parmigiana

LOIS OSTRANDER • LEBANON, PA

Prep Time: 20 minutes • Cooking Time: 6–8 hours • Ideal slow cooker size: 3½-qt.

1 egg

1 cup dry bread crumbs

6 bone-in chicken breast halves, divided

10½-oz. jar pizza sauce, divided

6 slices mozzarella cheese, or ½ cup grated Parmesan cheese

1. Beat egg in a shallow, oblong bowl. Place bread crumbs in another shallow, oblong bowl. Dip chicken halves into egg, and then into crumbs, using a spoon to coat meat on all sides with crumbs.

2. Sauté chicken in a large nonstick skillet sprayed with nonstick cooking spray.

3. Arrange 1 layer of browned chicken in slow cooker. Pour half of pizza sauce over top. Add a second layer of chicken. Pour remaining pizza sauce over top.

4. Cover and cook on Low 5¾–7¾ hours, or until chicken is tender but not dry.

5. Add mozzarella cheese or Parmesan cheese on top. Cover and cook 15 more minutes.

Makes 6 servings

Note: You can remove the chicken from the slow cooker after Step 4 and place the breasts on a microwave-proof serving platter. Put a slice of mozzarella on each chicken piece and then sprinkle each with Parmesan. Cook in the microwave on High 1 minute to melt cheese. Serve any extra sauce over pasta.

Italian Chicken

STARLA KREIDER • MOHRSVILLE, PA

Prep Time: 5 minutes • Cooking Time: 2½–8 hours • Ideal slow cooker size: 3-qt.

4 boneless, skinless chicken breast halves

28-oz. jar spaghetti sauce, your choice of special seasonings and ingredients

4 ozs. shredded mozzarella cheese

1. Place chicken in slow cooker.

2. Pour spaghetti sauce over chicken.

3. Cover and cook on High 2½–3½ hours, or on Low 6–8 hours.

4. Place chicken on a serving platter and sprinkle with cheese.

5. Serve with cooked rice or spaghetti.

Makes 4 servings

That's Amore Chicken Cacciatore

CAROL SHERWOOD • BATAVIA, NY

Prep Time: 20 minutes • Cooking Time: 7–9 hours • Ideal slow cooker size: 6-qt.

6 boneless, skinless chicken breast halves, divided

28-oz. jar spaghetti sauce

2 green peppers, chopped

1 onion, minced

2 Tbsp. minced garlic

1. Place a layer of chicken in slow cooker.

2. Mix remaining ingredients together in a bowl. Spoon half of sauce over first layer of chicken.

3. Add remaining breast halves. Top with remaining sauce.

4. Cover and cook on Low 7–9 hours, or until chicken is tender but not dry.

5. Serve with cooked spaghetti or linguine.

Makes 6 servings

Italian Chicken Nuggets

TINA GOSS • DUENWEG, MO

Prep Time: 5 minutes • Cooking Time: 1 hour • Ideal slow cooker size: 2-qt.

13½-oz. pkg. frozen chicken nuggets

⅓ cup grated Parmesan cheese

28-oz. jar spaghetti sauce

4 ozs. shredded mozzarella cheese

1 tsp. Italian seasoning

1. Put nuggets in bottom of slow cooker. Sprinkle with Parmesan cheese.

2. Layer in spaghetti sauce, mozzarella cheese, and Italian seasoning.

3. Cover and cook on High 1 hour, or until chicken is tender but not dry or mushy.

Makes 4 servings

Italian Chicken

COLLEEN HEATWOLE • BURTON, MI

Prep Time: 5–10 minutes • Cooking Time: 6–8 hours • Ideal slow cooker size: 3- to 4-qt.

4 boneless, skinless chicken breast halves

1 envelope dry Italian dressing mix

1 cup chicken broth

1. Place chicken in slow cooker. Sprinkle with dry Italian dressing mix.

2. Spoon chicken broth over top.

3. Cover and cook on High 6 hours, or on Low 8 hours, or until chicken is tender but not dry.

Makes 4 servings

Cooking Tip

Leave the lid on while the slow cooker cooks. The steam that condenses on the lid helps cook the food from the top. Every time you take off the lid, the cooker loses steam. After you put the lid back on, it takes up to 20 minutes to regain the lost steam and temperature. That means it takes longer for the food to cook.

—Pam Hochstedler, Kalona, IA

Chicken Stroganoff

MARY C. WIRTH • LANCASTER, PA

Prep Time: 10-15 minutes ▪ Cooking Time: 5½-6½ hours ▪ Ideal slow cooker size: 3-qt.

4 boneless, skinless, chicken breast halves, cubed

2 Tbsp. butter, melted

1- 2 envelopes dry Italian dressing mix

8-oz. pkg. light cream cheese, softened

10¾-oz. can cream of chicken soup

1. Put chicken, melted butter, and dressing mix in slow cooker. Stir together gently.

2. Cover and cook on Low 5–6 hours.

3. Stir in cream cheese and soup. Cover and cook on High 30 minutes, or until heated through.

4. Serve over cooked rice or noodles.

Makes 4 servings

Zesty Italian Chicken

YVONNE KAUFFMAN BOETTGER • HARRISONBURG, VA

Prep Time: 5 minutes ▪ Cooking Time: 4-8 hours ▪ Ideal slow cooker size: 4-qt.

2-3 lbs. boneless, skinless chicken breasts, cut into chunks

16-oz. bottle Italian dressing

¼ cup Parmesan cheese

1. Place chicken in bottom of slow cooker and pour dressing over chicken. Stir together gently.

2. Sprinkle cheese on top.

3. Cover and cook on High 4 hours, or on Low 8 hours, or until chicken is tender but not dry.

4. Serve over cooked rice, along with extra sauce from chicken.

Makes 4-6 servings

Chicken Cacciatore with Green Peppers

DONNA LANTGEN • CHADRON, NE

Prep Time: 10 minutes • Cooking Time: 6 hours • Ideal slow cooker size: 5-qt.

1 green pepper, chopped

1 onion, chopped

1 Tbsp. dry Italian seasoning

15½-oz. can diced tomatoes

6 boneless, skinless chicken
    breast halves, divided

1. In a small bowl, mix together green pepper, onion, Italian seasoning, and tomatoes. Place one-third in bottom of slow cooker.

2. Layer 3 chicken breasts over top. Spoon in one-third of tomato sauce.

3. Layer in 3 remaining chicken breasts. Top with remaining tomato mixture.

4. Cover and cook on Low 6 hours, or until chicken is done but not dry.

Makes 6 servings

Note: Top with grated mozzarella or Parmesan cheese when serving.

Can-You-Believe-It's-So-Simple Salsa Chicken

LEESA DEMARTYN • ENOLA, PA

Prep Time: 5 minutes • Cooking Time: 5–8 hours • Ideal slow cooker size: 3-qt.

4–6 boneless, skinless chicken
    breast halves

16-oz. jar chunky-style salsa,
    your choice of mild,
    medium, or hot

2 cups shredded cheese, your
    choice of flavor

1. Place chicken in slow cooker. Pour salsa over chicken.

2. Cover and cook on Low 5–8 hours, or until chicken is tender but not dry.

3. Top individual servings with shredded cheese.

4. Serve this over cooked rice, or in a whole wheat or cheddar cheese wrap.

Makes 4–6 servings

Chicken Cacciatore with Mushrooms

LUCY O'CONNELL • GOSHEN, MA

Prep Time: 30 minutes • Cooking Time: 8 hours • Ideal slow cooker size: 4-qt.

3-lb. broiler/fryer chicken, cut up

2 medium-sized onions, thinly sliced

1 lb. fresh mushrooms, sliced

48-oz. jar spaghetti sauce

$\frac{1}{2}$ cup red or white wine

$\frac{3}{4}$ tsp. salt, optional

$\frac{1}{2}$ tsp. pepper, optional

1. Remove skin from chicken.

2. Place chicken, onions, and mushrooms in slow cooker.

3. In a mixing bowl, combine spaghetti sauce, wine, and salt and pepper, if you wish. Pour over chicken.

4. Cover and cook on High 4 hours, and then on Low 4 hours.

5. Serve over spaghetti.

Makes 6–8 servings

Honey Chicken Wings

BONNIE WHALING • CLEARFIELD, PA

Prep Time: 20–30 minutes • Cooking Time: 3$\frac{1}{2}$–4$\frac{1}{2}$ hours • Ideal slow cooker size: 4-qt.

3 lbs. chicken wings, tips cut off, divided

2 Tbsp. vegetable oil

1 cup honey

$\frac{1}{2}$ cup soy sauce

2 Tbsp. ketchup

1. Cut each wing into 2 parts. Place a third of wings in a large nonstick skillet and brown in oil. (If skillet is crowded, wings will not brown.) Place in slow cooker.

2. Mix remaining ingredients and pour one-third of sauce over wings in cooker.

3. Repeat Steps 1 and 2 twice.

4. Cover and cook on High 3–4 hours, or until wings are tender but not dry.

Makes 6–8 servings

Five-Spice Chicken Wings

MARCIA PARKER • LANSDALE, PA

Prep Time: 30 minutes • Cooking Time: 2½–5½ hours • Ideal slow cooker size: 3½- to 4-qt.

3 lbs. (about 16) chicken wings

1 cup bottled plum sauce

2 Tbsp. butter, melted

1 tsp. five-spice powder

thinly sliced orange wedges, optional

pineapple slices, optional

1. In a foil-lined baking pan, arrange wings in a single layer. Bake at 375° for 20 minutes. Drain well.

2. Meanwhile, combine plum sauce, melted butter, and five-spice powder in slow cooker. Add wings. Then stir to coat wings with sauce.

3. Cover and cook on Low 4–5 hours, or on High 2–2½ hours.

4. Serve immediately, or keep them warm in cooker on Low up to 2 hours.

5. Garnish with orange wedges and pineapple slices to serve, if you wish.

Makes 6–8 servings

Variation: For Kentucky Chicken Wings, create a different sauce in Step 2. Use ½ cup maple syrup, ½ cup whiskey, and 2 Tbsp. melted butter. Then stir in the wings. Continue with Step 3.

Note: Plum sauce and five-spice powder can be found in Asian food stores or in the Asian food aisle of general grocery stores.

Chicken with Broccoli Rice

MARYANN MARKANO • WILMINGTON, DE

Prep Time: 20 minutes • Cooking Time: 6–8 hours • Ideal slow cooker size: 5-qt.

1¼ cups uncooked long-grain rice

pepper to taste

2 lbs. boneless, skinless chicken breasts, cut into strips

1 pkg. Knorr's cream of broccoli dry soup mix

2½ cups chicken broth

1. Spray slow cooker with nonstick cooking spray. Place rice in cooker. Sprinkle with pepper.

2. Top with chicken pieces.

3. In a mixing bowl, combine soup mix and broth. Pour over chicken and rice.

4. Cover and cook on Low 6–8 hours, or until rice and chicken are tender but not dry.

Makes 6 servings

Chicken and Rice in a Bag

DOROTHY VAN DEEST • MEMPHIS, TN

Prep Time: 15 minutes • Cooking Time: 8–10 hours • Ideal slow cooker size: 5-qt.

3-lb. fryer, cut into serving
pieces, or 3 lbs. legs and
thighs

1½ cups uncooked long-grain
rice

10¾-oz. can condensed
cream of chicken soup

1¾ cups water

1 envelope dry onion soup mix

1. Rinse chicken pieces and pat dry. Set aside.

2. Combine rice, cream of chicken soup, and water in slow
cooker. Stir until well blended.

3. Place chicken pieces in a see-through roasting bag. Add
onion soup mix. Shake bag to coat chicken thoroughly.
Puncture 4 to 6 holes in bottom of bag. Fold top of bag
over chicken and lay in slow cooker on top of rice.

4. Cover and cook on Low 8–10 hours, or until chicken is
tender and rice is cooked but not dry. Serve chicken and
rice together on a large platter.

Makes 4–6 servings

Chicken and Rice Casserole

DALE PETERSON • RAPID CITY, SD / JOYCE SHACKELFORD • GREEN BAY, WI

Prep Time: 20 minutes • Cooking Time: 4–5 hours • Ideal slow cooker size: 6-qt.

2 10¾-oz. cans cream of
celery soup, divided

2-oz. can sliced mushrooms,
undrained

½ cup uncooked long-grain rice

2 whole boneless, skinless
chicken breasts, uncooked
and cubed

1 Tbsp. dry onion soup mix

half a soup can water

1. Spray slow cooker with nonstick cooking spray. Combine
1 can of soup, mushrooms, and rice in cooker. Stir until
well blended.

2. Lay chicken on top. Pour remaining can of soup over all.

3. Sprinkle with onion soup mix. Add water.

4. Cover and cook on Low 4–5 hours, or until both chicken
and rice are fully cooked but not dry.

Makes 3–4 servings

Chicken with Brown or Wild Rice

CAROL EVELETH • WELLMAN, IA

Prep Time: 10 minutes • Cooking Time: 3–8 hours • Ideal slow cooker size: 6-qt.

1½ cups uncooked brown, or wild, rice

1 envelope dry onion soup mix

10¾-oz. can mushroom soup

10¾-oz. can cream of chicken soup

3½ cups water

8-10 pieces chicken

1. Spray slow cooker with nonstick cooking spray.

2. Pour rice, soup mix, and soups into slow cooker and mix thoroughly. Pour water on top.

3. Add chicken pieces.

4. Cook on Low 6–8 hours, or on High 3–4 hours, or until chicken and rice are tender but not dry.

Makes 8–10 servings

Chicken Curry with Rice

JENNIFER YODER SOMMERS • HARRISONBURG, VA

Prep Time: 10 minutes • Cooking Time: 5–10 hours • Ideal slow cooker size: 3- to 4-qt.

1½ lbs. boneless, skinless chicken thighs, quartered

1 onion, chopped

2 cups uncooked long-grain rice

2 Tbsp. curry powder

14½-oz. can chicken broth

1. Combine all ingredients in slow cooker.

2. Cover and cook on Low 8–10 hours, or on High 5 hours, or until chicken is tender but not dry.

Makes 6 servings

Variation: Add 1 chopped apple to Step 1. Thirty minutes before the end of the cooking time, stir in 2 cups frozen peas.

Cooking Tip

When camping, always prepare extra food. You'll likely need 6 servings to feed 4 ravenous campers!

Chinese Chicken with Rice

SHARON ANDERS • ALBURTIS, PA

Prep Time: 10 minutes • Cooking Time: 3½–6½ hours • Ideal slow cooker size: 3-qt.

⅔ cup soy sauce

½ cup honey

½ tsp. granulated garlic

2 cups hot water

4 boneless, skinless chicken breast halves

1 cup uncooked long-grain rice

1. Mix soy sauce, honey, and garlic with hot water in slow cooker.

2. Add chicken breasts, submerging them as much as possible in sauce.

3. Cover and cook on Low 5–6 hours, or on High 3–4 hours, or until chicken is tender but not dry.

4. Remove chicken to a platter and keep warm. Stir uncooked rice into sauce. Cover and cook on High 30 minutes, or until rice is tender. Add to platter with chicken and serve.

Makes 4 servings

Spicy Chicken with Rice

DAWN HAHN • LITITZ, PA

Prep Time: 10 minutes • Cooking Time: 4–6 hours • Ideal slow cooker size: 4- to 5-qt.

1 cup uncooked long-grain rice

1¼ cups chicken broth

1 cup salsa, your choice of mild, medium, or hot

4 boneless, skinless chicken breast halves

¾ cup shredded cheddar cheese

1. Spray slow cooker with nonstick cooking spray.

2. Pour rice into bottom of slow cooker.

3. Add chicken broth and salsa. Stir together well.

4. Place chicken breasts on top.

5. Cover and cook on Low 4–6 hours, or until chicken and rice are tender but not dry.

6. Garnish with cheese just before serving.

Makes 4 servings

Fiesta Chicken

STACIE SKELLY • MILLERSVILLE, PA

Prep Time: 5 minutes • Cooking Time: 6½ hours • Ideal slow cooker size: 4- to 5-qt.

8 boneless, skinless chicken breast halves

16-oz. jar salsa

2 cups instant rice

1. Place chicken in slow cooker. Pour salsa over chicken.

2. Cover and cook on Low 6 hours, or until chicken is tender but not dry.

3. Remove chicken to a serving platter and keep warm.

4. Add rice to hot salsa in slow cooker and cook on High 30 minutes. Serve chicken and rice together on a large platter.

Makes 8 servings

Spicy Chicken Curry

JOAN MILLER • WAYLAND, IA

Prep Time: 15–20 minutes • Cooking Time: 3–4½ hours • Ideal slow cooker size: 4- to 5-qt.

10 skinless, bone-in chicken breast halves, divided

16-oz. jar salsa, mild, medium, or hot

1 medium-sized onion, chopped

2 Tbsp. curry powder

1 cup sour cream

1. Place half of chicken in slow cooker.

2. Combine salsa, onion, and curry powder in a medium-sized bowl. Pour half of sauce over meat in cooker.

3. Repeat Steps 1 and 2.

4. Cover and cook on High 3 hours. Or cook on High 1½ hours, and then turn cooker to Low and cook 3 more hours.

5. Remove chicken to a serving platter and cover to keep warm.

6. Add sour cream to slow cooker and stir into salsa until well blended. Serve over chicken.

Makes 10 servings

Cooking Tip

Milk products such as cream, milk, and sour cream can curdle and separate when cooked for a long period. Add them during the last 10 minutes if cooking on High, or during the last 20–30 minutes if cooking on Low.

—Mrs. J. E. Barthold, Bethlehem, PA
—Marilyn Yoder, Archbold, OH

Cheesy Chicken Chili

JENNIFER KUH • BAY VILLAGE, OH

Prep Time: 5–7 minutes • Cooking Time: 6–8 hours • Ideal slow cooker size: 3- to 4-qt.

4 boneless, skinless chicken breast halves

16-oz. jar salsa, your choice of spiciness

2 16-oz. cans great northern beans, drained

8 ozs. shredded Colby Jack, or Pepper Jack, cheese

1. Place chicken in bottom of slow cooker.

2. Cover with salsa.

3. Cover and cook on Low $5\frac{1}{2}$–$7\frac{1}{2}$ hours, or until chicken is tender but not dry.

4. Shred or cube chicken in the sauce.

5. Stir in beans and cheese.

6. Cover and cook another 30 minutes on Low.

7. Serve over cooked rice or noodles.

Makes 4 servings

Spanish Chicken

NATALIA SHOWALTER • MT. SOLON, VA

Prep Time: 15–20 minutes • Cooking Time: 5–6 hours • Ideal slow cooker size: 3- to 6-qt.

8 chicken thighs, skinned

$\frac{1}{2}$–1 cup red wine vinegar, according to your taste preference

$\frac{2}{3}$ cup tamari, or low-sodium soy, sauce

1 tsp. garlic powder

4 6" cinnamon sticks

1. Brown chicken slightly in a nonstick skillet, if you wish, and then transfer to greased slow cooker.

2. Mix wine vinegar, tamari sauce, and garlic powder together in a bowl. Pour over chicken.

3. Break cinnamon sticks into several pieces and distribute among chicken thighs.

4. Cover and cook on Low 5–6 hours, or until chicken is tender but not dry.

Makes 4–6 servings

Note: You can skip browning the chicken if you're in a hurry, but browning gives the finished dish a better flavor.

Chicken Enchiladas

JENNIFER YODER SOMMERS • HARRISONBURG, VA

Prep Time: 20 minutes • Cooking Time: 4 hours • Ideal slow cooker size: 3-qt.

2 10¾-oz. cans cream of chicken or mushroom soup

4½-oz. can diced green chilies

2-3 boneless, skinless whole chicken breasts, cut into pieces

2 cups shredded cheddar cheese

5 6" flour tortillas

1. In a mixing bowl, combine soups, chilies, and chicken.

2. Spray slow cooker with nonstick cooking spray. Put foil handles in place (see Cooking Tip on page 162 for instructions).

3. Spoon in one-fifth of sauce on bottom of cooker. Top with one-fifth of cheese and then 1 tortilla. Continue layering in that order, and with those amounts, 4 more times, ending with cheese on top.

4. Cover cooker and cook on Low 4 hours.

Makes 4 servings

Green Enchiladas

JENNIFER YODER SOMMERS • HARRISONBURG, VA

Prep Time: 5-7 minutes • Cooking Time: 2-4 hours • Ideal slow cooker size: 3-qt.

2 10-oz. cans green enchilada sauce, divided

8 large tortillas, divided

2 cups cooked chicken, divided

1½ cups mozzarella cheese

1. Pour a little enchilada sauce on bottom of slow cooker.

2. Layer 1 tortilla, ¼ cup chicken, and ¼ cup sauce into slow cooker.

3. Repeat layers, until all 3 ingredients are used completely.

4. Sprinkle mozzarella cheese over top.

5. Cover and cook on Low 2-4 hours.

Makes 8 servings

Note: Green enchilada sauce can be found in the Mexican foods section of most grocery stores.

Hot Chicken Salad

AUDREY ROMONOSKY • AUSTIN, TX

Prep Time: 10 minutes • Cooking Time: 2 hours • Ideal slow cooker size: 2-qt.

2 Tbsp. onion, minced

1 cup mayonnaise

2 Tbsp. lemon juice

1½ cups shredded cooked
  chicken

½ cup slivered almonds or
  pecans

1. Mix together all ingredients in slow cooker.

2. Cover and cook on Low 2 hours, or until heated through.

3. Serve hot, or allow to cool and serve on lettuce leaves,
   along with sliced tomatoes.

   Makes 8 servings

Chicken and Noodles

ELENA YODER • CARLSBAD, NM

Prep Time: 15 minutes • Cooking Time: 2 hours • Ideal slow cooker size: 4-qt.

1 qt. chicken broth

1 qt. hot water

2 cups cooked chicken, cut
  into small pieces

10-oz. pkg. dry noodles

salt and pepper to taste

10¾-oz. can cream of
  mushroom soup

1. Combine all ingredients except soup in slow cooker.

2. Cover and cook on High 2 hours.

3. Ten minutes before serving, stir in soup.

   Makes 8 servings

Creamy Chicken or Turkey

CLARA YODER BYLER • HARTVILLE, OH

Prep Time: 30 minutes ▪ Cooking Time: 1½–2 hours ▪ Ideal slow cooker size: 4-qt.

10¾-oz. can cream of celery soup

10¾-oz. can chicken noodle soup

⅔ cup half-and-half

2 cups cooked chicken or turkey

10½-oz. can (or larger) chow mein noodles

1. Put all ingredients in slow cooker. Mix together gently until well mixed.

2. Cook on High 1½–2 hours, or until bubbly and hot.

   Makes 6–8 servings

Note: For a light meal, serve this with raw veggies. For a more stick-to-the-ribs meal, serve the creamy meat over rice or mashed potatoes.

Chicken Plus Stuffing

BETTY B. DENNISON • GROVE CITY, PA

Prep Time: 15 minutes ▪ Cooking Time: 2–5 hours ▪ Ideal slow cooker size: 5-qt.

12-serving-size pkg. chicken stuffing mix

4 cups cooked chicken

3 10¾-oz. cans cream of chicken soup

½ cup milk

2 cups cheddar cheese, shredded

1. Prepare stuffing mix as directed on package and put in slow cooker.

2. Add chicken, soup, and milk to slow cooker. Blend all ingredients together.

3. Sprinkle cheese over top.

4. Cover and cook on Low 4–5 hours, or on High 2–3 hours.

   Makes 8 servings

Chicken Dressing

MRS. MAHLON MILLER • HUTCHINSON, KS

Prep Time: 30 minutes • Cooking Time: 2 hours • Ideal slow cooker size: 1½-qt.

1 cup potatoes, diced and boiled

1 cup cooked chicken with
    some broth

3 eggs, beaten

½ cup milk

3 slices bread, cubed

¼-½ tsp. salt, optional

⅛-¼ tsp. pepper, optional

1 small onion, finely chopped,
    optional

1. Combine all ingredients in slow cooker.

2. Cover and cook on Low 2 hours.

   Makes 3–4 servings

Tender Turkey Breast

BECKY GEHMAN • BERGTON, VA

Prep Time: 5 minutes • Cooking Time: 2–9 hours • Ideal slow cooker size: 6-qt.

6-lb. turkey breast, boneless
    or bone-in

2-3 Tbsp. water

1. Place turkey breast in slow cooker. Add water.

2. Cover and cook on High 2–4 hours, or on Low 4–9 hours, or until tender but not dry and mushy.

3. Turn over once during cooking time.

4. If you'd like to brown the turkey, bake it uncovered in an oven at 325° for 15–20 minutes after it's finished cooking in slow cooker.

   Makes 10 servings

Notes:

• Save the drippings in the bottom of the slow cooker when you remove the meat. Transfer them to a nonstick skillet. Add ½ cup water to ½ cup drippings. Heat until simmering. In a small jar, blend 2 Tbsp. flour into 1 cup water. When smooth, stir into simmering broth, continuing to heat and stir until smooth and thickened. Use as gravy over sliced hot turkey.

• Slice cooked turkey and serve hot. Or allow to cool and then either shred, slice, or cut into chunks for making salads or sandwiches. Freeze any leftovers.

Slow Cooker Turkey Breast

LIZ ANN YODER • HARTVILLE, OH

Prep Time: 10 minutes • Cooking Time: 9–10 hours • Ideal slow cooker size: 6- to 7-qt.

6-lb. turkey breast

2 tsp. oil

salt to taste

pepper to taste

1 medium-sized onion, quartered

4 garlic cloves, peeled

½ cup water

1. Rinse turkey and pat dry with paper towels.

2. Rub oil over turkey. Sprinkle with salt and pepper. Place, meaty side up, in slow cooker.

3. Place onion and garlic around sides of cooker.

4. Cover. Cook on Low 9–10 hours, or until meat thermometer stuck in meaty part of breast registers 180°.

5. Remove from slow cooker and let stand 10 minutes before slicing.

6. Serve with mashed potatoes, cranberry salad, and corn or green beans.

Makes 8–10 servings

Variations: Add carrot chunks and chopped celery to Step 3 to add more flavor to the turkey broth. Reserve broth for soups, or thicken with flour-water paste and serve as gravy over sliced turkey. Freeze broth in pint-sized containers for future use. Debone turkey and freeze in pint-sized containers for future use. Or freeze any leftover turkey after serving the meal described above.

Turkey in the Slow Cooker

EARNEST ZIMMERMAN • MECHANICSBURG, PA

Prep Time: 5 minutes • Cooking Time: 1–5 hours • Ideal slow cooker size: 6-qt.

3-5-lb. bone-in turkey breast

salt to taste

2 carrots, cut in chunks

1 onion, cut in eighths

2 ribs celery, cut in chunks

pepper to taste

1. Rinse turkey breast and pat dry. Season well inside with salt.

2. Place vegetables in bottom of slow cooker. Sprinkle with pepper. Place turkey breast on top of vegetables.

3. Cover and cook on High 1–3 hours, or on Low 4–5 hours, or until tender but not dry or mushy.

Makes 6–8 servings

Note: Strain broth and reserve it. Discard vegetables. The broth makes excellent gravy or base for soups. You can freeze whatever you don't need immediately. Debone the turkey. Slice and serve hot, or chill and use for turkey salad or sandwiches.

Maple-Glazed Turkey Breast with Rice

JEANETTE OBERHOLTZER • MANHEIM, PA

Prep Time: 10–15 minutes • Cooking Time: 4–6 hours • Ideal slow cooker size: 3- to 4-qt.

6-oz. pkg. long-grain wild rice
   mix

1½ cups water

2-lb. boneless turkey breast,
   cut into 1½"–2" chunks

¼ cup maple syrup

1 onion, chopped

¼ tsp. cinnamon

½ tsp. salt, optional

1. Combine all ingredients in slow cooker.

2. Cook on Low 4–6 hours, or until turkey and rice are both tender but not dry or mushy.

Makes 4 servings

Saucy Turkey Breast

KELLY BAILEY • MECHANICSBURG, PA / MICHELE RUVOLA • SELDEN, NY
RUTH FISHER • LEICESTER, NY

Prep Time: 5 minutes • Cooking Time: 1–5 hours • Ideal slow cooker size: 4- to 6-qt.

3-5-lb. turkey breast, bone-in
   or boneless

1 envelope dry onion soup mix

salt and pepper to taste

16-oz. can cranberry sauce,
   jellied or whole-berry

2 Tbsp. cornstarch

2 Tbsp. cold water

1. Sprinkle salt and pepper and soup mix on top and bottom of turkey breast. Place turkey in slow cooker.

2. Add cranberry sauce to top of turkey breast.

3. Cover and cook on Low 4–5 hours, or on High 1–3 hours, or until tender but not dry and mushy. (A meat thermometer should read 180°.)

4. Remove turkey from cooker and allow to rest 10 minutes. (Keep sauce in cooker.)

5. Meanwhile, cover cooker and turn to High. In a small bowl, mix together cornstarch and cold water until smooth. When sauce is boiling, stir in cornstarch paste. Continue to simmer until sauce thickens.

6. Slice turkey and serve topped with sauce from cooker.

Makes 6–8 servings

Sage Turkey Thighs

CAROLYN BAER • CONRATH, WI

Prep Time: 15 minutes • Cooking Time: 6-8 hours • Ideal slow cooker size: 3-qt.

4 medium-sized carrots, halved

1 medium-sized onion, chopped

½ cup water

1½ tsp. dried sage, divided

2 skinless turkey thighs or drumsticks, about 2 lbs.

OPTIONAL INGREDIENTS:

1 tsp. browning sauce

¼ tsp. salt

⅛ tsp. pepper

1 Tbsp. cornstarch

¼ cup water

1. In slow cooker, combine carrots, onion, water, and 1 tsp. sage. Top with turkey. Sprinkle with remaining sage.

2. Cover and cook on Low 6-8 hours, or until a meat thermometer reads 180°.

3. Remove turkey and keep warm. Remove vegetables from cooker with a slotted spoon, reserving cooking juices.

4. Keep vegetables warm until ready to serve. Pour cooking juices into a saucepan.

5. Or, place vegetables in a food processor. Cover and process until smooth. Place in a saucepan. Add cooking juices.

6. Bring mixture in saucepan to a boil. Add browning sauce, salt, and pepper, if you wish.

7. In a small bowl, combine cornstarch and water until smooth. Stir into boiling juices. Cook and stir for 2 minutes, or until thickened. Serve over turkey.

8. If you've kept the vegetables warm, add to a serving platter with turkey.

Makes 4 servings

Note: Add a little minced garlic to Step 1 if you wish.

Sauerkraut and Turkey

CAROL LEAMAN • LANCASTER, PA

Prep Time: 5 minutes • Cooking Time: 7–8 hours • Ideal slow cooker size: 5-qt.

1 large boneless turkey breast, whole or half

32-oz. bag or can sauerkraut

1. Place turkey in slow cooker. Top with sauerkraut.

2. Cover and cook on Low 7–8 hours, or until turkey is tender but not dry or mushy.

   Makes 4–6 servings

Note: This is a great recipe to use if you prefer not to eat pork. Believe it or not, most people who eat this dish think they are eating pork! I like to slow-cook a turkey before I need it. I slice the cooked breast meat into serving pieces and freeze it. And I chop all the rest of the meat and freeze it in 3-cup batches. The chopped turkey is ready for any recipe calling for cooked turkey or chicken, such as turkey or chicken salad, turkey pot pie, and so on.

Sauerkraut and Turkey Sausage

VERA F. SCHMUCKER • GOSHEN, IN

Prep Time: 5 minutes • Cooking Time: 4–6 hours • Ideal slow cooker size: 3-qt.

1 large can sauerkraut

¼–½ cup brown sugar, according to your taste preference

8" link spicy or smoked turkey sausage

1. Pour sauerkraut into slow cooker.

2. Sprinkle with brown sugar.

3. Cut turkey sausage into ¼" slices and arrange over sauerkraut.

4. Cook on Low 4–6 hours.

   Makes 8 servings

Indonesian Turkey

ELAINE SUE GOOD • TISKILWA, IL

Prep Time: 10 minutes • Cooking Time: 6–8 hours • Ideal slow cooker size: 2- to 3½-qt.

3 turkey breast tenderloins
(about 1½–2 lbs.)

6 cloves garlic, pressed and
chopped

1½ Tbsp. grated fresh ginger

1 Tbsp. sesame oil

3 Tbsp. soy sauce, optional

½ tsp. cayenne pepper,
optional

⅓ cup peanut butter, your
choice of chunky or smooth

1. Place turkey on bottom of slow cooker.

2. Sprinkle with garlic, ginger, sesame oil, and soy sauce and cayenne pepper, if desired.

3. Cover and cook on Low 8 hours, or until a meat thermometer registers 180°.

4. With a slotted spoon, remove turkey pieces from slow cooker. Stir peanut butter into remaining juices. If sauce is thicker than you like, stir in ¼–⅓ cup water.

5. Spoon peanut butter sauce over turkey to serve.

Makes 4 servings

Note: If you like spicier foods, be sure to include the cayenne pepper as part of Step 2. And, if your diet allows, add the soy sauce during Step 2 also. You may substitute 4 whole boneless, skinless chicken breasts or 12 boneless, skinless chicken thighs for the 3 turkey breast tenderloins. I have used both and was pleased with the results. The more meat you have, the more evenly the dish will cook, especially if your slow cooker cooks hot.

Ground Turkey with Stuffing and Veggies

BRENDA HOCHSTEDLER • EAST EARL, PA

Prep Time: 10–15 minutes • Cooking Time: 3–8 hours • Ideal slow cooker size: 3-qt.

1 lb. lean ground turkey

2 cups frozen mixed
vegetables, your choice
of combination

¼ cup Italian dressing

1 tsp. steak sauce, optional

16-oz. can whole-berry
cranberry sauce

6-oz. pkg. stuffing mix for
turkey

1. Combine ground turkey, vegetables, Italian dressing, and steak sauce, if you wish, in slow cooker.

2. Pour cranberry sauce over top. Sprinkle with dry stuffing mix.

3. Cover and cook on Low 6–8 hours, or on High 3–4 hours.

Makes 6 servings

Cran-Orange Turkey Roll

BARBARA SMITH • BEDFORD, PA / CLARICE WILLIAMS • FAIRBANK, IA

Prep Time: 10–20 minutes • Cooking Time: 7–9 hours • Ideal slow cooker size: 4½-qt.

¼ cup sugar

2 Tbsp. cornstarch

¾ cup orange marmalade

1 cup fresh cranberries, chopped or finely ground

2-2½-lb. frozen turkey roll, partially thawed

salt and pepper to taste, optional

1. Mix sugar and cornstarch together in a 1- to 2-qt. microwave-safe bowl. Stir in marmalade and cranberries.

2. Cover with waxed paper and cook on High 1½ minutes. Stir. Cook on High 1 more minute. If sauce is slightly thickened, stop microwaving. If sauce is still thin, stir, cover, and cook another minute on High.

3. Place turkey in slow cooker. Sprinkle with salt and pepper, if you wish. Pour sauce over turkey.

4. Cover and cook on Low 7–9 hours, or until turkey reads 180° on a meat thermometer.

Makes 6 servings

Barbecued Turkey for Sandwiches

JOANNA BEAR • SALISBURY, MD

Prep Time: 10 minutes • Cooking Time: 1 hour • Ideal slow cooker size: 1½- to 2-qt.

½ cup ketchup

¼ cup brown sugar

1 Tbsp. prepared mustard

1 Tbsp. Worcestershire sauce

2 cups turkey, cooked and cut into bite-sized chunks

1 small onion, finely chopped, optional

1. Mix ketchup, sugar, mustard, and Worcestershire sauce together in slow cooker. Add turkey and onion, if you wish. Toss to coat well.

2. Cover and cook on High 1 hour, or until heated through.

3. Serve on buns.

Makes 4–5 servings

Hot Turkey Sandwiches

TRACEY HANSON SCHRAMEL • WINDOM, MN

Prep Time: 20–30 minutes • Cooking Time: 4–5 hours • Ideal slow cooker size: 3-qt.

6 cups cooked turkey, cut into bite-sized chunks

1½ cups mayonnaise or salad dressing

1 lb. Velveeta cheese, cubed

1½ cups celery, chopped

OPTIONAL INGREDIENTS:

1 small onion, minced

¼ tsp. salt

⅛ tsp. pepper

1. Combine all ingredients and place in slow cooker.

2. Cover and cook on Low 4–5 hours.

3. Serve in rolls.

   Makes 8 servings

Chipped Barbecued Turkey Ham

VELMA SAUDER • LEOLA, PA

Prep Time: 10 minutes • Cooking Time: 4 hours • Ideal slow cooker size: 4-qt.

2 lbs. chipped turkey ham or regular deli ham

1 small onion, chopped

1 cup ketchup

1 cup water

½ cup brown sugar

2 Tbsp. pickle relish

1. Combine all ingredients in slow cooker.

2. Cover and cook on Low 4 hours. If you're home, stir occasionally.

3. Serve in hamburger buns.

   Makes 8 servings

Note: Add a slice of your favorite cheese to the top of each filled bun, if you wish. Also, if there is too much liquid in your cooker, stick a toothpick under the edge of the lid to tilt it slightly and to allow the steam to escape.

Beef Main Dishes

So Easy Roast Beef

JEAN BINNS SMITH • BELLEFONTE, PA / SARAH MILLER • HARRISONBURG, VA
HEIDI HUNSBERGER • HARRISONBURG, VA

Prep Time: 5 minutes • Cooking Time: 6–8 hours • Ideal slow cooker size: 4-qt.

3-4-lb. beef roast

10¾-oz. can cream of
mushroom soup

half or whole envelope dry
onion soup mix

1. Rinse beef, pat dry, and place in slow cooker.

2. Pour mushroom soup over top. Sprinkle with dry soup mix.

3. Cover and cook on Low 6–8 hours, or until meat is tender
but not dry.

Makes 6–8 servings

Variation: You can add sliced carrots and halved potatoes after
4 hours of cooking.

Zesty Italian Beef

CAROL EVELETH • WELLMAN, IA

Prep Time: 5 minutes • Cooking Time: 4–10 hours • Ideal slow cooker size: 3½-qt.

1 envelope dry onion soup mix

½ tsp. garlic powder

1 tsp. dried basil

½ tsp. dried oregano

¼ tsp. paprika, optional

½ tsp. cayenne pepper, optional

2 cups water

2-lb. rump roast

1. Combine soup mix and seasonings with water in slow cooker. Add roast.

2. Cook on High 4–6 hours, or on Low 8–10 hours, or until meat is tender but not dry.

3. Allow meat to rest 10 minutes before slicing. Top slices with cooking juices.

Makes 6 servings

Italian Beef au Jus

CAROL SHERWOOD • BATAVIA, NY

Prep Time: 10 minutes • Cooking Time: 8 hours • Ideal slow cooker size: 4-qt.

3-5-lb. boneless beef roast

10-oz. pkg. dry au jus mix

1 pkg. dry Italian salad dressing mix

14½-oz. can beef broth

half a soup can water

1. Place beef in slow cooker.

2. Combine remaining ingredients. Pour over roast.

3. Cover. Cook on Low 8 hours.

4. Slice meat and spoon onto hard rolls with a straining spoon to make sandwiches. Or shred with 2 forks and serve over noodles or rice in broth thickened with flour.

Makes 8 servings

Note: To thicken broth, mix 3 Tbsp. cornstarch into ¼ cup cold water. Stir until smooth. Remove ½ cup beef broth from cooker and blend into cornstarch-water. Stir back into broth in cooker, stirring until smooth. Cook 10–15 minutes on High until broth becomes of gravy consistency.

Pot-Roasted Beef

RUTH HOFSTETTER • VERSAILLES, MO

Prep Time: 2 minutes • Cooking Time: 5–10 hours • Ideal slow cooker size: 3-qt.

3–4-lb. bottom round roast

1 envelope dry beef-stew
   seasoning mix

1 cup water

1. Place roast in slow cooker.

2. In a small bowl, mix together seasoning mix and water. Pour over meat.

3. Cook on Low 10 hours, or on High 5 hours.

Makes 8 servings

I-Forgot-to-Thaw-the-Roast Beef!

THELMA GOOD • HARRISONBURG, VA

Prep Time: 20 minutes • Cooking Time: 7–9 hours • Ideal slow cooker size: 4- to 5-qt.

3–4-lb. frozen beef roast

$1\frac{1}{2}$ tsp. salt

pepper to taste

1 large onion

$\frac{1}{4}$ cup flour

$\frac{3}{4}$ cup cold water

1. Place frozen roast in slow cooker. Sprinkle with $1\frac{1}{2}$ tsp. salt and pepper to taste. Slice onion and lay over top.

2. Cover and cook on High 1 hour. Turn heat to Low and roast 6–8 hours, or until meat is tender but not dry.

3. Spoon $1\frac{1}{4}$ cups broth from slow cooker into a saucepan. Bring to a boil.

4. While broth is heating, whisk together flour and cold water in a small bowl until smooth.

5. When broth boils, stir flour-water into broth, stirring continually, until broth is smooth and thickened.

6. Slice roast and return meat and onions to slow cooker. Pour gravy over top. Turn on Low until ready to serve.

Makes 10 servings

Note: This is a stress-free dish to serve to guests. To get the most flavor from herbs and spices when using them in a slow cooker, use them whole rather than ground or crushed. And use fresh herbs whenever you can.

Flavorful Pot Roast

MARY KAY NOLT • NEWMANSTOWN, PA

Prep Time: 10 minutes ▪ **Cooking Time: 7–8 hours** ▪ **Ideal slow cooker size: 5-qt.**

2 2½-lb. boneless beef chuck roasts

1 envelope dry ranch salad dressing mix

1 envelope dry Italian salad dressing mix

1 envelope dry brown gravy mix

½ cup water

OPTIONAL INGREDIENTS:

1 Tbsp. flour

½ cup water

1. Place chuck roasts in slow cooker.

2. In a small bowl, combine salad dressing and gravy mixes. Stir in water. Pour over meat.

3. Cover and cook on Low 7–8 hours, or until meat is tender but not dry.

4. If you wish, thicken cooking juices for gravy. Remove meat at end of cooking time and keep warm on a platter.

5. Turn cooker to High. Bring juices to a boil.

6. Meanwhile, mix 1 Tbsp. flour with ½ cup water in a jar with a tight-fitting lid. Shake until smooth.

7. When juices come to a boil, pour flour-water into cooker in a thin stream, stirring constantly. Continue cooking and stirring until juices thicken.

8. Serve over meat, or in a side dish along with meat.

Makes 10–12 servings

Italian Pot Roast

SANDY OSBORN • IOWA CITY, IA

Prep Time: 5-10 minutes • Cooking Time: 5–8 hours • Ideal slow cooker size: 3½-qt.

2½-lb. boneless beef round roast

1 medium-sized onion, sliced

¼ tsp. salt

¼ tsp. pepper

2 8-oz. cans no-salt-added tomato sauce

1 envelope dry Italian salad dressing mix

OPTIONAL INGREDIENTS:

½ cup flour or cornstarch

½ cup water

1. Slice roast in half for even cooking. Then place in slow cooker.

2. Add onion and remaining ingredients in the order listed.

3. Cover and cook on High 5 hours, or until roast is tender but not dry. You can also cook it on High 1 hour, then reduce heat to Low and cook 7 hours.

4. When meat is fully cooked, place it on a platter and cover to keep warm.

5. To turn cooking juices into gravy, turn cooker to High to bring juices to a boil.

6. If you wish, mix ½ cup flour or cornstarch into ½ cup water. When smooth, pour in a thin stream into boiling juices, stirring continually. Continue to cook until juices thicken.

7. Slice meat. Serve gravy over meat, or place gravy in a separate bowl to serve.

Makes 8 servings

Italian Roast Beef

DOROTHY VAN DEEST • MEMPHIS, TN

Prep Time: 15 minutes • Cooking Time: 10–12 hours • Ideal slow cooker size: 4- to 5-qt.

2 onions, divided

2 cloves garlic

1 large rib celery, finely chopped, optional

3 slices bacon

flour

4-lb. beef rump roast

1. Finely chop 1 onion, the garlic, celery, and bacon. Mix together.

2. Lightly flour roast. Rub on all sides with minced mixture.

3. Slice remaining onion. Place in slow cooker. Place roast on top of onion.

4. Sprinkle any remaining rub—or any that's fallen off—over roast.

5. Cover and cook on Low 10–12 hours.

Makes 6–8 servings

All-Day Pot Roast

CAROL SHIRK • LEOLA, PA

Prep Time: 15–20 minutes • Cooking Time: 5–12 hours • Ideal slow cooker size: 4-qt.

1½-lb. boneless eye of beef round roast, round rump roast, or chuck roast

4 medium-sized potatoes, quartered

16-oz. pkg. peeled baby carrots

10¾-oz. can golden mushroom soup

½ tsp. dried tarragon, or basil, crushed

1. In a large nonstick skillet, brown meat on all sides.

2. Place potatoes and carrots in slow cooker. Place browned meat on top of vegetables.

3. In a small bowl, mix together soup and tarragon or basil. Pour over meat and vegetables.

4. Cover and cook on Low 10–12 hours, or on High 5–6 hours, until meat and vegetables are tender but not dry.

Makes 5 servings

Cooking Tip

For more flavorful gravy, first brown the meat in a skillet. Scrape all browned bits from the bottom of the skillet and add to the slow cooker along with the meat.

—*Carolyn Baer, Conrath, WI*

Whole-Dinner Roast Beef

BETTY MOORE • PLANO, IL / RHONDA FREED • LOWVILLE, NY

Prep Time: 10 minutes • Cooking Time: 8–9 hours • Ideal slow cooker size: 3½- to 4-qt.

3-5-lb. beef roast

10¾-oz. can cream of mushroom soup

1 envelope dry onion soup mix

4-5 potatoes, quartered

4 cups baby carrots

1. Place roast in slow cooker.

2. Cover with mushroom soup. Sprinkle with onion soup mix.

3. Cover and cook on Low 6 hours.

4. Add potatoes and carrots, pushing down into sauce as much as possible.

5. Cover and cook another 2–3 hours, or until vegetables are tender but meat is not dry.

Makes 6–8 servings

Note: If desired, sprinkle carrots and potatoes with salt and pepper after placing in cooker.

Burgundy Roast

JANE HERSHBERGER • NEWTON, KS

Prep Time: 10 minutes • Cooking Time: 5 hours • Ideal slow cooker size: 4-qt.

4-lb. venison, or beef, roast

10¾-oz. can cream of mushroom soup

1 cup burgundy wine

1 large onion, finely chopped

2 Tbsp. chopped parsley

OPTIONAL INGREDIENTS:

4 medium-sized potatoes, quartered

4 medium-sized carrots, quartered

1. Place meat in slow cooker.

2. Blend soup and wine together in a mixing bowl. Pour over meat.

3. Top with onion and parsley.

4. Cover and cook on Low 5 hours, or until meat is tender but not dry.

Makes 6–8 servings

Note: If you choose to include potatoes and carrots, put them in the slow cooker first; then proceed with Step 1. Serve the sauce as a gravy over the sliced or cubed meat.

Uncle Tim's Pot Roast

TIM SMITH • RUTLEDGE, PA

Prep Time: 30 minutes • Cooking Time: 8 hours • Ideal slow cooker size: 5-qt.

4-lb. eye roast of beef

2 Tbsp. crushed garlic

8 medium-sized red potatoes, halved or quartered

1 lb. baby carrots, peeled

water

1 green pepper, cut in half and seeded

1. Place roast in center of slow cooker. Rub garlic into roast.

2. Add potatoes and carrots. Add water until carrots and potatoes are covered.

3. Cover and cook on Low 8 hours.

4. One hour before serving, place pepper halves on top of meat (moving vegetables aside as much as possible), cut side down. Cover and continue cooking.

Makes 4 servings

Note: If desired, sprinkle roast with salt and pepper in Step 1. And sprinkle potatoes and carrots with salt in Step 2.

Pot Roast with Carrots and Potatoes

LORETTA HANSON • HENDRICKS, MN

Prep Time: 30 minutes • Cooking Time: 4–12 hours • Ideal slow cooker size: 5- to 6-qt.

3–4 potatoes, pared, and thinly sliced

3–4 carrots, pared, and thinly sliced

1 onion, chopped, optional

salt and pepper to taste

3-lb. brisket, rump roast, or pot roast

1 cup beef consommé

1. Place vegetables in bottom of slow cooker.

2. Salt and pepper meat. Place meat in slow cooker.

3. Pour consommé around meat.

4. Cover and cook on Low 10–12 hours, or on High 4–5 hours.

Makes 6 servings

Roast Beef and Mushrooms

GLADYS M. HIGH • EPHRATA, PA

Prep Time: 10 minutes • Cooking Time: 8–10 hours • Ideal slow cooker size: 3-qt.

3-lb. boneless chuck roast

¼ lb. fresh mushrooms, sliced,
   or 4-oz. can mushroom
   stems and pieces, drained

1 cup water

1 envelope dry brown gravy mix

1 envelope dry Italian
   dressing mix

1. Place roast in slow cooker.

2. Top with mushrooms.

3. In a small bowl, mix together water, gravy mix, and
   dressing mix. Pour over roast and mushrooms.

4. Cover and cook on Low 8–10 hours, or until meat is tender
   but not dry.

Makes 4–6 servings

Quick and Easy Mushroom Brisket

DOROTHY VAN DEEST • MEMPHIS, TN / DEDE PETERSON • RAPID CITY, SD

Prep Time: 5 minutes • Cooking Time: 10–14 hours • Ideal slow cooker size: 4-qt.

4–5-lb. beef brisket

1 envelope dry onion soup mix

4-oz. can mushrooms,
   undrained

1. Place brisket in slow cooker with fat side up, cutting to fit
   into cooker, if necessary.

2. In a mixing bowl, combine soup mix with mushrooms
   and their liquid. Spread onion soup mixture over top of
   brisket.

3. Cover and cook on Low 10–14 hours, or until meat is
   tender but not dry.

4. Remove brisket from slow cooker and allow to rest
   10 minutes. Cut across the grain into thin slices. Serve
   with meat juices poured over top of sliced meat.

Makes 8–10 servings

Italian Roast with Potatoes

RUTHIE SCHIEFER • VASSAR, MI

Prep Time: 30–35 minutes • Cooking Time: 6–7 hours • Ideal slow cooker size: 5-qt.

6 medium-sized potatoes, peeled if you wish, and quartered

1 large onion, sliced

3–4-lb. boneless beef roast

26-oz. jar tomato and basil pasta sauce, divided

½ cup water

3 beef bouillon cubes

1. Place potatoes and onion in bottom of slow cooker.

2. Meanwhile, brown roast on top and bottom in a nonstick skillet.

3. Place roast on top of vegetables. Pour any drippings from skillet over beef.

4. Mix 1 cup pasta sauce and water together in a small bowl. Stir in bouillon cubes. Spoon mixture over meat.

5. Cover and cook on Low 6–7 hours, or until meat is tender but not dry.

6. Transfer roast and vegetables to serving platter. Cover with foil.

7. Take 1 cup cooking juices from slow cooker and place in a medium-sized saucepan. Stir in remaining pasta sauce. Heat.

8. Slice or cube beef. Serve with heated sauce.

Makes 8 servings

Roast with Hearty Vegetables

EDNA MAE HERSCHBERGER • ARTHUR, IL

Prep Time: 10 minutes • Cooking Time: 8 hours • Ideal slow cooker size: 4-qt.

4-lb. beef roast

2 tsp. salt

6 cups tomato juice

6 carrots, peeled and cut in half

6 potatoes, peeled and cut in half

1. Place roast in slow cooker. Sprinkle with salt. Pour tomato juice over all.

2. Cover and cook on High 6 hours. Add carrots and potatoes.

3. Cover and cook on High 2 hours.

Makes 6 servings

Onion Mushroom Pot Roast

DEB HERR • MOUNTAINTOP, PA

Prep Time: 10 minutes • Cooking Time: 5–12 hours • Ideal slow cooker size: 6-qt.

3-4-lb. pot roast or chuck
  roast

4-oz. can sliced mushrooms,
  drained

1 tsp. salt

1/4 tsp. pepper

1/2 cup beef broth

1 envelope dry onion soup mix

1. Place pot roast in slow cooker.

2. Add mushrooms, salt, and pepper.

3. In a small bowl, mix beef broth with onion soup mix. Spoon over roast.

4. Cover and cook on High 5–6 hours, or on Low 10–12 hours, or until meat is tender but not dry.

Makes 6 servings

Note: To make gravy, prepare a smooth paste in a jar or small bowl, mixing 1/2 cup flour or cornstarch with 1/2 cup water. After the roast is fully cooked, remove the meat and keep it warm on a platter. Turn cooker to High. When juices begin to boil, pour flour-water paste in a thin stream into the cooker, stirring continually. Continue cooking and stirring until juices thicken. Serve over sliced roast, or in a bowl along with the meat.

Barbecued Roast Beef

SHERRY H. KAUFFMAN • MINOT, ND

Prep Time: 15–20 minutes • Cooking Time: 6–7 hours • Ideal slow cooker size: 4-qt.

4-lb. beef roast

1 cup ketchup

1 onion, chopped

3/4 cup water

3 Tbsp. Worcestershire sauce

3/4 cup brown sugar

1. Place roast in slow cooker.

2. In a small bowl, mix together all remaining ingredients except brown sugar. Pour over roast.

3. Cover and cook on Low 6–7 hours. Approximately 1 hour before serving, sprinkle with brown sugar.

Makes 8 servings

Barbecued Beef Brisket

RUTHIE SCHIEFER • VASSAR, MI

Prep Time: 10 minutes • Cooking Time: 6½–8½ hours • Ideal slow cooker size: 5-qt.

2 cups Jack Daniel's Original No. 7 Recipe barbecue sauce, divided

1 medium-sized onion, cut in wedges

3 beef bouillon cubes

3–4 lb. beef roast or brisket

3 bay leaves

1. In bottom of slow cooker, combine 1 cup barbecue sauce, onion, and bouillon cubes.

2. Place roast on top of sauce. Top with bay leaves.

3. Cover and cook on Low 6–8 hours, or until beef is tender enough to shred easily.

4. Remove meat from slow cooker. Reserve cooking juices in slow cooker. Shred meat with 2 forks.

5. Return meat to slow cooker. Add remaining barbecue sauce. Mix well.

6. Cover and cook on High, until heated through.

7. Serve on sandwich buns.

   Makes 6–8 servings

Sweet 'n' Sour Roast

ROSALIE D. MILLER • MIFFLINTOWN, PA

Prep Time: 5 minutes • Cooking Time: 6–8 hours • Ideal slow cooker size: 2-qt.

2-lb. beef roast

½ cup pickle juice or apple cider vinegar

3 Tbsp. brown sugar

2 tsp. salt

1 Tbsp. Worcestershire sauce

1 cup water

1. Place roast in slow cooker.

2. In a small bowl, combine remaining ingredients. Pour over roast.

3. Cover and cook on Low 6–8 hours, or until meat is tender but not dry.

   Makes 5 servings

Variation: Place 5 medium-sized potatoes, cubed, in bottom of cooker. Add enough water to just cover the potatoes. Top with 1 qt. frozen green beans. Then add roast and continue with Step 2 above.

Cooking Tip

Browning the meat, onions, and vegetables before putting them in the cooker improves their flavor, but this extra step can be skipped in most recipes. The recipe will still be flavorful.
—*Dorothy M. Van Deest, Memphis, TN*

Roast Beef with Ginger Ale

MARTHA BENDER • NEW PARIS, IN

Prep Time: 15–20 minutes • Cooking Time: 8–10 hours • Ideal slow cooker size: 3½- to 4-qt.

3-lb. beef roast

½ cup flour

1 envelope dry onion soup mix

1 envelope dry brown gravy mix

2 cups ginger ale

1. Coat roast with flour. Reserve any flour that doesn't stick to roast. Place roast in slow cooker.

2. Combine dry soup mix, gravy mix, remaining flour, and ginger ale in a bowl. Mix well.

3. Pour sauce over roast.

4. Cover and cook on Low 8–10 hours, or until roast is tender.

5. Serve with mashed potatoes or rice.

Makes 6-8 servings

8-Hour Tangy Beef

MARY MARTINS • FAIRBANK, IA

Prep Time: 5 minutes • Cooking Time: 8–9 hours • Ideal slow cooker size: 4-qt.

3½-4-lb. beef roast

12-oz. can ginger ale

1½ cups ketchup

1. Put beef in slow cooker.

2. Pour ginger ale and ketchup over roast.

3. Cover. Cook on Low 8–9 hours.

4. Shred with 2 forks and serve on buns. Or break up into chunks and serve over rice, potatoes, or pasta.

Makes 6-8 servings

Variations: This recipe produces a lot of juice. You can add chopped onions, potatoes, and green beans in Step 2, if you want. Or stir in sliced mushrooms and/or peas 30 minutes before the end of the cooking time. For a tangier finished dish, add chili powder or cumin, along with black pepper, in Step 2.

Zippy Beef Roast

COLLEEN HEATWOLE • BURTON, MI / JOETTE DROZ • KALONA, IA
F. ELAINE ASPER • NORTON, OH / RUTH ANN HOOVER • NEW HOLLAND, PA

Prep Time: 10–15 minutes • Cooking Time: 5–10 hours • Ideal slow cooker size: 4- to 5-qt.

3–4-lb. beef roast

12-oz. can cola

10¾-oz. can cream of
   mushroom soup

1 envelope dry onion soup mix

1. Place beef in slow cooker.

2. In a small bowl, blend cola and mushroom soup together.
Pour over roast.

3. Sprinkle with dry onion soup mix.

4. Cover and cook on Low 10 hours, or on High 5 hours, or
until meat is tender but not dry.

Makes 6–8 servings

Piquant Chuck Roast

MARY JANE MUSSER • MANHEIM, PA

Prep Time: 5 minutes • Cooking Time: 5–10 hours • Ideal slow cooker size: 3- to 4-qt.

3-lb. chuck roast

½ cup orange juice

3 Tbsp. soy sauce

2 Tbsp. brown sugar

1 tsp. Worcestershire sauce

1. Place meat in slow cooker. In a mixing bowl, combine
remaining ingredients and pour over meat.

2. Cover and cook on Low 8–10 hours, or on High 5 hours.

Makes 6 servings

Note: Shred the meat with 2 forks. Mix well with sauce. Serve
over cooked rice, noodles, or mashed potatoes.

Tender Texas-Style Steaks

JANICE MULLER • DERWOOD, MD

Prep Time: 7 minutes • Cooking Time: 6 hours • Ideal slow cooker size: 3-qt.

4–6 steaks or chops

1 cup brown sugar

1 cup ketchup

salt to taste

pepper to taste

few dashes Worcestershire
   sauce

1. Lay steaks in bottom of slow cooker.

2. Combine sugar and ketchup. Pour over steaks. If you need
to layer the steaks or chops, make sure each one is covered
with sauce.

3. Sprinkle with salt and pepper and Worcestershire sauce.

4. Cover and cook on High 3 hours, and then on Low 3 hours.

Makes 4–6 servings

Sweet and Savory Brisket

DONNA NEITER • WAUSAU, WI / ELLEN RANCK • GAP, PA

Prep Time: 10–12 minutes • Cooking Time: 8–10 hours • Ideal slow cooker size: 5-qt.

3–3½-lb. fresh beef brisket, cut in half, divided

1 cup ketchup

¼ cup grape jelly

1 envelope dry onion soup mix

½ tsp. pepper

1. Place half of brisket in slow cooker.

2. In a bowl, combine ketchup, jelly, dry soup mix, and pepper.

3. Spread half of mixture over half of meat. Top with remaining meat and then remaining ketchup mixture.

4. Cover and cook on Low 8–10 hours, or until meat is tender but not dry.

5. Allow meat to rest 10 minutes. Then slice and serve with cooking juices.

Makes 8–10 servings

Note: Use fresh beef brisket, not corned beef.

Savory Sweet Roast

KIMBERLY BURKHOLDER • MILLERSTOWN, PA

Prep Time: 15 minutes • Cooking Time: 8–9 hours • Ideal slow cooker size: 4- to 5-qt.

3–4-lb. blade roast

10¾-oz. can cream of mushroom soup

½ cup water

¼ cup sugar

¼ cup vinegar

2 tsp. salt

1. Brown meat on both sides in a nonstick skillet. Place in slow cooker.

2. Mix together remaining ingredients in a bowl and pour over meat.

3. Cover and cook on Low 8–9 hours, or until meat is tender but not dry.

4. Remove meat from cooker and allow to rest 10 minutes before slicing or shredding with 2 forks.

Makes 6–8 servings

Note: Make a good gravy by following the directions with Peppercorn Roast Beef on page 117. Serve gravy alongside or over top of roast.

Barbecued Pot Roast

LEANN BROWN • RONKS, PA

Prep Time: 5 minutes • Cooking Time: 5–6 hours • Ideal slow cooker size: 5- to 6-qt.

5-lb. roast

16-oz. bottle honey barbecue
    sauce

1 small onion, chopped

1 clove garlic, minced

OPTIONAL INGREDIENTS:

black pepper

Montreal seasoning

1. Place roast in slow cooker.

2. Pour barbecue sauce over top.

3. Sprinkle onion over roast, and place garlic beside roast.

4. If you wish, sprinkle with pepper and/or seasoning.

5. Cover and cook on Low 5–6 hours.

6. Remove roast from cooker and allow to rest 10 minutes. Slice and serve with cooking juices.

Makes 10 servings

Beef Roast with Tomatoes, Onions, and Peppers

DONNA TRELOAR • HARTFORD CITY, IN

Prep Time: 15 minutes • Cooking Time: 8–10 hours • Ideal slow cooker size: 4-qt.

4–5-lb. beef roast

2 14½-oz. cans Mexican-style
    stewed tomatoes

16-oz. jar salsa, your choice of
    mild, medium, or hot

2 or 3 medium-sized onions,
    cut in chunks

1 or 2 green or red bell
    peppers, sliced

1. Brown roast on top and bottom in a nonstick skillet and place in slow cooker.

2. In a bowl, combine stewed tomatoes and salsa. Spoon over meat.

3. Cover and cook on Low 8–10 hours, or until meat is tender but not dry.

4. Add onions halfway through cooking time in order to keep them fairly crisp. Push down into sauce.

5. One hour before serving, add pepper slices. Push down into sauce.

6. Remove meat from cooker and allow to rest 10 minutes before slicing. Place slices on a serving platter and top with vegetables and sauce.

Makes 10 servings

Note: Make Easy Beef Burritos with the leftovers. Shred any leftover beef with 2 forks. Heat on the stovetop with the peppers, onions, and ½ cup sauce. Add 1 Tbsp. chili powder, 2 tsp. cumin, and salt to taste. Heat through. Spoon onto warm flour tortillas. Serve with salsa, sour cream, and/or guacamole.

Mexican Pot Roast

SUSAN SEGRAVES • LANSDALE, PA

Prep Time: 5 minutes • Cooking Time: 8–10 hours • Ideal slow cooker size: 5-qt.

1½ cups chunky salsa

6-oz. can tomato paste

1 envelope dry taco
    seasoning mix

1 cup water

3-lb. beef chuck roast

½ cup chopped cilantro

1. In a mixing bowl, combine first 4 ingredients.

2. Place roast in slow cooker and pour salsa mixture over top.

3. Cover and cook on Low 8–10 hours, or until beef is tender but not dry. Remove to a platter.

4. Stir cilantro into sauce before serving with beef.

   Makes 8 servings

Peppercorn Roast Beef

STACIE SKELLY • MILLERSVILLE, PA

Prep Time: 10–15 minutes • Cooking Time: 8–10 hours • Ideal slow cooker size: 4-qt.

3-4-lb. chuck roast

½ cup soy sauce

1 tsp. garlic powder

1 bay leaf

3-4 peppercorns

2 cups water

1 tsp. thyme, optional

OPTIONAL INGREDIENTS:

½ cup flour

½ cup water

1. Place roast in slow cooker.

2. In a mixing bowl, combine all other ingredients, except optional flour and ½ cup water, and pour over roast.

3. Cover and cook on Low 8–10 hours.

4. Remove meat to a platter and allow to rest before slicing or shredding.

   Makes 6–8 servings

Note: Serve the meat sliced with garlic mashed potatoes or macaroni and cheese, or shredded for roast beef sandwiches. To make gravy to go with the meat, turn cooker to High and bring cooking juices to a boil. In a small bowl, mix together ½ cup flour and ½ cup water until smooth. When cooking juices are boiling, pour flour-water paste into hot juices, stirring continually until juices thicken. Then turn off the cooker and serve gravy over the meat.

Green Chili Roast

ANNA KENAGY • CARLSBAD, NM

Prep Time: 15 minutes • Cooking Time: 8 hours • Ideal slow cooker size: 4-qt.

3-4-lb. beef roast

1 tsp. seasoned meat
tenderizer, optional

oil, optional

1 tsp. salt

3-4 green chili peppers, or
4-oz. can green chilies,
undrained

1 Tbsp. Worcestershire sauce

½ tsp. black pepper

1. Sprinkle roast with meat tenderizer. Brown under broiler or in oil in a skillet. Place in slow cooker.

2. Pour in water until roast is half covered.

3. Add remaining ingredients over top.

4. Cover. Cook on Low 8 hours.

5. Serve with mashed potatoes and green beans.

Makes 8–10 servings

Mexican Brisket

VERONICA SABO • SHELTON, CT

Prep Time: 20–30 minutes • Cooking Time: 2–10 hours • Ideal slow cooker size: 5-qt.

1 lb. baking potatoes, peeled
and cut into 1" cubes

1 lb. sweet potatoes, peeled
and cut into 1" cubes

3-3½-lb. beef brisket, fat
trimmed

1¼ cups salsa

2 Tbsp. flour, or quick-cooking
tapioca

1. Place both kinds of potatoes in slow cooker.

2. Top with brisket.

3. Put salsa and flour in a small bowl and mix well. Pour evenly over meat.

4. Cover and cook on Low 6½–10 hours, or on High 2–5½ hours, or until meat is tender but not dry.

5. To serve, remove meat from cooker, keep warm, and allow to rest 10 minutes. Then slice meat across the grain. Place slices on a platter and top with potatoes and sauce.

Makes 8 servings

Beef in Onion Gravy

DONNA NEITER • WAUSAU, WI

Prep Time: 20 minutes • Cooking Time: 6–8 hours • Ideal slow cooker size: 3-qt.

10¾-oz. can cream of
mushroom soup

1 Tbsp. dry onion soup mix

2 Tbsp. beef bouillon granules

1 Tbsp. quick-cooking tapioca

1 lb. beef stew meat, cut into
1″ cubes

1. Spray slow cooker with nonstick cooking spray.

2. In slow cooker, combine soup, soup mix, bouillon, and
tapioca. Let stand 15 minutes.

3. Stir in beef.

4. Cover and cook on Low 6–8 hours, or until meat is tender
but not dry.

   Makes 3 servings

Note: Serve over cooked noodles or mashed potatoes.

Easy Stroganoff

VICKI DINKEL• SHARON SPRINGS, KS / BARBARA SPARKS • GLEN BURNIE, MD

Prep Time: 5 minutes • Cooking Time: 6¼–8¼ hours • Ideal slow cooker size: 3-qt.

10¾-oz. can cream of
mushroom soup

14½-oz. can beef broth

1 lb. beef stewing meat or
round steak, cut in
1″ pieces

1 cup sour cream

2 cups cooked noodles

1. Combine soup and broth in slow cooker. Add meat.

2. Cover. Cook on High 3–4 hours. Reduce heat to Low and
cook 3–4 hours.

3. Stir in sour cream.

4. Stir in noodles.

5. Cook on High 20 minutes.

   Makes 6–8 servings

Note: Since I'm in school part-time and work two part-time jobs,
this nearly complete meal is great to come home to. It smells
wonderful when you open the door. A vegetable or salad and some
crispy French bread are good additions.

Herby French Dip

SARA WICHERT • HILLSBORO, KS

Prep Time: 5 minutes • Cooking Time: 5–6 hours • Ideal slow cooker size: 4-qt.

3-lb. chuck roast

2 cups water

½ cup soy sauce

1 tsp. garlic powder

1 bay leaf

3–4 whole peppercorns

1 tsp. dried rosemary, optional

1 tsp. dried thyme, optional

6–8 French rolls

1. Place roast in slow cooker.

2. Combine remaining ingredients in a mixing bowl. Pour over meat.

3. Cover and cook on High 5–6 hours, or until meat is tender but not dry.

4. Remove meat from broth and shred with a fork. Stir back into sauce.

5. Remove meat from cooker by large forkfuls and place on French rolls.

Makes 6–8 servings

Zesty French Dip

EARNEST ZIMMERMAN • MECHANICSBURG, PA / TRACEY HANSON SCHRAMEL • WINDOM, MN

Prep Time: 5 minutes • Cooking Time: 8 hours • Ideal slow cooker size: 4- to 6-qt.

4-lb. beef roast

10½-oz. can beef broth

10½-oz. can condensed French onion soup

12-oz. bottle beer

6–8 French rolls or baguettes

1. Pat roast dry and place in slow cooker.

2. In a mixing bowl, combine beef broth, onion soup, and beer. Pour over meat.

3. Cover and cook on Low 8 hours, or until meat is tender but not dry.

4. Split rolls or baguettes. Warm in oven or microwave until heated through.

5. Remove meat from cooker and allow to rest 10 minutes. Then shred with 2 forks, or cut on the diagonal into thin slices, and place in rolls. Serve with dipping sauce on the side.

Makes 6–8 servings

Beef Roast Sandwiches

KELLY BAILEY • MECHANICSBURG, PA

Prep Time: 15 minutes • Cooking Time: 24 hours • Ideal slow cooker size: 3-qt.

3-lb. beef roast

14 3/4-oz. can beef broth

1 envelope dry Italian salad
    dressing mix

10-12 crusty sandwich rolls

OPTIONAL INGREDIENTS:

1/2 cup mayonnaise

3 Tbsp. prepared mustard

1. Place beef in slow cooker.

2. Combine broth and dressing mix, and pour mixture
   over beef.

3. Cover and cook on Low 12 hours.

4. Remove beef from broth, and shred with 2 forks.

5. Return shredded beef to slow cooker, and continue to cook
   on Low another 12 hours.

6. Serve in crusty rolls, along with mayonnaise mixed with
   mustard, if you wish.

   Makes 10–12 servings

Beach Boy's Pot Roast

JEANETTE OBERHOLTZER • MANHEIM, PA

Prep Time: 10 minutes • Cooking Time: 8–12 hours • Ideal slow cooker size: 3- to 4-qt.

3-4-lb. chuck or top round
    roast

8-12 slivers garlic

32-oz. jar pepperoncini
    peppers, undrained

6-8 large hoagie rolls

12-16 slices cheese, your
    favorite

1. Cut slits into roast with a sharp knife and insert garlic
   slivers.

2. Place beef in slow cooker. Spoon peppers and all of their
   juice over top.

3. Cover and cook on Low 8–12 hours, or until meat is tender
   but not dry.

4. Remove meat from cooker and allow to cool. Then use
   2 forks to shred beef.

5. Spread on hoagie rolls and top with cheese.

   Makes 6–8 servings

Spicy French Dip

JOETTE DROZ • KALONA, IA

Prep Time: 10 minutes • Cooking Time: 8–10 hours • Ideal slow cooker size: 4-qt.

3-lb. boneless beef roast, cut in thirds

½ cup water

4-oz. can diced jalapeño peppers, drained

1 envelope dry Italian salad dressing mix

10–12 crusty sandwich rolls

1. Place 3 pieces of beef in slow cooker.

2. In a small bowl, combine water, jalapeños, and dry dressing mix. Pour over beef.

3. Cover and cook on Low 8–10 hours, or until meat is tender but not dry.

4. Remove beef and shred using 2 forks. Place shredded beef back in juices. Stir and serve on rolls.

Makes 10–12 servings

Slow-Cooked Steak

RADELLA VROLIJK • HINTON, VA

Prep Time: 10 minutes • Cooking Time: 6½–8½ hours • Ideal slow cooker size: 3- or 4-qt.

¾ cup flour

1 tsp. pepper

¼ tsp. salt

2 lbs. cubed or sirloin steak, cut into 6 serving pieces

10¾-oz. can cream of mushroom soup

1⅓ cups water

1. In a bowl, combine flour, pepper, and salt. Dredge steak in flour mixture.

2. Brown in a nonstick skillet, being careful not to crowd skillet. Transfer browned beef to slow cooker.

3. Combine remaining ingredients in a bowl. Pour over steak.

4. Cover and cook on Low 6–8 hours.

Makes 6 servings

Variation: Add 1 cup sliced celery and 1–3 tsp. beef bouillon granules or brown gravy mix to Step 3.

Cozy Cabin Casserole

ANNA MUSSER • MANHEIM, PA

Prep Time: 5 minutes • Cooking Time: 6–8 hours • Ideal slow cooker size: 4-qt.

1 lb. lean round steak

1 envelope dry beefy onion soup

10¾-oz. can cream of mushroom soup

10¾-oz. can cream of celery soup

½ cup sour cream

1. Layer first 4 ingredients in slow cooker.

2. Cover and cook on Low 6–8 hours, or until meat is tender but not overcooked.

3. Stir in sour cream 10 minutes before serving.

Makes 3–4 servings

Creamy Swiss Steak

MARGARET CULBERT • LEBANON, PA

Prep Time: 20 minutes • Cooking Time: 6–8 hours • Ideal slow cooker size: 5-qt.

2 lbs. round steak, ¾" thick, cut into serving-size pieces

salt and pepper to taste

1 large onion, thinly sliced

10¾-oz. can cream of mushroom soup

half a soup can water

1. Place meat in slow cooker. Sprinkle with salt and pepper.

2. Top with onion slices.

3. In small bowl, mix soup and water together until smooth. Spoon over top.

4. Cover and cook on Low 6–8 hours, or until meat is tender but not overcooked.

Makes 6 servings

Cooking Tip

A slow cooker is perfect for less tender meats such as round steak. Because the meat is cooked in liquid for hours, it turns out tender and juicy.

Swiss Steak and Gravy

SHERRY H. KAUFFMAN • MINOT, ND / VIRGINIA EBERLY • LOYSVILLE, PA / ESTHER BURKHOLDER • MILLERSTOWN, PA / RUTH RETTER • MANHEIM, PA / WILMA HABERKAMP • FAIRBANK, IA / PAULA KING • FLANAGAN, IL / CHRIS PETERSON • GREEN BAY, WI / PHYLLIS WYKES • PLANO, IL / LOIS OSTRANDER • LEBANON, PA / MARY LYNN MILLER • REINHOLDS, PA

Prep Time: 5 minutes ▪ Cooking Time: 4–7 hours ▪ Ideal slow cooker size: 5-qt.

2-2½-lb. round steak, cut into serving-size pieces

10¾-oz. can cream of mushroom soup

half a soup can milk or water

half or whole envelope dry onion soup mix, depending upon your taste preference

1. Place steak in slow cooker.

2. In a bowl, mix soup and milk or water together. Pour over steak.

3. Sprinkle dry onion soup mix over top.

4. Cover and cook on Low 4–7 hours, or until meat is tender but not overcooked.

Makes 6–8 servings

Slow-Cooked Round Steak

KATHY LAPP • HALIFAX, PA

Prep Time: 15 minutes ▪ Cooking Time: 4–5 hours ▪ Ideal slow cooker size: 4-qt.

1¾-lb. round steak

¼ cup flour

2 onions, thickly sliced

1 green pepper, sliced in strips

10¾-oz. can cream of mushroom soup

1. Cut steak into serving-size pieces. Dredge in flour. Brown in a nonstick skillet.

2. Place browned steak in slow cooker. Top with onion and pepper slices.

3. Pour soup over all, making sure steak pieces are covered.

4. Cover and cook on Low 4–5 hours.

Makes 4–6 servings

Variations: Add ½ tsp. salt and ¼ tsp. pepper to flour in Step 1. If you like a lot of gravy, add a second can of soup to Step 3.

Steak in a Crock

JUDITH A. GOVOTSOS • FREDERICK, MD

Prep Time: 10–20 minutes • Cooking Time: 8–12 hours • Ideal slow cooker size: 4- or 5-qt.

1 medium-sized onion, sliced
and separated into rings

4-oz. can sliced mushrooms,
liquid reserved

2½-lb. round steak, ¾" thick,
cut into 4–5 pieces

10¾-oz. can cream of
mushroom soup

2 Tbsp. dry sherry or water

1. Put onion rings and mushrooms in bottom of slow cooker.

2. Brown meat in a nonstick skillet on all sides. Place in slow cooker over top of vegetables.

3. In a bowl, mix reserved mushroom liquid, soup, and sherry together. Pour over all.

4. Cover and cook on Low 8–12 hours, or until meat is tender but not overcooked.

Makes 4–5 servings

Round Steak and Vegetables

JUDY A. WANTLAND • MENOMONEE FALLS, WI

Prep Time: 10–15 minutes • Cooking Time: 4–8 hours • Ideal slow cooker size: 4-qt.

1-1½-lb. round steak, cut into
1" cubes

10-oz. pkg. frozen peas,
optional

4 medium-sized carrots, sliced

4 medium-sized potatoes,
chunked

10¾-oz. can cream of
mushroom soup

1 envelope dry onion soup mix

1. Spray slow cooker with nonstick cooking spray. Then mix all ingredients together in cooker.

2. Cover and cook on Low 6–8 hours, or on High 4 hours, or until steak and vegetables are tender.

Makes 4 servings

Slow-Cooker Swiss Steak

JOYCE BOWMAN • LADY LAKE, FL

Prep Time: 30 minutes • Cooking Time: 7 hours • Ideal slow cooker size: 3-qt.

1-lb. round steak, ¾"–1" thick, cubed

16-oz. can stewed tomatoes

3 carrots, halved lengthwise

2 potatoes, quartered

1 medium-sized onion, quartered

garlic powder to taste, optional

1. Add all ingredients to slow cooker in the order listed.

2. Cover and cook on Low 7 hours, or until meat and vegetables are tender but not overcooked or dry.

Makes 4 servings

Note: Meats usually cook faster than vegetables in slow cookers. If you want to know if your dish is fully cooked, check the vegetables to see if they're tender. If the recipe allows, place vegetables on the bottom and along the sides of your cooker as you're preparing it.

Tomato-y Swiss Steak

LEONA YODER • HARTVILLE, OH / HEATHER HORST • LEBANON, PA

Prep Time: 5 minutes • Cooking Time: 4–6 hours • Ideal slow cooker size: 4-qt.

2-lb. round steak, ¾" thick and cut into serving-size pieces

1 tsp. salt

⅛–¼ tsp. pepper, depending on your taste preference

1 large onion, thinly sliced

14½-oz. can chopped or stewed tomatoes

1. Season steak with salt and pepper. Place in slow cooker and top with sliced onion.

2. Spoon tomatoes over top.

3. Cover and cook on Low 4–6 hours, or until meat is tender but not overcooked.

Makes 5–6 servings

Basil Swiss Steak

DENISE NICKEL • GOESSEL, KS

Prep Time: 10 minutes • Cooking Time: 6–8 hours ▪ Ideal slow cooker size: 3-qt.

2-lb. round steak, cut into
    serving-size pieces

1 onion, sliced

10³/₄-oz. can tomato soup, or
    14¹/₂-oz. can stewed
    tomatoes

1 tsp. salt

1 tsp. pepper

¹/₂ cup water

1 tsp. dried basil

1. Arrange steak in slow cooker. (Steak need not be browned first.)

2. Lay onion over meat.

3. Mix remaining ingredients together in a bowl. Spoon over meat and onion.

4. Cover and cook on Low 6–8 hours.

Makes 6–8 servings

Green-Pepper Swiss Steak

BETTY B. DENNISON • GROVE CITY, PA

Prep Time: 20 minutes • Cooking Time: 6–7 hours ▪ Ideal slow cooker size: 4-qt.

3 lbs. round steak, cut into
    serving-size pieces

¹/₂ cup flour

4-oz. can tomato sauce

1 medium-sized onion, sliced

1 green pepper, sliced

1. Dredge meat in flour.

2. In a nonstick skillet, brown meat on both sides, but do not cook.

3. Place browned steak in slow cooker.

4. Pour tomato sauce over steak.

5. Arrange onion and pepper over top.

6. Cover and cook on Low 6–7 hours, or until meat is tender but not overcooked.

Makes 6–8 servings

Note: If you wish, add 1 tsp. salt and ¹/₂ tsp. pepper to flour in Step 1.

Carrots and Swiss Steak

RUTH ZENDT • MIFFLINTOWN, PA

Prep Time: 10 minutes • Cooking Time: 8–10 hours • Ideal slow cooker size: 4- to 6-qt.

1 lb. baby carrots

1½-lb. round steak, cut into bite-size pieces

1 envelope dry onion soup mix

salt and pepper to taste

8-oz. can tomato sauce

½ cup water

1. Spray slow cooker with nonstick cooking spray. Place carrots in bottom of cooker. Top with steak.

2. In a bowl, combine soup mix, salt and pepper, tomato sauce, and water. Pour over meat.

3. Cover and cook on Low 8–10 hours.

Makes 5–6 servings

Italian Round Steak

CHRIS PETERSON • GREEN BAY, WI / PHYLLIS WYKES • PLANO, IL

Prep Time: 5–10 minutes • Cooking Time: 5–8 hours • Ideal slow cooker size: 4-qt.

1½ lbs. round steak

1 tsp. salt

½ tsp. oregano

¼ tsp. pepper

1 medium-sized or large onion, chopped coarsely

15½-oz. jar spaghetti sauce, your choice of flavors

1. Cut steak into 5–6 serving-size pieces.

2. In a bowl, mix together salt, oregano, and pepper. Sprinkle over both sides of pieces of meat. As you finish a piece, place meat into slow cooker.

3. Sprinkle with chopped onion.

4. Spoon spaghetti sauce over top, being careful not to disturb seasonings and onions.

5. Cover and cook on Low 5–8 hours, or until meat is tender but not overcooked.

Makes 5–6 servings

Fajita Steak

BECKY HARDER • MONUMENT, CO

Prep Time: 10 minutes • Cooking Time: 6–8 hours • Ideal slow cooker size: 4-qt.

15-oz. can tomatoes with
    green chilies

1/4 cup salsa, your choice of
    mild, medium, or hot

8-oz. can tomato sauce

2 lbs. round steak, cut in
    2" x 4" strips

1 envelope dry fajita spice mix

1 cup water, optional

1. Combine all ingredients—except water—in slow cooker.

2. Cover and cook on Low 6–8 hours, or until meat is tender but not over-cooked.

3. Check meat occasionally to make sure it isn't cooking dry. If it begins to look dry, stir in water, up to 1 cup.

Makes 6 servings

Note: Serve meat with fried onions and green peppers. Offer shredded cheese, avocado chunks, and sour cream as toppings. Let individual eaters wrap any or all of the ingredients in flour tortillas.

Pepper Steak

DARLENE G. MARTIN • RICHFIELD, PA

Prep Time: 15–20 minutes • Cooking Time: 5–6 hours • Ideal slow cooker size: 3 1/2- to 4-qt.

1-lb. round steak, cut 3/4"–1"
    thick

14 1/2-oz. can Italian-style
    stewed tomatoes,
    undrained

1 tsp. Worcestershire sauce

2 yellow, 2 red, and 2 green
    bell peppers, sliced in strips

1 large onion, sliced

1. Cut meat into 4 serving-size pieces. In a large nonstick skillet, brown meat on both sides. Transfer meat to slow cooker.

2. In a medium-sized bowl, stir together undrained tomatoes and Worcestershire sauce. Spoon over meat.

3. Arrange vegetables over top.

4. Cover and cook on Low 5–6 hours, or until meat and vegetables are tender but not overcooked.

Makes 4 servings

New Mexico Steak

MAMIE CHRISTOPHERSON • RIO RANCHO, NM

Prep Time: 10 minutes • Cooking Time: 4 hours • Ideal slow cooker size: 3-qt.

1 large onion, sliced

2-lb. round steak, cut into
    serving-size pieces

salt and pepper to taste

2 7-oz. cans green chili salsa

1. Place onion slices in bottom of slow cooker.

2. Sprinkle steak with salt and pepper. Add steak pieces to cooker.

3. Spoon chili salsa over all, being careful not to wash off seasonings.

4. Cover and cook on High 1 hour. Turn to Low and cook 3 hours, or until steak is tender but not overcooked.

Makes 4–6 servings

Note: If the chili salsa is too hot, sprinkle a little white sugar over mixture before cooking. Or choose a milder salsa. You can add a little liquid (water or beer) if the dish seems too dry toward the end of the cooking time.

Pigs in Blankets

LINDA SLUITER • SCHERERVILLE, IN

Prep Time: 30 minutes • Cooking Time: 6-8 hours • Ideal slow cooker size: 4-qt.

1-2-lb. round steak

1 lb. bacon

1 cup ketchup

¼ cup brown sugar

1 small onion

¼-½ cup water

1. Cut steak into long strips. Roll up each meat strip, and then wrap with a slice of bacon. Secure with a toothpick to hold the roll shape.

2. Warm remaining ingredients in a saucepan, bringing to a simmer to make a sauce.

3. Place meat rolls in slow cooker. Pour sauce over top.

4. Cover and cook on Low 6–8 hours, or until meat is tender but not overcooked.

Makes 4 servings

Beef Roulades

KAREN WAGGONER • JOPLIN, MO

Prep Time: 20 minutes ▪ Cooking Time: 2 hours ▪ Ideal slow cooker size: 5-qt.

4 lbs. round steak

4 cups prepared packaged
  herb-seasoned stuffing mix

2 10¾-oz. cans cream of
  mushroom soup

1-2 cups water

1. Cut steak (or ask your butcher to cut it) into 12 long pieces. Pound each piece until thin and flattened.

2. Place ⅓ cup prepared stuffing on each slice of meat. Roll up and fasten with a toothpick. Place in slow cooker.

3. In a bowl, mix soup and water together and then pour over steak.

4. Cover and cook on High 4–6 hours, or until meat is tender but not overcooked.

Makes 12 servings

Comforting Beef with Potatoes

DOROTHY VAN DEEST • MEMPHIS, TN

Prep Time: 20 minutes ▪ Cooking Time: 2-8 hours ▪ Ideal slow cooker size: 5-qt.

2-3 cups cut-up cooked beef
  roast

2 10-oz. pkgs. frozen hash
  brown potatoes, thawed

1 onion, finely chopped

¼ cup butter, melted

1 cup gravy or beef broth

1. Place all ingredients in slow cooker, either in layers or mixed together.

2. Cover and cook on Low 4–8 hours, or on High 2–3 hours, or until thoroughly heated.

Makes 4 servings

Note: This recipe can easily be doubled.

Buffet Beef

KATE JOHNSON • ROLFE, IA

Prep Time: 10 minutes • Cooking Time: 4–8 hours • Ideal slow cooker size: 4-qt.

12-oz. can beer

1 envelope dry brown gravy mix

$\frac{1}{3}$ cup flour

2$\frac{1}{2}$–3-lb. round steak, cut into
    cubes

1. In slow cooker, combine beer and gravy mix and mix together well.

2. In a plastic bag, shake flour and steak cubes together until meat is coated.

3. Empty entire contents of bag into slow cooker. Gently stir to coat meat with liquid.

4. Cover and cook on Low 6–8 hours, or on High 4 hours.

   Makes 8–10 servings

Quick and Tasty Beef-in-Gravy

DEDE PETERSON • RAPID CITY, SD / ROSALIE D. MILLER • MIFFLINTOWN, PA

Prep Time: 15–20 minutes • Cooking Time: 8–10 hours • Ideal slow cooker size: 6-qt.

3 lbs. stew meat

1 envelope dry onion soup mix

$\frac{1}{2}$ cup beef broth

10$\frac{3}{4}$-oz. can cream of
    mushroom soup

4-oz. can sliced mushrooms,
    drained

1. Combine all ingredients in slow cooker.

2. Cover and cook on Low 8–10 hours, or until meat is tender but not overcooked.

   Makes 8 servings

Creamy-Style Beef Tips

CATHY SELLERS • CEDAR RAPIDS, IA

Prep Time: 10 minutes • Cooking Time: 6–8 hours • Ideal slow cooker size: 4-qt.

2 lbs. stew meat

2 10¾-oz. cans cream of
   mushroom soup

1 soup can water

half a 12-oz. can evaporated milk

1 tsp. salt

1. Combine all ingredients in slow cooker. Mix well.

2. Cover and cook on Low 6–8 hours, or until meat is tender but not overcooked.

3. Serve over rice or noodles.

Makes 6 servings

Creamy Beef and Mushrooms

JOETTE DROZ • KALONA, IA / BETTY MOORE • PLANO, IL
MARY B. SENSENIG • NEW HOLLAND, PA

Prep Time: 10 minutes • Cooking Time: 6–8 hours • Ideal slow cooker size: 3-qt.

10¾-oz. can condensed
   golden mushroom soup

10¾-oz. can condensed
   cream of mushroom soup

10¾-oz. can condensed
   French onion soup

¼ cup seasoned bread crumbs

2 lbs. beef stew meat, cut into
   1" cubes

1. In slow cooker, combine soups and bread crumbs. Mix well.

2. Stir in beef.

3. Cover and cook on Low 6–8 hours, or until meat is tender but not overcooked.

Makes 6–8 servings

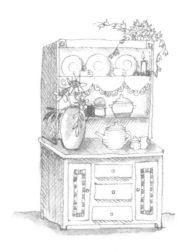

Slow-Cooker Beef Stroganoff

JENNIFER EBERLY • HARRISONBURG, VA

Prep Time: 5 minutes • Cooking Time: 6–8 hours • Ideal slow cooker size: 3-qt.

1 lb. lean round steak cubes

1 envelope dry beefy onion
    soup mix

10¾-oz. can cream of celery
    soup

10¾-oz. can cream of
    mushroom soup

½ cup sour cream

1. Place first 4 ingredients in slow cooker and mix together thoroughly.

2. Cover and cook on Low 6–8 hours, stirring occasionally if you're around the kitchen and able to do that.

3. Fifteen minutes before serving, stir in sour cream.

4. When hot and bubbly, serve over cooked rice or noodles.

Makes 6 servings

Sweet and Sour Beef Stew

HEATHER HORST • LEBANON, PA

Prep Time: 10 minutes • Cooking Time: 6–8 hours • Ideal slow cooker size: 3-qt.

1 cup chopped onions

2 lbs. stewing beef

1 Tbsp. Worcestershire sauce

½ cup vinegar

¼ cup brown sugar

1. Place onion in bottom of slow cooker.

2. In a bowl, mix meat and remaining ingredients together. Add to cooker.

3. Cover and cook on Low 6–8 hours, or until meat and onions are tender but not overcooked.

4. Serve over cooked rice or pasta.

Makes 6 servings

No-Peeking Beef Tips

RUTH C. HANCOCK • EARLSBORO, OK

Prep Time: 15 minutes • Cooking Time: 4 hours • Ideal slow cooker size: 4-qt.

2 lbs. stew meat

half or whole envelope dry
    onion soup mix

12-oz. can lemon-lime soda

10¾-oz. can cream of
    mushroom soup, or cream
    of chicken soup

1. Put meat in slow cooker. Sprinkle dry onion soup mix over meat.

2. Mix soda and cream of mushroom soup together in a bowl. Spoon over meat, being careful not to disturb onion soup mix.

3. Cover and cook on High 4 hours. Do not stir or remove lid until the time is up.

4. Serve over cooked rice or noodles.

   Makes 4 servings

Rainy Day Low-Fat Dinner

RUTH ZENDT • MIFFLINTOWN, PA

Prep Time: 10–15 minutes • Cooking Time: 6–10 hours • Ideal slow cooker size: 5-qt.

5–6 medium-sized potatoes,
    peeled or unpeeled, and
    cut into ½" cubes

1 lb. baby carrots

1½ lbs. lean beef cubes

10¾-oz. can fat-free cream of
    mushroom soup

12-oz. jar fat-free brown gravy

1. Layer potatoes, carrots, and beef in slow cooker in the order listed.

2. In a mixing bowl, blend together soup and gravy. Pour over cooker contents.

3. Cover and cook on Low 6–10 hours, or until vegetables and meat are tender.

   Makes 6–8 servings

Note: Add your favorite seasonings to the layers. Vary the vegetable ingredients as you want. You can prepare this recipe the night before, then refrigerate it overnight. Before you leave in the morning, put the crock in the cooker and turn it on. Dinner will be ready when you get home.

Golfer's Stew

LUCY O'CONNELL • GOSHEN, MA

Prep Time: 10 minutes • Cooking Time: 7 hours • Ideal slow cooker size: 4-qt.

1 lb. stew beef, cubed

12-oz. jar beef gravy or beef
   and mushroom gravy

6 medium-sized potatoes, cut
   in ½" chunks

6 carrots, cut in thick slices

3 ribs celery, cut in thick slices,
   optional

2-3 onions, cut in wedges

1. Place all ingredients in slow cooker. Stir together gently.

2. Cover and cook on High 1 hour, and then on Low 6 hours.

Makes 4–5 servings

Note: If you wish, add 1 tsp. salt and ¼–½ tsp. pepper in Step 1.

Beef Stew

LEANN BROWN • RONKS, PA

Prep Time: 10–15 minutes • Cooking Time: 5–6 hours • Ideal slow cooker size: 5- to 6-qt.

3 lbs. cubed beef

2 12-oz. jars beef gravy

2 cups chopped carrots

1 medium-sized onion, chopped

4 cups chopped potatoes

salt and pepper, optional

1. Place beef in slow cooker. Add remaining ingredients. Stir together well.

2. Cover and cook on Low 5–6 hours, or until meat and veggies are tender but not overcooked.

Makes 6–8 servings

Easy Beef Stew

JUDI MANOS • WEST ISLIP, NY

Prep Time: 20 minutes • Cooking Time: 7½–8½ hours • Ideal slow cooker size: 4-qt.

4 medium-sized red potatoes

1½ lbs. beef stew meat

⅓ cup flour

14-oz. can diced tomatoes, undrained

2 cups water

3 cups frozen stir-fry bell peppers and onions

1. Cut potatoes into quarters. Place on bottom of slow cooker.

2. In a mixing bowl, toss flour with beef to coat. Add to slow cooker.

3. Pour in undrained tomatoes and water.

4. Cover and cook on Low 7–8 hours, or until beef and potatoes are tender but not overcooked.

5. Gently fold stir-fry vegetables into stew. Cover and cook on Low 30–40 minutes, or until vegetables are hot and tender.

Makes 4–6 servings

Variations: Add 2-3 cups sliced carrots just after the potatoes in Step 1. Add 2 tsp. salt and ¾ tsp. pepper to the flour in Step 2, before tossing with the beef.

Lynn's Easy Stew

VERONICA SABO • SHELTON, CT

Prep Time: 10 minutes • Cooking Time: 5–8 hours • Ideal slow cooker size: 4- to 5-qt.

2 lbs. stew beef

4 ribs celery, cut into large pieces

3 cups carrots, cut into large pieces

1 large onion, chopped

1 envelope dry onion soup mix

water

1. Place all ingredients in slow cooker. Stir together gently, until well mixed. Add about 2" of water.

2. Cover and cook on High 5–8 hours, or until meat and vegetables are tender.

Makes 5–6 servings

Roast Beef Stew

THELMA GOOD • HARRISONBURG, VA

Prep Time: 10–15 minutes • Cooking Time: 10–13 hours • Ideal slow cooker size: 6-qt.

2-3-lb. roast, which may be frozen!

5-6 potatoes, quartered

4-5 carrots, sliced

2 small onions, sliced

half a head cabbage, sliced

1. In the evening, place roast in slow cooker.

2. Cover and cook on High 1 hour. Turn to Low and cook overnight, or 6–8 hours if you're doing this during the daytime.

3. In the morning, place potatoes, carrots, and onions around and over roast. Fill slow cooker one-half to two-thirds full with water, depending upon how soupy you like your stew.

4. Cover and cook on High 2–3 hours.

5. Lift the lid and put in cabbage, pushing it down into broth. Continue cooking on High 1 more hour, or until veggies are done to your liking. The stew should be ready at lunchtime—or dinnertime.

Makes 8 servings

Variations: Sprinkle the roast, top and bottom, with salt and pepper before placing it in the cooker in Step 1. Also, sprinkle the vegetables with salt after you've put them in the cooker in Step 3. Increase the amount of potatoes, carrots, onions, and cabbage to your liking. You may need to increase the cooking time in Steps 4 and 5 to make sure that they get as tender as you like.

Succulent Beef Stew

LINDA THOMAS • SAYNER, WI

Prep Time: 30 minutes • Cooking Time: 8 hours • Ideal slow cooker size: 3-qt.

1-1½ lbs. stew meat

1 medium-sized to large onion, chopped

14½-oz. can beef broth

1 broth can water

½ lb. baby carrots

5 medium-sized white potatoes, peeled or unpeeled, cut into ½" chunks

OPTIONAL INGREDIENTS:

salt and pepper

5 shakes Worcestershire sauce

2 bay leaves

1. In a nonstick skillet, brown stew meat and chopped onion. Sprinkle with salt and pepper, if you wish. Transfer mixture to slow cooker.

2. Add broth and water, and Worcestershire sauce and bay leaves, if you choose. Stir together well.

3. Cover and cook on Low 4 hours.

4. Layer in vegetables. Push down into liquid as much as you can. Cover and continue cooking on Low 4 more hours.

5. If the stew seems to get dry, add ½ cup water.

Makes 6 servings

Mediterranean Beef Stew

SANDY OSBORN • IOWA CITY, IA

Prep Time: 5-10 minutes • Cooking Time: 3-8 hours • Ideal slow cooker size: 3½-qt.

2 medium-sized zucchini, cut into bite-sized pieces

¾ pound beef stew meat, cut into ½" pieces

2 14½-oz. cans Italian-style diced tomatoes, undrained

½ tsp. pepper, optional

2" stick cinnamon, or ¼ tsp. cinnamon

1. Place zucchini in bottom of slow cooker.

2. Add beef and remaining ingredients in the order listed.

3. Cover and cook on High 3–5 hours, or until meat is tender but not overcooked. You can also cook the stew on High 1 hour, then on Low 7 hours, or until meat is tender but not overdone.

Makes 4 servings

Cooking Tip

When I want to warm rolls to go with a slow-cooker stew, I wrap them in foil and lay them on top of the stew until they're warm.

—*Donna Barnitz, Jenks, OK*

Italian Beef

PEGGY FORSYTHE • BARTLETT, TN

Prep Time: 20 minutes • Cooking Time: 8 hours • Ideal slow cooker size: 4- to 6-qt.

4-5-lb. beef roast, cut into
    1"-1½" cubes

2 or 3 beef bouillon cubes

1 tsp. garlic salt

2 Tbsp. Italian salad dressing

1. Place roast, bouillon, garlic salt, and dressing in slow cooker. Stir.

2. Add 1"-1½" water around beef, being careful not to disturb the seasoning on top of meat.

3. Cover and cook on Low 8 hours, or until tender but not overcooked.

4. Remove beef from cooker and shred with 2 forks. Return shredded meat to cooker and stir into broth.

5. Serve over rice, or on rolls or garlic bread for a delicious open-face sandwich.

Makes 6 servings

Beef a la Mode

GLORIA JULIEN • GLADSTONE, MI

Prep Time: 5-10 minutes • Cooking Time: 6-8 hours • Ideal slow cooker size: 4-qt.

2-lb. boneless beef roast, cut
    into 6 serving-size pieces

½ lb. salt pork or bacon, cut up

3 onions, chopped

pepper to taste

water

1. Place beef and pork in slow cooker.

2. Sprinkle onions over top of meat.

3. Add pepper to taste.

4. Pour water in alongside meat, about 1" deep.

5. Cook on Low 6-8 hours.

6. Serve over mashed potatoes, cooked rice, or pasta.

Makes 6 servings

Beef Brisket Barbecue

SHARON TIMPE • JACKSON, WI

Prep Time: 15 minutes • Cooking Time: 6¼–7¼ hours • Ideal slow cooker size: 4- to 5-qt.

2 cups barbecue sauce, divided

1 small onion, chopped

3 tsp. beef bouillon granules, or 2 beef bouillon cubes

3-4-lb. boneless beef brisket

8 sandwich rolls

1. In bottom of slow cooker, combine 1 cup barbecue sauce, chopped onion, and bouillon.

2. Place beef brisket on top.

3. Cover and cook on Low 6–7 hours, or until brisket shreds easily.

4. Remove brisket from cooker. Using 2 forks, shred meat.

5. Tilt cooker and spoon off fat from cooking broth. Discard fat.

6. Pour cooking broth into a bowl. Again, spoon off any remaining fat and discard.

7. Measure out 1 cup cooking broth. Pour back into slow cooker, along with remaining cup of barbecue sauce. Blend broth and sauce well.

8. Return shredded meat to slow cooker. Stir into sauce thoroughly.

9. Cover and cook on High 15 minutes, or until meat is hot.

10. Serve over sandwich rolls.

Makes 8 servings

Note: You can also serve this barbecue on small buns as a snack or appetizer. Serving from the slow cooker keeps the meat hot, and guests can help themselves whenever they want to.

Easy Roast Beef Barbecue

ROSE HANKINS • STEVENSVILLE, MD

Prep Time: 15 minutes • Cooking Time: 12 hours • Ideal slow cooker size: 4- to 5-qt.

12-oz. bottle barbecue sauce

½ cup water

½ cup ketchup

½ cup chopped onion

½ cup chopped green pepper

3–4-lb. beef roast

12–16 sandwich rolls

1. Combine first 5 ingredients in slow cooker. Smother roast in sauce.

2. Cover. Cook on Low 12 hours.

3. Shred meat using 2 forks. Mix thoroughly through sauce.

4. Serve on rolls with coleslaw.

Makes 12–16 servings

Pulled Beef or Pork

PAT BECHTEL • DILLSBURG, PA

Prep Time: 5–10 minutes • Cooking Time: 8–10 hours • Ideal slow cooker size: 3½-qt.

4-lb. beef or pork roast

2 envelopes dry ranch dressing mix

2 envelopes dry Italian dressing mix

1. Cook roast in slow cooker on Low 8–10 hours, or until tender but not overcooked. Do not add water or seasonings! By the end of cooking time, there will be broth from cooking—do not discard it!

2. Just before serving, remove meat from slow cooker. Using 2 forks, pull meat apart.

3. Add dry dressing mixes to broth and stir thoroughly. Stir pulled meat back into broth in cooker. Serve immediately in rolls, or over cooked rice or pasta, or over mashed potatoes.

Makes 16–18 servings

Barbecued Beef Sandwiches

ARIANNE HOCHSTETLER • GOSHEN, IN

Prep Time: 15 minutes • Cooking Time: 5½–6½ hours • Ideal slow cooker size: 4-qt.

4-lb. round steak, ¾" thick, cut into 3" cubes

2 cups ketchup

1 cup cola

½ cup chopped onion

2 garlic cloves, minced

1. Spray slow cooker with nonstick cooking spray.

2. Place beef pieces in cooker.

3. Mix remaining ingredients in a large bowl and pour over meat.

4. Cover and cook on High 5–6 hours.

5. About 30 minutes before serving, remove beef from slow cooker and shred with 2 forks. Return beef to slow cooker and mix well with sauce.

6. Cover and cook on High an additional 20 minutes.

7. Spoon about ⅓ cup beef mixture into individual sandwich buns.

Makes 24 servings

Super Beef Barbecue

LINDA E. WILCOX • BLYTHEWOOD, SC

Prep Time: 15 minutes • Cooking Time: 9–10 hours • Ideal slow cooker size: 6-qt.

3-4-lb. rump roast

1 clove garlic, minced, or ¼ cup finely chopped onion

18-oz. bottle barbecue sauce

1 cup ketchup

16-oz. jar whole dill pickles, undrained

1. Cut roast into quarters and place in slow cooker.

2. In a bowl, stir together garlic, barbecue sauce, and ketchup. When well blended, fold in pickles and their juice. Pour over meat.

3. Cover and cook on Low 8–9 hours, or until meat begins to fall apart.

4. Remove pickles and discard them.

5. Lift meat out onto a platter and shred by pulling it apart with 2 forks.

6. Return meat to sauce and heat thoroughly on Low, about 1 hour.

7. Serve in sandwich rolls.

Makes 10–12 servings

Braised Short Ribs

LEONA YODER • HARTVILLE, OH

Prep Time: 45 minutes • Cooking Time: 4–10 hours ▪ Ideal slow cooker size: 4-qt.

1 tsp. salt

1 cup flour

3 lbs. beef short ribs, cut into
    serving-size pieces

2–3 Tbsp. olive oil

2 medium-sized onions, sliced

1 cup water

1. Combine salt and flour in a shallow bowl. Roll short ribs in seasoned flour.

2. Brown ribs in oil on all sides in a large nonstick skillet. Rather than crowd the skillet, which prevents meat from browning, do the browning in batches. As you finish browning, place pieces of meat in slow cooker.

3. Add sliced onions and water.

4. Cover and cook on Low 8–10 hours, or on High 4–6 hours.

Makes 6 servings

Note: Add ½ tsp. pepper to the salt and flour in Step 1, if you wish. To make gravy, remove fully cooked ribs to a platter and keep warm. Place 1½ Tbsp. flour in a jar with a tight-fitting lid. Pour in ½ cup cold water. Shake together until lumps disappear. Turn cooker to High so that broth begins to simmer. When bubbling, pour in flour-water in a thin stream, whisking as you do it. Continue whisking until the broth thickens. Serve over, or alongside, ribs.

Tex-Mex Beef Ribs or Roast

JANIE STEELE • MOORE, OK

Prep Time: 5–10 minutes ▪ Cooking Time: 4–10 hours ▪ Ideal slow cooker size: 6-qt.

3–4 lbs. beef short ribs, or
    round steak, cut in
    serving-size pieces

1 cup sweet and tangy steak
    sauce

⅓ cup picante sauce

1 tsp. chili powder

½ tsp. dry mustard

1. Place ribs or steak in slow cooker.

2. Combine remaining ingredients in a bowl and pour over meat.

3. Cover and cook on Low 4–10 hours, or until meat is tender but not overcooked.

Makes 6 servings

Corned Beef and Cabbage

CARRIE DARBY • WAYLAND, IA / LEONA YODER • HARTVILLE, OH
ESTHER PORTER • MINNEAPOLIS, MN / BETTY K. DRESCHER • QUAKERTOWN, PA
KAREN CENEVIVA • NEW HAVEN, CT / BONITA ENSENBERGER • ALBUQUERQUE, NM
DOROTHY LINGERFELT • STONYFORD, CA

Prep Time: 30 minutes • Cooking Time: 4-7 hours • Ideal slow cooker size: 5- or 6-qt.

3-4-lb. corned beef brisket
(not in a brine), cut into
6-8 pieces

¾-1¼ cups water

5-6 carrots, cut in 2"-3" pieces

3 medium-sized onions,
quartered

salt and pepper

half to a whole head cabbage,
cut into wedges

1. Place corned beef in slow cooker. Add water.

2. Place carrots and onions around meat, if possible, pushing vegetables in so they're at least partly covered by water. Sprinkle salt and pepper over all.

3. Cover and cook on Low 4–5 hours, or on High 2½–3 hours.

4. Add cabbage to cooker, pushing down into liquid to moisten. Turn to High and cook an additional 1½–2 hours, or until vegetables and meat are tender but not overcooked.

Makes 6 servings

Note: You can prepare the cabbage separately in a large soup pot. Place wedges in kettle and add 1 cup broth from cooker. Cook 20 to 30 minutes, covered, or until just-tender. Stir into corned beef and vegetables right before serving.

Apple Corned Beef and Cabbage

DONNA TRELOAR • HARTFORD CITY, IN

Prep Time: 15 minutes • Cooking Time: 8-10 hours • Ideal slow cooker size: 5-qt.

3-4-lb. corned beef brisket
(not in a brine), cut into
6-8 pieces

1 small head cabbage, cut in
thin wedges

3-4 medium-sized potatoes,
cut in chunks

2-3 cups baby carrots, or sliced
full-sized carrots, optional

1 qt. pure apple juice

1 cup brown sugar

1. Place corned beef in slow cooker.

2. Place vegetables around and on top of meat.

3. Pour apple juice over everything. Sprinkle with brown sugar.

4. Cover and cook on Low 8–10 hours, or until meat and vegetables are tender but not overcooked.

Makes 6-8 servings

Reuben Casserole

MELANIE THROWER • MCPHERSON, KS

Prep Time: 10 minutes • Cooking Time: 2-4 hours • Ideal slow cooker size: 2-qt.

2 cups deli-style corned beef,
  torn into bite-sized pieces,
  divided

15-oz. can sauerkraut, drained,
  divided

$\frac{1}{2}$ cup shredded or 8 slices
  Swiss cheese, divided

$\frac{1}{4}$ cup Thousand Island salad
  dressing, divided

4 cups dry packaged stuffing
  mix, divided

1. Spray slow cooker with nonstick cooking spray.

2. Layer half of each ingredient in the order listed.

3. Repeat layers.

4. Cover and cook on Low 2–4 hours, until casserole is
   cooked through and cheese has melted.

Makes 4 servings

Noodle Casserole

MARY B. SENSENIG • NEW HOLLAND, PA

Prep Time: 5 minutes • Cooking Time: 3-3$\frac{1}{2}$ hours • Ideal slow cooker size: 4-qt.

8-oz. pkg. dry noodles

10$\frac{3}{4}$-oz. can cream of
  mushroom soup

1 cup milk

$\frac{1}{4}$ lb. dried beef, shredded

1 cup shredded cheese,
  optional

1. Cook noodles as directed on package. Drain and rinse
   with cold water.

2. In a mixing bowl, blend soup and milk together.

3. Spray cooker with nonstick cooking spray. Layer ingredients in cooker in this order: cooked noodles, soup-milk
   mixture, dried beef.

4. Cover and cook on Low 2$\frac{1}{2}$–3 hours. Sprinkle cheese over
   top, if you wish. Cover and continue cooking another half
   hour.

Makes 4 servings

Beef Tongue

LIZZIE ANN YODER • HARTVILLE, OH

Prep Time: 15–20 minutes • Cooking Time: 7–8 hours • Ideal slow cooker size: 4- to 5-qt.

1 beef tongue, fresh or smoked

2 scant Tbsp. salt

1½ cups water

1 bay leaf

2 lemons, squeezed, or
    2 onions, quartered

6 peppercorns

1. Place washed tongue in slow cooker.

2. In a bowl, mix all remaining ingredients together. Pour over tongue.

3. Cover and cook on Low 7–8 hours, or until meat is tender. Cool until you're able to handle meat, and then remove outer skin by pulling on it gently.

4. Slice meat and serve hot.

5. Use chilled leftovers in sandwiches.

Makes 6 servings

Roast Venison with Gravy

BECKY GEHMAN • BERGTON, VA

Prep Time: 5 minutes • Cooking Time: 6–7 hours • Ideal slow cooker size: 3-qt.

2-3-lb. venison roast

1-2 tsp. garlic powder, or onion powder

10¾-oz. can golden mushroom soup

¾ soup can water

1. Place roast in slow cooker. Sprinkle both sides with seasoning.

2. Cover and cook on Low 4–5 hours, turning roast twice while cooking.

3. In a bowl, mix together soup and water. Add to meat after it has cooked for 4–5 hours.

4. Cover and cook on Low 2 more hours, turning roast once during this time.

Makes 4–6 servings

Good and Easy Elk

EVELYN PAGE • LANCE CREEK, WY

Prep Time: 10–15 minutes • Cooking Time: 4–8 hours • Ideal slow cooker size: 3-qt.

1–2 lbs. elk, cubed

½ lb. sliced fresh mushrooms

1 cup beef broth

10¾-oz. can cream of
mushroom soup

1 envelope dry onion soup mix

1. Combine all ingredients in slow cooker. Mix gently but well.

2. Cover and cook on High 4 hours, or on Low 8 hours, or until meat is tender but not overcooked.

Makes 3–4 servings

Note: You may substitute venison or beef for the elk.

Elk Stroganoff

EVELYN PAGE • LANCE CREEK, WY

Prep Time: 20 minutes • Cooking Time: 6–8 hours • Ideal slow cooker size: 3-qt.

1 lb. cubed elk

½ cup chopped onion

10¾-oz. can cream of celery
soup

¼ tsp. garlic salt

4-oz. can mushroom pieces,
drained, optional

1 cup sour cream

1. Brown meat in a nonstick skillet. Add onions and sauté until wilted.

2. Combine meat and onions, soup, garlic salt, and mushrooms, if you wish, in slow cooker.

3. Cover and cook on Low 6–8 hours, or until tender.

4. Fifteen minutes before serving, stir in sour cream.

Makes 3–4 servings

Note: Serve over cooked rice or noodles. You may also substitute venison or beef for the elk.

Elk in Mushroom Soup

EVELYN PAGE • LANCE CREEK, WY

Prep Time: 15 minutes • Cooking Time: 5–8 hours • Ideal slow cooker size: 3-qt.

1–2 lbs. elk steak

10¾-oz. can cream of
  mushroom soup

1 soup can milk

1. Brown steak in a nonstick skillet. Then place in slow cooker.

2. In a bowl, combine soup and milk. Pour sauce over steak.

3. Cover and cook on Low 5–8 hours, or until meat is tender but not overcooked.

Makes 4–6 servings

Notes:
• I often serve this meat alongside cooked potatoes or rice. Then we pour the soup mixture over the meat and vegetables. You may substitute venison or beef for the elk.

Cheesy Hot Dish

LUCILLE MARTIN • BARNETT, MO

Prep Time: 30–40 minutes • Cooking Time: 2–3 hours • Ideal slow cooker size: 5-qt.

4–5 medium-sized potatoes,
  cooked and sliced, divided

1 lb. ground beef, browned and
  drained, divided

12-oz. pkg. frozen green beans,
  divided

½ lb. Velveeta cheese, sliced,
  divided

10¾-oz. can cream of
  mushroom soup

1. Place half of potatoes in bottom of buttered slow cooker.

2. Layer in half of ground beef, followed by half of green beans. Top with half of cheese slices.

3. Repeat all the layers.

4. Pour soup over all.

5. Cover and cook on Low 2 hours if food is hot when put into cooker, or on High 2 hours if food is cold when put into cooker.

Makes 6 servings

Cooking Tip

Invest in good-quality knives. They make preparation much easier.

Creamy Ground Beef

JOLEEN ALBRECHT • GLADSTONE, MI

Prep Time: 10–15 minutes • Cooking Time: 2–4 hours • Ideal slow cooker size: 3-qt.

1 lb. ground beef

garlic powder to taste

salt and pepper to taste

2 10¾-oz. cans cream of
    mushroom soup

half to whole soup can water

1. Brown ground beef in a nonstick skillet. Drain.

2. Place in slow cooker. Add seasonings. Taste and add more, if you like.

3. Mix in soup. Add water until mixture reaches consistency of gravy.

4. Cover and cook on Low 2–4 hours.

5. Serve over cooked noodles or rice.

Makes 5 servings

Note: You can also serve this dish over baked potatoes. Then sprinkle with grated cheddar cheese.

Tater Tot Casserole

SHARON WANTLAND • MENOMONEE FALLS, WI

Prep Time: 10 minutes • Cooking Time: 2–3 hours • Ideal slow cooker size: 3-qt.

1 lb. ground beef

¼ cup chopped onions

10¾-oz. can cream of chicken
    soup

16-oz. box Tater Tots

1. Brown ground beef with onions in a nonstick skillet until crumbly. Drain.

2. Place beef and onions in bottom of slow cooker.

3. Top with soup and then with Tater Tots.

4. Cover and cook on Low 2–3 hours.

Makes 4 servings

Spanish Rice

SHARON WANTLAND • MENOMONEE FALLS, WI / SHERRI MAYER • MENOMONEE FALLS, WI

Prep Time: 20 minutes • Cooking Time: 1½ hours • Ideal slow cooker size: 6-qt.

2 cups minute rice, cooked

1 qt. stewed tomatoes

½ cup chopped onions

½ cup chopped green pepper

1 envelope dry taco sauce
   seasoning, mixed with
   ¾ cup water, optional

¾ lb. ground beef, browned

1. Combine all ingredients in slow cooker and mix well.

2. Cover and cook 1½ hours on High, or until heated through.

   Makes 4 servings

Variation: Instead of the 2 cups of cooked Minute Rice, use 1½ cups uncooked long-grain rice and 2 Tbsp. oil or butter. Turn the slow cooker to High. Sauté the uncooked rice in the oil or butter until golden brown. Then proceed with Step 1.

Meaty Spanish Rice

SUSAN WENGER • LEBANON, PA

Prep Time: 20 minutes • Cooking Time: 4–8 hours • Ideal slow cooker size: 4- to 5-qt.

2 lbs. ground beef

44-oz. can stewed or diced
   tomatoes, or spaghetti
   sauce

1 cup water

2½ tsp. chili powder

2 tsp. Worcestershire sauce

1 cup long-grain rice, uncooked

OPTIONAL INGREDIENTS:

1 medium-sized onion,
   chopped

½ tsp. black pepper

1 green pepper, chopped

1½–2 tsp. salt

1. Brown beef in a nonstick skillet. (Include chopped onion and black pepper, if you wish.) Drain. Place mixture in slow cooker.

2. Add remaining ingredients to cooker (including green pepper and salt, if you wish), stirring well.

3. Cover and cook on Low 6–8 hours, or on High 4 hours.

   Makes 10 servings

Wild Rice Ground Beef Casserole

ESTHER GINGERICH • PARNELL, IA

Prep Time: 15 minutes • Cooking Time: 3–6 hours • Ideal slow cooker size: 3-qt.

1 lb. ground beef

1 medium-sized onion, chopped

6.2-oz. pkg. long-grain and wild rice, uncooked

4-oz. can mushrooms, drained

2 10¾-oz. cans cream of mushroom soup

½ cup water

1. In a nonstick skillet, brown ground beef and onion together. Drain.

2. In slow cooker, combine ground beef mixture with all remaining ingredients, including wild rice seasoning.

3. Cover and cook on High 3 hours, or on Low 5–6 hours, or until rice is tender but not mushy.

Makes 6 servings

Pizza Rice Casserole

JENNIE MARTIN • RICHFIELD, PA

Prep Time: 20 minutes • Cooking Time: 6 hours • Ideal slow cooker size: 5-qt.

1 lb. ground beef

1 medium-sized onion, chopped

3 cups uncooked long-grain rice

1 qt. pizza sauce

3 cups shredded cheese, your choice of flavor

1 cup cottage cheese, optional

4 cups water

1. Place ground beef and onion in a nonstick skillet. Brown and then drain.

2. Mix all ingredients in slow cooker.

3. Cover and cook on High 6 hours, or until rice is tender.

Makes 6–8 servings

Granny's Delight

ANNA B. STOLTZFUS • HONEY BROOK, PA

Prep Time: 20 minutes • Cooking Time: 1½ hours • Ideal slow cooker size: 6-qt.

1 lb. ground beef

1 small onion, chopped

3 cups dry macaroni

1 cup shredded cheddar
   cheese

4 cups spaghetti sauce, your
   favorite packaged or
   homemade

½ cup water

1. Brown beef with onion in a nonstick skillet. Drain.

2. Spray slow cooker with nonstick cooking spray. Place all ingredients into slow cooker and fold together gently.

3. Cover and cook on High 1½ hours, or until macaroni is tender but not mushy.

Makes 5 servings

Yumazetta

ANDREA CUNNINGHAM • ARLINGTON, KS

Prep Time: 15 minutes • Cooking Time: 3-5 hours • Ideal slow cooker size: 4- to 6-qt.

1 lb. ground beef

8 ozs. shredded cheese, your
   choice of flavors

1 onion, diced

10¾-oz. can cream of
   mushroom soup

12-oz. can diced tomatoes,
   undrained

1. Brown ground beef in a nonstick skillet. Drain.

2. Combine all ingredients in slow cooker.

3. Cook on Low 3–5 hours, or until heated through.

4. Serve over cooked pasta.

Makes 8 servings

Cooking Tip

Here's a real time-saver from our house: Brown large quantities (10 lbs.) of ground beef, seasoned with onion, basil, and oregano to taste. Drain and cool. Freeze in pint freezer containers. The meat is readily available, with no prep time or cleanup, when preparing a slow-cooker recipe or casserole that calls for browned ground beef.

—*Dale and Shari Mast, Harrisonburg, VA*

Easy Crock Taco Filling

JOANNE GOOD • WHEATON, IL

Prep Time: 20 minutes • Cooking Time: 6–8 hours • Ideal slow cooker size: 4-qt.

1 lb. ground beef

1 large onion, chopped

2 15-oz. cans chili beans

15-oz. can Santa Fe, or
   Mexican, or Fiesta corn

¾ cup water

OPTIONAL INGREDIENTS:

¼ tsp. cayenne pepper

½ tsp. garlic powder

1. Brown ground beef and onion in a nonstick skillet. Drain.

2. Mix all ingredients together in slow cooker, blending well.

3. Cover and cook on Low 6–8 hours.

Makes 4–6 servings

Note: You may want to add more or less than ¾ cup water to this recipe, depending upon how hot and fast your slow cooker cooks and how tight-fitting its lid is. Serve the filling in warmed, soft corn tortillas or hard taco shells. Or serve as a taco dip with plain corn tortilla chips. Good garnishes for this taco filling include sour cream, guacamole, shredded cheese, diced tomatoes, shredded lettuce, and salsa.

Halloween Hash

SHARON MILLER • HOLMESVILLE, OH

Prep Time: 20–25 minutes • Cooking Time: 2–4 hours • Ideal slow cooker size: 2-qt.

1 lb. lean ground beef

½ cup onion, chopped

16-oz. can whole-kernel corn,
   drained

16-oz. can kidney beans,
   drained

16-oz. can diced tomatoes

½ cup shredded cheddar
   cheese, optional

1. Brown beef and onion in a nonstick skillet until no longer pink. Drain. Place mixture in slow cooker.

2. Layer in all remaining ingredients except cheese.

3. Cover and cook on Low 2–4 hours, or until thoroughly hot.

4. Serve as is, or over a bed of rice or noodles. Sprinkle each serving with cheese, if you wish.

Makes 4 servings

Easy Beef Tortillas

KAREN WAGGONER • JOPLIN, MO

Prep Time: 20 minutes • Cooking Time: 1½–3 hours • Ideal slow cooker size: 4-qt.

1½ lbs. ground beef

10¾-oz. can cream of chicken soup

2½ cups crushed tortilla chips, divided

16-oz. jar salsa

1½ cups (6 ozs.) shredded cheddar cheese

1. Brown ground beef in a nonstick skillet. Drain. Stir in soup.

2. Spray slow cooker with nonstick cooking spray. Sprinkle 1½ cups tortilla chips in cooker. Top with beef mixture, then salsa, and then cheese.

3. Cover and cook on High 1½ hours, or on Low 3 hours.

4. Sprinkle with remaining chips just before serving.

Makes 6 servings

Tortilla Casserole

CHRISTIE DETAMORE-HUNSBERGER • HARRISONBURG, VA

Prep Time: 20 minutes • Cooking Time: 3¼–4¼ hours • Ideal slow cooker size: 3-qt.

4-6 white or whole wheat tortillas, divided

1 lb. ground beef

1 envelope dry taco seasoning

16-oz. can fat-free refried beans

1½ cups (6 ozs.) low-fat cheese of your choice, grated, divided

3-4 Tbsp. sour cream, optional

1. Spray slow cooker with nonstick cooking spray. Tear about three-quarters of tortillas into pieces and line sides and bottom of slow cooker.

2. Brown ground beef in a nonstick skillet. Drain. Return to skillet and mix in taco seasoning.

3. Layer refried beans, browned and seasoned meat, 1 cup cheese, and sour cream, if you wish, over tortilla pieces.

4. Place remaining tortilla pieces on top. Sprinkle with remaining cheese.

5. Cover and cook on Low 3–4 hours.

Makes 4 servings

Tamale Casserole

MAMIE CHRISTOPHERSON • RIO RANCHO, NM

Prep Time: 10 minutes • Cooking Time: 5-7 hours • Ideal slow cooker size: 4-qt.

2 lbs. frozen meatballs

28-oz. can chopped tomatoes

1 cup yellow cornmeal

14- to 16-oz. can cream-style corn

1 cup chopped stuffed green olives

½ tsp. chili powder, optional

1. Microwave frozen meatballs for 4 minutes on Power 3, or until thawed. Place in slow cooker.

2. Combine remaining ingredients in a mixing bowl. Pour over meatballs and mix well.

3. Cover and cook on High 1 hour. Turn to Low and cook 4-6 hours. Check after 4 hours of cooking. The casserole is finished when it reaches a "loaf" consistency.

Makes 6-8 servings

Stuffed Ground Beef

MARY B. SENSENIG • NEW HOLLAND, PA

Prep Time: 10 minutes • Cooking Time: 4-6 hours • Ideal slow cooker size: 4-qt.

2 cups ground beef

2 cups cabbage, shredded

salt and pepper to taste

2 cups stuffing mix

2 cups tomato juice

1. Brown ground beef in a nonstick skillet. Drain.

2. Spray slow cooker with nonstick cooking spray. Layer ingredients in slow cooker in this order: ground beef, cabbage, salt and pepper, bread filling.

3. Pour tomato juice over top.

4. Cook on Low 4-6 hours, or until cabbage is just-tender.

Makes 4 servings

German Dinner

AUDREY L. KNEER • WILLIAMSFIELD, IL

Prep Time: 15–20 minutes • Cooking Time: 4–8 hours • Ideal slow cooker size: 4- to 5-qt.

1 lb. lean ground beef

32-oz. bag sauerkraut, drained

1 small green bell pepper, finely chopped

2 11½-oz. cans vegetable juice

½ cup chopped celery

1. Brown ground beef in a nonstick skillet. Drain.

2. Combine all ingredients in slow cooker.

3. Cover and cook on High 1 hour, then on Low 3–7 hours, or until vegetables are done to your liking.

Makes 6 servings

Ground Beef Veggie Casserole

MARY B. SENSENIG • NEW HOLLAND, PA

Prep Time: 15–20 minutes • Cooking Time: 4 hours • Ideal slow cooker size: 4- to 5-qt.

1½ lbs. ground beef

half a medium-sized onion, sliced

2 10-oz. pkgs. petite mixed vegetables

1 cup tomato juice

8 ozs. cheese, your choice, shredded

1. Brown ground beef and onion in a nonstick skillet. Drain.

2. Place browned mixture in slow cooker. Stir in vegetables. Pour tomato juice over top.

3. Cover and cook on Low 4 hours, or until veggies are done to your liking.

4. Stir in cheese during last hour of cooking.

Makes 6–8 servings

Zucchini Hot Dish

SHARON WANTLAND • MENOMONEE FALLS, WI

Prep Time: 15–20 minutes • Cooking Time: 2–3 hours • Ideal slow cooker size: 1½-qt.

1 lb. ground beef

1 small onion, chopped, optional

salt and pepper to taste

4–5 6"-long zucchini, sliced

10¾-oz. can cream of
    mushroom soup

1–2 cups shredded cheddar
    cheese

1. In a nonstick skillet, brown ground beef with onion, if you wish, along with salt and pepper, until crumbly. Drain.

2. Layer zucchini and beef mixture alternately in slow cooker.

3. Top with soup. Sprinkle with cheese.

4. Cover and cook on Low 2–3 hours, or until zucchini is done to your liking.

Makes 4 servings

Green Bean, Potato, and Ground Beef Meal

ALICE MILLER • STUARTS DRAFT, VA

Prep Time: 15 minutes • Cooking Time: 4–6 hours • Ideal slow cooker size: 5-qt.

1 lb. ground beef

½–1 tsp. salt, according to
    your taste preference

¼–½ tsp. black pepper,
    according to your taste
    preference

1 qt. canned green beans,
    undrained

4 large potatoes, cut into
    1" chunks

1 cup chopped onions, optional

1. In a medium-sized nonstick skillet, brown ground beef until no longer pink. Drain. Add salt and pepper. Set aside.

2. Pour undrained green beans into slow cooker. Top with potatoes, onions if you wish, and then ground beef.

3. Cover and cook on High 4–6 hours, or until vegetables are tender.

Makes 4–6 servings

Potato-Beef-and-Beans

VERA MARTIN • EAST EARL, PA

Prep Time: 15–20 minutes • Cooking Time: 3 hours • Ideal slow cooker size: 4-qt.

1 lb. ground beef or turkey, divided

1 tsp. onion salt, celery salt, or both, divided

15½-oz. can kidney beans, undrained, divided

4 potatoes, French-fry cut, divided

26-oz. can tomato soup

1. Layer half of all ingredients—except tomato soup—into slow cooker in the order listed.

2. Repeat the layers. Pour tomato soup over all.

3. Cover and cook on High 3 hours, or until potatoes are tender.

4. Stir before serving.

Makes 6 servings

Variation: Mix 1–2 Tbsp. chili powder, depending upon your taste preference, with the tomato soup in Step 2.

Ground Beef Hot Dish

TRACEY HANSON SCHRAMEL • WINDOM, MN

Prep Time: 15 minutes • Cooking Time: 6–8 hours • Ideal slow cooker size: 3-qt.

1 lb. ground beef

small onion, chopped

4–5 medium-sized potatoes, sliced

½ tsp. salt, optional

14½-oz. can mixed vegetables, undrained

10¾-oz. can cream of chicken soup

1. Brown ground beef and onion in a nonstick skillet. Drain.

2. Spray slow cooker with nonstick cooking spray. Place all ingredients in cooker. Stir together gently until well mixed.

3. Cover and cook on Low 6–8 hours, or until potatoes are tender.

Makes 3–4 servings

Layered Ground Beef Casserole

DENISE NICKEL • GOESSEL, KS

Prep Time: 45 minutes • Cooking Time: 6-8 hours • Ideal slow cooker size: 4-qt.

1½ lbs. ground beef

3 large potatoes, cut into
1" chunks

16-oz. pkg. frozen peas

2-3 carrots, sliced

1 medium-sized onion, sliced,
optional

1 rib celery, diced, optional

10¾-oz. can tomato soup

1 soup can water

1. Brown ground beef in a nonstick skillet. Drain. Set aside.

2. Spray slow cooker with nonstick cooking spray. Layer all ingredients in cooker in this order: potato chunks, peas, carrot slices, onion slices and celery dice, if you wish, and browned ground beef.

3. Mix tomato soup and water together in a bowl until smooth. Pour over all other ingredients.

4. Cover and cook on Low 6-8 hours, or until vegetables are tender.

Makes 4-6 servings

Easy Meat Loaf

KAREN WAGGONER • JOPLIN, MO

Prep Time: 5 minutes • Cooking Time: 2 hours • Ideal slow cooker size: 3- to 4-qt.

2 lbs. ground beef, or turkey

6¼-oz. pkg. stuffing mix for
beef, plus seasoning

2 eggs, beaten

½ cup ketchup, divided

1. Mix beef or turkey, dry stuffing, eggs, and ¼ cup ketchup. Shape into an oval loaf.

2. Place in slow cooker. Pour remaining ketchup over top.

3. Cover and cook on High 2 hours.

Makes 5-6 servings

Meat Loaf

BECKY GEHMAN • BERGTON, VA

Prep Time: 10 minutes • Cooking Time: 2–6 hours • Ideal slow cooker size: 3-qt.

2 lbs. ground beef

½ cup cracker crumbs

1-2 tsp. onion powder

¼ cup ketchup

1. Combine ground beef, cracker crumbs, and onion powder. Form into a loaf. Place in slow cooker.

2. Spread ketchup over top of meat loaf.

3. Cover and cook on Low 4–6 hours, or on High 2 hours.

Makes 6–8 servings

Notes: You may mix all or half the ketchup into the meat loaf. Remove the cooked meat loaf from the cooker with a slotted spoon, and keep it warm on a platter. Pour the drippings from the slow cooker into a nonstick skillet. Turn the burner to medium and whisk 2 Tbsp. flour into the drippings until smooth. Add a beef bouillon cube and stir until the cube is dissolved and the drippings thicken. Serve the gravy with the sliced meat loaf.

Amazing Meat Loaf

SARA KINSINGER • STUARTS DRAFT, VA / MIRIAM NOLT • NEW HOLLAND, PA
RUTH ZENDT • MIFFLINTOWN, PA / KAREN CENEVIVA • NEW HAVEN, CT

Prep Time: 15 minutes • Cooking Time: 2–8 hours • Ideal slow cooker size: 4-qt.

½ cup ketchup, divided

2 lbs. ground beef

2 eggs

⅔ cup dry quick oats

1 envelope dry onion soup mix

1. Reserve 2 Tbsp. ketchup. Combine ground beef, eggs, dry oats, soup mix, and remaining ketchup. Shape into loaf. Place in slow cooker.

2. Top with remaining ketchup.

3. Cover and cook on Low 6–8 hours, or on High 2–4 hours.

Makes 8 servings

Note: Chill leftovers, and then slice for sandwiches.

Beef Barbecue

ANNA B. STOLTZFUS • HONEY BROOK, PA

Prep Time: 15 minutes • Cooking Time: 2½ hours • Ideal slow cooker size: 4-qt.

2 lbs. ground beef

2 small onions, chopped

2 Tbsp. Worcestershire sauce

1½ cups ketchup

4 Tbsp. brown sugar

1 cup water

1. Brown beef with onions in a large nonstick skillet, breaking up chunks of meat with a wooden spoon as it cooks. Drain.

2. Place beef and onions into cooker. Add remaining ingredients and mix together thoroughly.

3. Cover and cook on Low 2½ hours.

4. Pile into sandwich rolls.

   Makes 10 servings

Italian Barbecue Sandwiches

MARY B. SENSENIG • NEW HOLLAND, PA

Prep Time: 10 minutes • Cooking Time: 2–6 hours • Ideal slow cooker size: 3-qt.

1 lb. ground beef

1 cup tomato sauce

half an envelope dry spaghetti sauce mix

salt and pepper to taste

8 ozs. Velveeta or American cheese, cubed

1. In a nonstick skillet, brown ground beef. Drain.

2. Place meat in slow cooker. Stir in sauce and seasonings.

3. Cover and cook on Low 2–6 hours.

4. One hour before serving, stir in cheese.

5. Stir before serving over long rolls.

   Makes 4 servings

Cooking Tip

To remove meat loaf or other meats from your cooker, make foil handles to lift the food out. Use double strips of heavy foil to make 3 strips, each about 20" x 3". Crisscross them in the bottom of the pot and bring them up the sides in a spoke design before putting in the food.

—*John D. Allen, Rye, CO*
—*Esther Lehman, Croghan, NY*

Creamy Sloppy Joes

CLARA YODER BYLER • HARTVILLE, OH

Prep Time: 30 minutes • Cooking Time: 2–3 hours • Ideal slow cooker size: 4-qt.

2 lbs. ground beef

1 onion, finely chopped

$\frac{1}{2}$ cup ketchup

1 tsp. Worcestershire sauce

$10\frac{3}{4}$-oz. can cream of mushroom soup

1 tsp. salt, optional

1. Brown ground beef and onion together in a nonstick skillet. Drain.

2. Place in slow cooker. Stir in remaining ingredients.

3. Cook on High 2–3 hours, or until heated through.

4. Serve in rolls.

Makes 8–10 servings

Sloppy Joes

ROSALIE D. MILLER • MIFFLINTOWN, PA

Prep Time: 10–15 minutes • Cooking Time: 3–8 hours • Ideal slow cooker size: 3- to 4-qt.

3 lbs. ground beef

1 cup chopped onions

3 16-oz. cans Sloppy Joe sauce

4 Tbsp. brown sugar

4 Tbsp. Worcestershire sauce

1. Brown ground beef and onions in a nonstick skillet. Drain, but don't lose the onion pieces while you're doing it.

2. Place beef-onion mixture in slow cooker.

3. Stir in remaining ingredients.

4. Cover and cook on Low 6–8 hours, or on High 3–4 hours.

5. Spoon mixture into hamburger buns to serve.

Makes 8–10 servings

Party Meatball Subs

TAMARA MCCARTHY • PENNSBURG, PA

Prep Time: 15 minutes • Cooking Time: 8–10 hours • Ideal slow cooker size: 8- to 10-qt.

10-lb. bag prepared meatballs

1 large onion, sliced

10 good-sized fresh
mushrooms, sliced

2 26-oz. jars spaghetti sauce,
your choice of flavors

2 cloves garlic, minced

1 lb. grated mozzarella cheese,
optional

1. Combine all ingredients except cheese in slow cooker. Stir well to coat meatballs with sauce.

2. Cover and cook on Low 8–10 hours, stirring occasionally throughout cooking time to mix juices.

3. Serve in hoagie rolls and sprinkle mozzarella cheese over top, if you wish.

Makes 30 servings

Note: This makes a lot of meatball subs! The recipe also works if you reduce the ingredients by half, or even if you use only a quarter of the amounts that are called for.

Tangy Meatballs

LUCY O'CONNELL • GOSHEN, MA

Prep Time: 10 minutes • Cooking Time: 6–8 hours • Ideal slow cooker size: 5- to 6-qt.

3 lbs. Swedish-style meatballs
(frozen is fine)

16-oz. can whole-berry
cranberry sauce

18-oz. bottle barbecue sauce

½ cup spicy prepared mustard

1. Place meatballs in slow cooker.

2. Combine remaining ingredients in a bowl, then pour over meatballs.

3. Cover and cook on Low 6–8 hours.

Makes 12 main dish servings

Note: You can serve this as an appetizer, or as a main dish served over rice.

Sweet and Sour Meatballs

CHARLOTTE SHAFFER • EAST EARL, PA / MICHELE RUVOLA • SELDEN, NY
VELMA SAUDER • LEOLA, PA

Prep Time: 15 minutes • Cooking Time: 2 hours • Ideal slow cooker size: 3- to 4-qt.

2 lbs. precooked meatballs

1 cup grape jelly

2 cups cocktail sauce

1. Place precooked meatballs in slow cooker.

2. In a medium-sized bowl, mix jelly and cocktail sauce together with a whisk (it will be a little lumpy).

3. Pour jelly and cocktail sauce over meatballs. Stir well.

4. Cook on High 1–2 hours, or until sauce is heated through.

5. Turn heat to Low until you're ready to serve.

Makes 8–10 servings

Fruity Meatballs

DONNA LANTGEN • CHADRON, NE

Prep Time: 5–10 minutes • Cooking Time: 4–5 hours • Ideal slow cooker size: 4-qt.

2 lbs. frozen meatballs

1 cup brown sugar

16-oz. can crushed pineapple with juice

1. Combine ingredients in slow cooker.

2. Cover and cook on Low 4–5 hours. If you're home and able, stir every 2 hours.

Makes 8–10 servings

Tangy Cranberry Meatballs

CHAR HAGNER • MONTAGUE, MI

Prep Time: 10 minutes • Cooking Time: 3–4 hours • Ideal slow cooker size: 3-qt.

1 lb. frozen prepared meatballs

12-oz. bottle chili sauce

16-oz. can jellied cranberry sauce

½ cup brown sugar

1. Place meatballs in slow cooker.

2. In a mixing bowl, combine chili sauce, cranberry sauce, and brown sugar, breaking up the cranberry sauce as well as you can. Pour over meatballs.

3. Cover and cook on Low 3–4 hours.

Makes 4 servings

Note: You can serve this as an appetizer (with toothpicks), or as a main dish over rice, pasta, or mashed potatoes.

Cranberry Meatballs

MARY ANN WASICK • WEST ALLIS, WI

Prep Time: 5–10 minutes • Cooking Time: 2–4 hours • Ideal slow cooker size: 4-qt.

1 medium-sized onion, finely chopped

2 Tbsp. butter

16-oz. can jellied cranberry sauce

16-oz. pkg. prepared frozen beef or turkey meatballs (approx. 32)

1 tsp. dried orange peel

1. In a small saucepan, sauté onion in butter.

2. Stir cranberry sauce into saucepan. Heat on low until melted.

3. Combine all ingredients in slow cooker.

4. Cover and cook on Low 2–4 hours.

Makes 5–6 servings

Sweet Cranberry Meatballs

F. ELAINE ASPER • NORTON, OH

Prep Time: 15 minutes • Cooking Time: 2–6 hours • Ideal slow cooker size: 4-qt.

50 meatballs, about 1½ lbs.

1 cup brown gravy, from a jar, or made from a mix

1 cup whole-berry cranberry sauce

2 Tbsp. heavy cream

2 tsp. Dijon mustard

1. Put meatballs in slow cooker.

2. Mix remaining ingredients in a bowl. Pour over meatballs.

3. Cover and cook on High 2–3 hours, or on Low 5–6 hours.

   Makes 6 entrée servings, or 18–20 appetizers

Easy Meatballs

CARLENE HORNE • BEDFORD, NH

Prep Time: 7 minutes • Cooking Time: 4–5 hours • Ideal slow cooker size: 5-qt.

2 10¾-oz. cans cream of mushroom soup

2 8-oz. pkgs. cream cheese, softened

4-oz. can sliced mushrooms, undrained

1 cup milk

2–3 lbs. frozen meatballs

1. Combine soup, cream cheese, mushrooms, and milk in slow cooker.

2. Add meatballs. Stir.

3. Cover. Cook on Low 4–5 hours.

4. Serve over noodles.

   Makes 10–12 servings

Meatballs with Chili

COLLEEN KONETZNI • RIO RANCHO, NM

Prep Time: 10 minutes • Cooking Time: 8 hours • Ideal slow cooker size: 5-qt.

2 lbs. frozen beef meatballs

16-oz. jar 505 Southwestern green chili sauce, or any other good green chili sauce

chili-sauce jar water

1. Place frozen meatballs in slow cooker.

2. In a mixing bowl, combine green chili sauce and water.

3. Pour sauce and water over meatballs.

4. Cover and cook on Low 8 hours.

Makes 8 servings

Note: This is good as a main dish served with flour tortillas. Or put out toothpicks and serve the meatballs as party food.

My Norwegian Meatballs

MAMIE CHRISTOPHERSON • RIO RANCHO, NM

Prep Time: 5 minutes • Cooking Time: 45 minutes • Ideal slow cooker size: 3-qt.

2-2½-lb. pkg. frozen meatballs

2-3 10¾-oz. cans cream of mushroom soup, depending upon how saucy you'd like the finished dish to be

12-oz. can evaporated milk

1½ cups sour cream

1 cup beef broth

1 tsp. dill weed, optional

1. Lay frozen meatballs in a long, microwave-safe dish and microwave on High 4 minutes.

2. Meanwhile, in a large mixing bowl, combine all other ingredients.

3. Place meatballs in slow cooker. Cover with soup mixture.

4. Cover and cook on High 45 minutes (sauce should not boil).

5. Turn to Low. Keep warm until serving time.

Makes 10–12 servings

Note: Serve these as an appetizer (with toothpicks), or as a main dish with mashed potatoes or noodles. If you wish, substitute other herbs for the dill weed.

Meatballs with Cream Sauce

KAREN STOLTZFUS • ALTO, MI

Prep Time: 5 minutes • Cooking Time: 3–4 hours • Ideal slow cooker size: 2-qt.

1½ lbs. frozen fully cooked
   meatballs

8-oz. pkg. cream cheese,
   softened

10¾-oz. can cream of
   mushroom soup

½ cup water

1. Place meatballs in slow cooker.

2. In a mixing bowl, combine cream cheese and soup until well mixed. Add water and stir in thoroughly.

3. Pour sauce over meatballs.

4. Cover. Cook on High 1 hour, then turn to Low and cook 2–3 hours. (If meatballs are thawed, cook only on Low 2–3 hours.)

Makes 6–8 servings

Meatball Sauce

NORMA GRIESER • CLARKSVILLE, MI

Prep Time: 10 minutes • Cooking Time: 3–8 hours • Ideal slow cooker size: 6-qt.

32-oz. bottle ketchup

16 ozs. ginger ale

3 Tbsp. brown sugar

3 Tbsp. vinegar

3 Tbsp. Worcestershire sauce,
   optional

3 lbs. fully cooked meatballs

1. Combine sauce ingredients in slow cooker. Cover, turn to High, and bring to a simmer.

2. Gently spoon in meatballs, being careful not to splash yourself with hot sauce.

3. Cover and simmer 3–4 hours on Low if the meatballs are thawed when you put them in, 6–8 hours if they're frozen.

Makes 10 servings

Note: You can use little smokies instead of meatballs. In fact, this sauce is good on most meats you grill or barbecue. To serve as a sauce for grilled meat, follow Step 1, then brush on grilled meat.

Porcupine Meatballs

ESTHER J. YODER • HARTVILLE, OH / JEAN BINNS SMITH • BELLEFONTE, PA

Prep Time: 30 minutes • Cooking Time: 2–4 hours • Ideal slow cooker size: 4-qt.

1 lb. ground beef

1/4 cup uncooked long-grain rice

1/4–1/2 tsp. salt, optional

10 1/2-oz. can tomato soup, divided

2 Tbsp. shortening, or butter

1 cup water

1. In a medium-sized bowl, mix ground beef, rice, salt if you wish, and 1/4 cup of tomato soup. Shape into 1 1/2" balls.

2. Brown the balls in 2 Tbsp. shortening or butter in a large nonstick skillet, being careful not to crowd them. (If your skillet is small, brown them in two batches.)

3. Place browned meatballs in slow cooker.

4. In the bowl, mix together water and remaining tomato soup. Pour over meatballs.

5. Cover and cook on High 2–4 hours, or until rice is fully cooked.

Makes 8 servings

Meatball Stew

BETH PEACHEY • BELLEVILLE, PA

Prep Time: 15 minutes • Cooking Time: 6–8 hours • Ideal slow cooker size: 4-qt.

2 lbs. meatballs, frozen or homemade

10 1/2-oz. can tomato soup

1/4 cup water

1 cup carrots, sliced

1 onion, sliced

2 lbs. potatoes, sliced

1. Brown meatballs in a large nonstick skillet, being careful not to crowd the skillet. Brown in 2 batches rather than pile them up or squeeze them in.

2. When the meatballs are browned, place them and remaining ingredients in slow cooker. Stir together gently.

3. Cover and cook on Low 6–8 hours, or until vegetables are tender.

Makes 6 servings

Cooking Tip

Write in your cookbook the date when you tried a particular recipe and whether or not you liked it. Develop a rating system for each recipe you try (Excellent, Good, Yummy, Okay). Write notes about what might be a good addition or deletion the next time you make it.

PORK MAIN DISHES

Honey Barbecue Pork Chops

TAMARA MCCARTHY • PENNSBURG, PA

Prep Time: 15 minutes • Cooking Time: 6–8 hours • Ideal slow cooker size: 4-qt.

8 pork chops, divided

1 large onion, sliced, divided

1 cup barbecue sauce

⅓ cup honey

1. Place one layer of pork chops in slow cooker.

2. Arrange a proportionate amount of sliced onions over top.

3. Mix barbecue sauce and honey together in a small bowl. Spoon a proportionate amount of sauce over chops.

4. Repeat layers.

5. Cover and cook on Low 3–4 hours.

6. If sauce barely covers chops, flip them over at this point. If they're well covered, simply allow them to cook another 3–4 hours on Low, or until chops are tender but not dry.

Makes 8 servings

Pork Chops with Tomato Sauce

MARGARET H. MOFFITT • BARTLETT, TN

Prep Time: 25 minutes • Cooking Time: 3–7 hours • Ideal slow cooker size: 3-qt.

4 thickly cut pork chops

1 medium-sized onion, sliced
  or chopped

½ cup ketchup

¼ cup brown sugar

½ tsp. chili powder

½ cup water

1. Place pork chops in bottom of slow cooker. Top with onion.

2. In a bowl, mix ketchup, brown sugar, chili powder, and water together. Spoon sauce over all. (If chops need to be stacked to fit into slow cooker, make sure to top each one with sauce.)

3. Cover and cook on High 3–4 hours, or on Low up to 6–7 hours, or until meat is tender but not dry.

Makes 4–6 servings

Tangy Pork Chops

BARBARA GAUTCHER • HARRISONBURG, VA

Prep Time: 15 minutes • Cooking Time: 4–5 hours • Ideal slow cooker size: 3-qt.

4 thickly cut pork loin chops,
  or 6 thinner chops

seasoning salt to taste

pepper to taste

1 cup grape jelly

1 bottle prepared chili sauce

1. Rub pork chops with seasoning salt and pepper on both sides. Place chops in slow cooker.

2. In a small bowl, combine jelly and chili sauce. Spoon sauce over chops. (If chops need to be stacked to fit into slow cooker, make sure to top each one with sauce.)

3. Cover and cook on Low 4–5 hours, or until meat is tender but not dry.

Makes 4–6 servings

Cooking Tip

When sautéing or frying, turn a metal colander or strainer upside down over the skillet. This allows steam to escape and keeps fat from spattering.

Pork Chops with Suit-Yourself Sauce

CLARA NEWSWANGER • GORDONVILLE, PA

Prep Time: 15 minutes • Cooking Time: 4–5 hours • Ideal slow cooker size: 4-qt.

4-6 pork chops, divided

1 tsp. salt

¼ tsp. pepper

2 Tbsp. olive oil

½ cup water

10¾-oz. can condensed
    cream soup of your choice

1 cup barbecue sauce, optional

1. Season chops with salt and pepper. Brown on both sides in oil in a hot nonstick skillet. Brown chops in batches rather than crowding skillet. As they finish, place a layer in slow cooker.

2. Meanwhile, combine water, soup, and barbecue sauce, if you wish, in a bowl. Pour a proportionate amount of sauce mixture over first layer of chops. Add next layer of chops and pour remaining sauce over top.

3. Cover and cook on Low 4–5 hours, or until chops are tender but not dry.

Makes 4-6 servings

Creamy Pork Chops

JUDI MANOS • WEST ISLIP, NY

Prep Time: 5–7 minutes • Cooking Time: 4–5 hours • Ideal slow cooker size: 3-qt.

10¾-oz. can 98% fat-free
    cream of chicken soup

1 onion, chopped

3 Tbsp. ketchup

2 tsp. Worcestershire sauce

6 whole pork chops, boneless
    or bone-in, divided

1. Mix soup and chopped onions together in a bowl. Stir in ketchup and Worcestershire sauce. Pour half of mixture into slow cooker.

2. Place pork chops in slow cooker. If you have to stack them, spoon a proportionate amount of the remaining sauce over first layer of meat.

3. Add rest of chops. Cover with remaining sauce.

4. Cover and cook on Low 4–5 hours, or until meat is tender but not dry.

Makes 6 servings

Slow-Cooked Pork Chops

KIMBERLY BURKHOLDER • MILLERSTOWN, PA

Prep Time: 15 minutes • Cooking Time: 3–8 hours • Ideal slow cooker size: 3-qt.

½ cup flour

1 tsp. salt

½ tsp. garlic powder

6–8 lean pork chops, divided

10¾-oz. can chicken and rice soup, divided

1. Mix together flour, salt, and garlic powder in a shallow dish. Dredge pork chops in mixture.

2. Heat a nonstick skillet until hot. Then place several chops in skillet and brown on both sides. Do this in batches, rather than crowding skillet. As you finish browning chops, place one layer in slow cooker.

3. Top with a proportionate amount of soup. Finish browning meat, add it to cooker, and top with remaining soup.

4. Cover and cook on Low 6–8 hours, or High 3–4 hours.

Makes 6–8 servings

Smothered Pork Chops

MARILYN MOWRY • IRVING, TX

Prep Time: 10 minutes • Cooking Time: 6–8 hours • Ideal slow cooker size: 2-qt.

4 pork chops, center cut

10¾-oz. can cream of mushroom soup

1 cup milk

2 Tbsp. dry sherry

2 scallions, chopped

1. Place chops in slow cooker.

2. Mix remaining ingredients in a bowl. Pour over chops.

3. Cover and cook on Low 6–8 hours, or until meat is tender but not dry.

Makes 4 servings

Note: If you wish, add salt and pepper to taste to chops before placing in cooker.

Spicy Pork Chops

CYNTHIA MORRIS • GROTTOES, VA

Prep Time: 5 minutes • Cooking Time: 6–8 hours • Ideal slow cooker size: 4-qt.

4 frozen pork chops

1 cup Italian salad dressing

½ cup brown sugar

⅓ cup prepared spicy mustard

1. Place pork chops in slow cooker.

2. Mix remaining 3 ingredients together in a bowl. Pour over chops.

3. Cover and cook on Low 6–8 hours, or until meat is tender but not dry.

   Makes 4 servings

Variation: You can substitute chicken breasts for pork chops.

Note: Check the meat after cooking for 4 hours to make sure the meat is not getting dry or overcooked.

Pork Chops Hong Kong

MICHELLE HIGH • FREDERICKSBURG, PA

Prep Time: 65 minutes • Cooking Time: 3–6 hours • Ideal slow cooker size: 3- to 4-qt.

10-oz. bottle soy sauce

6–8 Tbsp. sugar

6–8 pork chops

10¾-oz. can cream of mushroom soup

1. Combine soy sauce and sugar. Pour over chops. Marinate 60 minutes.

2. Transfer pork chops to slow cooker. (Discard marinade.)

3. In a bowl, stir soup until creamy. Spoon over chops.

4. Cover and cook on Low 6 hours, or on High 3 hours.

   Makes 6–8 servings

Pork Chops and Apple Slices

DOROTHY VAN DEEST • MEMPHIS, TN / DALE PETERSON • RAPID CITY, SD

Prep Time: 15 minutes • Cooking Time: 6–8 hours • Ideal slow cooker size: 3- to 4-qt.

4 pork loin chops, about 1"
thick, well trimmed

2 medium-sized apples,
peeled, cored, and sliced

1 tsp. butter or margarine

¼ tsp. nutmeg, optional

salt and pepper to taste

1. Heat a nonstick skillet until hot. Add chops and brown quickly. Turn and brown on other side.

2. While chops are browning, place half of sliced apples in slow cooker. Top with 2 chops. Repeat layers.

3. Dot with butter and sprinkle with nutmeg. Sprinkle generously with salt and pepper.

4. Cover and cook on Low 6–8 hours, or until meat is tender but not dry.

Makes 4 servings

Slow-Cooked Pork Chops with Green Beans

VONNIE OYER • HUBBARD, OR

Prep Time: 10 minutes • Cooking Time: 4–8 hours • Ideal slow cooker size: 3-qt.

3–4 boneless pork chops

salt and pepper to taste

2 cups green beans, frozen or
fresh

2 slices bacon, cut up

½ cup water

1 Tbsp. lemon juice

1. Place pork chops in bottom of slow cooker. Salt and pepper to taste.

2. Top with remaining ingredients in the order listed.

3. Cover and cook on Low 4–8 hours, or until meat and green beans are tender but not dry or overcooked.

Makes 3–4 servings

Barbecued Pork Chops

SANDY OSBORN • IOWA CITY, IA

Prep Time: 10–15 minutes • Cooking Time: 7–8 hours • Ideal slow cooker size: 4-qt.

8 (5 ozs. each) center-cut pork chops, 1/2" thick

1/4 tsp. pepper

1/2 cup thick-and-spicy honey barbecue sauce

14 1/2-oz. can no-salt-added stewed tomatoes

10-oz. pkg. frozen vegetable blend

1. Trim fat from pork chops, and then sprinkle them with pepper.

2. Spray a large nonstick skillet with cooking spray. Set stove burner to medium-high.

3. When pan is hot, add pork chops in a single layer. Do not crowd pan or chops will not brown quickly. Brown on both sides.

4. Spray slow cooker with nonstick cooking spray. Place a layer of pork chops in slow cooker.

5. While chops are browning, combine barbecue sauce, tomatoes, and frozen vegetables in a bowl, stirring well.

6. Pour some of mixture over first layer of chops. When you've added rest of chops, pour remaining sauce with vegetables over top.

7. Cover and cook on High 1 hour.

8. Reduce heat to Low and cook 6–7 hours, or until meat is tender but not dry.

Makes 8 servings

Hassle-Free Pork Chops

CATHY SELLERS • CEDAR RAPIDS, IA

Prep Time: 15 minutes • Cooking Time: 3–8 hours • Ideal slow cooker size: 3- to 4-qt.

4 pork chops

1 small onion, sliced

4 potatoes, peeled and sliced

2 10¾-oz. cans tomato soup

½ cup milk

1. Heat a nonstick skillet until hot. Add chops and brown on both sides. Do in batches rather than crowd skillet.

2. Place chops in slow cooker. Brown onion in skillet drippings, and then place over top of chops.

3. Add layer of potatoes to cooker.

4. In a small bowl, combine soup and milk, mixing well. Pour mixture over potatoes.

5. Cover and cook on Low 6–8 hours, or on High 3–4 hours, or until meat and potatoes are tender but not dry.

Makes 4 servings

Note: If you wish, add salt and pepper to taste to the chops as you place them in the slow cooker. And add salt and pepper to taste to the layer of sliced potatoes after you've placed them in the cooker.

Pork and Sweet Potatoes

VERA F. SCHMUCKER • GOSHEN, IN

Prep Time: 15 minutes • Cooking Time: 4–4½ hours • Ideal slow cooker size: 4-qt.

4 pork loin chops

salt and pepper to taste

4 sweet potatoes, cut in large chunks

2 onions, cut in quarters

½ cup apple cider

1. Place meat in bottom of slow cooker. Salt and pepper to taste.

2. Arrange sweet potatoes and onions over top of pork.

3. Pour apple cider over all.

4. Cook on High 30 minutes, and then on Low 3½–4 hours, or until meat and vegetables are tender but not dry.

Makes 4 servings

Pork Chops and Yams

TAMARA MCCARTHY • PENNSBURG, PA

Prep Time: 15 minutes • Cooking Time: 6–7 hours • Ideal slow cooker size: 4-qt.

4–6 pork chops

16-oz. can yams, drained, or 3 medium-sized raw yams, peeled and sliced

10¾-oz. can cream of mushroom soup

½ cup sour cream

¼ cup water

1. In a nonstick skillet, brown pork chops over medium heat. Transfer to slow cooker.

2. Place yams over pork chops.

3. In a mixing bowl, combine soup, sour cream, and water. Stir until well blended.

4. Pour sauce over yams and pork chops.

5. Cover and cook on Low 6–7 hours, or until meat and yams are tender but not dry.

Makes 4 servings

Country Pork and Squash

JEAN HALLORAN • GREEN BAY, WI

Prep Time: 15 minutes • Cooking Time: 6–8 hours • Ideal slow cooker size: 5-qt.

6 boneless country-style pork ribs, trimmed of fat

2 medium-sized acorn squash

¾ cup brown sugar

2 Tbsp. orange juice

¾ tsp. Kitchen Bouquet browning and seasoning sauce

1. Place ribs on bottom of slow cooker.

2. Cut each squash in half. Remove seeds. Cut each half into 3 slices.

3. Place squash slices over top of ribs.

4. Combine remaining ingredients in a small bowl. Pour sauce over ribs and squash.

5. Cover and cook on Low 6–8 hours, or until meat is tender.

6. Serve 2 rings of squash with each pork rib.

Makes 6 servings

Note: If you wish, add ¾ tsp. salt to Step 4.

Pork Chops and Rice

DONNA LANTGEN • CHADRON, NE

Prep Time: 5-10 minutes • Cooking Time: 6–8 hours • Ideal slow cooker size: 4-qt.

1½ cups uncooked long-grain rice

2 cups water

4 pork chops

salt and pepper to taste

10¾-oz. can cream of mushroom, or celery, soup

1 Tbsp. chicken or beef bouillon granules, or 1 bouillon cube

1. Spray slow cooker with nonstick cooking spray. Place rice and water in cooker and mix together well.

2. Place chops over top of rice. Sprinkle with salt and pepper.

3. In a small bowl, stir soup and bouillon together. Spoon over chops.

4. Cover and cook on Low 6–8 hours, or until meat and rice are tender but not dry.

Makes 4 servings

Pork Chops with Sauerkraut

CHAR HAGNER • MONTAGUE, MI

Prep Time: 20 minutes • Cooking Time: 6–8 hours • Ideal slow cooker size: 5-qt.

6 pork chops

4 large potatoes, sliced

1 onion, chopped

1 qt. sauerkraut

½ cup apple juice

1. Heat a nonstick skillet over medium-high heat. Brown chops on each side. Brown in batches so as not to crowd skillet.

2. While chops are browning, place sliced potatoes and onion in slow cooker.

3. Add browned chops. Top with sauerkraut. Pour apple juice over all.

4. Cover and cook on Low 6–8 hours.

Makes 6 servings

Note: If you wish, salt and pepper chops to taste after browning and before placing in cooker.

Pork Chops 'n' Kraut

HEATHER HORST • LEBANON, PA

Prep Time: 15 minutes • Cooking Time: 3–8 hours • Ideal slow cooker size: 4- to 5-qt.

2 14-oz. cans sauerkraut, rinsed and drained

1 large apple, unpeeled and chopped

4 medium-sized red, or white, potatoes, quartered

1 large carrot, shredded

1 tsp. caraway seeds, optional

4 pork chops, fat trimmed

1. In slow cooker, mix together sauerkraut, apple, potatoes, carrot, and caraway seeds, if you wish.

2. Place chops on top.

3. Cover and cook on Low 6–8 hours, or on High 3–4 hours, or until meat and potatoes are tender but not dry.

Makes 4 servings

Pork Chops with Stuffing

MICHELLE HIGH • FREDERICKSBURG, PA

Prep Time: 20 minutes • Cooking Time: 4–5 hours • Ideal slow cooker size: 4-qt.

4 slices bread, cubed

1 egg

$\frac{1}{4}$ cup finely chopped celery

$\frac{1}{4}$–$\frac{1}{2}$ tsp. salt

$\frac{1}{8}$ tsp. pepper

2 thickly cut pork chops

1 cup water

1. In a mixing bowl, combine bread, egg, celery, salt, and pepper.

2. Lay pork chops flat. Cut horizontally partway through meat, making a cut at least 1" deep. Spread open and fill with stuffing.

3. Pour water into slow cooker. Add chops.

4. Cover and cook on Low 4–5 hours, or until meat is tender but not dry.

Makes 2 servings

Stuffed Pork Chops and Corn

PEGGY FORSYTHE • BARTLETT, TN

Prep Time: 15 minutes • Cooking Time: 3–6 hours • Ideal slow cooker size: 4- to 5-qt.

5–6 boneless pork chops

1 box stuffing mix for pork, prepared

14-oz. can whole corn, optional

10¾-oz. can cream of mushroom soup

1. Place pork chops in slow cooker. Spoon prepared stuffing mix over top of chops.

2. Spoon corn over stuffing. Pour soup over all—without adding water.

3. Cover and cook on Low 5–6 hours, or on High 3–4 hours, or until meat is tender but not dry.

Makes 5–6 servings

Note: Allow cooked meat to stand 10-15 minutes before slicing it, so that it can regather its juices.

Pork Chops and Stuffing with Curry

MARY MARTINS • FAIRBANK, IA

Prep Time: 15 minutes • Cooking Time: 6–7 hours • Ideal slow cooker size: 3- to 4-qt.

1 box stuffing mix

1 cup water

10¾-oz. can cream of mushroom soup

1 tsp., or more, curry powder, according to your taste preference

3–4 pork chops

1. Combine stuffing mix and water. Place half in bottom of slow cooker.

2. Combine soup and curry powder. Pour half over stuffing. Place pork chops on top.

3. Spread remaining stuffing over pork chops. Pour rest of soup on top.

4. Cover. Cook on Low 6–7 hours.

5. Serve with a tossed salad and a cooked vegetable.

Makes 3–4 servings

Cranberry Pork Roast

CHRIS PETERSON • GREEN BAY, WI / JOYCE KAUT • ROCHESTER, NY

Prep Time: 5 minutes • Cooking Time: 6–8 hours • Ideal slow cooker size: 5-qt.

3–4-lb. pork roast

salt and pepper to taste

1 cup finely chopped cranberries

$\frac{1}{4}$ cup honey

1 tsp. grated orange peel

$\frac{1}{2}$ tsp. nutmeg, optional

$\frac{1}{2}$ tsp. cloves, optional

1. Sprinkle roast with salt and pepper. Place in slow cooker.

2. Combine remaining ingredients in a bowl. Pour over roast.

3. Cover and cook on Low 6–8 hours, or until meat is tender.

   Makes 6–8 servings

Note: If you can't find fresh cranberries, substitute a 16-oz. can of either whole-berry or jellied cranberry sauce.

Cranberry Pork Loin

ANNABELLE UNTERNAHRER • SHIPSHEWANA, IN

Prep Time: 10 minutes • Cooking Time: 4–6 hours • Ideal slow cooker size: 5- to 6-qt.

3-lb. boneless pork loin

16-oz. can jellied cranberry sauce

$\frac{1}{4}$ cup sugar

$\frac{1}{2}$ cup cranberry juice

1 tsp. dry mustard

$\frac{1}{4}$ tsp. cloves, optional

1. Place pork loin in slow cooker.

2. Combine remaining ingredients in a bowl. Pour sauce over pork.

3. Cover and cook on Low 4–6 hours, or until meat is tender.

   Makes 6–8 servings

Note: To thicken the sauce, remove cooked meat to a platter and cover to keep warm. Mix 2 Tbsp. cornstarch with 2 Tbsp. water in a small bowl. Turn cooker to High. Stir cornstarch-water mixture into simmering sauce. Continue stirring until it is thoroughly combined. Then allow sauce to simmer until it thickens, about 10 minutes. Stir occasionally to keep it from getting lumpy. Serve thickened sauce over or alongside pork slices.

Fruited Pork

JEANETTE OBERHOLTZER • MANHEIM, PA

Prep Time: 10 minutes ▪ **Cooking Time: 4–6 hours** ▪ **Ideal slow cooker size: 3- to 4-qt.**

2-lb. boneless pork loin roast

½ tsp. salt

¼ tsp. pepper

1½ cups mixed dried fruit

½ cup apple juice

1. Place pork in slow cooker. Sprinkle with salt and pepper.

2. Top with fruit. Pour apple juice over top.

3. Cover and cook on Low 4–6 hours, or until pork is tender.

   Makes 6 servings

Tender Pork Roast

RENEE BAUM • CHAMBERSBURG, PA / MARY LYNN MILLER • REINHOLDS, PA

Prep Time: 10 minutes ▪ **Cooking Time: 3–8 hours** ▪ **Ideal slow cooker size: 5-qt.**

3-lb. boneless pork roast, cut
   in half

8-oz. can tomato sauce

¾ cup soy sauce

½ cup sugar

2 tsp. dry mustard

1. Place roast in slow cooker.

2. Combine remaining ingredients in a bowl. Pour over roast.

3. Cover and cook on Low 6–8 hours, or on High 3–4 hours, or until meat is tender but not dry.

4. Remove roast from slow cooker to a serving platter. Discard juices or thicken for gravy.

   Makes 8 servings

Note: To thicken the juices, remove cooked roast to a platter and keep warm. Turn cooker to High. Meanwhile, mix together 2 Tbsp. cornstarch and 2 Tbsp. water in a small bowl. When smooth, stir into bubbling juices. Continue stirring until thoroughly mixed in. Allow juices to simmer until thickened, about 10 minutes. Slice pork and serve juices over top or alongside.

Home-Style Pork

MARY B. SENSENIG • NEW HOLLAND, PA

Prep Time: 5 minutes • Cooking Time: 6–8 hours • Ideal slow cooker size: 4-qt.

4 lbs. boneless pork roast, cut into pieces

1 medium-sized onion, sliced

1 cup water

¼ cup brown sugar

¼ cup apple cider vinegar

3 tsp. prepared mustard

1. Place roast pieces in slow cooker. Top with onion.

2. Pour water around roast and onions.

3. In a bowl, blend together last 3 ingredients. Spoon over meat and onions.

4. Cover and cook on Low 6–8 hours, or until meat is tender.

Makes 8–10 servings

Note: If you wish, add ¾ tsp. salt and ¼ tsp. pepper to Step 3.

Pork Roast

KELLY BAILEY • MECHANICSBURG, PA

Prep Time: 5 minutes • Cooking Time: 6–12 hours • Ideal slow cooker size: 4- to 6-qt.

1 medium-sized to large onion, sliced and divided

3–4-lb. pork roast

12-oz. can cola

salt and pepper

1. Layer two-thirds of onions in bottom of slow cooker, reserving a few slices to place on top of roast.

2. Place roast in cooker. Pour cola over roast.

3. Season with salt and pepper. Top with remaining onion slices.

4. Cook on Low 6–12 hours, depending on size of roast, or until meat starts to fall apart.

Makes 8–10 servings

Carolina Pot Roast

JONATHAN GEHMAN • HARRISONBURG, VA

Prep Time: 20 minutes • Cooking Time: 3 hours • Ideal slow cooker size: 3-qt.

3 medium-large sweet
   potatoes, peeled and cut
   into 1" chunks

½ cup brown sugar

1-lb. pork roast

scant ¼ tsp. cumin

salt to taste

water

1. Place sweet potatoes in bottom of slow cooker. Sprinkle brown sugar over potatoes.

2. Heat a nonstick skillet over medium-high heat. Add roast and brown on all sides. Sprinkle meat with cumin and salt while browning. Place pork on top of potatoes.

3. Add an inch of water to cooker, being careful not to wash seasoning off meat.

4. Cover and cook on Low 3 hours, or until meat and potatoes are tender but not dry or mushy.

Makes 3–4 servings

As-Basic-as-It-Gets Pork and Sauerkraut

EARNEST ZIMMERMAN • MECHANICSBURG, PA

Prep Time: 5 minutes • Cooking Time: 3-8 hours • Ideal slow cooker size: 6- to 8-qt.

3-4-lb. pork roast

32-oz. bag, or 2 14½-oz. cans,
   sauerkraut, divided

salt and/or pepper, optional

1. Rinse pork roast; pat dry.

2. Place half of sauerkraut in bottom of slow cooker. Place roast on top.

3. Cover roast with remaining sauerkraut. Season with salt and/or pepper, if you wish.

4. Cover and cook on Low 6–8 hours, or on High 3–4 hours.

Makes 6–8 servings

No Fuss Sauerkraut

VERA M. KUHNS • HARRISONBURG, VA

Prep Time: 7 minutes • Cooking Time: 4–5 hours • Ideal slow cooker size: 7- to 8-qt.

3-lb. pork roast

3 2-lb. pkgs. sauerkraut (drain
    and discard juice from
    1 pkg.)

2 apples, peeled and sliced

½ cup brown sugar

1 cup apple juice

1. Place meat in slow cooker.

2. Place sauerkraut on top of meat.

3. Add apples and brown sugar. Add apple juice.

4. Cover. Cook on High 4–5 hours.

5. Serve with mashed potatoes.

Makes 12 servings

Note: If your slow cooker isn't large enough to hold all the ingredients, cook 1 package of sauerkraut and half the apples, brown sugar, and apple juice in second cooker. Mix the ingredients of both cookers together before serving.

Savory Pork Roast

ELEYA RAIM • OXFORD, IA

Prep Time: 10 minutes • Cooking Time: 3–6 hours • Ideal slow cooker size: 4-qt. oval

2-lb. pork roast

1 clove garlic, minced

1 medium-sized onion, sliced

1 pt. sauerkraut, or more if you
    wish

1 tsp. caraway seed

1. If you have time, heat a nonstick skillet over medium-high heat. Place roast in hot pan and brown on all sides.

2. Place roast, browned or not, in slow cooker.

3. Add remaining ingredients in the order listed.

4. Cover and cook on High 3 hours, or on Low 4–6 hours, or until meat is tender but not dry.

Makes 6 servings

Note: If you wish, salt and pepper the roast before you place it in the cooker.

Pork and Sauerdogs

LEESA DEMARTYN • ENOLA, PA

Prep Time: 5 minutes ▪ Cooking Time: 4½–12 hours ▪ Ideal slow cooker size: 5- to 6-qt.

5-lb. pork roast

32-oz. can sauerkraut, undrained

1 pkg. 8 hot dogs

1. Place pork in slow cooker. Spoon sauerkraut over pork.

2. Cover and cook on Low 9½–11½ hours, or on High 4–5½ hours, or until meat is tender but not dry.

3. Lift roast onto a platter and, using a fork, separate meat into small pieces.

4. Return pork to cooker and stir into sauerkraut.

5. Cut hot dogs into ½" slices and stir into pork and sauerkraut.

6. Cover and cook for an additional 30 minutes. Serve over a bed of mashed potatoes.

Makes 12–15 servings

Shredded Pork

CINDY KRESTYNICK • GLEN LYON, PA

Prep Time: 10 minutes ▪ Cooking Time: 4–10 hours ▪ Ideal slow cooker size: 4- to 5-qt.

3-4-lb. pork butt roast

1½ envelopes taco seasoning

3-5 cloves garlic, sliced, according to your taste preference

1 large onion, quartered

4-oz. can whole green chilies, drained

1 cup water

1. Place roast in slow cooker.

2. In a bowl, mix all remaining ingredients together. Spoon over meat in cooker.

3. Cover and cook on Low 8–10 hours, or on High 4–6 hours, or until meat is tender but not dry.

4. Place pork on a platter and shred with 2 forks. Stir shredded meat back into sauce.

5. Serve in tortillas, topped with shredded lettuce, tomato, and sour cream, or over steamed rice.

Makes 6–8 servings

North Carolina Barbecue

J. B. MILLER • INDIANAPOLIS, IN

Prep Time: 15 minutes • Cooking Time: 5–8 hours • Ideal slow cooker size: 4- to 5-qt.

3-4-lb. pork loin, roast or shoulder

1 cup apple cider vinegar

1/4 cup, plus 1 Tbsp., prepared mustard

1/4 cup, plus 1 Tbsp., Worcestershire sauce

2 tsp. red pepper flakes

1. Trim fat from pork. Place in slow cooker.

2. In a bowl, mix remaining ingredients together. Spoon over meat.

3. Cover and cook on High 5 hours, or Low 8 hours, or until meat is tender but not dry.

4. Slice or break meat apart, and serve drizzled with cooking juices. If you use the meat for sandwiches, you'll have enough for 8–12 sandwiches.

Makes 8–12 servings

Pork Barbecue

MARCIA S. MYER • MANHEIM, PA

Prep Time: 10 minutes • Cooking Time: 8–10 hours • Ideal slow cooker size: 4-qt.

3-4-lb. pork roast

16-oz. bottle hickory-smoked barbecue sauce

1 medium-large onion, chopped

1/8–1/4 tsp. cloves

1. Place meat in slow cooker.

2. Cover and cook on Low 6–8 hours, or until very tender.

3. Remove roast to platter. (Drain broth and save for a soup stock or for making gravy.) Using 2 forks, shred meat.

4. Return shredded meat to cooker. Stir in barbecue sauce, onion, and cloves.

5. Cover and cook on Low 2 hours. Serve on sandwich rolls.

Makes 9–12 servings

Slow-Cooked Pork Barbecue for a Group

LINDA E. WILCOX • BLYTHEWOOD, SC

Prep Time: 15 minutes • Cooking Time: 12-14 hours • Ideal slow cooker size: 6-qt.

6-lb. pork roast

18-oz. bottle favorite barbecue
  sauce

2 Tbsp. brown sugar

2 tsp. dry mustard

2 Tbsp. minced onion

1. Place roast in slow cooker and cook on Low 8–10 hours, or until meat is tender but not dry.

2. Remove roast to a platter. (Drain drippings and reserve for a soup stock or for a gravy.) Using 2 forks, shred pork.

3. Return shredded pork to slow cooker and stir in remaining ingredients.

4. Cook on Low 4 hours. Serve on rolls.

Makes 20-24 servings

Simply Pulled Pork Sandwiches

VIRGINIA BLISH • AKRON, NY

Prep Time: 10 minutes • Cooking Time: 5½ hours • Ideal slow cooker size: 5-qt.

3-4-lb. rolled pork loin roast

18-oz. bottle barbecue sauce
  of your choice

1. Leave pork roast tied as it came from the store. Rinse with cold water and pat dry with paper towel. Place roast in slow cooker.

2. Pour barbecue sauce over top and sides of roast.

3. Cover and cook on High 5½ hours, or until meat is tender but not dry.

4. Remove roast to a platter. Cut strings and discard. Use 2 forks to pull pork apart until it is shredded.

5. Return pork to slow cooker and mix thoroughly with sauce.

6. Serve on split kaiser rolls.

Makes 9-12 servings

Cooking Tip

Be sure to read a recipe the whole way through before you begin to cook, so that you are certain you have all the ingredients you need.

Pork and Sauerkraut

SHEILA SOLDNER • LITITZ, PA

Prep Time: 30 minutes • Cooking Time: 10–11 hours • Ideal slow cooker size: 6- to 7-qt.

4-5-lb. lean pork loin roast

1-2-lb. bag sauerkraut, divided

half a small head cabbage, thinly sliced, divided

1 large onion, thinly sliced, divided

1 apple, quartered, cored, and sliced, but not peeled, divided

1 tsp. dill weed, optional

½ cup brown sugar, optional

1 cup water

1. Brown roast for 10 minutes in a heavy nonstick skillet. Place roast in slow cooker.

2. Cover with a layer of half of sauerkraut, then half of cabbage, then half of onion, and then half of apple.

3. Repeat layers.

4. If you wish to use dill weed and brown sugar, mix them and water together in a bowl. Pour over layers. Or simply pour water over top.

5. Cover and cook on High 1 hour. Turn to Low and cook until meat is tender, about 9–10 hours.

Makes 10–15 servings

Pork and Potatoes

DOROTHY VAN DEEST • MEMPHIS, TN

Prep Time: 10 minutes • Cooking Time: 8–9 hours • Ideal slow cooker size: 5-qt.

3-4 small or medium-sized sweet potatoes, or baking potatoes, peeled or unpeeled, left whole

3-4-lb. pork loin roast, well trimmed

Kitchen Bouquet seasoning

garlic salt

salt and pepper

1. Place potatoes in bottom of slow cooker.

2. Brush roast well with Kitchen Bouquet. Sprinkle with garlic salt, salt, and pepper.

3. Place pork roast on "rack" of potatoes.

4. Cover and cook on Low 8–9 hours, or until potatoes and meat are tender but not dry or mushy.

Makes 4–6 servings

Veggie Pork Roast

PEGGY FORSYTHE • BARTLETT, TN

Prep Time: 10 minutes • Cooking Time: 8–10 hours • Ideal slow cooker size: 4- to 6-qt.

3 medium-sized potatoes, quartered

6 carrots, sliced or cut into ¾" chunks

1 onion, cut into wedges

3–4-lb. pork loin

1–1½ cups mild picante sauce

1. Place potatoes, carrots, and onion in bottom of slow cooker.

2. Place pork loin on top of vegetables.

3. Pour picante sauce over meat.

4. Cover and cook on Low 8–10 hours, or until meat and vegetables are tender but not dry or mushy.

5. When finished cooking, remove meat and allow to rest on a platter 10 minutes. Then slice and surround with vegetables. Ladle sauce over top. Serve additional sauce in a bowl.

Makes 8 servings

Saucy Pork Loin

CAROLYN SPOHN • SHAWNEE, KS

Prep Time: 5 minutes • Cooking Time: 3–8 hours • Ideal slow cooker size: 4- to 6-qt.

4 1" slices boneless pork loin

1 clove garlic, minced

scant ¼ tsp. dry sage

scant ¼ tsp. rosemary leaves

10¾-oz. can cream of celery soup

1. Place pork in slow cooker. Sprinkle evenly with garlic, sage, and rosemary.

2. Spoon soup over all.

3. Cover and cook on High 3–4 hours, or on Low 6–8 hours, or until tender but not dry.

4. Serve over cooked rice or bulgur.

Makes 4 servings

Spicy Pork Olé

MARY KENNELL • ROANOKE, IL

Prep Time: 10-15 minutes • Cooking Time: 3½-4 hours • Ideal slow cooker size: 4-qt.

1½ lbs. pork loin, cut into bite-sized pieces

2 Tbsp. taco seasoning

2 cups mild salsa

⅓ cup peach jam

2 Tbsp. cornstarch

¼ cup water

1. Spray slow cooker with nonstick cooking spray.

2. Place pork in cooker. Sprinkle with taco seasoning and stir to coat.

3. Add salsa and jam. Stir.

4. Cook on High 3–3½ hours, or until meat is tender. Remove meat to a serving dish and keep warm.

5. In a bowl, blend cornstarch and water. Turn cooker to High. When sauce simmers, stir in cornstarch-water mixture. Continue stirring until fully absorbed. Continue cooking, stirring occasionally, until sauce thickens. Serve over or alongside pork.

Makes 5 servings

Apricot-Glazed Pork Roast

JEAN BUTZER • BATAVIA, NY / VIRGINIA BLISH • AKRON, NY

Prep Time: 10 minutes • Cooking Time: 3-6 hours • Ideal slow cooker size: 5- to 6-qt.

10½-oz. can condensed chicken broth

18-oz. jar apricot preserves

1 large onion, chopped

2 Tbsp. Dijon mustard

3½-4-lb. boneless pork loin

1. Mix broth, preserves, onion, and mustard in a bowl.

2. Cut roast to fit, if necessary, and place in cooker. Pour glaze over meat.

3. Cover and cook on Low 4–6 hours, or on High 3 hours, or until tender.

Makes 10-12 servings

Note: If you prefer a thickened sauce, mix 2 Tbsp. cornstarch and 2 Tbsp. water in a small bowl. When the pork has finished cooking, remove it to a platter and cover to keep warm. Turn cooker to High. Stir cornstarch-water into simmering sauce. Stir until it is well mixed. Continue simmering about 10 minutes, or until sauce thickens. Serve over or alongside pork slices.

Fruity Slow-Cooked Pork

MARGARET MOFFITT • BARTLETT, TN

Prep Time: 15–20 minutes • Cooking Time: 3–6 hours • Ideal slow cooker size: 3-qt.

1½ lbs. pork tenderloin, cut in 2" pieces

20-oz. can pineapple chunks, undrained

half a pineapple can water

½ cup brown sugar

2 large cloves garlic, minced

⅓ cup soy sauce, or teriyaki sauce

1. Combine all ingredients in slow cooker.

2. Cover and cook on High 3–4 hours, or on Low 5–6 hours, or until meat is tender but not dry.

Makes 4–6 servings

Note: To thicken the sauce, remove cooked pork pieces and pineapple chunks with a slotted spoon to a serving dish. Keep warm. Mix together 2 Tbsp. cornstarch and 2 Tbsp. water in a small bowl until smooth. Turn cooker to High. When sauce is simmering, stir in cornstarch-water mixture until thoroughly absorbed. Continue simmering, stirring occasionally, until juices thicken, about 10 minutes. Serve over or alongside pork and pineapples.

Cranberry Mustard Pork Tenderloin

VALERIE DROBEL • CARLISLE, PA

Prep Time: 15 minutes • Cooking Time: 6–8 hours • Ideal slow cooker size: 5-qt.

16-oz. can whole-berry cranberry sauce

3 Tbsp. lemon juice

4 Tbsp. Dijon mustard

3 Tbsp. brown sugar

2 pork tenderloins, about 2 lbs. total

1. In a small bowl, combine first 4 ingredients. Place about a third of mixture in bottom of slow cooker.

2. Place tenderloins on top of sauce. Pour remaining sauce over tenderloins.

3. Cover and cook on Low 6–8 hours, or until meat is tender.

4. Allow meat to stand 10 minutes before slicing.

Makes 6 servings

Note: To thicken the juices, mix 2 Tbsp. cornstarch with 2 Tbsp. water in a small bowl. After removing meat from the cooker, turn it to High. When juices are simmering, stir in cornstarch-water mixture. Continue stirring until it is absorbed. Simmer until juices thicken, about 10 minutes, stirring occasionally. Serve over or alongside sliced pork.

Tangy Pork Tenderloin

JUNE S. GROFF • DENVER, PA

Prep Time: 3–4 hours for marinating • Cooking Time: 6–8 hours • Ideal slow cooker size: 4- to 5-qt.

2 pork tenderloins (a total of
   2 lbs.)

⅔ cup honey

½ cup Dijon mustard

½ tsp. chili powder

¼ tsp. salt

1. Place pork in glass or ceramic baking dish. Combine remaining ingredients and spoon over pork.

2. Cover and marinate in fridge at least 3–4 hours.

3. Place pork in slow cooker, cutting to fit if necessary. Spoon marinade over top.

4. Cover and cook on Low 6–8 hours, or until tender.

5. Remove to a serving platter and keep warm 10 minutes before slicing.

Makes 6 servings

Note: To thicken the sauce, turn the cooker to High after removing the pork. Meanwhile, blend together 2 Tbsp. cornstarch with 2 Tbsp. water in a small bowl. When the juices are simmering, stir in cornstarch-water mixture until absorbed. Continue simmering, stirring occasionally, until juices thicken, about 10 minutes. Serve over or alongside sliced pork.

Barbecued Ribs

SARA HARTER FREDETTE • GOSHEN, MA / MARGARET H. MOFFITT • BARTLETT, TN

Prep Time: 2 minutes • Cooking Time: 5–6 hours • Ideal slow cooker size: 4- to 5-qt.

6 lean pork ribs, or chops

salt and pepper to taste

19-oz. bottle hickory, or sweet
   and tangy, barbecue sauce

1. Place meat in slow cooker, cutting ribs to fit. Sprinkle each piece with salt and pepper.

2. Add barbecue sauce. If you need to create layers of meat, be sure to top each section of ribs with a proportionate amount of sauce.

3. Cover and cook on High 1 hour. Then cook on Low 4–5 hours, or until meat is tender but not dry.

4. When ready to serve, remove ribs from cooker and place on a serving platter. Cover to keep warm. Tilt cooker in order to spoon off any fat that has floated to top of sauce. Then spoon sauce over ribs, and serve any extra in a separate bowl.

Makes 6 servings

Seasoned Pork Ribs

MELANIE THROWER • MCPHERSON, KS

Prep Time: 5–10 minutes • Cooking Time: 4 hours • Ideal slow cooker size: 4- to 5-qt.

3 lbs. pork shoulder ribs, cut into serving-size pieces

2 tsp. chipotle seasoning spice

1 tsp. coarse black pepper, optional

1 Tbsp. prepared horseradish

¼ cup ketchup

¼ cup apricot jelly

1. Heat a nonstick skillet over medium-high heat.

2. Season pork with chipotle seasonings and then place in hot skillet, browning each piece on top and bottom. Do in batches so all pieces brown well.

3. As you finish browning ribs, place them in slow cooker.

4. Cover and cook on High 3 hours.

5. Meanwhile, mix together pepper, if you wish, horseradish, ketchup, and apricot jelly in a bowl. Spread over cooked pork.

6. Cover and cook on High 1 hour, or until meat is tender.

Makes 2–3 servings

Sweet and Saucy Ribs

JEAN BUTZER • BATAVIA, NY

Prep Time: 10–15 minutes • Cooking Time: 3–8 hours • Ideal slow cooker size: 3- to 4-qt.

2 lbs. pork baby back ribs

1 tsp. black pepper

2½ cups barbecue sauce (not mesquite flavor)

8-oz. jar cherry jam or preserves

1 Tbsp. Dijon mustard

¼ tsp. salt

1. Trim excess fat from ribs. Rub pepper over ribs. Cut into 2-rib portions and place in slow cooker.

2. Combine barbecue sauce, jam, mustard, and salt in a small bowl. Pour over ribs, making sure that each piece gets a good amount of sauce.

3. Cover and cook on Low 6–8 hours, or on High 3–4 hours, or until ribs are tender.

Makes 4 servings

Note: Try using different flavors of jam or preserves, such as apricot, plum, or grape.

Sweet BBQ Ribs

MICHELE RUVOLA • SELDEN, NY

Prep Time: 10 minutes • Cooking Time: 8–9 hours • Ideal slow cooker size: 3- to 4-qt.

3½ lbs. pork loin back ribs

½ tsp. salt

¼ tsp. pepper

½ cup cola

⅔ cup barbecue sauce

1. Cut ribs into 2–3 rib portions and put in slow cooker.

2. Sprinkle each portion with salt and pepper. Spoon cola over top, being careful not to wash off the seasonings.

3. Cover and cook on Low 7–8 hours, or until ribs are tender. Drain liquid.

4. Pour barbecue sauce into slow cooker. Mix gently with ribs so meat is coated.

5. Cover and cook on Low 1 hour, or until ribs are glazed.

Makes 6 servings

Spareribs

ELAINE RINEER • LANCASTER, PA

Prep Time: 35 minutes • Cooking Time: 7–8 hours • Ideal slow cooker size: 4- to 5-qt.

3 lbs. country-style spareribs

2 Tbsp. olive oil

2 small onions, chopped

1 cup ketchup

2 tsp. Worcestershire sauce

1 cup water

1. Brown spareribs on top and bottom in oil in a large nonstick skillet. As they brown, move ribs from nonstick skillet into slow cooker.

2. In a saucepan, mix together onions, ketchup, Worcestershire sauce, and water. Simmer 20 minutes, then pour over ribs.

3. Cover and cook on Low 7–8 hours, or until meat is tender.

4. Place ribs on a serving platter. Spoon sauce over top. Put additional sauce in a bowl and serve along with meat.

Makes 6 servings

Finger-Lickin' Pork Ribs

MARILYN MOWRY • IRVING, TX

Prep Time: 8–12 hours for marinating • Cooking Time: 6–8 hours • Ideal slow cooker size: 2- to 3-qt.

4–8 country-style pork ribs

1 cup water

½ cup white vinegar

4-oz. bottle liquid smoke

favorite bottled barbecue sauce

1. Place ribs in a covered dish. In a bowl, mix together water, vinegar, and liquid smoke. Pour over ribs. Turn ribs over once. Marinate overnight.

2. Next day, drain ribs and discard marinade.

3. Put ribs in slow cooker. Cover with barbecue sauce.

4. Cover cooker and cook on Low 6–8 hours, or until tender.

Makes 4 servings

A-Touch-of-Asia Ribs

SHARON SHANK • BRIDGEWATER, VA

Prep Time: 5–10 minutes • Cooking Time: 4–8 hours • Ideal slow cooker size: 5- to 6-qt.

6 lbs. country-style pork ribs, cut into serving-size pieces

¼ cup teriyaki sauce

¼ cup cornstarch

27-oz. jar duck sauce

2 Tbsp. minced garlic, optional

1. Place ribs in bottom of slow cooker.

2. In a large bowl, stir together teriyaki sauce and cornstarch. Blend in duck sauce and garlic, if you wish.

3. Pour sauce over ribs, making sure that each layer is well covered.

4. Cover and cook on Low 8 hours, or on High 4–5 hours.

Makes 8–10 servings

Italian Country-Style Pork Ribs

KAY KASSINGER • PORT ANGELES, WA

Prep Time: 20 minutes • Cooking Time: 7–8 hours • Ideal slow cooker size: 5-qt.

3–3½ lbs. country-style pork ribs, cut into serving-size pieces

2 14½-oz. cans Italian-seasoned diced tomatoes

1 cup frozen pearl onions

1½ tsp. Italian seasoning

1 tsp. salt

water as needed

1. Brown ribs on top and bottom in a nonstick skillet. Do in batches to ensure that each piece browns well.

2. Spray slow cooker with nonstick cooking spray. Transfer browned meat to cooker.

3. Drain tomatoes into hot skillet. Deglaze skillet with tomato juice by stirring up the drippings with a wooden spoon.

4. Layer tomatoes, onions, and seasonings over top of ribs. Pour deglazed pan drippings into slow cooker. Add about 2" of water.

5. Cover and cook on Low 7–8 hours, or until meat is tender but not overcooked.

Makes 8–10 servings

Easy Pork Riblets

RUTH C. HANCOCK • EARLSBORO, OK

Prep Time: 5–10 minutes • Cooking Time: 8 hours • Ideal slow cooker size: 3- to 4-qt.

2 lbs. pork riblets

8-oz. jar grape jelly

8-oz. bottle cocktail sauce

1. Place riblets in slow cooker.

2. Mix jelly and cocktail sauce together in a bowl. Pour over riblets.

3. Cover and cook on Low 8 hours, or until meat is tender.

Makes 3–4 servings

Cooking Tip

Thaw meat safely:
- In the refrigerator on the bottom shelf in a platter or deep dish.
- In the microwave.
- As part of the cooking process.
- In a bowl of cold water, changing the water every 20 minutes.
- Never at room temperature.

Apple Raisin Ham

BETTY B. DENNISON • GROVE CITY, PA

Prep Time: 10–15 minutes • Cooking Time: 4–5 hours • Ideal slow cooker size: 4-qt.

1½ lbs. fully cooked ham

21-oz. can apple pie filling

⅓ cup golden raisins

⅓ cup orange juice

¼ tsp. cinnamon

2 Tbsp. water

1. Cut ham into 6 equal slices.

2. In a mixing bowl, combine pie filling, raisins, juice, cinnamon, and water.

3. Place 1 slice of ham in slow cooker. Spread one-sixth of apple mixture over top.

4. Repeat layers until you have used all ham and all apple mixture.

5. Cover and cook on Low 4–5 hours.

Makes 6 servings

Note: This is a great way to use leftovers. And you can use any leftovers from this dish to make wonderful sandwiches.

Country Ham

ESTHER BURKHOLDER • MILLERSTOWN, PA

Prep Time: 10 minutes • Cooking Time: 6 hours • Ideal slow cooker size: 4-qt.

3-lb. boneless, fully cooked ham

½–¾ cup brown sugar, according to your taste preferences

2 Tbsp. prepared mustard

¼ cup peach preserves

1. Place ham in slow cooker.

2. Combine remaining ingredients in a small bowl. Spread over ham.

3. Cover and cook on Low 6 hours, or until heated through.

Makes 12 servings

Glazed Ham

DEDE PETERSON • RAPID CITY, SD

Prep Time: 20 minutes • Cooking Time: 4–6 hours • Ideal slow cooker size: 6-qt.

4 ham steaks

⅓ cup apricot jam

¾–1 cup honey, depending
upon how much sweetness
you like

⅓ cup soy sauce

¼ tsp. nutmeg

1. Place ham in slow cooker.

2. In a bowl, mix all other ingredients together. Pour over
ham.

3. Cook on Low 4–6 hours, or until meat is heated through
but not dry.

Makes 4 servings

Glazed Ham in a Bag

ELEANOR J. FERREIRA • NORTH CHELMSFORD, MA

Prep Time: 7 minutes • Cooking Time: 6–8 hours • Ideal slow cooker size: 6- to 7-qt.

5-lb. cooked ham

3 Tbsp. orange juice

1 Tbsp. Dijon mustard

1. Rinse meat. Place in a cooking bag.

2. Combine juice and mustard. Spread over ham.

3. Seal bag with twist tie. Poke 4 holes in top of bag. Place in
slow cooker.

4. Cover. Cook on Low 6–8 hours.

5. To serve, remove ham from bag, reserving juices. Slice
ham and spoon juices over. Serve additional juice alongside in a small bowl.

Makes 12 servings

Cranberry Ham

JANIE STEELE • MOORE, OK

Prep Time: 5–10 minutes • Cooking Time: 4½ hours • Ideal slow cooker size: 3-qt.

1–2-lb. fully cooked ham, or 2"-thick slice fully cooked ham

1 cup whole-berry cranberry sauce

2 Tbsp. brown sugar

1. Place ham in slow cooker. Cover with cranberry sauce. Sprinkle brown sugar over top.

2. Cook on Low 4½ hours, or until meat is heated through but not drying out.

Makes 4 servings

Fruited Ham Slice

ARLENE M. KOPP • LINEBORO, MD

Prep Time: 10 minutes • Cooking Time: 3–4 hours • Ideal slow cooker size: 3-qt.

1–1½-lb. fully cooked ham slice, 1" thick

8–10 whole cloves

prepared mustard

1-lb. can fruit cocktail, drained, with 1 cup syrup reserved

½ cup brown sugar, firmly packed

1. Stud edges of ham slice with cloves. Spread top with mustard. Place ham slice in slow cooker.

2. In a bowl, mix together fruit cocktail, 1 cup syrup, and brown sugar. Spoon over ham.

3. Cover and cook on Low 3–4 hours, or until ham is heated through but not drying out.

Makes 4 servings

Variations: Instead of the fruit cocktail, use 2 cups of any of the following: canned pineapple chunks, sliced peaches, apricot halves.

Succulent Ham

JUNE S. GROFF • DENVER, PA

Prep Time: 10 minutes • Cooking Time: 4–6 hours • Ideal slow cooker size: 3-qt.

1½ lbs. fully cooked smoked ham pieces

½ cup brown sugar

¼ cup butter, or margarine, melted

¼ cup red wine vinegar

1. Place ham in slow cooker.

2. In a bowl, blend sugar and melted butter. Stir in vinegar until sugar dissolves. Pour over ham.

3. Cover and cook on Low 4–6 hours, or until meat is heated through but not dried out.

4. Serve meat sliced, or in chunks, with juice spooned over top.

Makes 6 servings

Ham 'n' Cola

DOROTHY VAN DEEST • MEMPHIS, TN

Prep Time: 15 minutes • Cooking Time: 7–8 hours • Ideal slow cooker size: 4-qt.

½ cup brown sugar

1 tsp. dry mustard

1 tsp. prepared horseradish

¼-½ cup cola, divided

3-4-lb. precooked ham

1. In a mixing bowl, thoroughly combine brown sugar, mustard, and horseradish. Moisten with just enough cola to make a smooth paste. Reserve remaining cola.

2. Rub entire ham with brown sugar mixture. Place in slow cooker.

3. Pour remaining cola around edges of cooker.

4. Cover and cook on High 1 hour, then on Low 6–7 hours, or until ham is heated through but is not drying out.

Makes 9-12 servings

Easy and Elegant Ham

MARY LYNN MILLER • REINHOLDS, PA

Prep Time: 10–15 minutes • Cooking Time: 6–7 hours • Ideal slow cooker size: 5- to 6-qt.

2 20-oz. cans sliced pineapple, divided

6-lb. fully cooked boneless ham, halved

6-oz. jar maraschino cherries, well drained

12-oz. jar orange marmalade

1. Drain pineapple, reserving juice. Set juice aside. Place half of pineapple in ungreased slow cooker.

2. Top with ham halves.

3. Spoon cherries, remaining pineapple slices, and reserved pineapple juice over ham. Then spoon marmalade over ham.

4. Cover and cook on Low 6–7 hours, or until heated through.

5. Remove to a warm serving platter. Let stand 10–15 minutes before slicing.

6. Serve pineapple and cherries with sliced ham, either on top of or alongside slices.

Makes 18–20 servings

Potatoes and Green Beans with Ham

MARY B. SENSENIG • NEW HOLLAND, PA

Prep Time: 5 minutes • Cooking Time: 6–8 hours • Ideal slow cooker size: 3-qt.

1-lb. ham slice, cut in chunks

2 cups green beans, frozen or fresh

2 cups red-skinned potatoes, quartered, but not peeled

½ cup water

½ cup chopped onion

4 slices American cheese

1. Place all ingredients, except cheese, in slow cooker. Gently mix together.

2. Cover and cook on Low 6–8 hours, or until vegetables are tender.

3. One hour before end of cooking time, lay cheese slices over top.

Makes 4 servings

Ham and Vegetables

DOROTHY VAN DEEST • MEMPHIS, TN / BETTY HOSTETLER • ALLENSVILLE, PA

Prep Time: 15 minutes • Cooking Time: 3–4 hours • Ideal slow cooker size: 3- to 4-qt.

2 medium-sized potatoes, peeled if you want, and cut up

1 lb. green beans, Frenched, or cut in half

2½ cups water

½ tsp. salt

1 lb. lean cooked ham, in a piece or cut up, or a meaty ham hock

1. Place ingredients in slow cooker in order given.

2. Cover and cook on High 3–4 hours, or until vegetables are tender.

3. If you're home, check dish after it has cooked for 2 hours to make sure it isn't cooking dry. Add ½–1 cup water if it's looking dry.

4. If you use a ham hock, remove it, allow it to cool enough to handle, and debone it. Stir chunks of ham back into cooker.

Makes 5–6 servings

Green Beans and Ham

SARA KINSINGER • STUARTS DRAFT, VA

Prep Time: 5–7 minutes • Cooking Time: 1½–4 hours • Ideal slow cooker size: 4-qt.

2 qts. cooked, or canned, green beans, undrained

2 cups cooked ham, diced

1 stick (½ cup) butter, cut in chunks

1 tsp. hickory smoke seasoning

1. Place all ingredients in slow cooker. Stir together gently.

2. Cover and cook on High 1½ hours, or on Low 4 hours.

Makes 12 servings

Ham and Cabbage

TIM SMITH • RUTLEDGE, PA

Prep Time: 30 minutes • Cooking Time: 6–7 hours • Ideal slow cooker size: 6- to 7-qt.

2 lbs. ham, uncooked

12 whole cloves

8 medium-sized red potatoes

1 medium-sized head green
   cabbage

water

1. Rinse ham, then stick cloves evenly into ham. Place in center of slow cooker.

2. Cut potatoes in half. Add to slow cooker around ham.

3. Quarter cabbage and remove center stem. Add to cooker, again surrounding ham.

4. Fill with water to cover.

5. Cover and cook on High 6–7 hours, or until vegetables and meat are tender but not dry or mushy.

6. Serve with mustard for ham and butter for potatoes.

Makes 4 servings

Ham and Dumplings

DONNA LANTGEN • CHADRON, NE

Prep Time: 10 minutes • Cooking Time: 6–7 hours • Ideal slow cooker size: 5-qt.

2½-lb. piece of cooked ham

8 cups water

3 cups all-purpose baking mix

1 cup milk

1. Place ham and water in slow cooker.

2. Cover and cook on High 5–6 hours.

3. In a bowl, mix baking mix and milk together. Drop by spoonfuls into slow cooker.

4. Cover and cook on High 1 more hour.

Makes 6 servings

Note: Grate ends of cheese blocks (cheddar, Swiss, Monterey Jack, etc.) together into a zipper-lock bag and keep the grated cheese on hand for sprinkling over salads, casseroles, and toasted cheese bread.

Scalloped Potatoes and Ham

CAROL SHERWOOD • BATAVIA, NY / SHARON ANDERS • ALBURTIS, PA / MARY STAUFFER • EPHRATA, PA
ESTHER HARTZLER • CARLSBAD, NM / DAWN HAHN • LITITZ, PA / DIANN J. DUNHAM • STATE COLLEGE, PA

Prep Time: 20 minutes • Cooking Time: 6–8 hours • Ideal slow cooker size: 5-qt.

2–3 lbs. potatoes, peeled, sliced, and divided

12-oz. pkg., or 1 lb., cooked ham, cubed and divided

1 small onion, chopped and divided

2 cups shredded cheddar cheese, divided

10¾-oz. can cream of celery, or mushroom, soup

1. Spray slow cooker with nonstick cooking spray.

2. Layer one-third each of potatoes, ham, onion, and cheese into cooker.

3. Repeat twice.

4. Spread soup on top.

5. Cover and cook on Low 6–8 hours, or until potatoes are tender.

Makes 4–6 servings

Creamy Scalloped Potatoes and Ham

RHONDA FREED • LOWVILLE, NY

Prep Time: 20 minutes • Cooking Time: 4–5 hours • Ideal slow cooker size: 4-qt.

6 cups sliced potatoes

salt and pepper to taste

10¾-oz. can cream of mushroom, or celery, soup

1½ cups milk

1 lb. cooked ham, cubed

1. Place potatoes in slow cooker. Salt and pepper each layer.

2. In a bowl, mix soup, milk, and ham together. Pour over potatoes.

3. Cover and cook on High 3½ hours. Continue cooking ½–1½ hours more if needed, or until potatoes are tender.

Makes 6 servings

Cheesy Potatoes and Ham

BETH MAURER • HARRISONBURG, VA

Prep Time: 20 minutes • Cooking Time: 7–9 hours • Ideal slow cooker size: 4-qt.

6 cups peeled, sliced potatoes

2½ cups cooked ham, cubed

1½ cups shredded cheddar
cheese

10¾-oz. can cream of
mushroom soup

½ cup milk

1. In slow cooker, layer one-third each of potatoes, ham, and cheese. Repeat 2 more times.

2. Combine soup and milk. Pour over ingredients in slow cooker.

3. Cover. Cook on High 1 hour. Then cook on Low 6–8 hours, or just until potatoes are soft.

Makes 4–6 servings

Cottage Ham Dinner

ETHEL MUMAW • MILLERSBURG, OH

Prep Time: 10–15 minutes • Cooking Time: 8 hours • Ideal slow cooker size: 5-qt.

3-lb. boneless cottage ham

12-oz. can ginger ale

3 unpeeled medium-sized
potatoes, cut into strips

3 medium-sized onions, cut
into wedges

1. Place ham in slow cooker. Pour ginger ale over top.

2. Add potato strips and onion wedges around ham. Push down into liquid as much as possible.

3. Cover and cook on Low 8 hours, or until vegetables are tender.

Makes 8 servings

Ham Hocks and Kraut

KATHLEEN ROGGE • ALEXANDRIA, IN

Prep Time: 5 minutes • Cooking Time: 6–8 hours • Ideal slow cooker size: 6-qt.

6 meaty smoked ham hocks

15-oz. can sauerkraut

1 large onion, chopped

2 bay leaves

water

1. Place all ingredients in slow cooker. Fill with enough water to cover ham hocks.

2. Cover and cook on Low 6–8 hours, or until meat is tender.

3. Remove hocks and allow to cool enough to debone by hand. Stir ham chunks back into sauerkraut.

4. Remove bay leaves. Serve with mashed potatoes.

Makes 3–4 servings

Ham Balls

EDWINA F. STOLTZFUS • NARVON, PA

Prep Time: 10–15 minutes • Cooking Time: 3½ hours • Ideal slow cooker size: 3- to 4-qt.

1 cup brown sugar

1 Tbsp. prepared mustard

½ cup water

½ cup vinegar

4-oz. can crushed pineapple, undrained

2 lbs. prepared ham loaf, divided

1. In a saucepan, bring brown sugar, mustard, water, vinegar, and pineapple to a boil.

2. Meanwhile, shape ham loaf into balls. Place a layer in slow cooker.

3. Spoon a proportionate amount of boiling sauce over first layer of meat.

4. Continue with layers until all meat and sauce are in cooker, being sure to end with sauce.

5. Cook on High 3½ hours.

6. Before serving, tilt cooker carefully. Spoon off layer of fat and discard.

7. Place cooked balls on a serving platter and spoon sauce over top.

Makes 6 servings

Ham and Cheese Casserole

KENDRA DREPS • LIBERTY, PA

Prep Time: 15–30 minutes • Cooking Time: 2–4 hours • Ideal slow cooker size: 3½ qt.

12- or 16-oz. pkg. medium egg noodles, divided

10¾-oz. can condensed cream of celery soup

1 pt. sour cream

2 cups fully cooked ham, cubed, divided

2 cups shredded cheese, your choice, divided

1. Prepare noodles according to package instructions. Drain.

2. In a small bowl, combine soup and sour cream until smooth. Set aside.

3. In a greased slow cooker, layer one-third of cooked noodles, one-third of ham, and one-third of cheese.

4. Top with one-fourth of soup mixture.

5. Repeat Steps 3 and 4 twice until all ingredients are used. The final layer should be soup–sour cream mixture.

6. Cook 2–4 hours on Low, or until heated through.

Makes 8–10 servings

Ham and Hash Browns

JOETTE DROZ • KALONA, IA / JONICE CRIST • QUINTER, KS

Prep Time: 10 minutes • Cooking Time: 4–6 hours • Ideal slow cooker size: 4-qt.

26-oz. pkg. frozen hash browns

2 cups fully cooked ham, cubed

2-oz. jar diced pimentos, drained

10¾-oz. can cheddar cheese soup

¾ cup milk

¼ tsp. pepper, optional

1. In slow cooker, combine potatoes, ham, and pimentos.

2. Combine soup, milk, and pepper, if you wish, in a bowl until smooth. Mix well and pour over potato mixture. Stir.

3. Cover and cook on Low 4–6 hours, or until potatoes are tender.

Makes 4 servings

Sausage and Apples

LINDA SLUITER • SCHERERVILLE, IN

Prep Time: 10 minutes • Cooking Time: 1–3 hours • Ideal slow cooker size: 8-qt.

1 lb. smoked sausage

2 large apples, cored and sliced

¼ cup brown sugar

½ cup apple juice

1. Cut meat into 2" pieces.

2. Place all ingredients in slow cooker and mix together well.

3. Cover and cook on Low 1–3 hours, or until heated through and apples are as tender as you like them.

Makes 4 servings

Sausage and Sweet Potatoes

RUTH HERSHEY • PARADISE, PA

Prep Time: 15–20 minutes • Cooking Time: 4–10 hours • Ideal slow cooker size: 3-qt.

1 lb. bulk sausage

2 sweet potatoes, peeled and
  sliced

3 apples, peeled and sliced

2 Tbsp. brown sugar

1 Tbsp. flour

¼ cup water

1. Brown loose sausage in skillet, breaking up chunks of meat with a wooden spoon. Drain.

2. Layer sausage, sweet potatoes, and apples in slow cooker.

3. Combine remaining ingredients and pour over ingredients in slow cooker.

4. Cover. Cook on Low 8–10 hours, or on High 4 hours.

   Makes 4–6 servings

Sweet and Sour Sausage Dish

JENA HAMMOND • TRAVERSE CITY, MI

Prep Time: 15 minutes • Cooking Time: 3–6 hours • Ideal slow cooker size: 4-qt.

2 20-oz. cans pineapple
   chunks, drained

2 large green peppers, sliced
  into bite-sized strips

3 16-oz. pkgs. smoked
   sausage, cut into 1" chunks

18-oz. bottle honey barbecue
  sauce

1. Combine pineapple, peppers, and sausage chunks in slow cooker.

2. Pour barbecue sauce over mixture and stir.

3. Cover and cook on High 3 hours, or on Low 6 hours, or until dish is heated through.

   Makes 8–10 servings

Sausage and Scalloped Potatoes

MELISSA WARNER • BROAD TOP, PA / CAROLYN BAER • CONRATH, WI

Prep Time: 20 minutes • Cooking Time: 4–10 hours • Ideal slow cooker size: 3½- to 4-qt.

2 lbs. potatoes, sliced ¼" thick, divided

1 lb. fully cooked smoked sausage link, sliced ½" thick, divided

2 medium-sized onions, chopped, divided

10¾-oz. can condensed cheddar cheese soup, divided

10¾-oz. can condensed cream of celery soup

10-oz. pkg. frozen peas, thawed, optional

1. Spray slow cooker with nonstick cooking spray.

2. Layer into cooker one-third of potatoes, one-third of sausage, one-third of onions, and one-third of cheddar cheese soup.

3. Repeat layers two more times.

4. Top with cream of celery soup.

5. Cover and cook on Low 8–10 hours, or on High 4–5 hours, or until vegetables are tender.

6. If you wish, stir in peas. Cover and let stand 5 minutes. (If you forgot to thaw peas, stir them in but let stand 10 minutes.)

Makes 8 servings

Beans with Sausage

MARY B. SENSENIG • NEW HOLLAND, PA

Prep Time: 5 minutes • Cooking Time: 4–5 hours • Ideal slow cooker size: 4-qt.

16-oz. pkg. miniature smoked sausage links

1 qt. green beans, with most juice drained

1 small onion, chopped

½ cup brown sugar

¼ cup ketchup

1. Place sausage in slow cooker. Top with beans and then onion.

2. In a bowl, stir together sugar and ketchup. Spoon over top of sausage and vegetables.

3. Cover and cook on Low 4–5 hours.

Makes 4–5 servings

Sausage and Green Beans

JOY YODER • HARRISONBURG, VA

Prep Time: 15 minutes • Cooking Time: 2–5 hours • Ideal slow cooker size: 3- to 4-qt.

1½ lbs. link sausage, cut into 2" pieces

1 qt. green beans, frozen

1 apple, diced or sliced with peel

1 cup water

1. Place sausage in slow cooker.

2. Add beans, apple, and water. Mix together well.

3. Cover and cook on High 2 hours, or on Low 4–5 hours, or until sausage and beans are both tender.

Makes 6 servings

Creamy Sausage and Potatoes

JANET OBERHOLTZER • EPHRATA, PA

Prep Time: 15 minutes • Cooking Time: 6–8 hours • Ideal slow cooker size: 3½-qt.

3 lbs. small potatoes, peeled and quartered

1 lb. smoked sausage, cut into ¼" slices

8-oz. pkg. cream cheese, softened

10¾-oz. can cream of celery soup

1 envelope dry ranch salad dressing mix

1. Place potatoes in slow cooker. Add sausage.

2. In a bowl, beat together cream cheese, soup, and salad dressing mix until smooth. Pour over potatoes and sausage.

3. Cover and cook on Low 6–8 hours, or until potatoes are tender, stirring halfway through cooking time if you're home. Stir again before serving.

Makes 6 servings

Note: Small red potatoes are great in this dish. If you use them, don't peel them! Also, you may substitute smoked turkey sausage for the smoked pork sausage.

Sausage Comfort Casserole

KAY M. ZURCHER • MINOT, ND

Prep Time: 30 minutes • Cooking Time: 4–8 hours • Ideal slow cooker size: 4- to 5-qt.

2 lbs. beer brats, or spicy
    sausage, divided

2 14-oz. cans chicken broth,
    divided

3 lbs. potatoes, sliced
    $\frac{1}{4}$" thick, divided

salt and pepper, optional,
    divided

2 large onions, thinly sliced,
    divided

6 ozs. sharp cheddar cheese,
    shredded, divided

1. Spray slow cooker with nonstick cooking spray.

2. Brown sausage in a nonstick skillet until browned on all sides.

3. Meanwhile, pour 1 cup chicken broth into slow cooker. Spread one-third of potatoes on bottom of slow cooker. Sprinkle with salt and pepper, if you wish.

4. Then layer in one-third of onions, one-third of sausage, and one-third of cheese.

5. Repeat layers of potato, salt and pepper if you wish, onion, sausage, and cheese 2 more times.

6. Pour remaining chicken broth over top.

7. Cover and cook on Low 8 hours, or on High 4 hours, or until potatoes and onions are done to your liking.

Makes 6–8 servings

Note: Do not stir, but check potatoes to make sure they are finished but not overcooked.

Italian Sausage Dinner

JANESSA HOCHSTEDLER • EAST EARL, PA

Prep Time: 10 minutes ▪ Cooking Time: 5–10 hours ▪ Ideal slow cooker size: 4-qt.

$1\frac{1}{2}$ lbs. Italian sausage, cut in
    $\frac{3}{4}$" slices

2 Tbsp. A.1. steak sauce

28-oz. can diced Italian-style
    tomatoes, with juice

2 chopped green peppers

$\frac{1}{2}$ tsp. red pepper flakes,
    optional

2 cups uncooked minute rice

1. Place all ingredients, except rice, in slow cooker.

2. Cover and cook on Low $7\frac{1}{2}$–$9\frac{1}{2}$ hours, or on High $4\frac{1}{2}$ hours.

3. Stir in uncooked rice. Cover and cook an additional 20 minutes on High or Low.

Makes 6 servings

Sausage in Spaghetti Sauce

MARY ANN BOWMAN • EAST EARL, PA

Prep Time: 15 minutes • Cooking Time: 3–6 hours • Ideal slow cooker size: 5-qt.

4 lbs. sausage of your choice

1 red bell pepper

1 green bell pepper

1 large onion

26-oz. jar spaghetti sauce

1. Heat a nonstick skillet over medium-high heat. Brown sausage in skillet in batches. As a batch finishes browning on all sides, cut into 1½" chunks. Then place in slow cooker.

2. Slice or chop peppers and onion and put on top of sausage.

3. Add spaghetti sauce over all.

4. Cover and cook on Low 6 hours, or on High 3 hours.

Makes 10–12 servings

Super Sausage Supper

ANNE TOWNSEND • ALBUQUERQUE, NM

Prep Time: 5 minutes • Cooking Time: 1–6 hours • Ideal slow cooker size: 3-qt.

8-oz. pkg. hot sausage

16-oz. pkg. frozen mixed vegetables

10¾-oz. can cream of broccoli cheese soup

1. Slice sausage and place in slow cooker.

2. Distribute frozen vegetables over sausage.

3. Spread undiluted soup on top of vegetables.

4. Cover and cook on High 1 hour, or on Low 5–6 hours, or until meat is cooked and vegetables are tender.

Makes 3–4 servings

Note: This simple meal is quite thick and can be served on dinner plates rather than in soup bowls. It is delicious the next day, as well.

Sausage and Sauerkraut Supper

BONNIE GOERING • BRIDGEWATER, VA

Prep Time: 10 minutes • Cooking Time: 6–10 hours • Ideal slow cooker size: 4- to 5-qt.

1-lb. pkg. smoked sausage links, cut into 2" pieces

32-oz. bag refrigerated, or canned, sauerkraut, drained

half an onion, chopped

1 apple, cored and chopped

2–3 Tbsp. brown sugar

water

1. Combine all ingredients in slow cooker with water covering half of contents.

2. Cover and cook on Low 6–10 hours, or until vegetables are as tender as you like them.

3. Serve alongside mashed potatoes.

Makes 4–5 servings

Note: If you'll be cooking this dish for more than 8 hours, you may want to use enough water to nearly cover the ingredients in Step 1.

Sausage, Potatoes, and Sauerkraut

JANIE STEELE • MOORE, OK

Prep Time: 20 minutes • Cooking Time: 6–8 hours • Ideal slow cooker size: 4- to 5-qt.

32-oz. can sauerkraut, drained

2 cups peeled, thinly sliced potatoes

1/2 cup chopped onions

1 lb. Polish or Italian sausage, or any sausage of your choice, cut into 2"–3" pieces

1. Place sauerkraut on bottom of slow cooker. Layer in potatoes and onions.

2. Lay sausage pieces over top.

3. Cover and cook on Low 6–8 hours, or until vegetables are tender and sausage is cooked.

Makes 6–8 servings

Split Pea Soup with Ham ■ 4

Saucy Turkey Breast with Flavorful Fruited Rice ■ 95 and 277

Spicy French Dip

Round Steak and Vegetables ■ 125

Pork Chops with
Stuffing ■ 181

Pork Chops 'n'
Kraut ■ 181

Slow-Cooker Baked Beans

Acorn Squash

Artichoke Dip ■ 316

Easy Egg and Sausage Puff

Easy Autumn Cake

Upside-Down Chocolate
Pudding Cake

Sauerkraut and Kielbasa

COLLEEN HEATWOLE • BURTON, MI

Prep Time: 10 minutes • Cooking Time: 5–6 hours • Ideal slow cooker size: 3- to 4-qt.

2 14½-oz. cans sauerkraut

1 lb. Polish kielbasa

1. Drain sauerkraut. Place in slow cooker.

2. Cut kielbasa into 1"-thick slices. Combine with sauerkraut in slow cooker.

3. Cover and cook on Low 5–6 hours.

   Makes 4 servings

Sweet and Spicy Kielbasa

MICHELE RUVOLA • SELDEN, NY

Prep Time: 5 minutes • Cooking Time: 2½–3 hours • Ideal slow cooker size: 3-qt.

1 cup brown sugar

1 Tbsp. spicy mustard

2 lbs. smoked fully cooked
 kielbasa, cut into 1" pieces

1. Combine brown sugar and mustard in slow cooker.

2. Add kielbasa; stir to coat evenly.

3. Cover and cook on Low 2½–3 hours, stirring occasionally.

   Makes 6-8 servings

Harvest Kielbasa

CHRIST KACZYNSKI • SCHENECTADY, NY

Prep Time: 20 minutes • Cooking Time: 4–8 hours • Ideal slow cooker size: 4-qt.

2 lbs. smoked kielbasa

3 cups unsweetened
 applesauce

½ cup brown sugar

3 medium-sized onions, sliced

1. Slice kielbasa into ¼" slices. Brown in skillet. Drain.

2. Combine applesauce and brown sugar.

3. Layer kielbasa, onions, and applesauce mixture in slow cooker.

4. Cover. Cook on Low 4–8 hours.

   Makes 6 servings

Note: The longer it cooks, the better the flavor.

Melt-in-Your-Mouth Sausage

SUSAN WENGER • LEBANON, PA

Prep Time: 15 minutes • Cooking Time: 4–6 hours • Ideal slow cooker size: 4-qt.

2 lbs. fresh sausage, cut in ³/₄" slices

24-oz. jar spaghetti sauce

6-oz. can tomato paste

tomato paste can water

1 Tbsp. Parmesan cheese

OPTIONAL INGREDIENTS:

1 tsp. parsley flakes

1 onion, thinly sliced

half or whole bell pepper, sliced

1–2 cups fresh mushrooms, sliced

1. Heat a nonstick skillet over medium-high heat. Brown sausage on all sides.

2. Put browned sausage and all remaining ingredients in slow cooker. Stir together gently but thoroughly.

3. Cover and cook on High 4–6 hours. Serve on steak rolls, or over mashed potatoes or corkscrew pasta.

Makes 6–8 servings

Easy Sausage Sandwiches

RENEE SUYDAM • LANCASTER, PA

Prep Time: 10 minutes • Cooking Time: 5½–8 hours • Ideal slow cooker size: 5-qt.

8 pieces sausage of your choice, sub-roll length

water

26-oz. jar spaghetti sauce, your favorite

8 sub rolls

2–3 cups shredded mozzarella cheese

1. Place sausage pieces in slow cooker. Add 1"–2" water.

2. Cover and cook on Low 5–7 hours. Drain water.

3. Stir in spaghetti sauce.

4. Cover and cook 30–60 minutes more, until sauce is heated through.

5. Serve on rolls topped with mozzarella cheese.

Makes 8 servings

Note: Serve with sautéed peppers and onions as condiments for topping the sandwiches.

Cooking Tip

If you want to verify that meat in your cooker is fully cooked, use a meat thermometer to check that the internal temperature of poultry has reached 180°F. Medium-done beef and pork should reach an internal temperature of 160°F. Well-done beef and pork should reach an internal temperature of 170°F.

Saucy Hot Dogs

DONNA CONTO • SAYLORSBURG, PA

Prep Time: 15 minutes • Cooking Time: 2 hours • Ideal slow cooker size: 5-qt.

1 lb. all-beef hot dogs

10-oz. jar grape jelly

1/3 cup prepared mustard

1/4 cup red wine

1/4 tsp. dry mustard

1. Cut hot dogs into 1/2" slices. Place in slow cooker.

2. Mix remaining ingredients together with hot dogs in cooker.

3. Cover and cook on Low 2 hours.

4. Serve in rolls or over cooked pasta.

Makes 8 servings

Barbecued Smokies

RADELLA VROLIJK • HINTON, VA

Prep Time: 5 minutes • Cooking Time: 4–6 hours • Ideal slow cooker size: 3-qt.

12-oz. bottle barbecue sauce

8-oz. jar grape jelly

1 1/2 lbs. little smokies, or hot dogs, cut into 3/4" slices

1. Mix barbecue sauce and jelly in slow cooker. Add cut-up meat.

2. Cover and cook on Low 4–6 hours.

3. Serve in hot dog buns or over cooked pasta. Or serve on a buffet from warm cooker, with toothpicks to spear meat pieces.

Makes 10-12 servings

Barbecued Hot Dogs

SHELIA HEIL • LANCASTER, PA

Prep Time: 15 minutes • Cooking Time: 2–2½ hours • Ideal slow cooker size: 2- or 3-qt.

16–20 hot dogs, cut into
    1" chunks

1 jar cocktail sauce

½ cup brown sugar

½ cup ketchup

1. Place hot dog chunks in slow cooker.

2. Add remaining ingredients to cooker and mix with hot dogs.

3. Cover and cook on Low 2–2½ hours.

4. Serve with mashed potatoes or French fries. Or serve on a buffet from warm cooker, with toothpicks to spear meat pieces.

Makes 10 servings

Zesty Wieners

SHERRIL BIEBERLY • SALINA, KS

Prep Time: 5 minutes • Cooking Time: 1–2 hours • Ideal slow cooker size: 2- to 3-qt.

12-oz. bottle chili sauce

12-oz. jar hot pepper jelly

1½ lbs. little smokie wieners

1. Combine chili sauce and jelly in slow cooker. Add wieners.

2. Simmer on High until sauce thickens, about 1–2 hours.

3. Serve in buns, or over cooked rice or pasta. Or serve on a buffet from warm cooker, along with toothpicks to spear wieners.

Makes 10–12 servings

Cranberry Franks

LORETTA KRAHN • MOUNTAIN LAKE, MN

Prep Time: 10 minutes • Cooking Time: 1–2 hours • Ideal slow cooker size: 3-qt.

2 pkgs. cocktail wieners or
    little smoked sausages

16-oz. can jellied cranberry
    sauce

1 cup ketchup

3 Tbsp. brown sugar

1 Tbsp. lemon juice

1. Combine all ingredients in slow cooker.

2. Cover. Cook on High 1–2 hours.

Makes 15–20 servings

Note: This makes great picnic, potluck, or buffet food.

Smoked Sausage with Green Beans and New Potatoes

SHEILA SOLDNER • LITITZ, PA

Prep Time: 15 minutes • Cooking Time: 8–10 hours • Ideal slow cooker size: 4-qt.

2 cups water

1½ lbs. smoked sausage, cut into 4" pieces

2 medium-sized onions, quartered

1 qt. small new potatoes

2 qts. fresh green beans

salt and pepper to taste

1. Put water in slow cooker. Add sausage and then onions.

2. Layer potatoes on top. Place green beans over top. Salt and pepper to taste.

3. Cover and cook on Low 8–10 hours, or until vegetables are tender.

Makes 4–6 servings

Potluck Wiener Bake

RUTH ANN PENNER • HILLSBORO, KS

Prep Time: 8 minutes • Cooking Time: 3 hours • Ideal slow cooker size: 3-qt.

4 cups cooked potatoes, peeled and diced

10¾-oz. can cream of mushroom soup

1 cup mayonnaise

1 cup sauerkraut, drained

1 lb. wieners, sliced

1. Mix all ingredients in slow cooker.

2. Cover and cook on Low 3 hours.

Makes 6 servings

Cooking Tip

You'll get the best results from your slow cooker when it's two-thirds full. Then it's less likely to scorch around the edges (sometimes a problem with a too-empty cooker), or to not cook through (if the cooker's full to the brim). And if you're driving your two-thirds-full cooker to a potluck meal, the contents won't run out into your trunk as you go around corners.

Frankfurter Succotash

JUNE S. GROFF • DENVER, PA

Prep Time: 10 minutes • Cooking Time: 4–6 hours • Ideal slow cooker size: 2-qt.

1 lb. hot dogs, cut into ½" slices

2 10-oz. pkgs. frozen succotash, thawed and drained

10¾-oz. can cheddar cheese soup

1. Stir all ingredients together in slow cooker.

2. Cover and cook on Low 4–6 hours, or until vegetables are tender.

Makes 4–6 servings

Variation: Substitute cooked ham chunks for the hot dogs.

Sloppy Jane Sandwiches

KATHLEEN ROGGE • ALEXANDRIA, IN

Prep Time: 5–10 minutes • Cooking Time: 2–3 hours • Ideal slow cooker size: 2-qt.

1 pkg. hot dogs, cut into ¾" slices

28-oz. can baked beans

1 tsp. prepared mustard

1 tsp. instant minced onion

⅓ cup chili sauce

1. In slow cooker, combine all ingredients.

2. Cover and cook on Low 2–3 hours.

3. Spoon into toasted hot dog buns.

Makes 4–5 servings

Note: This recipe doubles easily.

Convenient Slow-Cooker Lasagna

RACHEL YODER • MIDDLEBURY, IN

Prep Time: 30–45 minutes • Cooking Time: 4 hours • Ideal slow cooker size: 6-qt.

1 lb. ground beef

29-oz. can tomato sauce

8-oz. pkg. lasagna noodles, uncooked

4 cups shredded mozzarella cheese

1½ cups cottage cheese

1. Spray slow cooker with nonstick cooking spray.

2. Brown ground beef in a large nonstick skillet. Drain off drippings.

3. Stir in tomato sauce. Mix well.

4. Spread one-fourth of meat sauce on bottom of slow cooker.

5. Arrange one-third of uncooked noodles over sauce. (I usually break them up so they fit better.)

6. Combine cheeses in a bowl. Spoon one-third of cheeses over noodles.

7. Repeat these layers twice.

8. Top with remaining sauce.

9. Cover and cook on Low 4 hours.

Makes 6–8 servings

Variations: Add 1 chopped onion to the ground beef in Step 2; or add 1 tsp. salt to the tomato sauce and beef in Step 3; or add ½ cup grated Parmesan cheese to the mozzarella and cottage cheeses in Step 6; or add ½ cup additional shredded mozzarella cheese to the top of the lasagna 5 minutes before serving.

Slow-Cooker Lasagna

MARY JANE MUSSER • MANHEIM, PA / JANET OBERHOLTZER • EPHRATA, PA
ELEYA RAIM • OXFORD, IA / ORPHA HERR • ANDOVER, NY

Prep Time: 15 minutes • Cooking Time: 4 hours • Ideal slow cooker size: 4-qt.

12-oz. pkg. lasagna noodles

half a stick (¼ cup) butter

1½ lbs. ground beef

1 qt. spaghetti sauce

8 ozs. Velveeta cheese, cubed,
   or your choice of cheeses

1. Cook noodles according to package directions. Drain. Return cooked noodles to saucepan and stir in butter until melted.

2. While noodles are cooking, brown beef in a nonstick skillet. Drain off drippings.

3. Then layer into slow cooker one-fourth of sauce, one-third of browned beef, one-third of cooked noodles, and one-third of cubed cheese.

4. Repeat these layers 2 more times, ending with one-fourth of sauce.

5. Cover and cook on Low 3–4 hours, or until heated through and cheese has melted.

Makes 6–8 servings

Cheesy Cheddar Lasagna

LUANNA J. HOCHSTEDLER • EAST EARL, PA

Prep Time: 15 minutes • Cooking Time: 3–8 hours • Ideal slow cooker size: 3-qt.

1 lb. ground beef

14-oz. jar spaghetti sauce, or
   about 1½ cups if you're
   using homemade sauce

1 cup water

12-oz. box macaroni and
   cheese, uncooked, divided

8 ozs. cottage cheese

½ cup shredded mozzarella
   cheese

1. Brown ground beef in a nonstick skillet. Drain off drippings. Then mix spaghetti sauce and water into beef in skillet.

2. Place half of meat mixture into slow cooker. Top with half of uncooked macaroni and cheese dinner and half of its sauce packet.

3. Spoon cottage cheese over top.

4. Add remaining meat.

5. Then add remaining macaroni and cheese and remainder of sauce packet.

6. Sprinkle with mozzarella cheese.

7. Cover and cook on Low 6–8 hours, or on High 3–4 hours, or until macaroni is tender and cheeses are melted.

Makes 4 servings

Lazy Lasagna

BARB HARVEY • QUARRYVILLE, PA

Prep Time: 30 minutes • Cooking Time: 3¼–4¼ hours • Ideal slow cooker size: 4-qt.

1 lb. ground beef

12-oz. pkg. egg noodles

32-oz. jar spaghetti sauce, your choice of flavors

8 ozs. mozzarella cheese, shredded

16 ozs. cottage cheese

1. Brown ground beef in a nonstick skillet. Drain off drippings.

2. While beef is browning, cook noodles according to package directions. Drain. Return cooked noodles to saucepan.

3. Stir spaghetti sauce into browned and drained ground beef.

4. Stir mozzarella and cottage cheeses into cooked noodles.

5. Layer one-third of sauce into bottom of slow cooker. Top with half of noodles, followed by half of cheeses.

6. Layer in half of remaining sauce, followed by all remaining noodles and cheeses. Top with rest of sauce.

7. Cover and cook on Low 3–4 hours.

Makes 10 servings

Cooking Tip

Allow cooked pasta dishes, especially those with cheese, as well as egg dishes, to stand 10–15 minutes before serving so that they can absorb their juices and firm up.

Quick-'n'-Easy Meat-Free Lasagna

RHONDA FREED • LOWVILLE, NY

Prep Time: 10 minutes • Cooking Time: 3–4 hours • Ideal slow cooker size: 4-qt.

28-oz. jar spaghetti sauce, your choice of flavors

6–7 uncooked lasagna noodles

2 cups shredded mozzarella cheese, divided

15 ozs. ricotta cheese

¼ cup grated Parmesan cheese

1. Spread one-fourth of sauce in bottom of slow cooker.

2. Lay 2 noodles, broken into 1" pieces, over sauce.

3. In a bowl, mix together 1½ cups mozzarella cheese and all ricotta and Parmesan cheeses.

4. Spoon half of cheese mixture onto noodles and spread out to edges.

5. Spoon in one-third of remaining sauce, and then 2 more broken noodles.

6. Spread remaining cheese mixture over top, then one-half of remaining sauce and all remaining noodles.

7. Finish with remaining sauce.

8. Cover and cook on Low 3–4 hours, or until noodles are tender and cheeses are melted.

9. Add ½ cup mozzarella cheese and cook until cheese melts.

Makes 6 servings

Note: Always taste the food you've prepared before serving it, so you can correct the seasonings, if necessary.

Spaghetti and Sauce

BEVERLY FLATT GETZ • WARRIORS MARK, PA

Prep Time: 15 minutes • Cooking Time: 4–8 hours • Ideal slow cooker size: 4-qt.

1½ lbs. ground beef

1 large onion, chopped

26-oz. jar spaghetti sauce with mushrooms

10½-oz. can tomato soup

14-oz. can stewed, or petite diced, tomatoes

1 soup can water

OPTIONAL SEASONINGS:

minced garlic, to taste

Italian seasoning, to taste

onion salt, to taste

1. Sauté ground beef and onion in a large nonstick skillet just until meat is browned.

2. Place meat and onion in slow cooker. Stir in spaghetti sauce, tomato soup, tomatoes, water, and any optional seasonings you would like.

3. Cover and cook on High 4 hours, or on Low 6–8 hours.

4. It's ready to serve over your favorite pasta!

Makes 8 servings

Creamy Spaghetti

KENDRA DREPS • LIBERTY, PA

Prep Time: 30 minutes • Cooking Time: 2–4 hours • Ideal slow cooker size: 4- to 5-qt.

1 lb. dry spaghetti

1 lb. ground beef, or loose sausage

1 lb. 10-oz. jar spaghetti sauce, your favorite flavor

1 lb. Velveeta cheese, cubed

10¾-oz. can cream of mushroom soup

1. Cook spaghetti according to package directions. Drain. Then place in a large mixing bowl.

2. In a nonstick skillet, brown ground beef or sausage. Drain off drippings. Then add to cooked spaghetti in large bowl.

3. Stir remaining ingredients into bowl. Mix together well, and then place in slow cooker.

4. Cook on Low 2–4 hours, or until heated through.

Makes 10–12 servings

Slow-Cooker Pizza

LIZ RUGG • WAYLAND, IA

Prep Time: 30 minutes ▪ Cooking Time: 2–3 hours ▪ Ideal slow cooker size: 4-qt.

12-oz. bag Kluski, or sturdy, noodles

1½ lbs. ground beef

32-oz. jar spaghetti sauce, your choice of flavors

16 ozs. mozzarella cheese, shredded

8 ozs. pepperoni, thinly sliced

1. Cook noodles according to directions on package. Drain.

2. While noodles are cooking, brown ground beef in a nonstick skillet. Drain off drippings.

3. Meanwhile, grease slow cooker.

4. Pour in one-fourth of spaghetti sauce. Follow with half of noodles, and then half of browned ground beef. Top with one-third of shredded cheese. Follow with half of pepperoni.

5. Repeat the layers, beginning with one-third of sauce, followed by a layer of remaining noodles, a layer of remaining ground beef, half of cheese, and remaining pepperoni.

6. Top with remaining spaghetti sauce. Finish with rest of cheese.

7. Cover and cook on Low 2–3 hours, or until heated through and until cheese has melted.

Makes 8–10 servings

Variation: Add sliced mushrooms, chopped or sliced onions, sliced black olives, and diced green peppers to one or more of the layers, if you wish.

Tortellini with Broccoli

SUSAN KASTING • JENKS, OK

Prep Time: 10 minutes ▪ Cooking Time: 2½–3 hours ▪ Ideal slow cooker size: 4-qt.

½ cup water

26-oz. jar pasta sauce, your favorite

1 Tbsp. Italian seasoning

9-oz. pkg. frozen spinach and cheese tortellini

16-oz. pkg. frozen broccoli florets

1. In a bowl, mix water, pasta sauce, and seasoning together.

2. Pour one-third of sauce into bottom of slow cooker. Top with all tortellini.

3. Pour one-third of sauce over tortellini. Top with broccoli.

4. Pour remaining sauce over broccoli.

5. Cook on High 2½–3 hours, or until broccoli and pasta are tender but not mushy.

Makes 4 servings

Beef Ravioli Casserole

ELIZABETH COLUCCI • LANCASTER, PA

Prep Time: 30 minutes • Cooking Time: 2½–3 hours • Ideal slow cooker size: 3-qt.

10-oz. pkg. beef ravioli

16-oz. jar spaghetti sauce, with peppers, mushrooms, and onions, divided

½ cup Italian bread crumbs

1 cup mozzarella cheese

¼ cup Parmesan cheese, optional

½ cup cheddar cheese

1. Cook ravioli according to package directions. Drain.

2. Spoon enough spaghetti sauce into slow cooker to cover bottom. Place ravioli on top.

3. Cover with remaining sauce. Top with bread crumbs. Sprinkle with cheeses.

4. Stir to mix together well.

5. Cover and cook on Low 2½–3 hours, or until heated through but without overcooking pasta.

Makes 4–6 servings

Chicken Broccoli Alfredo

MRS. MAHLON MILLER • HUTCHINSON, KS

Prep Time: 30 minutes • Cooking Time: 1–2 hours • Ideal slow cooker size: 3-qt.

8-oz. pkg. noodles, or spaghetti (half a 16-oz. pkg.)

1½ cups fresh or frozen broccoli

1 lb. uncooked boneless, skinless chicken breasts, cubed

10¾-oz. can cream of mushroom soup

½ cup grated mild cheddar cheese

1. Cook noodles according to package directions, adding broccoli during last 4 minutes of cooking time. Drain.

2. Sauté chicken in a nonstick skillet, or cook in the microwave, until no longer pink in center.

3. Combine all ingredients in slow cooker.

4. Cover and cook on Low 1–2 hours, or until heated through and cheese is melted.

Makes 4 servings

Cheesy Chicken and Macaroni

LUANNA J. HOCHSTEDLER • EAST EARL, PA

Prep Time: 5–10 minutes • Cooking Time: 4–7 hours • Ideal slow cooker size: 3- to 4-qt.

4 small boneless, skinless chicken breast halves

7¼-oz. pkg. macaroni and cheese dinner, uncooked

1 cup shredded cheddar cheese

2 cups water

2 cups frozen vegetable blend, thawed

½ cup water, optional

1. Place chicken in slow cooker.

2. Sprinkle contents of macaroni and cheese dinner's sauce packet over chicken.

3. Pour dry macaroni on top.

4. Sprinkle with cheddar cheese.

5. Pour water over all, being careful not to wash off cheddar cheese.

6. Cover and cook on High 2 hours, or on Low 4 hours.

7. Stir in thawed vegetables, mixing them in thoroughly. Add ½ cup water if needed to keep dish from cooking dry.

8. Cover and cook on High another hour, or on Low another 2–3 hours, or until vegetables are tender but pasta is not mushy or dry.

Makes 4–6 servings

Creamy Cooker Dinner

ANNA MUSSER • MANHEIM, PA

Prep Time: 7 minutes • Cooking Time: 2½–3 hours • Ideal slow cooker size: 5-qt.

2 cups shredded cheese, your choice

2 cups macaroni, uncooked

3 cups milk

2 10¾-oz. cans cream of mushroom soup

2 cups cooked ham, or sliced hot dogs, or cooked, cubed chicken, or cooked ground beef

1. Place all ingredients in slow cooker. Mix together gently, until well blended.

2. Cover and cook on High 2½–3 hours, or until macaroni is cooked but not overdone.

Makes 6 servings

Macaroni and Cheese

CYNTHIA MORRIS • GROTTOES, VA / JENNIFER A. CROUSE • MT. CRAWFORD, VA / ESTHER S. MARTIN • EPHRATA, PA / AUDREY L. KNEER • WILLIAMSFIELD, IL / VIRGINIA EBERLY • LOYSVILLE, PA

Prep Time: 5 minutes • Cooking Time: 3 hours • Ideal slow cooker size: 3-qt.

1-3 Tbsp. butter, melted, depending upon how rich you'd like the dish to be

1½ cups uncooked macaroni

1 qt. milk

8-12 ozs. grated sharp cheddar cheese, or cubed Velveeta cheese (not the low-fat variety)

½-1 tsp. salt, depending upon your taste and dietary preferences

¼ tsp. pepper

1. Stir all ingredients together in slow cooker.

2. Cover and cook on Low 3 hours.

   Makes 4–5 servings

Lotsa Cheese Macaroni and Cheese

RENEE BAUM • CHAMBERSBURG, PA

Prep Time: 15 minutes • Cooking Time: 3 hours • Ideal slow cooker size: 3-qt.

1 lb. dry macaroni

1 lb. Velveeta cheese, cubed

8 ozs. extra-sharp cheddar cheese, shredded

1 qt. milk

1 stick (½ cup) butter, cut into small chunks

1. Follow package instructions for preparing macaroni, but cook macaroni only half the amount of time called for. Drain. Pour macaroni into slow cooker.

2. Add remaining ingredients and stir together well.

3. Cover and cook on High 3 hours, stirring occasionally.

   Makes 10 servings

Cheesy Macaronis

RENEE SUYDAM • LANCASTER, PA / PATRICIA FLEISCHER • CARLISLE, PA
RUTH ZENDT • MIFFLINTOWN, PA

Prep Time: 30 minutes • Cooking Time: 3 hours • Ideal slow cooker size: 6-qt.

1 lb. dry macaroni

12-oz. can evaporated milk

3 cups milk

2 lbs. Velveeta cheese, cubed,
or sharp cheese, shredded

1. Cook macaroni according to package directions. Drain.

2. Put both milks in slow cooker. Cube cheese and add to milk.

3. Stir in cooked macaroni.

4. Cover and cook on Low 3 hours.

Makes 10–12 servings

Variations: Add ¼ cup onion, finely chopped, to Step 2. Or add ¼ tsp. chili powder to Step 2.

Two-Cheeses Macaroni

MARY STAUFFER • EPHRATA, PA / RUTH ANN BENDER • COCHRANVILLE, PA
ESTHER BURKHOLDER • MILLERSTOWN, PA

Prep Time: 8–10 minutes • Cooking Time: 2½ hours • Ideal slow cooker size: 4- to 5-qt.

1 stick (½ cup) butter, cut in
pieces

2 cups uncooked macaroni

2 cups grated sharp cheese,
divided

24 ozs. small-curd cottage
cheese

2½ cups boiling water

1. Place butter in bottom of slow cooker. Add uncooked macaroni, 1½ cups shredded cheese, and cottage cheese. Stir together until well mixed.

2. Pour boiling water over everything. Do not stir.

3. Cover and cook on High 2 hours.

4. Stir. Sprinkle with remaining ½ cup grated cheese.

5. Allow dish to stand 10–15 minutes before serving to allow sauce to thicken.

Makes 6 servings

Creamy Spirals

JANET OBERHOLTZER • EPHRATA, PA / RENEE BAUM • CHAMBERSBURG, PA

Prep Time: 30 minutes • Cooking Time: 2–2½ hours • Ideal slow cooker size: 4- to 5-qt.

1 lb. uncooked spiral pasta

¾ stick (6 Tbsp.) butter

2 cups half-and-half

10¾-oz. can cheddar cheese soup

2–4 cups shredded cheddar cheese, depending upon how creamy you'd like the dish to be

1. Cook pasta according to package directions, being careful not to overcook. Drain.

2. Return pasta to saucepan. Stir in butter until it melts.

3. Combine half-and-half and soup in slow cooker, blending well.

4. Stir pasta and shredded cheese into mixture in cooker.

5. Cover and cook on Low 2–2½ hours, or until heated through and cheese melts. (If you're home, stir dish at end of first hour of cooking.)

Makes 10–12 servings

Lemon Dijon Fish

JUNE S. GROFF • DENVER, PA

Prep Time: 10 minutes • Cooking Time: 3 hours • Ideal slow cooker size: 2-qt.

1½ lbs. orange roughy fillets

2 Tbsp. Dijon mustard

3 Tbsp. butter, melted

1 tsp. Worcestershire sauce

1 Tbsp. lemon juice

1. Cut fillets to fit in slow cooker.

2. In a bowl, mix remaining ingredients together. Pour sauce over fish. (If you have to stack fish, spoon a portion of sauce over first layer of fish before adding second layer.)

3. Cover and cook on Low 3 hours, or until fish flakes easily but is not dry or overcooked.

Makes 4 servings

Salmon Soufflé

BETTY B. DENNISON • GROVE CITY, PA / ANNE TOWNSEND • ALBUQUERQUE, NM

Prep Time: 5 minutes • Cooking Time: 2–3 hours • Ideal slow cooker size: 2- to 3-qt.

15-oz. can salmon, drained and flaked

2 eggs, beaten well

2 cups seasoned croutons

1 cup grated cheddar cheese

2 chicken bouillon cubes

1 cup boiling water

1/4 tsp. dry mustard, optional

1. Grease slow cooker with nonstick cooking spray.

2. Combine salmon, eggs, croutons, and cheese in cooker.

3. Dissolve bouillon cubes in boiling water in a small bowl. Add mustard, if you wish, and stir. Pour over salmon mixture and stir together lightly.

4. Cover and cook on High 2–3 hours, or until mixture appears to be set. Allow to stand 15 minutes before serving.

Makes 4 servings

Tuna Loaf

TINA GOSS • DUENWEG, MO

Prep Time: 5 minutes • Cooking Time: 1 hour • Ideal slow cooker size: 2-qt.

10 3/4-oz. can cream of mushroom soup, divided

3/4 cup milk, divided

2 eggs, beaten

2 cups dry stuffing mix

12-oz. can tuna, drained and flaked

1. Place two-thirds of undiluted soup and 1/2 cup milk in a small saucepan. Blend together; then set aside.

2. Grease slow cooker with nonstick cooking spray. Mix remaining ingredients, except reserved soup and milk, together in slow cooker.

3. Cover and cook on High 1 hour. Allow to stand 15 minutes before serving.

4. Meanwhile, heat reserved soup and milk in saucepan. Serve over cooked tuna as a sauce.

Makes 4 servings

Note: If you wish, add 1/2 tsp. salt and 1/4 tsp. pepper to Step 2.

VEGETABLES

Barbecued Beans

MARY ANN BOWMAN • EAST EARL, PA

Prep Time: 10 minutes • Cooking Time: 3–4 hours • Ideal slow cooker size: 4-qt.

2 16-oz. cans baked beans, your choice of variety

2 15-oz. cans kidney or pinto beans, or one of each, drained

½ cup brown sugar

1 cup ketchup

1 onion, chopped

1. Combine all ingredients in slow cooker. Mix well.

2. Cover and cook on Low 3–4 hours, or until heated through.

Makes 8–10 servings

Barbecued Baked Beans

ANNE NOLT • THOMPSONTOWN, PA

Prep Time: 15 minutes • Cooking Time: 3 hours • Ideal slow cooker size: 3-qt.

6 slices uncooked bacon, cut into pieces

2 15-oz. cans pork and beans

1 tsp. dry mustard, or 1 Tbsp. prepared mustard

½ cup ketchup

¾ cup brown sugar

1. Brown bacon in a nonstick skillet until crispy. Drain.

2. Mix with all remaining ingredients in slow cooker.

3. Cover and cook on High 3 hours. Remove cover during last 30 minutes to allow some of juice to cook off.

Makes 6–8 servings

Bonnie's Baked Beans

F. ELAINE ASPER • NORTON, OH

Prep Time: 15–20 minutes • Cooking Time: 3–8 hours • Ideal slow cooker size: 4-qt.

½ lb. bacon, cut into ½" pieces

2 28-oz. cans pork and beans

2 medium-sized onions,
    chopped into 1½" pieces

¾ cup brown sugar

1 cup ketchup

1. Brown bacon in a nonstick skillet until crispy. Drain.

2. Place all ingredients into slow cooker.

3. Cover and cook on High 3 hours, or on Low 7–8 hours.

   Makes 12–14 servings

Variation: Add 2 green peppers in Step 2, cut into 1" pieces.

Mac's Beans

WILMA HABERKAMP • FAIRBANK, IA / MABEL SHIRK • MOUNT CRAWFORD, VA

Prep Time: 20 minutes • Cooking Time: 4 hours • Ideal slow cooker size: 3- to 4-qt.

4 slices bacon

3 15-oz. cans kidney beans,
    drained, or other beans of
    your choice

1 cup chili sauce

½ cup sliced scallions, or red
    onions

⅓ cup brown sugar

1. In a small nonstick skillet, brown bacon until crisp. Reserve drippings. Crumble bacon.

2. Combine all ingredients except brown sugar in slow cooker. Sprinkle brown sugar over top.

3. Cover and cook on Low 4 hours.

4. Serve beans directly from slow cooker.

   Makes 6–8 servings

Variations: Use regular onions instead of green onions. Or use canned lima beans instead of kidney beans.

Barbecued Beans and Beef

JOAN MILLER • WAYLAND, IA

Prep Time: 20–25 minutes • Cooking Time: 9–11 hours • Ideal slow cooker size: 3½- to 4-qt.

1 medium-sized onion, chopped

3 slices bacon, cut into squares

1½ lbs. boneless beef chuck roast, or ribs

½ cup barbecue sauce

3 16-oz. cans baked beans (not pork and beans!)

1. Mix onion and bacon together in slow cooker.

2. Top with beef. Pour barbecue sauce over beef.

3. Cover and cook on Low 8–10 hours, or until beef is tender but not dried out.

4. Remove beef from slow cooker and place on cutting board. Cut beef into ½" pieces.

5. Pour juices from slow cooker through a strainer into a small bowl. Reserve onion, bacon, and only ½ cup of cooking juices.

6. Return cut-up beef, onions, bacon, and reserved ½ cup juices to slow cooker. Stir in baked beans.

7. Cover and cook on High 40–50 minutes, or until heated throughout.

Makes 6 servings

Slow-Cooker Baked Beans

KIMBERLY BURKHOLDER • MILLERSTOWN, PA

Prep Time: 15 minutes • Cooking Time: 6 hours, after beans are soaked • Ideal slow cooker size: 4-qt.

2½ cups dry pinto, or kidney, beans

2½ qts. water

4 cups water

2 cups pizza sauce

3 Tbsp. sorghum molasses

2 tsp. chili powder

2 tsp. salt

2 slices bacon, fried and crumbled, optional

1. Place dry beans in a large soup kettle. Cover with 2½ qts. water. Allow to soak 8 hours or overnight. Drain. Or, for a quicker method, bring beans to a boil after covering with 2½ qts. water. Boil, covered, for 2 minutes. Turn off heat and allow beans to stand 1 hour, covered. Drain.

2. Place beans and 4 cups fresh water in slow cooker.

3. Add remaining ingredients, stirring together well.

4. Cook on Low 6 hours, or until beans are tender.

Makes 6 servings

Full Meal Deal Beans

REITA YODER • CARLSBAD, NM

Prep Time: 25 minutes • Cooking Time: 7–8 hours, after beans are soaked • Ideal slow cooker size: 2-qt.

3 cups dry pinto beans, sorted
and washed

3 qts. water

1 ham bone with lots of ham
still hanging on!

1 bunch scallions, chopped

1 Tbsp. cumin, optional

5½ cups water

10¾-oz. can Rotel chili and
tomatoes

salt to taste, optional

1. Place dry beans in a large soup kettle and cover with 3 qts.
water. Cover and allow to stand 8 hours or overnight. Or
for a quicker method, follow the same directions, but
instead of having beans stand 8 hours, bring them to a
boil and cook 2 minutes. Keep beans covered, remove
from heat, and allow to stand 1 hour. Drain beans.

2. Place ham bone, green onions, and cumin, if you wish, in
bottom of slow cooker.

3. Put drained beans on top. Add 5½ cups fresh water and
tomatoes.

4. Cover and cook on High 7–8 hours, or until beans are soft.

5. Stir in salt, if you wish. Let stand 15 minutes before serving.

Makes 10–12 servings

Makes-a-Meal Baked Beans

RUTH FISHER • LEICESTER, NY

Prep Time: 15 minutes • Cooking Time: 3 hours • Ideal slow cooker size: 3-qt.

1 lb. ground beef

½ cup chopped onions

½ tsp. taco seasoning, or more

1 or 2 15-oz. cans pork and
beans

¾ cup barbecue sauce

1. Brown ground beef and onions in a nonstick skillet. Drain.

2. Stir all ingredients together in slow cooker, including
browned ground beef and onions.

3. Cover and cook on Low 3 hours.

Makes 6–8 servings

Baked Limas

ELEANOR LARSON • GLEN LYON, PA

Prep Time: 1½–8 hours • Cooking Time: 4–8 hours • Ideal slow cooker size: 10- to 12-qt.

1 lb. dried lima beans

2½ qts. water

¼ lb. bacon, cut into squares

¼ cup molasses

2 Tbsp. brown sugar

1 cup tomato sauce

1. Wash beans. Place in a large soup kettle. Cover with 2½ qts. water. Cover and soak 8 hours or overnight. Drain, reserving soaking water. Or for a quicker method, bring beans to a boil in 2½ qts. water. Cover and continue boiling 2 minutes. Remove from heat, keep covered, and allow to stand 1 hour. Drain, reserving soaking water.

2. Meanwhile, brown bacon in a nonstick skillet until crispy. Drain.

3. Place soaked beans in slow cooker. Add remaining ingredients and stir. Add enough bean water to cover beans.

4. Cover and cook on Low 8 hours, or on High 4 hours, or until beans are tender but not mushy.

Makes 6 servings

Barbecued Black Beans with Sweet Potatoes

BARBARA JEAN FABEL • WAUSAU, WI

Prep Time: 15 minutes • Cooking Time: 2–4 hours • Ideal slow cooker size: 3-qt.

4 large sweet potatoes, peeled and cut into 8 chunks each

15-oz. can black beans, rinsed and drained

1 medium-sized onion, diced

2 ribs celery, sliced

9 ozs. Sweet Baby Ray's Barbecue Sauce

1. Place sweet potatoes in slow cooker.

2. Combine remaining ingredients. Pour over sweet potatoes.

3. Cover. Cook on High 2–3 hours, or on Low 4 hours.

Makes 4–6 servings

Cooking Tip

Yams and sweet potatoes are not the same. Yams are much drier. Likewise, there are many varieties of apples, from very tart to very sweet, from firm texture to soft. Experiment with different kinds to discover your favorite for a recipe.

Creamy Broccoli

CAROLYN FULTZ • ANGOLA, IN

Prep Time: 10 minutes • Cooking Time: 2½–6 hours • Ideal slow cooker size: 3-qt.

2 10-oz. pkgs. frozen broccoli spears, thawed and cut up

10¾-oz. can cream of celery soup

1¼ cups grated sharp cheddar cheese, divided

¼ cup minced scallions

1 cup saltine crackers, crushed

1. Spray slow cooker with nonstick cooking spray.

2. Combine broccoli, soup, 1 cup cheese, and onion in slow cooker.

3. Sprinkle top with crackers and remaining cheese.

4. Cover and cook on Low 5–6 hours, or on High 2½–3 hours.

Makes 4–5 servings

Golden Cauliflower

ROSALIE D. MILLER • MIFFLINTOWN, PA / DEDE PETERSON • RAPID CITY, SD

Prep Time: 5–10 minutes • Cooking Time: 1½–5 hours • Ideal slow cooker size: 3-qt.

2 10-oz. pkgs. frozen cauliflower, thawed

salt and pepper

10¾-oz. can condensed cheddar cheese soup

4 slices bacon, crisply fried and crumbled

1. Place cauliflower in slow cooker. Season with salt and pepper.

2. Spoon soup over top. Sprinkle with bacon.

3. Cover and cook on High 1½ hours, or on Low 4–5 hours, or until cauliflower is tender.

Makes 4–6 servings

Note: If you forgot to thaw the cauliflower, cook the dish 30 minutes longer.

Steamed Carrots

DEDE PETERSON • RAPID CITY, SD

Prep Time: 15–20 minutes • Cooking Time: 4–6 hours • Ideal slow cooker size: 4-qt.

8 large carrots, sliced
   diagonally

1/4 cup water

2 Tbsp. butter

1 tsp. sugar

1/4 tsp. salt

1. Layer carrots in slow cooker. Add water and pieces of butter. Sprinkle with sugar and salt.

2. Cover and cook on Low 4–6 hours.

   Makes 4 servings

Slow-Cooked Glazed Carrots

MICHELE RUVOLA • SELDEN, NY

Prep Time: 5 minutes • Cooking Time: 6½–8½ hours • Ideal slow cooker size: 3- to 4-qt.

2-lb. bag baby carrots

1½ cups water

1/4 cup honey

2 Tbsp. butter

1/4 tsp. salt

1/8 tsp. pepper

1. Combine carrots and water in slow cooker.

2. Cover and cook on Low 6–8 hours, or until carrots are tender.

3. Drain carrots and return to slow cooker.

4. Stir in honey, butter, salt, and pepper. Mix well.

5. Cover and cook on Low 30 minutes, or until glazed.

   Makes 6–7 servings

Golden Carrots

JAN MAST • LANCASTER, PA

Prep Time: 5 minutes • Cooking Time: 3–4 hours • Ideal slow cooker size: 2-qt.

2-lb. pkg. baby carrots

$\frac{1}{2}$ cup golden raisins

1 stick ($\frac{1}{2}$ cup) butter, melted
    or softened

$\frac{1}{3}$ cup honey

2 Tbsp. lemon juice

$\frac{1}{2}$ tsp. ginger, optional

1. Combine all ingredients in slow cooker.

2. Cover and cook on Low 3–4 hours, or until carrots are tender-crisp.

Makes 6 servings

Note: To use whole carrots, cut into 1"-long chunks. If the carrots are thick, you may need to cook them 5–6 hours until they become tender-crisp.

Apricot-Glazed Carrots

MARCIA S. MYER • MANHEIM, PA

Prep Time: 5 minutes • Cooking Time: 9 hours, plus 10–15 minutes • Ideal slow cooker size: 4-qt.

2 lbs. baby carrots

1 onion, chopped

$\frac{1}{2}$ cup water

$\frac{1}{3}$ cup honey

$\frac{1}{3}$ cup apricot preserves

2 Tbsp. chopped fresh parsley

1. Place carrots and onions in slow cooker. Add water.

2. Cover and cook on Low 9 hours.

3. Drain liquid from slow cooker.

4. In a small bowl, mix honey and preserves together. Pour over carrots.

5. Cover and cook on High 10–15 minutes.

6. Sprinkle with parsley before serving.

Makes 8 servings

Glazed Carrots

GLORIA FREY • LEBANON, PA

Prep Time: 10–15 minutes • Cooking Time: 2½–3½ hours • Ideal slow cooker size: 2-qt.

16-oz. pkg. frozen baby carrots

¼ cup apple cider, or apple juice

¼ cup apple jelly

1½ tsp. Dijon mustard

1. Put carrots and apple juice in slow cooker.

2. Cover and cook on High 2–3 hours, until carrots are tender.

3. Blend jelly and mustard together in a small bowl.

4. During last 45 minutes of cooking time, after carrots are tender, stir in blended apple jelly and mustard. Continue to heat until steaming hot.

Makes 4 servings

Candied Carrots

ARLENE M. KOPP • LINEBORO, MD

Prep Time: 10 minutes • Cooking Time: 2½–3½ hours • Ideal slow cooker size: 3-qt.

1 lb. carrots, cut into 1" pieces

½ tsp. salt

¼ cup water

2 Tbsp. butter

½ cup light brown sugar, firmly packed

2 Tbsp. chopped nuts

1. Place carrots in slow cooker. Sprinkle with salt.

2. Pour water in along side of cooker.

3. Cover and cook on High 2–3 hours, or until carrots are just tender. Drain.

4. Stir in butter. Sprinkle with sugar.

5. Cover and cook on High 30 minutes.

6. Sprinkle with nuts about 10 minutes before end of cooking time.

Makes 3–4 servings

Carrot Casserole

JANESSA HOCHSTEDLER • EAST EARL, PA

Prep Time: 20 minutes • Cooking Time: 4–5 hours • Ideal slow cooker size: 2-qt.

4 cups sliced carrots

1 medium-sized onion, chopped

10¾-oz. can cream of celery soup

½ cup Velveeta cheese, cubed

¼–½ tsp. salt

1. Mix all ingredients in slow cooker.

2. Cover and cook on Low 4–5 hours, or until carrots are tender but not mushy.

Makes 4–5 servings

Zippy Vegetable Medley

GLORIA FREY • LEBANON, PA

Prep Time: 10–15 minutes • Cooking Time: 2½ hours • Ideal slow cooker size: 2-qt.

16-oz. pkg. frozen broccoli, cauliflower, and carrots

16-oz. pkg. frozen corn

2 10½-oz. cans fiesta nacho cheese soup

½ cup milk

1. Combine broccoli mixture and corn in slow cooker.

2. Combine soups and milk in a microwave-safe bowl. Microwave 1 minute on High, or just enough to mix well. When blended, pour over vegetables.

3. Cover and cook on High 2½ hours, or until hot and bubbly and vegetables are done to your liking.

Makes 4–5 servings

Garden Vegetables

ESTHER GINGERICH • PARNELL, IA / JUDY A. AND SHARON WANTLAND • MENOMONEE FALLS, WI

Prep Time: 15 minutes • Cooking Time: 2½–4 hours • Ideal slow cooker size: 3-qt.

16-oz. pkg. frozen vegetables, thawed (combination of broccoli, carrots, cauliflower, etc.)

10¾-oz. can cream of mushroom soup

half a soup can water

⅓ cup sour cream

1–2 cups shredded Swiss, or mozzarella, cheese, divided

6-oz. can French-fried onions, divided

1. In slow cooker, combine thawed vegetables, soup, water, sour cream, half of cheese, and half of onions.

2. Cover and cook on Low 2½–4 hours, or until vegetables are as soft as you like them.

3. Fifteen minutes before end of cooking time, sprinkle remaining cheese and onions on top.

Makes 6 servings

Creamy Vegetables

GLORIA FREY • LEBANON, PA

Prep Time: 5–10 minutes • Cooking Time: 2½–3½ hours • Ideal slow cooker size: 2- to 3-qt.

16-oz. pkg. frozen broccoli and cauliflower

10¾-oz. can cream of mushroom soup

8-oz. carton spreadable garden vegetable cream cheese

1 cup seasoned croutons

1. Place frozen vegetables in slow cooker.

2. Put soup and cream cheese in a microwave-safe bowl. Microwave on High 1 minute. Stir soup and cheese together until smooth. Microwave 30–60 seconds more, if necessary, to melt the ingredients.

3. Pour cheesy soup over vegetables in slow cooker and mix well.

4. Cover and cook on Low 2½–3½ hours, or until vegetables are tender.

5. Thirty minutes before end of cooking time, sprinkle croutons over top. Continue to cook, uncovered.

Makes 4–5 servings

Company Corn

SHERRIL BIEBERLY • SALINA, KS / JEANNINE JANZEN • ELBING, KS

Prep Time: 5-10 minutes • Cooking Time: 5 hours • Ideal slow cooker size: 3- to 4-qt.

2 20-oz. pkgs. frozen corn

½ tsp. salt

2-4 Tbsp. sugar, according to your taste preference

1 stick (½ cup) butter

8-oz. pkg. cream cheese

1. Place frozen corn in slow cooker. Stir in salt and sugar.

2. Cut butter and cream cheese into little pieces and place on top of corn.

3. Cook on Low for 5 hours, stirring occasionally if you're at home and able to do so.

Makes 8-10 servings

Corn Pudding

CLARA NEWSWANGER • GORDONVILLE, PA

Prep Time: 10-15 minutes • Cooking Time: 4 hours • Ideal slow cooker size: 3-qt.

¼-½ cup sugar, according to your taste preference

3 Tbsp. cornstarch

2 eggs, slightly beaten

12-oz. can evaporated milk

16-oz. can cream-style corn

1. Combine all ingredients except corn in slow cooker until well blended.

2. Add corn. Mix well.

3. Cook on Low 4 hours. Allow to stand 15 minutes before serving.

Makes 4-5 servings

Cooking Tip

If there is too much liquid in your cooker, stick a toothpick under the edge of the lid to tilt it slightly and to allow the steam to escape.

—*Carol Sherwood, Batavia, NY*

Sweet Dried Corn

SHELIA HEIL • LANCASTER, PA

Prep Time: 5 minutes ▪ Cooking Time: 2–2½ hours ▪ Ideal slow cooker size: 4-qt.

5 15-oz. cans whole-kernel corn, drained

1 stick (½ cup) butter, at room temperature

¾ cup brown sugar

1. Place corn in slow cooker. Add butter and brown sugar. Stir to combine.

2. Cook on High until hot, about 1½ hours. Stir. Continue cooking on Low another 30–60 minutes, or until corn is very hot.

Makes 14 servings

Dried Corn

MARY B. SENSENIG • NEW HOLLAND, PA

Prep Time: 3–5 minutes ▪ Cooking Time: 4 hours ▪ Ideal slow cooker size: 3-qt.

15-oz. can froze-dried corn

2 Tbsp. sugar

3 Tbsp. butter, softened

1 tsp. salt

1 cup half-and-half

2 Tbsp. water

1. Place all ingredients in slow cooker. Mix together well.

2. Cover and cook on Low 4 hours.

Makes 4 servings

Note: If you're able, check after cooking 3 hours to make sure the corn isn't cooking dry. If it appears to be, stir in an additional ¼–½ cup half-and-half. Cover and continue cooking.

Green Beans au Gratin

DONNA LANTGEN • CHADRON, NE

Prep Time: 10 minutes • Cooking Time: 5–6 hours • Ideal slow cooker size: 4-qt.

2 lbs. frozen green beans, or
    4 14½-oz. cans, drained

1–2 cups cubed Velveeta
    cheese, depending upon
    how much you like cheese

½ cup chopped onion

½ cup milk

1 Tbsp. flour

1. Place beans, cheese, and onion in slow cooker. Stir together well.

2. Place milk first, and then flour, in a jar with a tight-fitting lid. Shake together until smooth. Or mix together in a small bowl until smooth. Then stir into other ingredients.

3. Cover and cook on Low 5–6 hours, or until beans are fully cooked and heated through.

Makes 12–14 servings

Dressed-Up Green Beans

PAT UNTERNAHRER • WAYLAND, IA

Prep Time: 5–10 minutes • Cooking Time: 2½–2¾ hours • Ideal slow cooker size: 3- to 4-qt.

3 14½-oz. cans green beans,
    drained

2 10¾-oz. cans mushroom
    soup

6-oz. can cheddar, or original,
    French-fried onions, divided

1. Spray slow cooker with nonstick cooking spray.

2. Put drained green beans into cooker.

3. Put 2 cans mushroom soup on top of beans. Stir together gently.

4. Cook on High 2 hours.

5. Add half a can French-fried onions. Stir and continue to cook 30–45 minutes.

6. Sprinkle remaining onions on top and serve.

Makes 10–12 servings

Barbecued Green Beans

SHARON TIMPE • JACKSON, WI / RUTH E. MARTIN • LOYSVILLE, PA

Prep Time: 15 minutes • Cooking Time: 3-4 hours • Ideal slow cooker size: 4-qt.

3 14½-oz. cans cut green
beans (drain 2 cans
completely; reserve liquid
from 1 can)

1 small onion, diced

1 cup ketchup

¾ cup brown sugar

4 strips bacon, cooked crisp
and crumbled

1. Combine green beans, diced onion, ketchup, and brown sugar in slow cooker.

2. Add ⅓ cup reserved bean liquid. Mix gently.

3. Cover and cook on Low 3–4 hours, until beans are tender and heated through. Stir at end of 2 hours of cooking, if you're home.

4. Pour in a little reserved bean juice if sauce thickens more than you like.

5. Sprinkle bacon over beans just before serving.

Makes 10-12 servings

Special Green Beans

SARA KINSINGER • STUARTS DRAFT, VA

Prep Time: 30-45 minutes • Cooking Time: 1-2 hours • Ideal slow cooker size: 4-qt.

4 14½-oz. cans green beans,
drained

10¾-oz. can cream of
mushroom soup

14½-oz. can chicken broth

1 cup Tater Tots

3-oz. can French-fried onion
rings

1. Put green beans in slow cooker.

2. In a bowl, mix soup and broth together. Spread over beans.

3. Spoon Tater Tots over all. Top with onion rings.

4. Cover and bake on High 1–2 hours, or until heated through and potatoes are cooked.

Makes 12-14 servings

Creole Green Beans

JAN MAST • LANCASTER, PA

Prep Time: 10 minutes • Cooking Time: 3–4 hours • Ideal slow cooker size: 2-qt.

2 small onions, chopped

half a stick (¼ cup) butter

4 cups green beans, fresh or frozen

½ cup salsa

2–3 Tbsp. brown sugar

½ tsp. garlic salt, optional

1. Sauté onions in butter in a saucepan.

2. Combine with remaining ingredients in slow cooker.

3. Cover and cook on Low 3–4 hours, or longer, depending on how soft or crunchy you like your beans.

   Makes 4–6 servings

Greek-Style Green Beans

DIANN J. DUNHAM • STATE COLLEGE, PA

Prep Time: 5 minutes • Cooking Time: 2-5 hours • Ideal slow cooker size: 4-qt.

20 ozs. whole or cut-up frozen beans (not French cut)

2 cups tomato sauce

2 tsp. dried onion flakes, optional

pinch of dried marjoram or oregano

pinch of nutmeg

pinch of cinnamon

1. Combine all ingredients in slow cooker, mixing together thoroughly.

2. Cover and cook on Low 2–4 hours if beans are defrosted, or 3–5 hours on Low if beans are frozen, or until beans are done to your liking.

   Makes 6 servings

Green Beans Portuguese-Style

JOYCE KAUT • ROCHESTER, NY

Prep Time: 20 minutes • Cooking Time: 3–8 hours • Ideal slow cooker size: 5-qt.

¼ lb. salt pork, or bacon

2 lbs. fresh green beans

2 medium-sized tomatoes

½ tsp. each salt and pepper

2 cups beef bouillon, or 2 beef
    bouillon cubes dissolved in
    2 cups water

1. Dice salt pork or bacon, and spread across bottom of slow cooker.

2. Wash beans, then break into 2"–3" pieces. Layer beans over pork or bacon.

3. Peel, seed, and cube tomatoes. Spoon over beans.

4. Sprinkle with salt and pepper. Pour bouillon over all ingredients in slow cooker.

5. Cook on High 3–4 hours, or on Low 6–8 hours, or until beans are done to your liking.

Makes 8 servings

Variations: You may use a 14½-oz. can of tomatoes instead of fresh ones. And you may use canned green beans instead of fresh. If you use canned tomatoes and/or beans, cook on High 2–3 hours, or on Low 4–5 hours.

Super Green Beans

ESTHER J. YODER • HARTVILLE, OH

Prep Time: 15 minutes • Cooking Time: 1–2 hours • Ideal slow cooker size: 3-qt.

2 14½-oz. cans green beans,
    undrained

1 cup cooked cubed ham

⅓ cup finely chopped onion

1 Tbsp. melted butter, or bacon
    drippings

1. Place undrained beans in cooker. Add remaining ingredients and mix well.

2. Cook on High 1–2 hours, or until steaming hot.

Makes 5 servings

Fresh Green Beans

LIZZIE ANN YODER • HARTVILLE, OH

Prep Time: 20 minutes • Cooking Time: 6–24 hours • Ideal slow cooker size:: 4- to 5-qt.

¼ lb. ham, or bacon, pieces

2 lbs. fresh green beans, washed and cut into pieces, or Frenched

3-4 cups water

1 scant tsp. salt

1. If using bacon, cut it into squares and brown in a nonstick skillet. When crispy, drain and set aside.

2. Place all ingredients in slow cooker. Mix together well.

3. Cover and cook on High 6–10 hours, or on Low 10–24 hours, or until beans are done to your liking.

Makes 6–8 servings

Cheese-y Potatoes

BARBARA SPARKS • GLEN BURNIE, MD

Prep Time: 10 minutes • Cooking Time: 5½–8 hours • Ideal slow cooker size: 4-qt.

30-oz. pkg. frozen shredded hash brown potatoes, partially thawed

10¾-oz. can cheddar cheese soup

12-oz. can evaporated milk

2 Tbsp. butter, softened or melted

½ tsp. salt

pepper to taste, optional

1. Spray slow cooker with nonstick cooking spray.

2. Break up partially thawed potatoes in slow cooker.

3. In a bowl, stir together soup, milk, butter, and salt, and pepper, if you wish. Pour over potatoes. Mix together gently.

4. Cover and cook on Low 5½–8 hours, or until potatoes are tender and fully cooked.

Makes 8–10 servings

Slow-Cooked Cheese-y Potatoes

TRACEY HANSON SCHRAMEL • WINDOM, MN / SHERRY H. KAUFFMAN • MINOT, ND

Prep Time: 8-10 minutes • Cooking Time: 3-9 hours • Ideal slow cooker size: 5-qt.

30-oz. pkg. frozen hash
browns, shredded or sliced

2 10¾-oz. cans cheddar
cheese soup

12-oz. can evaporated milk

3-oz. can French-fried onion
rings, divided

¾ tsp. salt

¼ tsp. pepper

1. Spray slow cooker with nonstick cooking spray.

2. Combine potatoes, soup, milk, half of onion rings, salt,
and pepper in slow cooker.

3. Cover and cook on Low 7–9 hours, or on High 3–4 hours,
or until potatoes are heated through.

4. Sprinkle remaining onion rings over top before serving.

Makes 10–12 servings

Creamy Easy Potatoes

LORETTA HANSON • HENDRICKS, MN

Prep Time: 15 minutes • Cooking Time: 4-6 hours • Ideal slow cooker size: 4-qt.

30-oz. pkg. frozen cubed hash
browns, thawed

12-oz. can evaporated milk

10¾-oz. can cream of celery
soup

10¾-oz. can cream of potato
soup

½ cup diced onion, optional

1 cup shredded cheddar cheese

1. Spray slow cooker with nonstick cooking spray.

2. Combine hash browns, milk, soups, and onion, if you
wish, in slow cooker.

3. Sprinkle cheese over top.

4. Cover and cook on Low 4–6 hours, stirring occasionally if
you're around, until potatoes are tender and cooked through.

Makes 6–8 servings

Easy Cheese-y Potatoes

CAROL SHERWOOD • BATAVIA, NY

Prep Time: 20 minutes • Cooking Time: 3–8 hours • Ideal slow cooker size: 4-qt.

30-oz. pkg. frozen hash brown
  potatoes, partially thawed

1-lb. pkg. kielbasa, chopped

1 medium-sized onion, diced

10¾-oz. can cheddar cheese
  soup

1 soup can milk

1. Spray slow cooker with nonstick cooking spray.

2. Place first 3 ingredients in slow cooker. Stir together.

3. Mix soup and milk together in a bowl, stirring until well blended. Pour into slow cooker.

4. Fold all ingredients together.

5. Cover and cook on High 3 hours, or on Low 7–8 hours.

   Makes 4 servings

Sour Cream Hash Browns

KATRINA EBERLY • STEVENS, PA / STACY PETERSHEIM • MECHANICSBURG, PA
JEANETTE OBERHOLTZER • MANHEIM, PA

Prep Time: 5 minutes • Cooking Time: 3½–4½ hours • Ideal slow cooker size: 4- to 6-qt.

10¾-oz. can cream of
  mushroom soup, plain, or
  with roasted garlic

1 cup sour cream, fat-free or
  regular

1½–3 cups shredded cheddar,
  or Monterey Jack, cheese

30-oz. pkg. frozen cubed hash
  brown potatoes

1. Spray slow cooker with nonstick cooking spray.

2. Combine soup, sour cream, and cheese in a medium-sized bowl. Mix well.

3. Pour half of potatoes into slow cooker.

4. Top with half of soup mixture.

5. Repeat layers. Spread soup mixture evenly over top.

6. Cook on Low 3½–4½ hours, or until potatoes are tender and cooked through.

   Makes 10–12 servings

Satisfyingly Creamy Potatoes

SHERRY KAUFFMAN • MINOT, ND

Prep Time: 15 minutes ▪ Cooking Time: 3–4 hours ▪ Ideal slow cooker size: 5-qt.

1 pt. sour cream

10¾-oz. can cream of chicken
    soup

2 cups Velveeta cheese, cubed

½ cup chopped onions

30-oz. pkg. frozen hash browns

1. Spray slow cooker with nonstick cooking spray.

2. Combine all ingredients in slow cooker.

3. Cover and cook on Low 3–4 hours, or until potatoes are tender and cooked through.

Makes 8–10 servings

Creamy Hash Browns

STARLA KREIDER • MOHRSVILLE, PA

Prep Time: 10 minutes ▪ Cooking Time: 4–5 hours ▪ Ideal slow cooker size: 5-qt.

30-oz. package frozen, diced
    hash browns

2 cups cubed or shredded
    cheese of your choice

2 cups sour cream

2 10¾-oz. cans cream of
    chicken soup

half a stick (¼ cup) butter,
    melted

1. Place hash browns in ungreased slow cooker.

2. Combine remaining ingredients and pour over potatoes. Mix well.

3. Cover and cook on Low 4–5 hours, or until potatoes are tender and heated through.

Makes 14 servings

Cooking Tip

It's quite convenient to use a slow cooker to cook potatoes for salads or for fried potatoes or as baked potatoes. Just fill the slow cooker with cleaned potatoes and cook all day until done.

—*Darla Sathre, Baxter, MN*

Scalloped Potatoes

EDNA MAE HERSCHBERGER • ARTHUR, IL

Prep Time: 5 minutes • Cooking Time: 4½–5½ hours • Ideal slow cooker size: 4-qt.

1 pt. half-and-half

1 stick (½ cup) butter,
    softened or melted

30-oz. pkg. hash browns

1 tsp. garlic powder

¼ tsp. pepper, optional

1 lb. Velveeta, cubed

1. Spray slow cooker with nonstick cooking spray.

2. Place all ingredients except Velveeta in slow cooker. Stir together gently, until well mixed.

3. Cover and cook on Low 4–5 hours, or until potatoes are tender and cooked through.

4. Stir in Velveeta. Cook until melted, approximately 30 minutes.

Makes 6–8 servings

Onion-y Potatoes

JEANNINE JANZEN • ELBING, KS

Prep Time: 5–10 minutes • Cooking Time: 4 hours • Ideal slow cooker size: 4-qt.

30-oz. pkg. frozen hash brown
    potatoes, thawed

½ cup diced onion, optional

5⅔ Tbsp. (⅓ cup) butter,
    melted

2 cups French onion dip

16-oz. pkg. American cheese,
    cut up

1. Spray slow cooker with nonstick cooking spray.

2. Combine all ingredients in slow cooker. Mix well.

3. Cover and cook on Low 4 hours, or until potatoes are tender and cooked through.

Makes 6–8 servings

Bacon Hash Browns

TIERRA WOODS • DUENWEG, MO

Prep Time: 15 minutes • Cooking Time: 4 hours • Ideal slow cooker size: 4-qt.

$\frac{1}{4}$ lb. bacon

6 cups frozen hash brown potatoes, partially thawed

1 cup mayonnaise

$\frac{1}{2}$ cup processed cheese sauce

1. Cut up bacon. Brown in a nonstick skillet until crispy. Drain and set aside.

2. Spray slow cooker with nonstick cooking spray.

3. Measure out $\frac{1}{4}$ cup bacon and reserve. Place remainder of bacon and rest of ingredients into slow cooker. Mix together well.

4. Cover and cook on Low 4 hours.

5. Sprinkle with reserved bacon just before serving.

Makes 5–6 servings

Ranch Hash Browns

JEAN BUTZER • BATAVIA, NY

Prep Time: 5 minutes • Cooking Time: 4–7 hours • Ideal slow cooker size: 6-qt.

30-oz. bag frozen hash browns, partially thawed

8-oz. pkg. cream cheese, softened

1 envelope dry ranch dressing mix

10$\frac{3}{4}$-oz. can cream of potato soup

1. Spray slow cooker with nonstick cooking spray.

2. Place potatoes in slow cooker. Break up with a spoon if frozen together.

3. Mix remaining ingredients in a bowl. Stir gently into potatoes.

4. Cook on Low 4–7 hours, or until potatoes are cooked through. Stir carefully before serving.

Makes 5–6 servings

Creamy Scalloped Potatoes

NANCY WAGNER GRAVES • MANHATTAN, KS

Prep Time: 5–15 minutes, depending upon the kind of potatoes you use • Cooking Time: 3–4 hours for fresh potatoes; 2–5 hours for frozen hash browns • Ideal slow cooker size: 4- to 5-qt.

2 Tbsp. dried minced onion

1 medium-sized clove garlic, minced

1 tsp. salt

8–10 medium-sized fresh potatoes, sliced, or 30-oz. bag frozen hash browns, divided

8-oz. pkg. cream cheese, cubed, divided

½ cup shredded cheddar cheese, optional

1. Spray slow cooker with nonstick cooking spray.

2. In a small bowl, combine onion, garlic, and salt.

3. Layer about one-fourth of potatoes into slow cooker.

4. Sprinkle one-fourth of onion-garlic mixture over potatoes.

5. Spoon about one-third of cream cheese cubes over top.

6. Repeat layers, ending with seasoning.

7. If using fresh potatoes, cook on High 3–4 hours, or until potatoes are tender. If using frozen hash browns, cook on High 2 hours, or on Low 4–5 hours, or until potatoes are tender and cooked through.

8. Stir potatoes to spread out cream cheese. If you wish, you can mash potatoes at this point.

9. If you like, sprinkle shredded cheese over top of sliced or mashed potatoes.

10. Cover and cook an additional 10 minutes, or until cheese is melted.

Makes 8–10 servings

Plain Old Scalloped Potatoes

RUTH ANN PENNER • HILLSBORO, KS

Prep Time: 10 minutes • Cooking Time: 2 hours • Ideal slow cooker size: 3-qt.

2 cups thinly sliced raw
   potatoes, divided

1 Tbsp. flour

1 tsp. salt

pepper

1 cup milk

1 Tbsp. butter

1. Spray slow cooker with nonstick cooking spray.

2. Put half of thinly sliced potatoes in bottom of slow cooker.

3. In a small bowl, mix together flour, salt, and pepper. Sprinkle half over top of potatoes.

4. Repeat layering.

5. Pour milk over all. Dot with butter.

6. Cover and cook on High 2 hours.

Makes 3–4 servings

Note: Pour milk over all as soon as possible to avoid having potatoes turn dark. A cup of fully cooked ham cubes could be stirred in before serving. Top the dish with shredded cheese, if you wish.

Speedy Potato Dish

ESTHER J. YODER • HARTVILLE, OH

Prep Time: 15 minutes • Cooking Time: 3–4 hours • Ideal slow cooker size: 4-qt.

5 medium-sized potatoes,
   peeled and sliced

10¾-oz. can cream of chicken
   soup

¼ cup chicken broth

¼–½ tsp. pepper

1. Spray slow cooker with nonstick cooking spray.

2. Gently fold ingredients together in slow cooker.

3. Cover and cook on High 3–4 hours, or until potatoes are soft but not mushy or dry.

Makes 3–4 servings

From-Scratch Scalloped Potatoes

HEATHER HORST • LEBANON, PA

Prep Time: 20 minutes • Cooking Time: 4–5 hours • Ideal slow cooker size: 5- to 6-qt.

6 lbs. potatoes, peeled and thinly sliced, divided

2 cups cheddar cheese, shredded

1 cup chopped onion

2 10¾-oz. cans cream of mushroom soup

1 cup water

½ tsp. each salt and pepper

1 tsp. garlic powder, optional

1. Place one-third of sliced potatoes in slow cooker.

2. In a medium-sized bowl, mix together shredded cheese, onion, soup, water, and seasonings.

3. Pour one-third of creamy mixture over potatoes.

4. Repeat layers 2 more times.

5. Cover and cook on High 4–5 hours, or until potatoes are tender.

Makes 12–15 servings

Gourmet Scalloped Potatoes

JEAN HINDAL • GRANDIN, MO

Prep Time: 15 minutes • Cooking Time: 4–8 hours • Ideal slow cooker size: 6-qt.

8 raw potatoes (peeled or not), shredded

2 cups sour cream

10¾-oz. can cream of chicken, or mushroom, soup

2 cups shredded cheddar cheese

1 tsp. salt

¼ tsp. pepper, optional

1 tsp. dried onion flakes, optional

1. Spray slow cooker with nonstick cooking spray.

2. Combine all ingredients gently in slow cooker.

3. Cover and cook on High 4 hours, or on Low 6–8 hours, or until potatoes are tender.

Makes 10–12 servings

From-Scratch Creamy Potatoes

MARY STAUFFER • EPHRATA, PA

Prep Time: 1 hour preparing; 3 hours chilling • Cooking Time: 5 hours • Ideal slow cooker size: 6-qt.

5½ lbs. potatoes

2 10½-oz. cans cheddar
cheese soup

3 cups sour cream

1 cup chopped onion

1 tsp. salt

½ tsp. pepper

1. Cook unpeeled whole potatoes in water in a large saucepan until soft. Allow to cool to room temperature. Then refrigerate until fully chilled.

2. Spray cooker with nonstick cooking spray.

3. Skin chilled potatoes. Then grate into cooker.

4. Add remaining ingredients to slow cooker and stir together well.

5. Cover and cook on High 5 hours, or until hot and bubbly.

Makes 15 servings

Scalloped Potatoes and Bacon

JEAN BUTZER • BATAVIA, NY

Prep Time: 10 minutes • Cooking Time: 8–10 hours • Ideal slow cooker size: 3- to 4-qt.

6 large potatoes, peeled and
sliced, divided

1 small onion, diced

2 cups shredded cheddar
cheese, divided

8 strips bacon, uncooked and
diced, divided

10¾-oz. can cream of
mushroom soup

1. Spray slow cooker with nonstick cooking spray.

2. Place half of sliced potatoes in bottom of slow cooker. Top with half each of chopped onion, cheese, and bacon.

3. Repeat layers in order. Top with soup.

4. Cover and cook on Low 8–10 hours, or until potatoes are tender but not mushy or dry.

Makes 6–8 servings

Note: You may want to brown the bacon in a nonstick skillet until crispy, and then drain the drippings, before placing bacon in the cooker. That adds some time to the process, but it cuts down on the fat content.

Sausage and Scalloped Potatoes

MRS. MAHLON MILLER • HUTCHINSON, KS

Prep Time: 15 minutes • Cooking Time: 4 hours • Ideal slow cooker size: 3-qt.

½ lb. loose sausage

4 cups raw potatoes, finely diced

½ cup shredded cheddar cheese

½ cup sour cream

10¾-oz. can cream of mushroom soup

1. Cook sausage in a nonstick skillet until it loses its pink color. Drain.

2. Spray slow cooker with nonstick cooking spray.

3. Combine all ingredients in slow cooker.

4. Cover and cook on Low for 4 hours, or until potatoes are tender.

Makes 3–4 servings

Simple Saucy Potatoes

MARY LYNN MILLER • REINHOLDS, PA

Prep Time: 15–20 minutes • Cooking Time: 4–5 hours • Ideal slow cooker size: 5-qt.

10 bacon slices

4 15-oz. cans sliced white potatoes, drained

2 10¾-oz. cans cream of celery soup

2 cups sour cream

6 scallions, thinly sliced

1. Brown bacon in a nonstick skillet. Drain. Crumble and set aside.

2. Place potatoes in slow cooker.

3. In a large bowl, combine remaining ingredients, including bacon. Pour over potatoes and mix well.

4. Cover and cook on High 4–5 hours, or until potatoes are cooked through.

Makes 8–10 servings

Ranch Potatoes

JEAN BUTZER • BATAVIA, NY

Prep Time: 10–15 minutes • Cooking Time: 3½–8 hours • Ideal slow cooker size: 4-qt.

2½ lbs. small red potatoes, quartered

1 cup sour cream

1 envelope dry buttermilk ranch salad dressing mix

10¾-oz. can cream of mushroom soup

1. Spray slow cooker with nonstick cooking spray.

2. Place potatoes in slow cooker.

3. Combine remaining ingredients in a bowl. Spoon over potatoes and stir gently.

4. Cover and cook on Low 7–8 hours, or on High 3½–4 hours, or until potatoes are tender but not dry or mushy.

5. Stir carefully before serving.

Makes 6 servings

Creamy Red Potatoes

ORPHA HERR • ANDOVER, NY

Prep Time: 25 minutes • Cooking Time: 8 hours • Ideal slow cooker size: 5-qt.

2 lbs. small red potatoes, scrubbed, quartered, unpeeled

8-oz. pkg. cream cheese, softened

10¾-oz. cream of potato soup

half a soup can milk or water

1 envelope dry ranch salad dressing mix

1. Place potatoes in slow cooker.

2. In a small bowl, beat remaining ingredients together until blended. Stir into potatoes.

3. Cover and cook on Low 8 hours, or until potatoes are tender but not mushy or dry.

Makes 4–6 servings

Note: Barbecued pork chops are a great match with this dish. In a bowl, mix a 10¾-oz. can of cream of mushroom soup with 1 cup ketchup, 1 Tbsp. Worcestershire sauce, and ½ cup chopped onion. Place 4 or 5 pork chops in a second slow cooker! Pour sauce over top, making sure all the chops have sauce over them. Cover and cook on High 4–6 hours, or on Low 6–8 hours, or until chops are tender but not dry.

Lemon Red Potatoes

CAROL LEAMAN • LANCASTER, PA

Prep Time: 15–20 minutes • Cooking Time: 2½–3 hours • Ideal slow cooker size: 3- to 4-qt.

10-12 small to medium-sized
    red potatoes

¼ cup water

¼ cup butter, melted

1 Tbsp. lemon juice

3 Tbsp. fresh, or dried, parsley

salt and pepper to taste

1. Cut a strip of peel from around middle of each potato, using a potato peeler.

2. Place potatoes and water in slow cooker.

3. Cover and cook on High 2½–3 hours, or until tender. Do not overcook.

4. Drain water.

5. Combine butter, lemon juice, and parsley. Mix well. Pour over potatoes and toss to coat. Season with salt and pepper.

Makes 6 servings

Rosemary New Potatoes

CAROL SHIRK • LEOLA, PA

Prep Time: 15 minutes • Cooking Time: 2-6 hours • Ideal slow cooker size: 3- to 4-qt.

1½ lbs. new red potatoes,
    unpeeled

1 Tbsp. olive oil

1 Tbsp. fresh chopped
    rosemary, or 1 tsp. dried
    rosemary

1 tsp. garlic and pepper
    seasoning, or 1 large clove
    garlic, minced, plus ½ tsp.
    salt, and ¼ tsp. pepper

1. If potatoes are larger than golf balls, cut them in half or in quarters.

2. In a bowl or plastic bag, toss potatoes with olive oil, coating well.

3. Add rosemary and garlic and pepper seasoning (or minced garlic, salt, and pepper). Toss again until potatoes are well coated.

4. Place potatoes in slow cooker. Cook on High 2–3 hours, or on Low 5–6 hours, or until potatoes are tender but not mushy or dry.

Makes 4–5 servings

Parmesan Potato Wedges

CAROL AND JOHN AMBROSE • MCMINNVILLE, OR

Prep Time: 15 minutes • Cooking Time: 4 hours • Ideal slow cooker size: 3-qt.

2 lbs. red potatoes, cut into
    ½" wedges or strips

¼ cup chopped onion

2 Tbsp. butter, cut into pieces

1½ tsp. dried oregano

¼ cup grated Parmesan
    cheese

1. Layer potatoes, onion, butter, and oregano in slow cooker.

2. Cover and cook on High 4 hours, or until potatoes are tender but not dry or mushy.

3. Spoon into a serving dish and sprinkle with cheese.

    Makes 6 servings

Garlicky Potatoes

DONNA LANTGEN • CHADRON, NE

Prep Time: 30 minutes • Cooking Time: 4½–6 hours • Ideal slow cooker size: 3- to 4-qt.

6 potatoes, peeled and cubed

6 cloves garlic, minced

¼ cup diced onion, or one
    medium-sized onion,
    chopped

2 Tbsp. olive oil

1. Spray slow cooker with nonstick cooking spray.

2. Combine all ingredients in slow cooker.

3. Cover and cook on Low 4½–6 hours, or until potatoes are tender but not mushy or dry.

    Makes 4–5 servings

Onion Potatoes

DONNA LANTGEN • CHADRON, NE

Prep Time: 20-30 minutes • Cooking Time: 5-6 hours • Ideal slow cooker size: 4-qt.

6 medium-sized potatoes, diced

1/3 cup olive oil

1 envelope dry onion soup mix

1. Combine potatoes and olive oil in plastic bag. Shake well.

2. Add onion soup mix. Shake well.

3. Pour into slow cooker.

4. Cover and cook on Low 5-6 hours.

Makes 6 servings

Note: Slow cookers fit any season. When it's hot outside, they don't heat up your kitchen. So turn on your cooker before heading to the pool or the beach—or the garden. Or put your dinner in the slow cooker, and then go play or watch your favorite sport.

The Simplest "Baked" Potatoes

MARY KATHRYN YODER • HARRISONVILLE, MO

Prep Time: 20 minutes • Cooking Time: 4-10 hours • Ideal slow cooker size: 3½- to 5-qt.

4-12 potatoes

1. Prick potatoes. Wrap each in foil. Place potatoes in slow cooker. (Do not add water.)

2. Cover and cook on High 4-5 hours, or on Low 8-10 hours, or until potatoes are tender when jagged.

Makes 4-12 servings

Seasoned "Baked" Potatoes

DONNA CONTO • SAYLORSBURG, PA

Prep Time: 5 minutes • Cooking Time: 4–10 hours • Ideal slow cooker size: large enough to hold the potatoes!

potatoes

olive, or vegetable, oil

Season-All, or your choice of favorite dry seasonings

1. Wash and scrub potatoes. Rub each unpeeled potato with oil.

2. Put about 1 tsp. seasoning per potato in a mixing bowl or a plastic bag. Add potatoes one at a time and coat with seasonings.

3. Place potatoes in slow cooker as you finish coating them.

4. Cover and cook on High for 4 hours, or on Low 8–10 hours, or until potatoes are tender when jagged.

Makes as many servings as you need!

Stress-Free "Baked" Potatoes

LEONA YODER • HARTVILLE, OH

Prep Time: 10 minutes • Cooking Time: 4–10 hours • Ideal slow cooker size: 4- to 5-qt.

12 potatoes

butter, softened

1. Spray slow cooker with nonstick cooking spray.

2. Rub butter over unpeeled whole potatoes. Place in slow cooker.

3. Cover and cook on High 4–5 hours, or on Low 8–10 hours, or until potatoes are tender when jagged.

Makes 12 servings

Cooking Tip

Mix 1 Tbsp. pesto into ½ cup sour cream for a luscious baked potato topping.

Cornflake Cooker Potatoes

ANNE NOLT • THOMPSONTOWN, PA

Prep Time: 15 minutes ▪ Cooking Time: 4 hours ▪ Ideal slow cooker size: 3-qt.

6–8 potatoes, peeled

2 tsp. salt

2–3 Tbsp. butter

1 cup cornflakes, slightly
crushed

1. Place potatoes in slow cooker.

2. Fill cooker with hot water. Sprinkle with salt.

3. Cover and cook on High 4 hours, or until potatoes are
tender.

4. While potatoes are cooking, melt butter. Continue melting
until butter browns but does not burn. (Watch carefully!)
Stir in cornflakes. Set aside.

5. Drain potatoes. Spoon buttered cornflakes over potatoes.
Or mash potatoes and then top with buttered cornflakes.

Makes 4–6 servings

Mashed Potatoes

ALICE MILLER • STUARTS DRAFT, VA

Prep Time: 15 minutes ▪ Cooking Time: 3–5 hours ▪ Ideal slow cooker size: 3- to 4-qt.

8 large potatoes, peeled and
cut into 1" chunks

water

half a stick (¼ cup) butter,
softened

1½ cups milk, heated until skin
forms on top

1 tsp. salt

1. Place potatoes in slow cooker; add water to cover.

2. Cover and cook on High 3–5 hours, or until potatoes are
very tender but not watery.

3. Lift potatoes out with a slotted spoon into a bowl. Beat
with an electric mixer on high speed, scraping sides down.

4. Cut butter in chunks. Add to potatoes. Slowly add milk,
being careful not to splash yourself with hot milk. Add
salt. Beat until creamy.

Makes 4 servings

Tip: Put the potatoes in the slow cooker and forget about them
while you're occupied otherwise. Come back to the kitchen
3–5 hours later, and you've got soft potatoes, ready to mash!

Refrigerator Mashed Potatoes

ELSIE SCHLABACH • MILLERSBURG, OH

Prep Time: 15–20 minutes • Cooking Time: 2–3 hours • Ideal slow cooker size: 4- to 5-qt.

5 lbs. potatoes (not baking potatoes), peeled and cut into chunks

8-oz. pkg. cream cheese, softened

1–2 cups sour cream

2 Tbsp. butter, softened

1 tsp. salt

1. Cook potatoes in 2"–3" water in a large kettle until tender. Drain, reserving 1–2 cups cooking water.

2. Mash until smooth. Add cooking water as needed to keep potatoes from being too stiff.

3. Mash in remaining ingredients and beat until light and fluffy.

4. Cool. Cover and refrigerate.

5. When ready to use, spray slow cooker with nonstick cooking spray.

6. Stir chilled potatoes and then place in slow cooker. Cover and cook on Low 2–3 hours, or until hot throughout.

Makes 8–10 servings

Note: This dish is great for a Sunday noon dinner, or anytime when you're away from the kitchen but want a comforting potato dish for a meal.

Individual Mashed Potatoes

MRS. AUDREY L. KNEER • WILLIAMSFIELD, IL

Prep Time: 25 minutes • Cooking Time: up to 3 hours • Ideal slow cooker size: 1- to 2-qt.

1–2 medium-sized potatoes per person

3 Tbsp. milk per potato

$\frac{1}{2}$ Tbsp. butter per potato, melted

$\frac{1}{8}$ tsp. salt per potato

1. Peel and boil potatoes until soft. Mash.

2. While mashing potatoes, heat milk to scalding. Then add hot milk, butter, and salt to mashed potatoes, stirring in well.

3. Put in slow cooker a couple of hours before serving. Set cooker on Low. Stir once in a while. These will be the same as fresh mashed potatoes.

Note: This saves needing to mash potatoes at the last minute.

Seasoned Mashed Potatoes

ELENA YODER • CARLSBAD, NM

Prep Time: 30 minutes • Cooking Time: 3–4 hours • Ideal slow cooker size: 4-qt.

potatoes to fill a 4-qt. slow cooker, peeled and cut into chunks

boiling water to cover potatoes

8-oz. pkg. cream cheese, softened

2 cups buttermilk

1 cup dry milk

1 envelope dry ranch dressing mix

1. Place potatoes in slow cooker. Cover with boiling water.

2. Cover and cook on High 3–4 hours, or until very tender.

3. Drain, reserving liquid.

4. Mash potatoes.

5. Beat in cream cheese.

6. Beat in buttermilk, dry milk, and ranch dressing mix.

7. If needed, beat in as much reserved potato water as you want, until potatoes reach desired consistency.

Makes 12 servings

Garlic Mashed Potatoes

KATRINE ROSE • WOODBRIDGE, VA

Prep Time: 20 minutes • Cooking Time: 6–9 hours • Ideal slow cooker size: 4-qt.

2 lbs. baking potatoes, unpeeled and cut into ½" cubes

¼ cup water

3 Tbsp. butter, sliced

1 tsp. salt

¾ tsp. garlic powder

¼ tsp. pepper

1 cup milk

1. Combine all ingredients, except milk, in slow cooker. Toss to combine.

2. Cover. Cook on Low 7 hours, or on High 4 hours.

3. Add milk to potatoes during last 30 minutes of cooking time.

4. Mash potatoes with a potato masher or an electric mixer until fairly smooth.

5. Place in slow cooker 2 hours before serving. Cover. Set cooker on Low.

6. Stir before serving.

Makes 6 servings

Note: These potatoes will taste freshly mashed, and they will spare you last-minute work.

Make-Ahead Mashed Potatoes

TRACEY HANSON SCHRAMEL • WINDOM, MN

Prep Time: 45–60 minutes • Cooking Time: 4–5 hours in slow cooker • Ideal slow cooker size: 2 6-qt. cookers

5 lbs. potatoes, peeled and cubed

8-oz. pkg. cream cheese, softened

1 cup half-and-half

1 stick (½ cup) butter, softened

salt and pepper to taste

1. Cook potatoes in water in a large saucepan until tender but not mushy. Drain, reserving 1 cup cooking water.

2. In a large bowl, beat softened cream cheese and half-and-half together until smooth.

3. Stir in hot potatoes and reserved cooking water and blend well.

4. Stir in butter, salt, and pepper.

5. Place meal-sized portions of mixture in freezer containers. Cool; then freeze.

6. When needed, thaw a container of potatoes. Spray slow cooker. Then place potato mixture in slow cooker.

7. Stir in 1–2 Tbsp. softened butter and ½–1 tsp. paprika.

8. Cover and cook on Low 4–5 hours, or until potatoes are heated through but not dry.

Makes 8–12 servings

Cheddar Mashed Potatoes

GLORIA GOOD • HARRISONBURG, VA

Prep Time: 10 minutes • Cooking Time: 3–5 hours • Ideal slow cooker size: 2-qt.

10¾-oz. condensed cheddar cheese soup

½ cup sour cream

2 Tbsp. chopped scallions

dash of pepper

3 cups leftover, or stiff, seasoned mashed potatoes

1. Spray slow cooker with nonstick cooking spray.

2. Mix all ingredients together in slow cooker.

3. Cover and cook on High 3 hours, or on Low 5 hours, or until potatoes are thoroughly hot.

Makes 5–6 servings

Simply Sweet Potatoes

LEONA YODER • HARTVILLE, OH

Prep Time: 5 minutes • Cooking Time: 6–9 hours • Ideal slow cooker size: 2- to 3-qt.

3 large sweet potatoes

¼ cup water

1. Place unpeeled sweet potatoes into slow cooker.

2. Add ¼ cup water.

3. Cover and cook on High 1 hour. Then turn to Low and cook 5–8 hours, or until potatoes are tender.

Makes 4 servings

Fruity Sweet Potatoes

JEAN BUTZER • BATAVIA, NY / EVELYN PAGE • LANCE CREEK, WY

Prep Time: 15 minutes • Cooking Time: 6–8 hours • Ideal slow cooker size: 3- to 4-qt.

2 lbs. (about 6 medium-sized) sweet potatoes, or yams

1½ cups applesauce

⅔ cup brown sugar

3 Tbsp. butter, melted

1 tsp. cinnamon

chopped nuts, optional

1. Peel sweet potatoes, if you wish. Cut into cubes or slices. Place in slow cooker.

2. In a bowl, mix together applesauce, brown sugar, butter, and cinnamon. Spoon over potatoes.

3. Cover and cook on Low 6–8 hours, or until potatoes are tender.

4. Mash potatoes and sauce together, if you wish, with a large spoon—or spoon potatoes into a serving dish and top with sauce.

5. Sprinkle with nuts, if you want.

Makes 6 servings

Variation: Instead of raw sweet potatoes, substitute a 40-oz. can of cut-up sweet potatoes, drained. Then cook on Low for only 3–4 hours.

Apples 'n' Yams

REBECCA PLANK LEICHTY • HARRISONBURG, VA

Prep Time: 25 minutes • Cooking Time: 4–6 hours • Ideal slow cooker size: 4- to 5-qt.

6 apples, peeled and sliced

6 large yams, or sweet potatoes, peeled and thinly sliced

1 Tbsp. lemon juice, or lemonade

¼ cup apple juice

1 Tbsp. butter, melted

1. Toss sliced apples and yams in lemon juice.

2. Combine apple juice and butter. Pour over apples and sweet potatoes. Pour into greased slow cooker.

3. Cover. Cook on High 4 hours, or Low 6 hours.

Makes 8–10 servings

Note: This is a tasty vegetable dish to add to a meal when serving children. The apples smell wonderful when cooking and truly moisten the potatoes. It is a well-rounded and easy way to serve sweet potatoes.

Cinnamon Sweet Potatoes

DEBORAH HEATWOLE • WAYNESBORO, GA

Prep Time: 10–15 minutes • Cooking Time: 3 hours • Ideal slow cooker size: 2- to 3-qt.

¼ cup brown sugar

¼ tsp. cinnamon

3 medium-sized sweet potatoes, peeled and thinly sliced (about 4–6 cups of slices), divided

half a stick (¼ cup) butter, melted, divided

salt to taste

1. Spray slow cooker with nonstick cooking spray.

2. Combine brown sugar and cinnamon in a small bowl.

3. Place one-third of sweet potato slices in slow cooker.

4. Drizzle with one-third of butter. Sprinkle with salt and one-third of brown sugar mixture.

5. Repeat layers 2 more times.

6. Cover and cook on High 3 hours, or until potatoes are tender.

Makes 4–6 servings

Glazed Sweet Potatoes

JAN MAST • LANCASTER, PA

Prep Time: 20 minutes • Cooking Time: 3–4 hours • Ideal slow cooker size: 2-qt.

8-10 medium-sized sweet
    potatoes
½ tsp. salt
¾ cup brown sugar
2 Tbsp. butter
1 Tbsp. flour
¼ cup water

1. Cook sweet potatoes in 2"–3" water in a large saucepan until barely soft. Drain. When cool enough to handle, peel and slice into slow cooker.

2. While potatoes are cooking in the saucepan, combine remaining ingredients in a microwave-safe bowl.

3. Microwave on High 1½ minutes. Stir. Repeat until glaze thickens slightly.

4. Pour glaze over peeled, cooked sweet potatoes in slow cooker.

5. Cover and cook on High 3–4 hours.

Makes 8–10 servings

Glazed Maple Sweet Potatoes

JEANNINE JANZEN • ELBING, KS

Prep Time: 5–10 minutes • Cooking Time: 7–9 hours • Ideal slow cooker size: 4-qt.

5 medium-sized sweet
    potatoes, cut in ½"-thick
    slices
¼ cup brown sugar, packed
¼ cup pure maple syrup
¼ cup apple cider
2 Tbsp. butter

1. Place potatoes in slow cooker.

2. In a small bowl, combine brown sugar, maple syrup, and apple cider. Mix well. Pour over potatoes. Stir until all potato slices are covered.

3. Cover and cook on Low 7–9 hours, or until potatoes are tender.

4. Stir in butter before serving.

Makes 5 servings

Tasty Rice

STARLA KREIDER • MOHRSVILLE, PA

Prep Time: 5–10 minutes • Cooking Time: 2–3 hours • Ideal slow cooker size: 2-qt.

1½ cups uncooked long-grain rice

3–3½ cups water, divided

10¾-oz. can cream of celery soup

2 tsp. chicken bouillon granules

1 onion, chopped

salt and pepper to taste

1. Spray slow cooker with nonstick cooking spray.

2. Combine rice, 3 cups water, soup, bouillon, onion, and a dash of salt and pepper in slow cooker.

3. Cover and cook on High 2–3 hours. If rice begins to dry out after 2 hours, stir in ½ cup water and continue cooking until heated through.

Makes 6–8 servings

Cooked Rice

MARY KATHRYN YODER • HARRISONVILLE, MO

Prep Time: 5 minutes • Cooking Time: 1½–2½ hours • Ideal slow cooker size: 4-qt.

1 Tbsp. butter

3 cups uncooked long-grain rice

6 cups water

salt to taste, about 3 tsp.

1. Grease slow cooker with butter.

2. If you have time, heat water to boiling in a saucepan on stovetop or in a microwave-safe bowl in microwave. Then pour rice, water (heated or not), and salt into slow cooker and stir together.

3. Cover and cook on High 1½–2½ hours. If you're home and able to do so, stir occasionally.

Makes 8 servings

Cooking Tip

When I use mushrooms or green peppers in the slow cooker, I usually stir them in during the last hour, so they don't get mushy.

—*Trudy Kutter, Corfu, NY*

Wild Rice Casserole

LORETTA HANSON • HENDRICKS, MN

Prep Time: 15 minutes • Cooking Time: 2 hours • Ideal slow cooker size: 4-qt.

6-oz. box long-grain and wild rice

10¾-oz. can cream of mushroom soup

¾ cup water

2 Tbsp. chopped onion, optional

2 Tbsp. butter, melted

1 Tbsp. beef bouillon

dash of Worcestershire sauce

1. Place all ingredients in slow cooker, including seasonings packet from rice box.

2. Cover and cook on High 2 hours. Fluff with fork before serving.

Makes 4 servings

Wild Rice Pilaf

JUDI MANOS • WEST ISLIP, NY

Prep Time: 10 minutes • Cooking Time: 3½–5 hours • Ideal slow cooker size: 3- to 4-qt.

1½ cups uncooked wild rice

½ cup finely chopped onion

14-oz. can chicken broth

2 cups water

4-oz. can sliced mushrooms, drained

½ tsp. dried thyme leaves

1. Spray slow cooker with nonstick cooking spray.

2. Rinse rice and drain well.

3. Combine rice, onion, chicken broth, and water in slow cooker. Mix well.

4. Cover and cook on High 3–4 hours.

5. Add mushrooms and thyme and stir gently.

6. Cover and cook on Low 30–60 minutes longer, or until wild rice pops and is tender.

Makes 6 servings

Note: If you wish, add ¾ tsp. salt in Step 3.

Flavorful Fruited Rice

SANDRA HAVERSTRAW • HUMMELSTOWN, PA

Prep Time: 7 minutes • Cooking Time: 2 hours • Ideal slow cooker size: 2- to 3½-qt.

⅓ cup chopped onion

6-oz. pkg. long-grain and wild
   rice mix

2 cups chicken broth

¼ cup dried cranberries

¼ cup chopped dried apricots

1. Spray a small skillet with nonstick cooking spray. Add chopped onions and cook on medium heat about 5 minutes, or until onions begin to brown.

2. Place onions and remaining ingredients in slow cooker, including seasonings from rice package. Stir well to dissolve seasonings.

3. Cover and cook on High 2 hours. Fluff with fork to serve.

Makes 4 servings

Variations: Just before serving, sprinkle dish with ½ cup toasted pecans or other nuts. Or use other dried fruits instead of the cranberries, such as raisins or dried cherries.

Cheddar Rice

NATALIA SHOWALTER • MT. SOLON, VA

Prep Time: 10–15 minutes • Cooking Time: 2–3 hours • Ideal slow cooker size: 3-qt.

2 cups uncooked brown rice

3 Tbsp. butter

½ cup thinly sliced scallions,
   or shallots

1 tsp. salt

5 cups water

½ tsp. pepper

2 cups shredded cheddar
   cheese

1 cup slivered almonds, optional

1. Combine rice, butter, green onions, and salt in slow cooker.

2. Bring water to boil and pour over rice mixture.

3. Cover and cook on High 2–3 hours, or until rice is tender and liquid is absorbed.

4. Five minutes before serving, stir in pepper and cheese.

5. Garnish with slivered almonds, if you wish.

Makes 8–10 servings

Red Bean and Brown Rice Stew

BARBARA GAUTCHER • HARRISONBURG, VA

Prep Time: 15 minutes, plus 8 hours for soaking beans • Cooking Time: 6 hours • Ideal slow cooker size: 6-qt.

2 cups dried red beans

water

¾ cup uncooked brown rice

4 cups water

6 carrots, peeled if you wish, and cut into chunks

1 large onion, cut into chunks

1 Tbsp. cumin

1. Place dried beans in slow cooker and cover with water. Allow to soak 8 hours. Drain. Discard soaking water.

2. Return soaked beans to cooker. Stir in all remaining ingredients.

3. Cover and cook on Low 6 hours, or until all vegetables are tender.

Makes 6 servings

Note: If you wish, add 1 Tbsp. salt to Step 2.

Broccoli Rice Casserole

LIZ RUGG • WAYLAND, IA

Prep Time: 5 minutes • Cooking Time: 3–4 hours • Ideal slow cooker size: 3- to 4-qt.

1 cup uncooked minute rice

1-lb. pkg. frozen chopped broccoli

8-oz. jar processed cheese spread

10¾-oz. can cream of mushroom soup

1. Mix all ingredients together in slow cooker.

2. Cover and cook on High 3–4 hours, or until rice and broccoli are tender but not mushy or dry.

Makes 6 servings

Cheese-y Rice

JANICE MULLER • DERWOOD, MD

Prep Time: 20 minutes • Cooking Time: 4–6 hours • Ideal slow cooker size: 3½- to 4-qt.

2 cups hot cooked rice

3-oz. can French-fried onions, divided

1 cup sour cream

16-oz. jar medium salsa, divided

1 cup shredded cheddar, or taco-blend, cheese, divided

1. Spray slow cooker with nonstick cooking spray.

2. In a bowl, combine rice and ⅔ cup onions. Spoon half of rice mixture into slow cooker.

3. Spread sour cream over rice. Layer half of salsa and half of cheese over sour cream.

4. Top with remaining rice, salsa, and cheese.

5. Cook on Low 4–6 hours, or until cheese is melted and casserole is heated through.

Makes 6 servings

Hometown Spanish Rice

BEVERLY FLATT-GETZ • WARRIORS MARK, PA

Prep Time: 20 minutes • Cooking Time: 2–4 hours • Ideal slow cooker size: 4-qt.

1 large onion, chopped

1 bell pepper, chopped

1 lb. bacon, cooked, and broken into bite-sized pieces

2 cups cooked long-grain rice

28-oz. can stewed tomatoes with juice

grated Parmesan cheese, optional

1. Sauté onion and pepper in a small nonstick skillet until tender.

2. Spray slow cooker with nonstick cooking spray.

3. Combine all ingredients except Parmesan cheese in slow cooker.

4. Cover and cook on Low 4 hours, or on High 2 hours, or until heated through.

5. Sprinkle with Parmesan cheese just before serving, if you wish.

Makes 6-8 servings

Rice 'n' Beans 'n' Salsa

HEATHER HORST • LEBANON, PA

Prep Time: 7 minutes • Cooking Time: 4–10 hours • Ideal slow cooker size: 3- to 5-qt.

2 16-oz. cans black, or navy,
   beans, drained

14-oz. can chicken broth

1 cup uncooked long-grain
   white, or brown, rice

1 qt. salsa, mild, medium, or hot

1 cup water

½ tsp. garlic powder

1. Combine all ingredients in slow cooker. Stir well.

2. Cover and cook on Low 8–10 hours, or on High 4 hours.

   Makes 6–8 servings

New Year's Sauerkraut

JUDITH A. GOVOTSOS • FREDERICK, MD

Prep Time: 10-15 minutes • Cooking Time: 2-10 hours • Ideal slow cooker size: 3-qt.

3 cups sauerkraut, rinsed and
   drained

½-¾ cup brown sugar

1 apple, cored and chopped

1 small onion, chopped

water to cover

1. Place sauerkraut in slow cooker. Add sugar, apple, and onion. Stir.

2. Cover with water.

3. Cover with lid and cook on High 2–3 hours, or on Low all day.

   Makes 4–6 servings

Acorn Squash

JANET L. ROGGIE • LOWVILLE, NY / MARY STAUFFER • EPHRATA, PA
LEONA YODER • HARTVILLE, OH / JUNE S. GROFF • DENVER, PA / TRUDY KUTTER • CORFU, NY

Prep Time: 5 minutes • Cooking Time: 7–8 hours, depending on the size of the squash • Ideal slow cooker size: 4- to 5-qt., depending on the size of the squash

whole acorn squash

water

salt

cinnamon

butter

brown sugar or maple syrup,
   optional

1. Wash squash. Cut off stem. Place whole squash in slow cooker. Add water to a depth of about 1".

2. Cover and cook on Low 7–8 hours, depending on size of squash. Jag with a sharp fork to see if it's tender. Cook longer if it isn't. Check every 2 hours during cooking time, if you can, to make sure squash isn't cooking dry. Add water if it drops below 1" deep.

3. Remove squash from cooker and allow to cool until you can handle it.

4. Cut in half with a long-bladed knife. Scoop seeds out of both halves.

5. Sprinkle flesh with salt and cinnamon. Dot with butter. Drizzle with brown sugar or maple syrup, if you wish. Serve. Or scoop out the flesh with a spoon into a mixing bowl. Add remaining ingredients and mash together until well blended and smooth.

Makes 4–6 servings, depending on the size of the squash

Artichokes

GERTRUDE DUTCHER • HARTVILLE, OH

Prep Time: 15 minutes • Cooking Time: 6–8 hours • Ideal slow cooker size: 4-qt.

4–6 artichokes

1–1½ tsp. salt

1 cup lemon juice, divided

2 cups hot water

1 stick (½ cup) melted butter

1. Wash and trim artichokes. Cut off about 1" from top. If you wish, trim tips of leaves. Stand chokes upright in slow cooker.

2. Sprinkle each choke with ¼ tsp. salt and 2 Tbsp. lemon juice.

3. Pour hot water around base of artichokes.

4. Cover and cook on Low 6–8 hours.

5. Serve with melted butter and lemon juice for dipping.

Makes 4–6 servings

Red Cabbage

KRISTIN TICE • SHIPSHEWANA, IN

Prep Time: 30 minutes • Cooking Time: 6 hours • Ideal slow cooker size: 3-qt.

5 cups shredded red cabbage

1 cup white sugar

1 cup white vinegar

1 apple, chopped

1 tsp. salt

1 cup water

1. Combine all ingredients in slow cooker.

2. Cover and cook on Low 6 hours.

   Makes 8 servings

Note: This is a great side dish to serve with pork.

Cheese-y Onions

JANESSA HOCHSTEDLER • EAST EARL, PA

Prep Time: 10–20 minutes • Cooking Time: 2–4 hours • Ideal slow cooker size: 2-qt.

1½ lbs. small onions

4 slices bacon, cooked and crumbled

10½-oz. can cheddar cheese soup

½ cup milk

¼ cup grated Parmesan cheese

1. Peel onions, but leave whole. Place in slow cooker.

2. Mix remaining ingredients together in a bowl.

3. Pour into slow cooker. Gently mix in onions.

4. Cook on High 2 hours, or on Low 4 hours, or until onions are fully tender.

   Makes 6–8 servings

Caramelized Onions

JEANETTE OBERHOLTZER • MANHEIM, PA

Prep Time: 15 minutes • Cooking Time: 10–12 hours • Ideal slow cooker size: 4- to 6-qt.

4-6 large sweet onions

1 stick (½ cup) butter, melted, or olive oil

1. Peel onions and slice off top and bottom ends.

2. Place onions in slow cooker.

3. Pour butter or olive oil on top of onions. Stir together.

4. Cook on Low 10–12 hours.

5. Use caramelized onions as filling for omelets or sandwiches, as an ingredient in soup, or as a condiment with grilled meat.

Makes 6-8 servings

Fresh Zucchini and Tomatoes

PAULINE MORRISON • ST. MARYS, ONTARIO

Prep Time: 15 minutes • Cooking Time: 2½–3 hours • Ideal slow cooker size: 3½-qt.

1½ lbs. zucchini, peeled if you wish, and cut into ¼" slices

19-oz. can stewed tomatoes, broken up and undrained

1½ cloves garlic, minced

½ tsp. salt

1½ Tbsp. butter

1. Place zucchini slices in slow cooker.

2. Add tomatoes, garlic, and salt. Mix well.

3. Dot surface with butter.

4. Cover and cook on High 2½–3 hours, or until zucchini is done to your liking.

Makes 6-8 servings

Note: Sprinkle with grated Parmesan cheese when serving, if you wish.

Stewed Tomatoes

MICHELLE SHOWALTER • BRIDGEWATER, VA

Prep Time: 15 minutes • Cooking Time: 3–4 hours • Ideal slow cooker size: 3-qt.

2 qts. canned tomatoes

1/3 cup sugar

1 1/2 tsp. salt

dash of pepper

2 cups bread cubes

3 Tbsp. butter, melted

1. Place tomatoes in slow cooker.

2. Sprinkle with sugar, salt, and pepper.

3. Lightly toast bread cubes in melted butter. Spread over tomatoes.

4. Cover. Cook on High 3–4 hours.

   Makes 10–12 servings

Note: If you prefer bread that is less moist and soft, add bread cubes 15 minutes before serving and continue cooking without lid.

Mushrooms in Red Wine

DONNA LANTGEN • CHADRON, NE

Prep Time: 10 minutes • Cooking Time: 4–6 hours • Ideal slow cooker size: 2-qt.

1 lb. fresh mushrooms, cleaned

4 cloves garlic, chopped

1/4 cup onion, chopped

1 Tbsp. olive oil

1 cup red wine

1. Combine all ingredients in slow cooker. Cook on Low 4–6 hours, or until done to your liking.

2. Serve as a side dish with your favorite meat.

   Makes 4 servings

Stuffed Mushrooms

MELANIE L. THROWER • MCPHERSON, KS

Prep Time: 20–30 minutes • Cooking Time: 2–4 hours • Ideal slow cooker size: 3-qt.

8-10 large mushrooms

1 Tbsp. oil

¼ tsp. minced garlic

dash of salt

dash of pepper

dash of cayenne pepper, optional

¼ cup grated Monterey Jack cheese

1. Remove stems from mushrooms. Dice stems.

2. Heat oil in skillet. Sauté diced stems with garlic until softened. Remove skillet from heat.

3. Stir in seasonings and cheese. Stuff into mushroom shells. Place in slow cooker.

4. Cover. Heat on Low 2–4 hours.

Makes 4–6 servings

Variations: Add 1 Tbsp. minced onion to Step 2. Or use Monterey Jack cheese with jalapeños.

Stuffed Peppers

VIRGINIA BLISH • AKRON, NY

Prep Time: 15–25 minutes • Cooking Time: 3 hours • Ideal slow cooker size: 5-qt.

4 medium-sized green, yellow, or red, sweet peppers, or a mixture of colors

1 cup cooked rice

15-oz. can chili beans with chili gravy

1 cup (4 ozs.) shredded cheese, divided

14½-oz. can petite diced tomatoes, with onion, celery, and green pepper

1. Wash and dry sweet peppers. Remove tops, membranes, and seeds, but keep peppers whole.

2. In a bowl, mix together rice, beans, and half of cheese. Spoon mixture into peppers.

3. Pour tomatoes into slow cooker. Place filled peppers on top, keeping them upright. Do not stack peppers.

4. Cover and cook on High 3 hours.

5. Carefully lift peppers out of cooker and place on a serving platter. Spoon hot tomatoes over top. Sprinkle remaining cheese over peppers.

Makes 4 servings

Southwest Hominy

REITA YODER • CARLSBAD, NM

Prep Time: 10 minutes • Cooking Time: 1½–3 hours • Ideal slow cooker size: 3- to 4-qt.

3 29-oz. cans hominy, drained

10¾-oz. can cream of chicken
    soup

½ lb. Velveeta, or cheddar,
    cheese, grated or cubed

1 lb. cubed cooked ham, or
    sliced hot dogs

2 2¼-oz. cans green chilies,
    undrained

1. Mix all ingredients together in slow cooker.

2. Cover and cook on High 1½ hours, on Low 2–3 hours, or
   until bubbly and cheese is melted.

   Makes 12–14 servings

Note: Serve with fresh salsa.

Mexican Hominy

JANIE STEELE • MOORE, OK

Prep Time: 10 minutes • Cooking Time: 1 hour • Ideal slow cooker size: 3- to 4-qt.

2 29-oz. cans hominy, drained

4-oz. can chopped green
    chilies, mild or hot

1 cup sour cream

8-oz. jar Cheez Whiz

1. Combine ingredients in slow cooker.

2. Cover and heat on Low 1 hour, or until cheese is melted
   and dish is thoroughly hot.

   Makes 6–8 servings

Cooking Tip

Many stovetop and oven recipes can be adapted for a slow
cooker. If you want to experiment, use these conversion
factors:

• Low (in a slow cooker) = 200° in an oven, approximately.

• High (in a slow cooker) = 300° in an oven, approximately.

• In a slow cooker, 2 hours on Low = 1 hour, approximately,
  on High.

Apple Stuffing

JUDI MANOS • WEST ISLIP, NY / JEANETTE OBERHOLTZER • MANHEIM, PA

Prep Time: 20 minutes • Cooking Time: 4–5 hours • Ideal slow cooker size: 4- to 6-qt.

1 stick (½ cup) butter, divided

1 cup chopped walnuts

2 onions, chopped

14-oz. pkg. dry herb-seasoned stuffing mix

1½ cups applesauce

water, optional

1. In a nonstick skillet, melt 2 Tbsp. butter. Sauté walnuts over medium heat until toasted, about 5 minutes, stirring frequently. Remove from skillet and set aside.

2. Melt remaining butter in skillet. Add onions and cook 3–4 minutes, or until almost tender. Set aside.

3. Spray slow cooker with nonstick cooking spray. Place dry stuffing mix in slow cooker.

4. Add onion-butter mixture and stir. Add applesauce and stir.

5. Cover and cook on Low 4–5 hours, or until heated through. Check after stuffing has cooked 3½ hours. If it's sticking to cooker, drying out, or becoming too brown on edges, stir in ½–1 cup water. Continue cooking.

6. Sprinkle with walnuts before serving.

Makes 4–5 servings

Pineapple Stuffing

EDWINA F. STOLTZFUS • NARVON, PA / KRISTA HERSHBERGER • ELVERSON, PA

Prep Time: 10 minutes • Cooking Time: 3–4 hours • Ideal slow cooker size: 4-qt.

1 stick (½ cup) butter, softened

½ cup sugar

3 eggs

20-oz. can crushed pineapple, drained

6 slices stale bread, cubed

1. In a large mixing bowl, blend together butter and sugar.

2. Blend in 1 egg at a time, mixing until thoroughly combined.

3. Stir in drained pineapple. Fold in bread cubes.

4. Spoon into slow cooker.

5. Cook 3–4 hours on Low, or until heated through.

6. Allow to stand 15 minutes before serving.

Makes 4–6 servings

Corny Cornbread

PAT UNTERNAHRER • WAYLAND, IA

Prep Time: 5 minutes • Cooking Time: 3 hours 45 minutes • Ideal slow cooker size: 4-qt.

1 egg

½ cup sour cream

1 stick (½ cup) butter, melted

2 14¾-oz. cans cream-style corn

8½-oz. box cornbread mix

1. Spray slow cooker with nonstick cooking spray.

2. Mix all ingredients together in a bowl. Spoon into greased slow cooker.

3. Cook on High 3 hours and 45 minutes.

Makes 8 servings

Spicy Cheese Dip with Ground Beef

SUSAN TJON • AUSTIN, TX

Prep Time: 25 minutes • Cooking Time: 2½ hours • Ideal slow cooker size: 2- to 3-qt.

1 lb. lean ground beef

¼ cup onions, finely chopped

half a large onion, finely chopped

1½ lbs. Velveeta cheese, cubed

15-oz. can Rotel tomatoes with green chili peppers

1. Brown ground beef and ¼ cup onions in a large nonstick skillet. Break beef apart as needed. Drain.

2. Combine beef with remaining ingredients in slow cooker.

3. Cook on Low 2½ hours, or until cheese is melted.

4. Serve from slow cooker with scoop-shaped tortilla chips.

Makes 12–15 servings

Note: The smaller the Velveeta chunks, the faster they will melt.

Hot Ground Beef Dip

JENNIFER YODER SOMMERS • HARRISONBURG, VA

Prep Time: 10 minutes • Cooking Time: 1 hour • Ideal slow cooker size: 3-qt.

1 lb. ground beef

1 lb. Velveeta cheese, cubed

15-oz. can tomato sauce

Worcestershire sauce, to taste

green pepper, diced, to taste

1. Brown ground beef in a nonstick skillet. Drain.

2. Combine all ingredients in slow cooker.

3. Cover and cook on High 1 hour.

   Makes 10–12 servings

Note: Serve hot with tortilla chips for dipping.

Aunt Cheri's Dip

CYNTHIA MORRIS • GROTTOES, VA

Prep Time: 20–30 minutes • Cooking Time: 45 minutes–1 hour • Ideal slow cooker size: 6-qt.

1 lb. lean ground beef

2 lbs. Velveeta cheese, cubed

2 10¾-oz. cans tomato soup

2 10¾-oz. cans cream of celery soup

chopped green pepper, optional

chopped onion, optional

1. Brown ground beef in a large nonstick skillet. Drain.

2. Return drained beef to skillet. Turn heat to low. Stir cubed cheese into beef in skillet. Heat gently until cheese melts, stirring occasionally.

3. Place browned beef and melted cheese in slow cooker. Add remaining ingredients and stir well.

4. Cook on High 45–60 minutes, or until heated through.

5. Serve with nacho chips.

   Makes 20–30 servings

Ground Beef Cheese Dip

CAROL EBERLY • HARRISONBURG, VA

Prep Time: 20 minutes • Cooking Time: 2 hours • Ideal slow cooker size: 2-qt.

2-lb. box Velveeta cheese, cubed

1 lb. ground beef

1 onion, chopped

10¾-oz. can cream of mushroom soup

14½-oz. can diced tomatoes with green chilies

1. While cutting up cheese, brown beef and onions in skillet. Drain meat mixture and place in slow cooker.

2. Place all remaining ingredients in slow cooker and combine.

3. Cover. Cook on Low 2 hours, or until cheese is melted, stirring occasionally.

4. Serve over baked potatoes or with tortilla chips.

   Makes about 6 cups dip

Variation: For more snap, add 4¼-oz. can green chilies in Step 2.

Cheesy Ground Beef Salsa Dip

MARY JANE MUSSER • MANHEIM, PA / COLLEEN HEATWOLE • BURTON, MI

Prep Time: 15 minutes • Cooking Time: 1 hour • Ideal slow cooker size: 3- to 4-qt.

2 lbs. ground beef

2 lbs. Velveeta cheese, cubed

16-, or 32-oz., jar salsa, according to your taste preference

tortilla chips

1. Brown beef in a nonstick skillet. Drain.

2. Place beef in slow cooker while hot. Stir in cheese until melted.

3. Add salsa.

4. Turn slow cooker to High and cook 1 hour. Turn to Low. Serve with tortilla chips for dipping.

   Makes 20 servings

Note: You can make this dip ahead of time and refrigerate it, then reheat it in the slow cooker for an hour or two before you're ready to serve it.

Salsa Dip

BARBARA SMITH • BEDFORD, PA

Prep Time: 20 minutes • Cooking Time: 4 hours • Ideal slow cooker size: 3- to 4-qt.

½ lb. lean ground beef

1 lb. Velveeta cheese, cubed

3-oz. pkg. cream cheese

half an envelope dry taco
    seasoning

14-oz. jar salsa, your choice of
    hotness

1. Brown ground beef in a nonstick skillet. Drain.

2. Place in slow cooker. Add remaining ingredients. Stir well.

3. Cover and cook on Low 4 hours.

4. Stir, and then serve with taco chips.

Makes 20 servings

Note: To remove onion odor from your fingers, rub a metal spoon between your finger and thumb under running water.

Mexican Ground Beef–Cheese Dip

LIZ RUGG • WAYLAND, IA

Prep Time: 15 minutes • Cooking Time: 4–5 hours • Ideal slow cooker size: 2-qt.

1 lb. ground beef

15-oz. can enchilada sauce

1 lb. Velveeta cheese, cubed

1. Brown ground beef in a nonstick skillet. Drain.

2. Place in slow cooker. Add sauce and cubed cheese. Stir well.

3. Cover and cook on Low 4–5 hours.

4. When heated through, serve with your favorite taco chips.

Makes 10 servings

Taco Pizza Dip

ARLENE SNYDER • MILLERSTOWN, PA

Prep Time: 15 minutes • Cooking Time: 1½–2 hours • Ideal slow cooker size: 2- to 3-qt.

2 8-oz. pkgs. cream cheese, softened

8-12-oz. container French onion dip

1 lb. ground beef

half an envelope dry taco seasoning mix

1 cup shredded cheddar cheese

OPTIONAL INGREDIENTS:

green pepper, diced

mushrooms, sliced

1. Combine cream cheese and onion dip. Spread in slow cooker.

2. Brown ground beef in a skillet. Drain. Stir taco seasoning into meat.

3. Place seasoned meat on top of cream cheese mixture.

4. Sprinkle cheddar cheese on top of meat. Top with peppers and mushrooms, if you wish.

5. Cover and cook on Low 1½–2 hours. Serve with white corn chips.

Makes 8–10 servings

Creamy Taco Dip

ELAINE RINEER • LANCASTER, PA

Prep Time: 15 minutes • Cooking Time: 2–3 hours • Ideal slow cooker size: 2- to 3- qt.

1½ lbs. ground beef

1 envelope dry taco seasoning mix

16-oz. jar salsa

2 cups sour cream

1 cup cheddar cheese, grated

1. Brown ground beef in a nonstick skillet. Drain.

2. Return beef to skillet. Add taco seasoning and salsa.

3. Remove from stove and add sour cream and cheese. Pour mixture into slow cooker.

4. Cover and cook on Low 2–3 hours, or until hot.

5. Serve with tortilla chips.

Makes 10–12 servings

Hearty Broccoli-Beef Dip

RENEE BAUM • CHAMBERSBURG, PA

Prep Time: 15–20 minutes • Cooking Time: 2–3 hours • Ideal slow cooker size: 3-qt.

1 lb. ground beef

1 lb. American cheese, cubed

10¾-oz. can cream of
    mushroom soup

10-oz. pkg. frozen chopped
    broccoli, thawed

2 Tbsp. salsa, hot, medium, or
    mild

1. Brown ground beef in a nonstick skillet. Drain.

2. Combine all ingredients in slow cooker. Mix well.

3. Cover and cook on Low 2–3 hours, or until heated
through, stirring after 1 hour.

4. Serve with tortilla chips.

Makes 24 servings

Note: Serve as a main dish over baked potatoes or cooked rice.
—*Cindy Harney, Lowville, NY*

Hot Chip Dip

SHARON WANTLAND • MENOMONEE FALLS, WI

Prep Time: 15 minutes • Cooking Time: 1½ hours • Ideal slow cooker size: 4-qt.

1 lb. ground beef

1-lb. can chili without beans

1 bunch scallions, chopped

4¼-oz. can green chilies,
    chopped

1 lb. Velveeta cheese, cubed

1. Brown beef in a nonstick skillet until crumbly. Drain.

2. Place in slow cooker and add all other ingredients. Mix
together well.

3. Cover and cook on High 1½ hours.

4. Turn cooker to Low, and serve dip with large tortilla chips.

Makes 8 servings

Chili-Cheese Dip

DOROTHY LINGERFELT • STONYFORD, CA / GERTRUDE DUTCHER • HARTVILLE, OH
CORINNA HERR • STEVENS, PA

Prep Time: 10 minutes • Cooking Time: 1 hour • Ideal slow cooker size: 4-qt.

1 lb. lean ground beef

1 lb. American cheese, cubed

8–10-oz. can tomatoes and green chilies

2 tsp. Worcestershire sauce

½ tsp. chili powder

1. Brown ground beef in a nonstick skillet. Drain.

2. Place browned beef in slow cooker. Add all remaining ingredients. Stir well.

3. Cover and cook on High 1 hour, stirring occasionally, until cheese is fully melted.

4. Serve immediately, or turn to Low for serving up to 6 hours later.

Makes 10–12 servings

Note: Serve with tortilla or corn chips. For a thicker dip, stir 2 Tbsp. flour and 3 Tbsp. water together in a small bowl until smooth. When dip is hot and cheese is melted, stir paste into slow cooker. Continue to stir until thoroughly blended.

Nacho Dip

GLADYS M. HIGH • EPHRATA, PA

Prep Time: 15 minutes • Cooking Time: 1 hour • Ideal slow cooker size: 5- to 6-qt.

1 lb. ground beef

2 lbs. American cheese, cubed

16-oz. jar salsa, your choice of heat

1 Tbsp. Worcestershire sauce

1. Brown ground beef in a nonstick skillet. Drain.

2. Place beef in slow cooker. Add all other ingredients and blend well.

3. Cover and cook on High 1 hour. Stir occasionally until cheese is fully melted.

4. Serve immediately, or turn to Low for serving up to 6 hours later.

5. Serve with tortilla or corn chips.

Makes 10–12 servings

Easy Pizza Appetizers

SHARON WANTLAND • MENOMONEE FALLS, WI

Prep Time: 15 minutes • Cooking Time: 1 hour • Ideal slow cooker size: 4-qt.

1 lb. ground beef

1 lb. bulk Italian sausage

1 lb. Velveeta cheese, cubed and divided

4 tsp. pizza seasoning

½ tsp. Worcestershire sauce

1. In a large nonstick skillet, brown beef and sausage until crumbly. Drain.

2. Add remaining ingredients and place mixture in slow cooker.

3. Cover and heat on Low 1 hour.

4. When thoroughly warmed, offer a small spoon or knife for spreading and serve with party rye bread.

   Makes 8 servings

Meaty Queso Dip

JANIE STEELE • MOORE, OK

Prep Time: 50 minutes • Cooking Time: 30–60 minutes • Ideal slow cooker size: 3- to 4-qt.

1 lb. ground beef

1 lb. bulk hot Italian sausage

1 lb. jalapeño Velveeta cheese, cubed

10¾-oz. can golden mushroom soup

tortilla chips

1. Brown ground beef in a nonstick skillet. Drain. Place in slow cooker.

2. Brown loose sausage in skillet. Drain. Add to slow cooker.

3. Add all remaining ingredients except tortilla chips to slow cooker. Mix together well.

4. Cook on High 30–60 minutes, stirring frequently, until cheese is melted.

5. Turn to Low, stirring occasionally to prevent scorching. Serve with chips.

   Makes 15 appetizer servings

Hearty Pizza Dip

NATALIA SHOWALTER • MT. SOLON, VA

Prep Time: 30 minutes • Cooking Time: 3 hours • Ideal slow cooker size: 3-qt.

1 lb. bulk smoked sausage

2 8-oz. pkgs. cream cheese, cubed

2 cups pizza sauce

2 cups grated mozzarella cheese

1 cup grated cheddar cheese

1. Brown sausage in a skillet, breaking the meat into small pieces with a spoon as it browns. Drain.

2. Place sausage in slow cooker. Stir in all remaining ingredients.

3. Cover and cook on High 1 hour. Stir.

4. Cook on Low until heated through, about 2 more hours.

   Makes 18 servings

Note: Serve with corn chips.

Hot Beef Dip

SARAH MILLER • HARRISONBURG, VA

Prep Time: 30 minutes • Cooking Time: 2-3 hours • Ideal slow cooker size: 1- to 2-qt.

2 8-oz. pkgs. cream cheese, softened

8 ozs. grated cheddar cheese

1 green pepper, finely chopped

1 small onion, finely chopped

¼ lb. dried beef, shredded

1. In a medium-sized mixing bowl, combine cream cheese and grated cheese.

2. Fold in pepper, onion, and dried beef. Place stiff mixture in slow cooker.

3. Cover and cook on Low 2–3 hours. Stir occasionally.

4. Serve hot with crackers.

   Makes 12–15 servings

Reuben Appetizers

JOLEEN ALBRECHT • GLADSTONE, MI

Prep Time: 15 minutes • Cooking Time: 1–2 hours • Ideal slow cooker size: 2-qt.

½ cup mayonnaise

2 cups (10 ozs.) Swiss cheese, shredded

½ lb. thinly sliced corned beef, cut up

14-oz. can sauerkraut, drained

1 loaf or pkg. party rye bread

1. Combine all ingredients, except bread, in slow cooker.

2. Cover and cook on High 1–2 hours, or until heated through and cheese is melted.

3. Spread on slices of rye bread. Serve hot.

   Makes 10 servings

Note: The consistency is better if you do not use low-fat cheese or mayonnaise.

Reuben Spread

RENEE BAUM • CHAMBERSBURG, PA

Prep Time: 15 minutes • Cooking Time: 3 hours • Ideal slow cooker size: 2½-qt.

2½ cups cubed, cooked corned beef

16-oz. jar sauerkraut, rinsed and drained well

2 cups (8 ozs.) shredded Swiss cheese

2 cups (8 ozs.) shredded cheddar cheese

1 cup mayonnaise

1. Combine all ingredients in slow cooker. Mix well.

2. Cover and cook on Low 3 hours, stirring occasionally. Serve warm.

   Makes 18–20 servings

Sweet 'n' Sour Meatballs

VALERIE DROBEL • CARLISLE, PA / SHARON HANNABY • FREDERICK, MD

Prep Time: 10 minutes • Cooking Time: 2–4 hours • Ideal slow cooker size: 3- to 4-qt.

12-oz. jar grape jelly

12-oz. jar chili sauce

2 1-lb. bags prepared frozen
   meatballs, thawed

1. Combine jelly and sauce in slow cooker. Stir well.

2. Add meatballs. Stir to coat.

3. Cover and heat on Low 4 hours, or on High 2 hours. Keep slow cooker on Low while serving.

   Makes 15–20 servings

Note: If your meatballs are frozen, add another hour to the cooking time.

Tangy Meatballs

PENNY BLOSSER • BEAVERCREEK, OH

Prep Time: 15 minutes • Cooking Time: 2–4 hours • Ideal slow cooker size: 4-qt.

2 lbs. precooked meatballs

16-oz. bottle barbecue sauce

8 ozs. grape jelly

1. Place meatballs in slow cooker.

2. Combine barbecue sauce and jelly in a medium-sized mixing bowl.

3. Pour over meatballs and stir well.

4. Cover and cook on High 2 hours, or on Low 4 hours.

5. Turn to Low and serve.

   Makes 50–60 meatballs

Mini–Hot Dogs and Meatballs

MARY KAY NOLT • NEWMANSTOWN, PA

Prep Time: 5 minutes • Cooking Time: 2–3 hours • Ideal slow cooker size: 5- to 6-qt.

36 frozen cooked Italian
    meatballs (1/2 oz. each)

16-oz. pkg. miniature hot dogs,
    or little smoked sausages

26-oz. jar meatless spaghetti
    sauce

18-oz. bottle barbecue sauce

12-oz. bottle chili sauce

1. Combine all ingredients in slow cooker.

2. Cover and cook on High 2 hours, or on Low 3 hours, until heated through.

Makes 15 servings

Variation: Add 3½-oz. pkg. sliced pepperoni to Step 1.

Bacon Cheddar Dip

ARLENE SNYDER • MILLERSTOWN, PA

Prep Time: 10–15 minutes • Cooking Time: 1½–2 hours • Ideal slow cooker size: 4-qt.

2 8-oz. pkgs. cream cheese,
    softened

2 cups sour cream

1 lb. bacon, fried and crumbled

4 cups shredded cheddar
    cheese, divided

1. In a mixing bowl, beat cream cheese and sour cream until smooth.

2. Fold in bacon and 3 cups cheddar cheese.

3. Place mixture in slow cooker and sprinkle with remaining cheese.

4. Cover and cook on Low 1½–2 hours, or until heated through.

5. Serve with white corn chips.

Makes 15 servings

Variation: For a spicier version, stir some fresh herbs, or some chopped chilies, into Step 2.

Note: Save a few bacon crumbs to sprinkle on top.

Swiss Cheese Dip

JENNIFER YODER SOMMERS • HARRISONBURG, VA

Prep Time: 5 minutes • Cooking Time: 1–2 hours • Ideal slow cooker size: 1½-qt.

2 cups (8 ozs.) shredded Swiss cheese

1 cup mayonnaise

½ cup bacon bits

2 Tbsp. chopped onion

½ cup snack cracker crumbs

1. Combine cheese, mayonnaise, bacon bits, and onion in slow cooker.

2. Sprinkle cracker crumbs over top.

3. Cover and cook on Low 1–2 hours.

4. Serve with a variety of snack crackers or cut-up fresh vegetables.

Makes 12 servings

Pepperoni Pizza Dip

ANNABELLE UNTERNAHRER • SHIPSHEWANA, IN

Prep Time: 10 minutes • Cooking Time: 2 hours • Ideal slow cooker size: 3-qt.

2 8-oz. pkgs. cream cheese, cubed

14-oz. can pizza sauce

8-oz. pkg. sliced pepperoni, chopped

1 small can sliced ripe olives, drained

2 cups (8 ozs.) shredded mozzarella cheese

1. Place cream cheese in slow cooker.

2. In a small bowl, combine pizza sauce, pepperoni, and olives. Pour over cream cheese.

3. Sprinkle mozzarella cheese over top.

4. Cover and cook on Low 2 hours, or until cheese is melted.

5. Stir and serve with tortilla chips, bagel chips, or little garlic toasts.

Makes 10–15 servings

Mustard-Lovers' Party Dogs

BARB HARVEY • QUARRYVILLE, PA

Prep Time: 15 minutes • Cooking Time: 1–2 hours • Ideal slow cooker size: 3-qt.

12 hot dogs cut into bite-size pieces

1 cup grape jelly

1 cup prepared mustard

1. Place all ingredients in slow cooker. Stir well.

2. Turn on High until mixture boils. Stir.

3. Turn to Low and bring to the buffet table.

Makes 12 servings

Meaty Buffet Favorites

JUDY A. WANTLAND • MENOMONEE FALLS, WI

Prep Time: 5 minutes • Cooking Time: 2 hours • Ideal slow cooker size: 2- to 3-qt.

1 cup tomato sauce

1 tsp. Worcestershire sauce

1/2 tsp. prepared mustard

2 Tbsp. brown sugar

1 lb. prepared meatballs, or
    1 lb. mini-wieners

1. Mix first 4 ingredients in slow cooker.

2. Add meatballs or mini-wieners.

3. Cover and cook on High 2 hours. Turn to Low, and serve as an appetizer from the slow cooker.

Makes 24 servings

Note: If you wish, double the sauce and add both wieners and meatballs. Or add 1/4–1/2 cup onion for extra flavor and texture.

Mini–Hot Dogs

CAROLYN FULTZ • ANGOLA, IN

Prep Time: 5 minutes • Cooking Time: 4–5 hours • Ideal slow cooker size: 4-qt.

2 cups brown sugar

1 Tbsp. Worcestershire sauce

14-oz. bottle ketchup

2 or 3 lbs. mini-hot dogs

1. In slow cooker, mix together brown sugar, Worcestershire sauce, and ketchup.

2. Stir in hot dogs.

3. Cover and cook on High 1 hour. Turn to Low and cook 3–4 hours.

4. Serve from the cooker while turned to Low.

Makes 20–30 appetizer servings

Sausages in Wine

MARY E. WHEATLEY • MASHPEE, MA

Prep Time: 15 minutes • Cooking Time: 45 minutes–1 hour • Ideal slow cooker size: 3-qt.

1 cup dry red wine

2 Tbsp. currant jelly

6–8 mild Italian sausages, or
   Polish sausages

1. Place wine and jelly in slow cooker. Heat until jelly is dissolved and sauce begins to simmer. Add sausages.

2. Cover and cook on High 45 minutes–1 hour, or until sausages are cooked through and lightly glazed.

3. Transfer sausages to a cutting board and slice. Serve with juices spooned over.

Makes 6 servings or 24 appetizers

Zippy Sausage Cheese Dip

REITA YODER • CARLSBAD, NM

Prep Time: 15 minutes • Cooking Time: 1–2 hours • Ideal slow cooker size: 1-qt.

1 lb. pork sausage, sliced thin,
   or squeezed out of casing
   and crumbled

2 lbs. Velveeta cheese, cubed

2 10¾-oz. cans Rotel
   tomatoes with chilies,
   undrained

1. Brown sausage in a large nonstick skillet. Drain.

2. Return browned sausage to skillet and stir in cubed Velveeta cheese.

3. Cook over low heat until cheese melts. Stir occasionally.

4. Place pork and melted cheese in slow cooker. Stir in tomatoes.

5. Cover and cook on Low 1–2 hours, or until heated through.

6. Serve warm with raw, cut-up veggies or chips.

Makes 12 servings

Note: If the dip gets too dry, add ¼–½ cup warm water. If the cheese looks curdled, it's okay. Stir the mixture and reduce the heat, or turn off the cooker.

Cooking Tip

Use light brown sugar for a caramel flavor. Use dark brown sugar when you prefer a molasses flavor and color.

Simmered Smoked Sausages

JONICE CRIST • QUINTER, KS / MARY LYNN MILLER • REINHOLDS, PA
JOETTE DROZ • KALONA, IA / RENEE BAUM • CHAMBERSBURG, PA

Prep Time: 15 minutes • Cooking Time: 4 hours • Ideal slow cooker size: 2-qt.

2 16-oz. pkgs. miniature
   smoked sausage links

1 cup brown sugar, packed

½ cup ketchup

¼ cup prepared horseradish

1. Place sausages in slow cooker.

2. Combine remaining ingredients in a bowl and pour over sausages.

3. Cover and cook on Low 4 hours.

   Makes 16–20 servings

Slow-Cooked Smokies

RENEE BAUM • CHAMBERSBURG, PA

Prep Time: 5 minutes • Cooking Time: 6–7 hours • Ideal slow cooker size: 3- to 4-qt.

2 lbs. miniature smoked
   sausage links

28-oz. bottle barbecue sauce

1¼ cups water

3 Tbsp. Worcestershire sauce

3 Tbsp. steak sauce

½ tsp. pepper

1. In a slow cooker, combine all ingredients. Mix well.

2. Cover and cook on Low 6–7 hours.

   Makes 12–16 servings

Barbecued Lil' Smokies

JENA HAMMOND • TRAVERSE CITY, MI

Prep Time: 5 minutes • Cooking Time: 4 hours • Ideal slow cooker size: 4-qt.

4 16-oz. pkgs. little smokies

18-oz. bottle barbecue sauce

1. Mix ingredients together in slow cooker.

2. Cover and cook on Low 4 hours.

   Makes 48–60 appetizer servings

Apple-y Kielbasa

JEANETTE OBERHOLTZER • MANHEIM, PA

Prep Time: 15 minutes • Cooking Time: 6–8 hours • Ideal slow cooker size: 3-qt.

2 lbs. fully cooked kielbasa
    sausage, cut into 1" pieces

³/₄ cup brown sugar

1 cup chunky applesauce

2 cloves garlic, minced

1. Combine all ingredients in slow cooker.

2. Cover and cook on Low 6–8 hours, or until thoroughly heated.

Makes 12 servings

Easy Barbecue Smokies

RUTH ANN BENDER • COCHRANVILLE, PA

Prep Time: 5 minutes • Cooking Time: 2 hours • Ideal slow cooker size: 3¹/₂-qt.

18-oz. bottle barbecue sauce

8 ozs. salsa

2 16-oz. pkgs. little smokies

1. Mix barbecue sauce and salsa in slow cooker.

2. Add the little smokies.

3. Heat on High 2 hours.

4. Stir. Turn to Low to serve.

Makes 12–16 servings

Crab Spread

JEANETTE OBERHOLTZER • MANHEIM, PA

Prep Time: 20 minutes • Cooking Time: 4 hours • Ideal slow cooker size: 1- to 3-qt.

¹/₂ cup mayonnaise

8 ozs. cream cheese, softened

2 Tbsp. apple juice

1 onion, minced

1 lb. lump crabmeat, picked
    over to remove cartilage
    and shell bits

1. Mix mayonnaise, cheese, and juice in a medium-sized bowl until blended.

2. Stir in onions, mixing well. Gently stir in crabmeat.

3. Place in slow cooker, cover, and cook on Low 4 hours.

4. Dip will hold for 2 hours. Stir occasionally. Serve with snack crackers, snack bread, or crudités.

Makes 8 servings

Hot Cheese Melt

TIERRA WOODS • DUENWEG, MO

Prep Time: 5–10 minutes • Cooking Time: 1½–2 hours • Ideal slow cooker size: 3- to 4-qt.

12-oz. can whole, or chopped, jalapeño peppers, drained

15-oz. can Mexican stewed, or Rotel, tomatoes, undrained

2 lbs. Velveeta cheese, cubed

4 slices bacon, cooked crisp and crumbled

1. Put chopped jalapeños in bottom of slow cooker. Spoon in tomatoes and then top with chunks of cheese.

2. Cover and cook on Low 1½ hours, or until cheese is melted.

3. When ready to serve, sprinkle bacon on top.

4. Keep cooker turned to Low, and serve with tortilla chips, bread chunks, or fresh, cut-up vegetables.

Makes 9–10 servings

Pizza Fondue

BONNIE WHALING • CLEARFIELD, PA

Prep Time: 15 minutes • Cooking Time: 1 hour • Ideal slow cooker size: 3½-qt.

1-lb. block of cheese, your choice of good melting cheese(s), cut in ½" cubes

2 cups grated mozzarella cheese

19-oz. can Italian-style stewed tomatoes with juice

loaf Italian bread, slices toasted and then cut into 1" cubes

1. Place cheese cubes, grated mozzarella cheese, and tomatoes in lightly greased slow cooker.

2. Cover and cook on High 45–60 minutes, or until cheese is melted.

3. Stir occasionally and scrape down sides of slow cooker with rubber spatula to prevent scorching.

4. Reduce heat to Low and serve. (Fondue will keep a smooth consistency up to 4 hours.)

5. Serve with toasted bread cubes for dipping.

Makes 4–6 servings

Variation: Add ¼ lb. thinly sliced pepperoni to Step 1.

Mexican Bean and Cheese Dip

MARY SOMMERFELD • LANCASTER, PA

Prep Time: 5 minutes • Cooking Time: 2–3 hours • Ideal slow cooker size: 2-qt.

15-oz. can refried beans

8-oz. jar taco sauce

1 lb. Velveeta cheese, cubed

1 pkg. dry taco seasoning

1. Combine ingredients in slow cooker.

2. Cover. Cook on Low 2–3 hours, or until cheese is melted.

3. Serve warm from cooker with tortilla chips.

   Makes about 5 cups dip

Note: If you're cautious about salt, choose minimally salted chips.

Mexican Cheese Dip

DALE PETERSON • RAPID CITY, SD

Prep Time: 10 minutes • Cooking Time: 2–3 hours • Ideal slow cooker size: 3-qt.

2 lbs. Velveeta cheese, cubed

2 tsp. taco seasoning

10-oz. can tomatoes and green chilies, undrained

1. Place cubed cheese in slow cooker.

2. Cover and cook on Low 1–1½ hours, or until cheese is melted.

3. Stir in seasoning and tomatoes with green chilies.

4. Cover and cook on Low another 1–1½ hours. Stir occasionally to keep cheese from sticking to bottom of cooker.

5. Serve with your favorite sturdy chips.

   Makes 12 servings

Chili Con Queso

ARLENE LEAMAN KLIEWER • LAKEWOOD, CO

Prep Time: 15 minutes • Cooking Time: 2 hours • Ideal slow cooker size: 2-qt.

1 medium-sized onion, chopped

2 Tbsp. oil

2 4¼-oz. cans chopped green chilies

14½-oz. can Mexican-style stewed tomatoes, drained

1 lb. Velveeta cheese, cubed

1. In skillet, sauté onion in oil until transparent. Add chilies and tomatoes. Bring to a boil.

2. Add cheese. Pour into slow cooker set on Low. Cook 2 hours.

3. Keep warm in slow cooker, stirring occasionally.

4. Serve with tortilla chips.

Makes 12–16 servings

Chili Rellanos

ANDREA CUNNINGHAM • ARLINGTON, KS

Prep Time: 15 minutes • Cooking Time: 6–8 hours • Ideal slow cooker size: 4-qt.

1¼ cups milk

4 eggs, beaten

3 Tbsp. flour

12-oz. can chopped green chilies

2 cups grated cheddar cheese

1. Combine all ingredients in slow cooker until well blended.

2. Cover and cook on Low 6–8 hours.

3. Serve with tortilla chips and salsa.

Makes 8 servings

Note: You can serve this dish as a burrito filling.

Chili-Cheese Dip

SHARON TIMPE • JACKSON, WI

Prep Time: 5 minutes • Cooking Time: 2–3 hours • Ideal slow cooker size: 2-qt.

1 lb. pasteurized cheese spread

15–16-oz. can chili without
    beans

¼ cup chopped onion

4-oz. can chopped green chilies

1. Mix all ingredients in slow cooker.

2. Cover and cook on Low 2–3 hours, or until heated through.

   Makes 10-12 servings

Note: Serve hot from the pot with scoop-shaped corn chips or
tortilla chips.

Chili Con Queso Dip

JANIE STEELE • MOORE, OK

Prep Time: 5–10 minutes • Cooking Time: 1–2 hours • Ideal slow cooker size: 4-qt.

1 lb. Velveeta cheese, cubed

15-oz. can of chili with beans

4-oz. can chopped green
    chilies

1 medium-sized onion, chopped

1. Combine all ingredients in slow cooker.

2. Cover and cook on High 30 minutes, stirring frequently,
   until cheese is melted.

3. Turn to Low, keeping the cooker covered, and cook
   30–60 minutes. Stir occasionally to prevent scorching.

4. Serve with chips.

   Makes 12–15 servings

Mommy Trapp's Chip Dip

PENNY BLOSSER • BEAVERCREEK, OH

Prep Time: 15 minutes • Cooking Time: 1 hour • Ideal slow cooker size: 3-qt.

2 pounds Velveeta cheese, cubed

1/4 cup milk

1 cup sharp cheddar cheese, grated

2 2³/4-oz. cans green chilies

1 small jar pimentos

1. Combine all ingredients in slow cooker.

2. Cover and cook on High 1 hour, or until cheese melts. Stir frequently.

3. Turn cooker to Low and serve with chips of your choice.

Makes 18–24 servings

Note: Add chopped jalapeño peppers if you want a spicier dip.

Revved-Up Chili Dip

RENEE BAUM • CHAMBERSBURG, PA / SHIRLEY SEARS • SARASOTA, FL
MARY LYNN MILLER • REINHOLDS, PA

Prep Time: 5–10 minutes • Cooking Time: 2 hours • Ideal slow cooker size: 2- to 3-qt.

24-oz. jar salsa

15-oz. can chili with beans

2 2¹/4-oz. cans sliced ripe olives, drained

12 ozs. American cheese, cubed

1. In slow cooker, combine salsa, chili, and olives. Stir in cheese.

2. Cover and cook on Low 2 hours, or until cheese is melted, stirring halfway through.

3. Serve with sturdy tortilla chips.

Makes 15 servings

Curried Cheese Dip

SUSAN KASTING • JENKS, OK

Prep Time: 10 minutes • Cooking Time: 45 minutes–1 hour • Ideal slow cooker size: 1- to 2-qt.

2 cups shredded cheddar cheese

8-oz. pkg. cream cheese, softened

1/2 cup milk

1/4 cup chopped scallions

1¹/2 tsp. curry powder

1. Mix ingredients together in slow cooker.

2. Cover and heat on High 45 minutes–1 hour, or until cheeses are melted and dip is heated through. Stir occasionally.

3. Turn cooker to Low and serve dip with crackers or veggies.

Makes 9–10 servings

Cider Cheese Fondue—for a Buffet Table

RUTH ANN BENDER • COCHRANVILLE, PA

Prep Time: 15 minutes • Warming Time: until the cooker is empty! • Ideal slow cooker size: 1-qt.

¾ cup apple juice or cider

2 cups (8–10 ozs.) shredded cheddar cheese

1 cup (4–5 ozs.) shredded Swiss cheese

1 Tbsp. cornstarch

⅛ tsp. pepper

1-lb. loaf French bread, cut into chunks

1. In a large saucepan, bring cider to a boil. Reduce heat to medium-low.

2. In a large mixing bowl, toss together cheeses with cornstarch and pepper.

3. Stir mixture into cider. Cook and stir for 3–4 minutes, or until cheese is melted.

4. Transfer to a 1-qt. slow cooker to keep warm. Stir occasionally.

5. Serve with bread cubes or apple wedges for dipping.

Makes 4 servings

Super-Bowl Dip

LIZ RUGG • WAYLAND, IA

Prep Time: 15 minutes • Cooking Time: 2–3 hours • Ideal slow cooker size: 3- to 4-qt.

2 lbs. ground beef

1 envelope dry taco seasoning mix

24-oz. jar salsa, your choice of heat

1 lb. Velveeta cheese, cubed

16-oz. can refried beans

1. Brown beef in a nonstick skillet. Drain.

2. Place beef in slow cooker. Stir in remaining ingredients.

3. Cover and cook on Low 2–3 hours, or until cheese is melted.

Makes 30 servings

Note: Serve with your favorite tortilla chips.

Refried Bean Dip

MABEL SHIRK • MOUNT CRAWFORD, VA / WILMA HABERKAMP • FAIRBANK, IA

Prep Time: 5–10 minutes • Cooking Time: 2–2½ hours ▪ Ideal slow cooker size: 1- to 2-qt.

20-oz. can refried beans

1 cup shredded cheddar, or hot pepper, cheese

½ cup chopped scallions

¼ tsp. salt

2–4 Tbsp. bottled taco sauce (depending on your taste preference)

1. In slow cooker, combine beans with cheese, onions, salt, and taco sauce.

2. Cover and cook on Low 2–2½ hours.

3. Serve hot from the pot with tortilla chips.

   Makes 8–10 servings

Easy Refried Bean Dip

KATRINA EBERLY • STEVENS, PA

Prep Time: 10 minutes • Cooking Time: 1½ hours ▪ Ideal slow cooker size: 2-qt.

2 15-oz. cans refried beans

1 envelope taco seasoning mix (use all, or ¾, depending on your taste preference)

½ cup chopped onions

2 cups shredded Monterey Jack, or Mexican Blend, cheese

chopped jalapeños, or mild chilies, to taste

2–4 drops Tabasco sauce, optional

1. Place beans, taco seasoning, onions, and cheese in slow cooker. Stir well to blend.

2. Stir in jalapeños or chilies and Tabasco sauce.

3. Cook on Low until cheese is melted, about 1½ hours.

4. Add a little water if dip seems too thick.

   Makes 12 servings

Note: If you have leftovers (unlikely!), wrap the remaining dip in a flour tortilla and top with some sour cream for a light lunch or dinner.

—Joleen Albrecht, Gladstone, MI

Cheesy Bean Dip

DEBORAH HEATWOLE • WAYNESBORO, GA

Prep Time: 5–10 minutes • Cooking Time: 1½–3 hours • Ideal slow cooker size: 2-qt.

16-oz. can refried beans

2 8-oz. pkgs. cream cheese, cubed

2 cups salsa, hot, medium, or mild

2 cups shredded cheddar cheese

1 envelope dry taco seasoning mix

1. Mix all ingredients in slow cooker. Stir to combine well.

2. Cover and heat on High 1½ hours, or on Low 3 hours, stirring occasionally.

3. Serve with corn chips.

Makes 18–20 servings

Note: A potato masher works well for blending the ingredients together.

Fiesta Dip

MELISSA WARNER • BROAD TOP, PA

Prep Time: 10 minutes • Cooking Time: 30–60 minutes • Ideal slow cooker size: 1-qt.

16-oz. can refried beans

1 cup shredded cheddar cheese

½ cup Mexican salsa

1 green chili pepper, chopped, optional

1. Combine all ingredients and place in slow cooker.

2. Cover and heat on High 30–60 minutes, or until cheese is melted.

3. Serve with tortilla chips or corn chips.

Makes 8 servings

Cooking Tip

The Warm setting on a slow cooker holds food at a temperature between 145° and 165°F.

Cheese and Broccoli Dip

MARYANN MARKANO • WILMINGTON, DE

Prep Time: 20–25 minutes ▪ Cooking Time: 1½–2 hours ▪ Ideal slow cooker size: 3- to 4-qt.

2 10-oz. pkgs. frozen chopped broccoli

1 lb. cubed Mexican Velveeta cheese, or plain Velveeta, or a combination of the two

2 10¾-oz. cans cream of mushroom soup

¼ cup sour cream

1 tsp. garlic powder

1. Cook broccoli until just-tender in a saucepan. Drain.

2. Melt cheese in slow cooker on Low about 1½–2 hours. (You can jumpstart things by melting cheese in the microwave—30 seconds on High. Stir. Continue heating on High in 15-second increments, followed by stirring each time, until cheese is melted).

3. In a large mixing bowl, mix together soup, sour cream, broccoli, and garlic powder. Stir in melted cheese.

4. Spoon into slow cooker. Keep slow cooker on warm while serving with tortilla chips. Stir occasionally.

Makes 24 servings

Hot Broccoli Dip

BRENDA HOCHSTEDLER • EAST EARL, PA

Prep Time: 20 minutes ▪ Cooking Time: 1 hour ▪ Ideal slow cooker size: 2-qt.

2 cups fresh or frozen broccoli, chopped

4 Tbsp. chopped red bell pepper

2 8-oz. containers ranch dip

½ cup grated Parmesan cheese

2 cups shredded cheddar cheese

1. Mix together all ingredients in slow cooker.

2. Cook on Low 1 hour.

3. Serve with pita chips, veggie chips, or raw, cut-up vegetables.

Makes 24 servings

Hot Mushroom Dip

CAROL L. STROH • AKRON, NY

Prep Time: 30 minutes • Cooking Time: 3–4 hours • Ideal slow cooker size: 1½- to 2-qt.

8-oz. pkg. cream cheese

10¾-oz. can cream of
mushroom soup

4-oz. can mushrooms,
chopped and drained

⅔ cup chopped shrimp, crab,
or ham

½ cup milk

1. Cut cream cheese into small pieces and place in slow cooker with remaining ingredients. Stir to mix.

2. Heat on Low 3–4 hours, stirring occasionally during first hour.

3. Serve with your choice of dippers—French bread, veggies, or crackers.

Makes 6–8 servings

Artichokes

DOROTHY LINGERFELT • STONYFORD, CA

Prep Time: 10 minutes • Cooking Time: 2½–4 hours • Ideal slow cooker size: 4-qt.

4 whole, fresh artichokes

1 tsp. salt

4 Tbsp. lemon juice, divided

2 Tbsp. butter, melted

1. Wash and trim off tough outer leaves and around bottom of artichokes. Cut off about 1" from tops of each, and trim off tips of leaves. Spread top leaves apart and use a long-handled spoon to pull out fuzzy chokes in their centers.

2. Stand prepared artichokes upright in slow cooker. Sprinkle each with ¼ tsp. salt.

3. Spoon 2 Tbsp. lemon juice over artichokes. Pour in enough water to cover bottom half of artichokes.

4. Cover and cook on High 2½–4 hours.

5. Serve with melted butter and remaining lemon juice for dipping.

Makes 4 servings

Artichoke Dip

COLLEEN HEATWOLE • BURTON, MI

Prep Time: 20 minutes • Cooking Time: 1–1½ hours • Ideal slow cooker size: 2-qt.

12-oz. jar marinated artichoke hearts

1 cup grated Parmesan cheese

⅔ cup sour cream

⅔ cup mayonnaise

2 Tbsp. diced pimento

1. Drain artichoke hearts very well. Chop finely.

2. Place chopped artichokes in slow cooker. Combine with remaining ingredients.

3. Cover and cook on Low 1–1½ hours, stirring occasionally.

4. Serve with tortilla chips.

Makes 9–12 servings

Apple Dip

LETICIA A. ZEHR • LOWVILLE, NY

Prep Time: 15 minutes • Cooking Time: 20 minutes • Ideal slow cooker size: 2- to 3-qt.

2 sticks (1 cup) butter

2 cups brown sugar, packed

2 14-oz. cans sweetened, condensed milk

1 cup corn syrup

1 cup peanut butter, optional

apple slices to dip

1. Combine all ingredients except apple slices in a saucepan until smooth. Heat until scalding, watching to make sure dip doesn't stick to bottom of pan.

2. Transfer dip to slow cooker.

3. Cover and cook on Low 20 minutes.

4. While dip is warming, slice apples and place on a serving plate.

5. Serve dip from cooker turned on Low to keep it creamy.

Makes 24 servings

Butterscotch Dip

RENEE BAUM • CHAMBERSBURG, PA

Prep Time: 5–10 minutes • Cooking Time: 45–50 minutes • Ideal slow cooker size: 1-qt.

2 10-11-oz. pkgs. butterscotch chips

5-oz. can evaporated milk

⅔ cup chopped pecans

1 Tbsp. rum extract, optional

apple and pear wedges

1. Combine butterscotch chips and milk in slow cooker.

2. Cover and cook on Low 45–50 minutes, or until chips are softened. Stir until smooth.

3. Stir in pecans and extract.

4. Serve warm with fruit wedges for dipping.

Makes 10–15 servings

Slow-Cooker Candy

EILEEN M. LANDIS • LEBANON, PA / SARAH MILLER • HARRISONBURG, VA
JANET OBERHOLTZER • EPHRATA, PA

Prep Time: 5–10 minutes • Cooking Time: 2 hours • Chilling Time: 45 minutes • Ideal slow cooker size: 2- to 3-qt.

1½ lbs. almond bark, broken

4-oz. Baker's Brand German sweet chocolate bar, broken

8 ozs. chocolate chips

8 ozs. peanut butter chips

2 lbs. lightly salted, or unsalted, peanuts

1. Spray slow cooker with nonstick cooking spray.

2. Layer ingredients into slow cooker in the order listed.

3. Cook on Low 2 hours. Do not stir or lift lid during cooking time.

4. After 2 hours, mix well.

5. Drop by teaspoonfuls onto waxed paper. Refrigerate for approximately 45 minutes before serving or storing.

Makes 80–100 pieces

Peanut Clusters

JEANNINE JANZEN • ELBING, KS / MARCIA PARKER • LANSDALE, PA

Prep Time: 20 minutes • Cooking Time: 3 hours • Cooling Time: 30 minutes • Ideal slow cooker size: 4-qt.

2 lbs. white candy coating, chopped

12-oz. pkg. semi-sweet chocolate chips

4-oz. milk chocolate bar, or 4-oz. pkg. German sweet chocolate, chopped

24-oz. jar dry roasted peanuts

1. Spray slow cooker with nonstick cooking spray.

2. In slow cooker, combine white candy coating, chocolate chips, and milk chocolate.

3. Cover and cook on Low 3 hours. Stir every 15 minutes.

4. Add peanuts to melted chocolate. Mix well.

5. Drop by tablespoonfuls onto waxed paper. Cool until set. Serve immediately, or store in a tightly covered container, separating layers with waxed paper. Keep cool and dry.

Makes 3½–4 dozen pieces

Note: This rich mixture can be lumpy as it melts. Stir often, using a wooden spoon to flatten out the lumps. This recipe makes great holiday gifts. And the taste improves a day after it's been made.

Haystacks

CATHY BOSHART • LEBANON, PA

Prep Time: 15 minutes • Cooking Time: 15 minutes • Cooling Time: 30 minutes • Ideal slow cooker size: 2-qt.

2 6-oz. pkgs. butterscotch chips

¾ cup chopped almonds

5-oz. can chow mein noodles

1. Turn cooker to High. Place chips in slow cooker. Stir every few minutes until they're melted.

2. When chips are completely melted, gently stir in almonds and noodles.

3. When well mixed, drop by teaspoonfuls onto waxed paper.

4. Let stand until haystacks are set, or speed things up by placing them in fridge until set.

5. Serve, or store in a covered container, placing waxed paper between layers of candy. Keep in a cool, dry place.

Makes 3 dozen pieces

Old-Fashioned Hot Chocolate Syrup

JENNIE MARTIN • RICHFIELD, PA

Prep Time: 10 minutes • Warming Time: 4 hours • Ideal slow cooker size: 5-qt.

1 cup dry cocoa powder

2 cups sugar

1½ cups hot water

½ tsp. vanilla

3 qts. milk

1. Mix first 3 ingredients together with a whisk in a 2-qt. saucepan. Bring to a boil and boil 2 minutes.

2. Remove from heat and stir in vanilla.

3. Add this syrup to approximately 3 qts. milk. You can heat milk in a 5-qt. saucepan, stir syrup into it, and then pour the hot chocolate into slow cooker. Or you can heat milk in slow cooker and add syrup to it there.

4. Either way, you can maintain hot chocolate in slow cooker throughout an evening party.

Makes 18 servings

Slow-Cooker Apple Butter

SARAH MILLER • HARRISONBURG, VA

Prep Time: 15 minutes • Cooking Time: 12-15 hours • Ideal slow cooker size: 5-qt.

4 qts. unsweetened applesauce

3½ cups sugar

¼ tsp. oil of cinnamon (look in the cake/candy ingredients aisle of your grocery store)

¼ tsp. oil of cloves (look in the cake/candy ingredients aisle of your grocery store)

¼ cup vinegar

dash or two of cinnamon, optional

1. Put applesauce in slow cooker. Cover, and cook on Low overnight.

2. In the morning, add remaining ingredients. Cook on High, stirring occasionally, until apple butter reaches the thickness you like. This could take several hours, depending on variety of apples.

3. Pour into hot sterilized jars and process according to standard canning methods.

Makes 10 cups

Traditional Apple Butter

WILMA HABERKAMP • FAIRBANK, IA / VERA MARTIN • EAST EARL, PA

Prep Time: 15 minutes • Cooking Time: 10-13 hours • Ideal slow cooker size: 3-qt.

12-14 medium-sized tart cooking apples (about 16 cups chopped)

2 cups cider

2 cups sugar

1 tsp. cinnamon

⅛-¼ tsp. cloves (add ⅛ tsp. cloves first; taste about halfway through the cooking time to decide if you want to add the other ⅛ tsp.)

1. Core and chop apples. Do not peel them. Combine apples and cider in slow cooker.

2. Cover and cook on Low 9–12 hours, or until apples turn mushy and then thicken.

3. Puree apples in a food mill or sieve.

4. Return pureed mixture to slow cooker.

5. Add sugar, cinnamon, and cloves and mix together well.

6. Cover and cook on Low 1 hour.

Makes 8 cups

Note: This will keep several weeks in your refrigerator. You may also can or freeze it. This is good on bread or toast. Or use it as a topping over ice cream. Or try it as a filling for apple turnovers. If you can't find cider, you can use apple juice instead.

Lotsa-Apples Apple Butter

MARY KATHRYN YODER • HARRISONVILLE, MO

Prep Time: 30 minutes • Cooking Time: all day • Ideal slow cooker size: 3½-qt.

crock full of chopped apples

2 cups sugar

3 tsp. cinnamon

¼ tsp. salt

1. Peel, core, and finely chop apples. You can make the cooker so heaping full that the lid doesn't fit at first, but apples will cook down so that the lid will eventually fit.

2. Drizzle sugar, cinnamon, and salt over apples.

3. Cover and cook on High 1 hour. Reduce heat to Low. Cook all day, or until mixture becomes thick and dark in color. Stir occasionally.

4. Place in small jars, cool, and freeze, leaving room for expansion.

Makes 5 cups

Apricot Butter

JANET L. ROGGIE • LOWVILLE, NY

Prep Time: 10 minutes • Cooking Time: 8 hours • Ideal slow cooker size: 5-qt.

4 28-oz. cans apricots, drained

3 cups sugar

2 tsp. cinnamon

½ tsp. cloves

2 Tbsp. lemon juice

1. Puree fruit in food processor. Pour into slow cooker.

2. Stir in remaining ingredients.

3. Cover and cook on Low 8 hours.

4. Pour into hot, sterilized 1-cup, or 1-pt., jars and process according to standard canning methods.

5. Serve as a spread with bread, or as a sauce with pork or chicken dishes.

Makes 15 cups

BEVERAGES

Home-Style Tomato Juice

WILMA HABERKAMP • FAIRBANK, IA

Prep Time: 20 minutes • Cooking Time: 4–6 hours • Ideal slow cooker size: 3-qt.

10–12 large ripe tomatoes

1 tsp. salt

1 tsp. seasoned salt

¼ tsp. pepper

1 Tbsp. sugar

1. Wash and drain tomatoes. Remove core and blossom ends.

2. Place whole tomatoes in slow cooker. (Do not add water.)

3. Cover and cook on Low 4–6 hours, or until tomatoes are very soft.

4. Press them through a sieve or food mill.

5. Add seasonings. Chill.

Makes 4 cups

Note: If you have more than 10–12 tomatoes, you can use a larger slow cooker and double the recipe.

Spicy Hot Cider

MICHELLE HIGH • FREDERICKSBURG, PA

Prep Time: 5 minutes • Cooking Time: 3 hours • Ideal slow cooker size: 5-qt.

1 gallon apple cider

4 cinnamon sticks

2 Tbsp. allspice

¼-½ cup brown sugar

1. Combine all ingredients in slow cooker. Begin with ¼ cup brown sugar. Stir to dissolve. If you'd like cider to be sweeter, add more sugar, up to ½ cup total.

2. Cover and cook on Low 3 hours.

3. Serve warm from cooker.

Makes 16 servings

Red Hot Apple Cider

ALLISON INGELS • MAYNARD, IA

Prep Time: 5 minutes • Cooking Time: 1½-2 hours • Ideal slow cooker size: 5-qt.

1 gallon apple cider, or apple juice

1¼ cups red cinnamon hearts

16 4"-long cinnamon sticks

1. Combine cider and cinnamon hearts in slow cooker.

2. Cover. Cook on Low 1½–2 hours.

3. Serve hot with a cinnamon stick in each cup.

Makes 16 servings

Hot Apple Cider

JEANNINE JANZEN • ELBING, KS

Prep Time: 5 minutes • Cooking Time: 2–3 hours • Ideal slow cooker size: 3-qt.

1 qt. apple cider

⅛ tsp. nutmeg

½ cup red cinnamon hearts

1. Combine all ingredients in slow cooker.

2. Cover and cook on High 2–3 hours, or until very hot. If you're at home and available, stir the cider occasionally to help candy dissolve.

3. Serve warm from slow cooker.

Makes 4 servings

Wassail

DAWN HAHN • LITITZ, PA

Prep Time: 5 minutes ▪ Cooking Time: 3–5 hours ▪ Ideal slow cooker size: 5-qt.

½ cup red cinnamon hearts

1 gallon apple cider

16 orange slice halves

16 3"–4"-long cinnamon sticks

1. Pour cinnamon hearts into bottom of slow cooker.

2. Add apple cider.

3. Cook on Low 3–5 hours, or until cider is very hot and candy has melted. If you're able, stir occasionally to help candy dissolve.

4. Place 1 orange slice half and 1 cinnamon stick in each cup. Pour hot cider over top.

Makes 16 servings

Note: Slow cookers come in a variety of sizes, from 2 to 8 qts. The best size for a family of four or five is a 5- to 6-qt. size.

—*Dorothy M. Van Deest, Memphis, TN*

Citrus Cider

VALERIE DROBEL • CARLISLE, PA

Prep Time: 10 minutes ▪ Cooking Time: 2–5 hours ▪ Ideal slow cooker size: 3- to 5-qt.

2 qts. apple cider

½ cup packed brown sugar

2 4"-long cinnamon sticks

1 tsp. whole cloves

1 orange or lemon, sliced

1. Pour cider into slow cooker. Stir in brown sugar.

2. Place cinnamon sticks and cloves in cheesecloth and tie with string to form a bag. Float in slow cooker.

3. Add fruit slices on top.

4. Cover and cook on Low 2–5 hours. Remove spice bag. Stir before serving.

Makes 8-10 servings

Orange Spiced Cider

CAROLYN BAER • CONRATH, WI

Prep Time: 5 minutes • Cooking Time: 2–3 hours • Ideal slow cooker size: 2- to 3-qt.

4 cups unsweetened apple juice

12-oz. can orange juice concentrate, thawed

½ cup water

1 Tbsp. red cinnamon hearts

½ tsp. nutmeg

1 tsp. whole cloves

8 3"–4"-long cinnamon sticks, optional

8 fresh orange slice halves, optional

1. Combine first 5 ingredients in slow cooker.

2. Place cloves on a piece of cheesecloth. Tie with string to create a bag. Submerge bag in juices in slow cooker.

3. Cover and cook on Low 2–3 hours, or until cider is very hot.

4. Remove bag before serving. Stir cider.

5. If you wish, place a cinnamon stick, topped with an orange slice, in each cup. Pour in hot cider.

Makes 8 servings

Fruit Cider Punch

BECKY FREY • LEBANON, PA

Prep Time: 5–10 minutes • Cooking Time: 4–10 hours • Ideal slow cooker size: 3½-qt.

4 cups apple cider

2 cups cranberry juice

1 cup orange juice

12-oz. can apricot nectar

¼ cup sugar, optional

2 4"-long cinnamon sticks

1. Combine all ingredients thoroughly in slow cooker.

2. Cover and cook on Low 4–10 hours.

3. Serve warm from cooker.

Makes 10–12 servings

Note: Taste the punch before adding the sugar to see if you think it's needed.

Cranberry-Apple Cider

NORMA GRIESER • CLARKSVILLE, MI

Prep Time: 10 minutes • Cooking Time: 2–3 hours • Ideal slow cooker size: 8-qt.

1 gallon cider, or apple juice

64-oz. can cranberry juice
    cocktail

½ cup brown sugar

1 cup red cinnamon hearts

2 tsp. cinnamon

1. Pour ingredients in slow cooker. Stir together well.

2. Cover and heat on High 2–3 hours, or until cider is very hot. If you're home and able to do so, stir occasionally to help candy dissolve.

3. Serve warm from cooker.

Makes 20 servings

Fruity Wassail

MELISSA WARNER • BROAD TOP, PA

Prep Time: 5 minutes • Cooking Time: 5–9 hours • Ideal slow cooker size: 3-qt.

2 qts. apple juice, or cider

2 cups cranberry juice cocktail

2 4"-long cinnamon sticks

1 tsp. whole allspice

10-oz. can mandarin oranges,
    with juice

1. Place apple juice, or cider, and cranberry juice in slow cooker.

2. Place cinnamon sticks and whole allspice on a piece of cheesecloth. Tie with a string to make a bag. Place in cooker.

3. Cover and cook on High 1 hour, and then cook on Low 4–8 hours.

4. Add oranges and their juice 15 minutes before serving.

5. Remove cheesecloth bag before serving.

Makes 10 servings

Spiced Cranberry Cider

ESTHER BURKHOLDER • MILLERSTOWN, PA

Prep Time: 5–10 minutes • Cooking Time: 3–5 hours • Ideal slow cooker size: 3-qt.

1 qt. apple cider

3 cups cranberry juice cocktail

3 Tbsp. brown sugar

2 3"-long cinnamon sticks

3/4 tsp. whole cloves

1/2 lemon, thinly sliced, optional

1. Pour apple cider and cranberry juice into slow cooker.

2. Stir in brown sugar.

3. Put spices on a piece of cheesecloth. Tie with a string to create a bag. Place in slow cooker.

4. Stir in lemon slices, if you wish.

5. Cover and cook on Low 3–5 hours, or until cider is very hot. If you're able, stir occasionally to be sure brown sugar is dissolving.

6. Remove spice bag, and lemon slices, if you've included them, before serving warm from cooker.

Makes 7 servings

Lime-Cranberry Punch

SANDRA HAVERSTRAW • HUMMELSTOWN, PA

Prep Time: 5 minutes • Cooking Time: 3–4 hours • Ideal slow cooker size: 4-qt.

8 cups cranberry juice cocktail

3 cups water

1/2 cup fresh lime juice

2/3 cup sugar

3 4"-long cinnamon sticks, broken in half

8 half-slices of an orange, optional

1. Place all ingredients except oranges slices in slow cooker. Stir until sugar is dissolved.

2. Cover and simmer on Low 3–4 hours, or until very hot.

3. With a slotted spoon, remove cinnamon sticks and discard before serving.

4. If you wish, float a half-slice of orange on each individual serving of hot punch.

Makes 10–12 servings

Note: Refrigerate any leftover punch; then reheat it or enjoy it cold.

Spiced Apricot Cider

JANET OBERHOLTZER • EPHRATA, PA

Prep Time: 5 minutes • Cooking Time: 3–4 hours • Ideal slow cooker size: 2-qt.

2 12-oz. cans apricot nectar

¼ cup lemon juice

2 cups water

¼ cup sugar

3 whole cloves

3 3"–4"-long cinnamon sticks

1. Combine juices, water, and sugar in slow cooker. Mix well.

2. Place whole cloves and cinnamon sticks on a piece of cheesecloth. Tie with a string to create a bag. Submerge in juices in cooker.

3. Cover and cook on Low 3–4 hours, or until cider is very hot.

4. Remove cloves and cinnamon sticks before serving. Serve warm from cooker.

Makes 4–6 servings

Delta Tea

VERA F. SCHMUCKER • GOSHEN, IN

Prep Time: 5 minutes • Cooking Time: 3–4 hours • Ideal slow cooker size: 2- to 3-qt.

6-oz. can frozen lemonade

5 cups water

1 tsp. vanilla

1 tsp. almond flavoring

3 tsp. dry instant tea

1. Combine all ingredients in slow cooker.

2. Cover and cook on High 3–4 hours, or until very hot.

3. Serve hot from cooker, or ice it and serve cold.

Makes 6 cups

Johnny Appleseed Tea

SHEILA PLOCK • BOALSBURG, PA

Prep Time: 15–20 minutes • Cooking Time: 1–2 hours • Ideal slow cooker size: 3-qt.

2 qts. water, divided

6 tea bags of your favorite flavor

6 ozs. frozen apple juice, thawed

¼ cup, plus 2 Tbsp., firmly packed brown sugar

1. Bring 1 qt. water to boil. Add tea bags. Remove from heat. Cover and let steep 5 minutes. Pour into slow cooker.

2. Add remaining ingredients and mix well.

3. Cover. Heat on Low until hot. Continue heating on Low while serving from slow cooker.

Makes 8–9 cups

Spicy Tea

RUTH RETTER • MANHEIM, PA

Prep Time: 15 minutes • Cooking Time: 2–3 hours • Ideal slow cooker size: 3½-qt.

6 cups water

6 tea bags, experiment with various flavors, or use your favorite

⅓ cup sugar

2 Tbsp. honey

1½ cups orange juice

1½ cups pineapple juice

1. Place water in a saucepan and bring to a boil. Add tea bags to boiling water. Let stand 5 minutes.

2. Remove tea bags. Pour tea into slow cooker.

3. Stir in remaining ingredients.

4. Cover and cook on Low 2–3 hours, or until very hot.

Makes 9–10 servings

Note: If you wish, float half an orange slice on each cup of tea.

Hot Chocolate

COLLEEN HEATWOLE • BURTON, MI

Prep Time: 10 minutes • Cooking Time: 2–3 hours • Ideal slow cooker size: 3-qt.

8 cups water

3 cups dried milk

⅓ cup nondairy coffee creamer

1 cup instant hot chocolate mix (the kind you mix with milk, not water)

marshmallows

1. Pour water into slow cooker.

2. Gradually stir in dried milk until blended.

3. Cover and cook on High 2–3 hours, or until milk is hot.

4. Stir in coffee creamer and hot chocolate mix.

5. Turn on Low until serving time, up to 3–4 hours.

6. Serve in mugs topped with marshmallows.

Makes 10–12 servings

Hot Mint Malt

CLARICE WILLIAMS • FAIRBANK, IA

Prep Time: 5 minutes • Cooking Time: 2–3 hours • Ideal slow cooker size: 2- to 3-qt.

6 chocolate-covered cream-filled mint patties

5 cups milk

½ cup chocolate malted milk powder

1 tsp. vanilla

whipping cream, whipped stiff

1. In slow cooker, combine mint patties with milk, malted milk powder, and vanilla.

2. Heat on Low 2–3 hours. If you're able, stir occasionally to help melt patties.

3. When drink is thoroughly heated, beat with a rotary beater until frothy.

4. Pour into cups and top with whipped cream.

Makes 6 servings

Hot Chocolate Malted

SHARON TIMPE • JACKSON, WI

Prep Time: 10 minutes ▪ Cooking Time: 3 hours ▪ Ideal slow cooker size: 3½-qt.

1½ cups hot cocoa mix

½ cup chocolate malted milk
   powder

6 caramels, unwrapped

1 tsp. vanilla

8 cups water or milk

whipped topping, optional

25–30 miniature
   marshmallows, optional

1. Mix all ingredients, except last 2 optional ones, in slow
   cooker.

2. Heat on High 3 hours, stirring occasionally if you're home
   and able to do so.

3. Taste before serving. Depending on the hot cocoa mix
   you've used, you may want to add more water or milk.
   (Heat additional liquid in the microwave before adding to
   hot chocolate.)

4. Ladle into cups and top each with a dollop of whipped
   cream or marshmallows, if you wish.

   Makes 8–10 servings

Creamy Hot Chocolate

DEBORAH HEATWOLE • WAYNESBORO, GA

Prep Time: 15 minutes ▪ Cooking Time: 2–4 hours ▪ Ideal slow cooker size: 3-qt.

½ cup dry baking cocoa

14-oz. can sweetened
   condensed milk

⅛ tsp. salt

7½ cups water

1½ tsp. vanilla

24, or more, miniature
   marshmallows, optional

1. In slow cooker, combine dry cocoa, milk, and salt. Stir
   until smooth. Add water gradually, stirring until smooth.

2. Cover and cook on High 2 hours, or on Low 4 hours, or
   until very hot.

3. Just before serving, stir in vanilla.

4. Top each serving with 3 or more marshmallows, if you wish.

   Makes 8 servings

Note: To speed things up, heat the water before adding it to the
chocolate mixture. Keep hot chocolate warm on Low up to 4 hours
in the slow cooker. Add a mocha flavor by stirring in instant coffee
in Step 3.

Italian Hot Chocolate

CYNDIE MARRARA • PORT MATILDA, PA

Prep Time: 3–5 minutes • Cooking Time: 1–2 hours • Ideal slow cooker size: 1- to 2-qt.

2 cups brewed strong coffee

½ cup instant hot chocolate mix

1 4"-long cinnamon stick, broken into large pieces

1 cup whipping cream

1 Tbsp. confectioners' sugar

1. Put coffee, hot chocolate mix, and cinnamon sticks into slow cooker. Stir.

2. Cover and cook on High 1–2 hours, or until very hot. Discard cinnamon pieces.

3. Immediately after you've turned on cooker, place electric mixer beaters and a mixer bowl in fridge to chill (this makes cream more likely to whip).

4. Just before serving, pour whipping cream into chilled electric mixer bowl. Beat cream on high speed until soft peaks form.

5. Fold sugar into whipped cream. Beat again on high speed until stiff peaks form.

6. Ladle hot chocolate coffee into small cups. Top each with a dollop of whipped cream.

Makes 4–6 small servings

Party Mocha

BARBARA SPARKS • GLEN BURNIE, MD

Prep Time: 5 minutes • Cooking Time: 3 hours • Ideal slow cooker size: 3- to 4-qt.

½ cup instant coffee granules

6 envelopes instant cocoa mix

2 qts. hot water

2 cups milk

whipped topping, optional

10 4"-long cinnamon sticks, optional

10 peppermint sticks, optional

1. Combine all ingredients, except last 3 optional ones, in slow cooker. Stir well.

2. Cover and cook on High 3 hours.

3. Stir and turn to Low to keep warm while serving.

4. To serve, pour mocha into cups. Top each with a dollop of whipped topping, or add a cinnamon stick or peppermint stick to each cup, if you wish.

Makes 10 servings

Spiced Coffee

ESTHER BURKHOLDER • MILLERSTOWN, PA

Prep Time: 10 minutes • Cooking Time: 3 hours • Ideal slow cooker size: 3-qt.

8 cups brewed coffee

⅓ cup sugar

¼ cup chocolate syrup

4 3"-long cinnamon sticks

1½ tsp. whole cloves

1. Pour coffee into slow cooker. Stir in sugar and chocolate syrup.

2. Place cinnamon sticks and whole cloves on a piece of cheesecloth. Tie with string to create a bag. Submerge in slow cooker.

3. Cover and cook on Low 3 hours, or until coffee is very hot. Remove cheesecloth bag.

4. Turn to Low and serve warm from cooker.

Makes 8 servings

BREAKFASTS AND BRUNCHES

Breakfast Sausage Casserole

KENDRA DREPS • LIBERTY, PA

Prep Time: 15 minutes ▪ Chilling Time: 8 hours ▪ Cooking Time: 4 hours ▪ Ideal slow cooker size: 3-qt.

1 lb. loose sausage

6 eggs

2 cups milk

8 slices bread, cubed

2 cups shredded cheddar
    cheese

1. In a nonstick skillet, brown and drain sausage.

2. Mix together eggs and milk in a large bowl.

3. Stir in bread cubes, cheese, and sausage.

4. Place in greased slow cooker.

5. Refrigerate overnight.

6. Cook on Low 4 hours.

   Makes 8 servings

Variation: Use cubed cooked ham instead of sausage.

Easy Egg and Sausage Puff

SARA KINSINGER • STUARTS DRAFT, VA

Prep Time: 10–15 minutes • Cooking Time: 2–2½ hours • Ideal slow cooker size: 2- to 4-qt.

1 lb. loose sausage

6 eggs

1 cup all-purpose baking mix

1 cup shredded cheddar cheese

2 cups milk

¼ tsp. dry mustard, optional

1. Brown sausage in a nonstick skillet. Break up chunks of meat as it cooks. Drain.

2. Meanwhile, spray slow cooker with nonstick cooking spray.

3. Mix all ingredients in slow cooker.

4. Cover and cook on High 1 hour. Turn to Low and cook 1–1½ hours, or until dish is fully cooked in the center.

Makes 6 servings

Note: Save the end pieces of loaves of bread in a bag in the freezer. When you have a bag full, run them through a food processor or blender to make bread crumbs. (My children love to do this.) Use the crumbs for breading chicken, in meat loaf, or with melted butter as a topping for macaroni and cheese.

Layered Breakfast Casserole

CATHY BOSHART • LEBANON, PA

Prep Time: 30 minutes • Cooling Time: 4–8 hours • Cooking Time: 1 hour • Ideal slow cooker size: 6-qt.

6 medium-sized potatoes

2 dozen eggs

1 lb. chopped ham

12 ozs. Velveeta cheese, shredded

1. The day before you want to serve the casserole, boil potatoes in their skins until soft. Chill. When thoroughly chilled, grate potatoes. Spread in bottom of greased slow cooker.

2. Scramble and cook eggs in a nonstick skillet. When just set, spoon cooked eggs over top of potatoes.

3. Layer ham evenly over eggs. Sprinkle with cheese.

4. Bake on Low 1 hour, or until cheese is melted.

Makes 8–10 servings

Note: This is a perfect dish to serve on a buffet. Or prepare through the first instruction in Step 3 a day ahead (chill in the fridge overnight), but sprinkle the cheese over top just before cooking. If you've refrigerated the slow cooker overnight, allow it to reach room temperature before turning it on and reheating the dish. Serve with toasted English muffins and fresh fruit.

Breakfast Bake

KRISTI SEE • WESKAN, KS

Prep Time: 15 minutes • Cooking Time: 3–4 hours • Ideal slow cooker size: 4- to 5-qt.

12 eggs

1½–2 cups grated cheese,
　　your choice

1 cup diced cooked ham

1 cup milk

1 tsp. salt

½ tsp. pepper

1. Beat eggs. Pour into slow cooker.

2. Mix in remaining ingredients.

3. Cover and cook on Low 3–4 hours.

　　Makes 10 servings

Almond Date Oatmeal

AUDREY L. KNEER • WILLIAMSFIELD, IL

Prep Time: 10 minutes • Cooking Time: 4–8 hours, or overnight • Ideal slow cooker size: 3-qt.

2 cups dry rolled oats

½ cup dry Grape-Nuts cereal

½ cup almonds, chopped

¼ cup dates, chopped

4½ cups water

1. Combine all ingredients in slow cooker.

2. Cover and cook on Low 4–8 hours, or overnight.

3. Serve with fat-free milk.

　　Makes 8 servings

Slow Cooker Oatmeal

MARTHA BENDER • NEW PARIS, IN

Prep Time: 10–15 minutes • Cooking Time: 8–9 hours • Ideal slow cooker size: 4- to 5-qt.

2 cups dry rolled oats

4 cups water

1 large apple, peeled and
　　chopped

1 cup raisins

1 tsp. cinnamon

1–2 Tbsp. orange peel

1. Combine all ingredients in slow cooker.

2. Cover and cook on Low 8–9 hours.

3. Serve topped with brown sugar, if you wish, and milk.

　　Makes 7–8 servings

Breakfast Oatmeal

DONNA CONTO • SAYLORSBURG, PA

Prep Time: 5 minutes • Cooking Time: 8 hours • Ideal slow cooker size: 4-qt.

2 cups dry rolled oats

4 cups water

1 tsp. salt

½–1 cup chopped dates, or
    raisins, or cranberries, or a
    mixture

1. Combine all ingredients in slow cooker.

2. Cover and cook on Low 8 hours, or overnight.

Makes 6 servings

Note: This is a great dish when you have company for breakfast.
No last-minute preparation needed!

Overnight Oatmeal

JODY MOORE • PENDLETON, IN

Prep Time: 5 minutes • Cooking Time: 8 hours • Ideal slow cooker size: 3-qt.

1 cup dry steel-cut oats

4 cups water

1. Combine ingredients in slow cooker.

2. Cover and cook on Low 8 hours, or overnight.

3. Stir before serving. Serve with brown sugar, ground
cinnamon, fruit preserves, jam, jelly, pumpkin pie spice,
fresh fruit, maple syrup, or your other favorite toppings.

Makes 4–5 servings

Note: Please note that steel-cut oats are called for. They are
different—with more texture, requiring a longer cooking time—
than old-fashioned or rolled oatmeal.

Pineapple Baked Oatmeal

SANDRA HAVERSTRAW • HUMMELSTOWN, PA

Prep Time: 5 minutes • Cooking Time: 1½ -2½ hours • Ideal slow cooker size: 2- to 3½-qt.

1 box 8 instant oatmeal packets (approx. a 12- to 14-oz. box), any flavor

1½ tsp. baking powder

2 eggs, beaten

½ cup milk

8-oz. can crushed pineapple in juice, undrained

1. Spray slow cooker with nonstick cooking spray.

2. Empty packets of oatmeal into a large bowl. Add baking powder and mix.

3. Stir in eggs, milk, and undrained pineapple. Mix well. Pour mixture into slow cooker.

4. Cover and cook on High 1½ hours, or on Low 2½ hours.

Makes 5–6 servings

Note: Serve warm as is, or with milk, for breakfast. This is also a good, hearty, not-too-sweet dessert served with ice cream. Individual servings reheat well in the microwave for a quick breakfast.

Breakfast Apples

JOYCE BOWMAN • LADY LAKE, FL / JEANETTE OBERHOLTZER • MANHEIM, PA

Prep Time: 10–15 minutes • Cooking Time: 2–8 hours • Ideal slow cooker size: 3-qt.

4 medium-sized apples, peeled and sliced

¼ cup honey

1 tsp. cinnamon

2 Tbsp. melted butter

2 cups dry granola cereal

1. Place apples in slow cooker.

2. Combine remaining ingredients. Sprinkle mixture evenly over top of apples.

3. Cover and cook on Low 6–8 hours, or overnight, or on High 2–3 hours.

4. Serve as a side dish to bacon and bagels, or use as a topping for waffles, French toast, pancakes, or cooked oatmeal.

Makes 4 servings

Polenta or Cornmeal Mush

DOROTHY VAN DEEST • MEMPHIS, TN

Prep Time: 10 minutes • **Cooking Time:** 2–9 hours • **Chilling Time:** 8 hours, or overnight • **Ideal slow cooker size:** 1½-qt.

4 Tbsp. butter, melted, divided

¼ tsp. paprika and/or dash of cayenne pepper

6 cups boiling water

2 cups dry cornmeal

2 tsp. salt

1. Use 1 Tbsp. butter to lightly grease slow cooker. Sprinkle in paprika and/or cayenne. Turn to High setting.

2. Add remaining ingredients to slow cooker in the order listed, including 1 Tbsp. butter. Stir well.

3. Cover and cook on High 2–3 hours, or on Low 6–9 hours. Stir occasionally.

4. Pour hot cooked polenta/mush into 2 lightly greased loaf pans. Chill overnight.

5. To serve, cut into ¼"-thick slices. Melt 2 Tbsp. butter in a large nonstick skillet, then lay in slices and cook until browned. Turn to brown other side.

6. For breakfast, serve with maple syrup, honey, or your choice of sweetener.

Makes 8–10 servings

Breakfast Hominy

BONNIE GOERING • BRIDGEWATER, VA

Prep Time: 5 minutes • **Cooking Time:** 8 hours • **Ideal slow cooker size:** 2-qt.

1 cup dry cracked hominy

1 tsp. salt

black pepper, optional

3 cups water

2 Tbsp. butter

1. Stir all ingredients together in greased slow cooker.

2. Cover and cook on Low 8 hours, or overnight.

3. Serve warm for breakfast.

Makes 5 servings

Variation: You can make cheesy hominy by decreasing the salt to ¾ tsp. and adding 1 cup grated cheese (we like American cheese best) to Step 1.

Cheesy Hominy

DEBORAH HEATWOLE • WAYNESBORO, GA

Prep Time: 5 minutes • Cooking Time: 2½ hours • Ideal slow cooker size: 2-qt.

1 29-oz., or 2 15½-oz., cans hominy, drained

1 cup diced cheese (cheddar or Velveeta works well)

½ tsp. salt

dash pepper

8 saltine crackers, crumbled

½ cup milk

butter, optional

1. Spray slow cooker with nonstick cooking spray. Add hominy, cheese, salt, pepper, and saltines. Stir to mix.

2. Pour milk over all. Dot with butter, if you wish.

3. Cover and cook on High 2½ hours.

Makes 6-8 servings

Note: Serve for breakfast with sausage and fruit, or for a main meal with a meat and green vegetable.

Blueberry Fancy

LETICIA A. ZEHR • LOWVILLE, NY

Prep Time: 10-15 minutes • Cooking Time: 3-4 hours • Ideal slow cooker size: 5-qt.

1 loaf Italian bread, cubed, divided

1 pint blueberries, divided

8 ozs. cream cheese, cubed, divided

6 eggs

1½ cups milk

1. Place half of bread cubes in slow cooker.

2. Drop half of blueberries over top of bread.

3. Sprinkle half of cream cheese cubes over blueberries.

4. Repeat all 3 layers.

5. In a mixing bowl, whisk together eggs and milk. Pour over all ingredients.

6. Cover and cook on Low 3-4 hours, until the dish is custardy and set.

7. Serve with maple syrup or blueberry sauce.

Makes 12 servings

Variation: Add 1 tsp. vanilla to Step 5.

Streusel Cake

JEAN BUTZER • BATAVIA, NY

Prep Time: 10 minutes • Cooking Time: 3–4 hours • Ideal slow cooker size: 3-qt.

16-oz. pkg. pound cake mix, prepared according to package directions

¼ cup packed brown sugar

1 Tbsp. flour

¼ cup chopped nuts

1 tsp. cinnamon

1. Liberally grease and flour a 2-lb. coffee can, or a slow-cooker baking insert, that fits into slow cooker. Pour prepared cake mix into coffee can or baking insert.

2. In a small bowl, mix brown sugar, flour, nuts, and cinnamon together. Sprinkle over top of cake mix.

3. Place coffee tin or baking insert in slow cooker. Cover top of tin or insert with several layers of paper towels.

4. Cover cooker itself and cook on High 3–4 hours, or until toothpick inserted in center of cake comes out clean.

5. Remove baking tin from slow cooker and allow to cool 30 minutes before cutting cake into wedges to serve.

Makes 8–10 servings

Cooking Tip

Keep spatulas, wire whisks, wooden spoons, etc., near the stove, within arm's reach.

DESSERTS

Cherry Cobbler

MICHELE RUVOLA • SELDEN, NY

Prep Time: 5 minutes ▪ Cooking Time: 2½–5½ hours ▪ Ideal slow cooker size: 3-qt.

16-oz. can cherry pie filling

1¾ cups dry cake mix of your choice

1 egg

3 Tbsp. evaporated milk

½ tsp. cinnamon

1. Lightly spray slow cooker with nonstick cooking spray.

2. Place pie filling in slow cooker and cook on High 30 minutes.

3. Meanwhile, mix together remaining ingredients in a bowl until crumbly. Spoon onto hot pie filling.

4. Cover and cook on Low 2–5 hours, or until a toothpick inserted into center of topping comes out dry.

5. Serve warm or cooled.

Makes 6–8 servings

Just Peachy

BETTY B. DENNISON • GROVE CITY, PA

Prep Time: 2–3 minutes • Cooking Time: 4–5 hours • Ideal slow cooker size: 3-qt.

4 cups sliced peaches, fresh or canned (if using canned peaches, reserve the juice)

²⁄₃ cup rolled dry oats

¹⁄₃ cup all-purpose baking mix

¹⁄₂ cup sugar

¹⁄₂ cup brown sugar

¹⁄₂ tsp. cinnamon, optional

¹⁄₂ cup water, or reserved peach juice

1. Spray slow cooker with nonstick cooking spray.

2. Place peaches in slow cooker.

3. In a bowl, mix together all dry ingredients. When blended, stir in water or juice until well mixed.

4. Spoon batter into cooker and stir into peaches, just until blended.

5. Cover and cook on Low 4–5 hours.

6. Serve warm with vanilla ice cream or frozen yogurt.

Makes 4–6 servings

Peanut Butter Cake

VELMA SAUDER • LEOLA, PA

Prep Time: 5–10 minutes • Cooking Time: 2–3 hours • Ideal slow cooker size: 4-qt.

2 cups yellow cake mix

¹⁄₃ cup crunchy peanut butter

¹⁄₂ cup water

1. Combine all ingredients in an electric mixer bowl. Beat with electric mixer about 2 minutes.

2. Pour batter into greased and floured baking-pan insert designed to fit inside slow cooker.

3. Place baking-pan insert in slow cooker. Cover with 8 paper towels.

4. Cover cooker. Cook on High 2–3 hours, or until toothpick inserted into center of cake comes out clean. About 30 minutes before end of cooking time, remove lid of cooker, but keep paper towels in place.

5. When cake is fully cooked, remove insert from slow cooker. Turn insert upside down on a serving plate and remove cake.

Makes 6 servings

Fruity Cake

JANICE MULLER • DERWOOD, MD

Prep Time: 15 minutes • Cooking Time: 3–5 hours • Ideal slow cooker size: 3½- to 4-qt.

1, or 2, 21-oz. can(s) apple, blueberry, or peach pie filling

18¼-oz. pkg. yellow cake mix

1 stick (½ cup) butter, melted

⅓ cup chopped walnuts

1. Spray slow cooker with nonstick cooking spray.

2. Place pie filling in slow cooker.

3. In a mixing bowl, combine dry cake mix and butter. Spoon over filling.

4. Drop walnuts over top.

5. Cover and cook on Low 3–5 hours, or until a toothpick inserted into center of topping comes out clean.

Makes 10–12 servings

Note: You can use a 2-lb. coffee can, 2 1-lb. coffee cans, 3 16-oz. vegetable cans, a 6–7 cup mold, or a 1½–2-qt. baking dish for "baking" cakes in a slow cooker. Leave the cooker lid slightly open to let extra moisture escape.

—*Eleanor J. Ferreira, North Chelmsford, MA*

Pineapple Upside-Down Cake

VERA M. KUHNS • HARRISONBURG, VA

Prep Time: 20 minutes • Cooking Time: 4–5 hours • Ideal slow cooker size: 4-qt.

1 stick (½ cup) butter, or margarine, melted

1 cup brown sugar

1 medium-sized can pineapple slices, drained, juice reserved

6–8 maraschino cherries

1 box dry yellow cake mix

1. Combine butter and brown sugar. Spread over bottom of well-greased slow cooker.

2. Add pineapple slices and place cherries in center of each slice.

3. Prepare cake according to package directions, using pineapple juice for part of liquid. Spoon cake batter into cooker over top of fruit.

4. Cover cooker with 2 tea towels and then with its own lid. Cook on High 1 hour, and then on Low 3–4 hours.

5. Allow cake to cool 10 minutes. Then run a knife around edge and invert cake onto a large platter.

Makes 10 servings

Pumpkin Pie Dessert

BONNIE WHALING • CLEARFIELD, PA

Prep Time: 15–20 minutes • Cooking Time: 3–4 hours • Ideal slow cooker size: 5- to 6-qt.

19-oz. can pumpkin pie filling

12-oz. can evaporated milk

2 eggs, lightly beaten

boiling water

1 cup gingersnap cookie
    crumbs

1. In a large mixing bowl, stir together pie filling, milk, and eggs until thoroughly mixed.

2. Pour into an ungreased baking-pan insert designed to fit into slow cooker.

3. Place filled baking insert in slow cooker. Cover insert with its lid, or with 8 paper towels.

4. Carefully pour boiling water into cooker around baking insert, to a depth of 1".

5. Cover cooker. Cook on High 3–4 hours, or until a tester inserted in center of custard comes out clean.

6. Remove baking insert from slow cooker. Remove its lid. Sprinkle dessert with cookie crumbs. Serve warm from baking insert.

Makes 4–6 servings

Black Forest Cake

MARLA FOLKERTS • HOLLAND, OH

Prep Time: 10 minutes • Cooking Time: 2–2½ hours • Ideal slow cooker size: 4- to 5-qt.

20-oz. can cherry pie filling
    (lite or regular)

18¼-oz. box chocolate cake
    mix, butter-style

1. Preheat slow cooker on High 10 minutes.

2. Meanwhile, spray baking-pan insert designed to fit into slow cooker with nonstick cooking spray.

3. In a bowl, stir together pie filling and cake mix until mix is thoroughly moistened. Spoon into insert.

4. Place insert in cooker. Cover insert with 8 paper towels. Cover slow cooker.

5. Cook on High 1¾ hours. Remove paper towels and cooker lid. Continue cooking another 30 minutes, or until a toothpick inserted in center of cake comes out clean.

6. Remove baking insert from cooker. Serve cake warm directly from insert.

Makes 8–10 servings

Brownies with Nuts

DOROTHY VAN DEEST • MEMPHIS, TN

Prep Time: 10–15 minutes • Cooking Time: 3 hours • Ideal slow cooker size: 5-qt.

half a stick (¼ cup) butter, melted

1 cup chopped nuts, divided

23-oz. pkg. brownie mix

1. Pour melted butter into a baking-pan insert designed to fit into slow cooker. Swirl butter around to grease sides of insert.

2. Sprinkle butter with half of nuts.

3. In a bowl, mix brownies according to package directions. Spoon half of batter into baking insert, trying to cover nuts evenly.

4. Add remaining half of nuts. Spoon in remaining batter.

5. Place insert in slow cooker. Cover insert with 8 paper towels.

6. Cover cooker. Cook on High 3 hours. Do not check or remove cover until last hour of cooking. Then insert toothpick into center of brownies. If it comes out clean, brownies are finished. If it doesn't, continue cooking another 15 minutes. Check again. Repeat until pick comes out clean.

7. When finished cooking, uncover cooker and baking insert. Let brownies stand 5 minutes.

8. Invert insert onto a serving plate. Cut brownies with a plastic knife (so the crumbs don't drag). Serve warm.

Makes 24 brownies

Cooking Tip

Always cut brownies with a plastic knife. It prevents clumping and ragged edges.

Upside-Down Chocolate Pudding Cake

SARAH HERR • GOSHEN, IN

Prep Time: 15 minutes • Cooking Time: 2-3 hours • Ideal slow cooker size: 3½-qt.

1 cup dry all-purpose baking
   mix

1 cup sugar, divided

3 Tbsp. unsweetened cocoa
   powder, plus ⅓ cup,
   divided

½ cup milk

1 tsp. vanilla

1⅔ cups hot water

1. Spray slow cooker with nonstick cooking spray.

2. In a bowl, mix together baking mix, ½ cup sugar, 3 Tbsp. cocoa powder, milk, and vanilla. Spoon batter evenly into slow cooker.

3. In a clean bowl, mix remaining ½ cup sugar, ⅓ cup cocoa powder, and hot water together. Pour over batter in slow cooker. Do not stir.

4. Cover and cook on High 2–3 hours, or until toothpick inserted in center of cakey part comes out clean.

Makes 8 servings

Note: The batter will rise to the top and turn into cake. Underneath will be a rich chocolate pudding.

Chocolate Soufflé

RACHEL YODER • MIDDLEBURY, IN

Prep Time: 5 minutes • Cooking Time: 6 hours • Ideal slow cooker size: 6-qt.

18¼-oz. pkg. chocolate cake
   mix

½ cup vegetable oil

2 cups sour cream

4 eggs, beaten

3-oz. box instant chocolate
   pudding mix

1 cup chocolate chips, optional

1. Combine all ingredients in a large mixing bowl.

2. Spray slow cooker with nonstick cooking spray. Pour soufflé mixture into cooker.

3. Cover and cook on Low 6 hours. (Do not lift lid until end of cooking time!)

4. Insert toothpick into center of cake to see if it comes out clean. If it does, soufflé is finished. If it doesn't, continue cooking another 15 minutes. Check again. Repeat until it's finished cooking.

5. Serve warm from cooker with ice cream or frozen yogurt.

Makes 10–12 servings

Chocolate Peanut Butter Cake

ESTHER HARTZLER • CARLSBAD, NM

Prep Time: 7 minutes • Cooking Time: 2–2½ hours • Ideal slow cooker size: 5- to 6-qt.

2 cups dry milk chocolate cake mix

½ cup water

6 Tbsp. peanut butter

2 eggs

½ cup chopped nuts

1. Combine all ingredients in an electric mixer bowl. Beat 2 minutes.

2. Spray a baking-pan insert designed to fit into slow cooker with nonstick cooking spray. Flour interior of greased insert. Pour batter into insert. Place insert in slow cooker.

3. Cover insert with 8 paper towels.

4. Cover cooker. Cook on High 2–2½ hours, or until toothpick inserted into center of cake comes out clean.

5. Allow cake to cool. Then invert onto a serving plate, cut, and serve.

Makes 8–10 servings

Chocolate Fondue

DIANN J. DUNHAM • STATE COLLEGE, PA

Prep Time: 5 minutes • Cooking Time: 2½ hours • Ideal slow cooker size: 2-qt.

1 stick (½ cup) butter, melted

1½ cups sugar

¼ cup whipping cream

3 Tbsp. creme de cocoa, rum, or orange-flavored liqueur (or 1 tsp. orange, rum, or vanilla flavoring)

6 1-oz. squares unsweetened chocolate

1. Combine butter and sugar in slow cooker until well mixed.

2. Stir in whipping cream until well blended. Stir in liqueur or flavoring until well blended.

3. Stir in squares of chocolate.

4. Cover and cook on High 30 minutes.

5. Stir well, turn cooker to Low, and cook 2 hours.

6. Serve warm from cooker with angel food or pound cake cut into bite-sized pieces, marshmallows, apple slices, banana chunks, and strawberries, whole or halved.

Makes 2½–3 cups

Note: As long as an inch or more of the fondue remains in the cooker, you can keep the cooker turned on Low for up to 6 hours. Stir occasionally.

Dessert Fondue

SARA KINSINGER • STUARTS DRAFT, VA / BONITA ENSENBERGER • ALBUQUERQUE, NM

Prep Time: 10–15 minutes • Cooking Time: 2 hours • Ideal slow cooker size: 4-qt.

1 Tbsp. butter

16 1-oz. candy bars, half milk chocolate; half semi-sweet chocolate, broken

30 large marshmallows

⅓ cup milk

1 cup whipping cream

1. Grease slow cooker with butter. Turn on High 10 minutes.

2. Meanwhile, mix broken candy bars, marshmallows, and milk together in a bowl.

3. Put candy/milk mixture into slow cooker.

4. Cover and cook on Low 30 minutes. Stir. Cover and cook another 30 minutes. Stir.

5. Gradually stir in whipping cream. Cover and cook on Low another hour.

6. Serve fondue warm from cooker with pieces of pound cake, angel food cake, bananas, and pretzels for dipping.

Makes about 3 cups

Best Bread Pudding

BETTY B. DENNISON • GROVE CITY, PA

Prep Time: 10 minutes • Cooking Time: 2–3 hours • Ideal slow cooker size: 5-qt.

¾ cup brown sugar

6 slices raisin-and-cinnamon-swirl bread, buttered and cubed

4 eggs

1 qt. milk

1½ tsp. vanilla

½ tsp. lemon extract, optional

1. Spray slow cooker with nonstick cooking spray.

2. Spread brown sugar in bottom of cooker. Add cubed bread. (Do not stir sugar and bread together.)

3. In a mixing bowl, beat eggs well. Beat in milk and vanilla, and lemon extract, if you wish. Pour over bread.

4. Cover and cook on High 2–3 hours, or until pudding is no longer soupy. Do not stir. Brown sugar will form a sauce on the bottom.

5. When pudding is finished, spoon it into a serving dish, drizzling sauce over top of bread.

Makes 8–10 servings

Baked Custard

BARBARA SMITH • BEDFORD, PA

Prep Time: 10–15 minutes • Cooking Time: 2–3 hours • Ideal slow cooker size: 4- to 5-qt.

2 cups whole milk

3 eggs, slightly beaten

⅓ cup, plus ½ tsp., sugar, divided

1 tsp. vanilla

¼ tsp. cinnamon

1. Heat milk in a small uncovered saucepan until a skin forms on top. Remove from heat and let cool slightly.

2. Meanwhile, in a large mixing bowl, combine eggs, ⅓ cup sugar, and vanilla.

3. Slowly stir cooled milk into egg-sugar mixture.

4. Pour into a greased 1-qt. baking dish that fits into slow cooker, or into a baking-pan insert designed for slow cooker.

5. Mix cinnamon and ½ tsp. reserved sugar in a small bowl. Sprinkle over custard mixture.

6. Cover baking dish or insert with foil. Set container on a metal rack or trivet in slow cooker. Pour hot water around dish to a depth of 1".

7. Cover cooker. Cook on High 2–3 hours, or until custard is set. (When blade of a knife inserted in center of custard comes out clean, custard is set.)

8. Serve warm from baking dish or insert.

Makes 5–6 servings

Tapioca

RUTH ANN HOOVER • NEW HOLLAND, PA / SHARON ANDERS • ALBURTIS, PA
PAT UNTERNAHRER • WAYLAND, IA

Prep Time: 5-10 minutes • Cooking Time: 3 hours and 20 minutes • Chilling Time: 4-5 hours • Ideal slow cooker size: 3-qt.

2 qts. whole milk

1¼ cups sugar

1 cup dry small pearl tapioca

4 eggs

1 tsp. vanilla

whipped topping, optional

1. Combine milk and sugar in slow cooker, stirring until sugar is dissolved as well as possible. Stir in tapioca.

2. Cover and cook on High 3 hours.

3. In a small mixing bowl, beat eggs slightly. Beat in vanilla and about 1 cup hot milk from slow cooker. When well mixed, stir into slow cooker.

4. Cover and cook on High 20 more minutes.

5. Chill. Serve with whipped topping, if you wish.

   Makes 10-12 servings

Pineapple Tapioca

JANESSA K. HOCHSTEDLER • EAST EARL, PA

Prep Time: 15 minutes • Cooking Time: 3 hours • Chilling Time: 2-3 hours • Ideal slow cooker size: 3-qt.

2½ cups water

2½ cups pineapple juice

½ cup dry small pearl tapioca

¾-1 cup sugar

15-oz. can crushed pineapple, undrained

1. Mix first 4 ingredients together in slow cooker.

2. Cover and cook on High 3 hours.

3. Stir in crushed pineapple. Chill for several hours.

   Makes 4-6 servings

Slow-Cooker Rice Pudding

NADINE MARTINITZ • SALINA, KS

Prep Time: 5–20 minutes, depending upon whether or not you need to cook the rice • Cooking Time: 2–4 hours • Ideal slow cooker size: 2-qt.

2½ cups cooked rice

12-oz. can evaporated milk

½ cup sugar

2 eggs, beaten

1 tsp. vanilla

½ cup raisins, optional

1. Spray slow cooker with nonstick cooking spray.

2. Mix all ingredients together in slow cooker.

3. Cover and cook on High 2 hours, or on Low 4 hours.

4. Stir after first hour. If rice seems to be nearly done, check again after another 30 minutes, and adjust cooking time accordingly.

5. Serve warm or cold.

Makes 6 servings

Old-Fashioned Rice Pudding

RUTH ZENDT • MIFFLINTOWN, PA / ARIANNE HOCHSTETLER • GOSHEN, IN

Prep Time: 5 minutes • Cooking Time: 4–7 hours • Ideal slow cooker size: 3- to 4-qt.

2 qts. skim, or 2%, milk

1 cup uncooked long-grain rice

1 cup sugar

pinch of salt

¼ cup butter, melted, optional

½–¾ cup raisins, optional

1. Spray slow cooker with nonstick cooking spray.

2. Place all ingredients in slow cooker. Stir thoroughly.

3. Cook on High 4–5 hours, or on Low 6–7 hours, stirring occasionally if you're home and able to do so. Cooking time varies depending on how thick and stiff you'd like finished rice to be. Rice pudding will thicken slightly as it cools.

Makes 10–12 servings

Note: To serve, sprinkle with cinnamon or sugar, or pour a little milk over each serving.

Rice Pudding from Scratch

RHONDA FREED • LOWVILLE, NY

Prep Time: 25 minutes • Cooking Time: 3¼–3¾ hours • Ideal slow cooker size: 4-qt.

8 cups milk

1 cup uncooked long-grain rice

1 cup sugar

2 Tbsp. butter

2 tsp. vanilla

1. In a large microwave-safe bowl, mix milk, rice, sugar, and butter together. Cover.

2. Microwave on High 5 minutes, and then stir. Cover, microwave 4 minutes, and then stir. Repeat for 3, 2, and 1 minutes of cooking time, stirring between each cooking time.

3. Pour into slow cooker. Stir in vanilla.

4. Cover and cook on High 1½ hours. Stir occasionally if you're home and able to do so.

5. Cook on High an additional 1½–2 hours with cover off, or until rice is cooked through and creamy but not dry or mushy.

Makes 8–10 servings

Note: Rice pudding thickens as it cools. If you like a thinner pudding, reduce the cooking time.

Sugarless Applesauce

LAUREN M. EBERHARD • SENECA, IL

Prep Time: 20 minutes • Cooking Time: 3–5 hours • Ideal slow cooker size: 3-qt.

8 cups apples, peeled and thinly sliced

1–2 tsp. cinnamon

half to a whole 12-oz. can Diet 7Up, or any sugar-free clear soda

1. Toss apples with cinnamon in slow cooker.

2. Pour enough soda over apples to cover one-third of them.

3. Cover and cook on Low 3–4 hours, or until apples are tender enough to mash into sauce.

4. Remove cover and turn cooker to High. Cook until sauce reaches thickness you prefer. Stir occasionally, breaking up chunks.

5. Remove from cooker and allow to reach room temperature. Chill and then serve.

Makes 12 servings

Homestyle Applesauce

PAULA KING • FLANAGAN, IL / LIZZIE ANN YODER • HARTVILLE, OH / DOROTHY LINGERFELT • STONYFORD, CA / ELLEN RANCK • GAP, PA / JANET L. ROGGIE • LOWVILLE, NY / MARY E. WHEATLEY • MASHPEE, MA / SHARON MILLER • HOLMESVILLE, OH / DONNA TRELOAR • HARTFORD CITY, IN

Prep Time: 15–20 minutes • Cooking Time: 4½–6½ hours • Ideal slow cooker size: 3- to 4-qt.

8–10 medium-sized cooking apples, peeled, cored, and diced

½ cup water

scant ½–¾ cup sugar, according to the kind of apples you use

½–1 tsp. cinnamon, optional

1. In slow cooker, combine apples and water.

2. Cover and cook on Low 4–6 hours, or until apples are very soft. Add sugar, and cinnamon if you wish (or reserve cinnamon and sprinkle over finished sauce), and cook on Low another 30 minutes.

3. Sprinkle with cinnamon at serving time if you wish (unless you've already added it in Step 2).

Makes 6–8 servings

Note: This applesauce will be slightly chunky. If you prefer a smoother sauce, puree or sieve the apples after they've been cooked.

Applesauce

JEAN BUTZER • BATAVIA, NY / TRUDY CUTTER • CORFU, NY

Prep Time: 15 minutes • Cooking Time: 1½–2 hours • Ideal slow cooker size: 4- to 5-qt.

8 medium-sized tart apples, peeled, cored, and cut into quarters

⅔ cup sugar

¾ cup apple juice, or water, or cranberry juice

2 Tbsp. butter, melted

1 tsp. cinnamon

2 tsp. lemon juice, optional

1. Mix all ingredients, except lemon juice, in slow cooker.

2. Cover and cook on High 1½–2 hours.

3. Stir well to break up larger pieces of apples.

4. Do a taste test. If sauce is sweeter than you like, stir in up to 2 tsp. lemon juice.

5. Serve warm or chilled. Applesauce is especially good served with pork roast or chops. It's also good as a breakfast fruit or over toast.

Makes 8 servings

Variation: Adjust the amount of cinnamon to suit your personal or family tastes. You may also use ½ tsp. nutmeg in place of the cinnamon.

Chunky Cranberry Applesauce

CHRISTIE ANNE DETAMORE-HUNSBERGER • HARRISONBURG, VA

Prep Time: 15 minutes • Cooking Time: 3–4 hours • Ideal slow cooker size: 3-qt.

6 McIntosh, or Winesap, or favorite baking apples, peeled or unpeeled, cut into 1" cubes

½ cup apple juice

½ cup fresh or frozen cranberries

¼ cup sugar

¼ tsp. cinnamon, optional

1. Combine all ingredients in slow cooker.

2. Cover and cook on Low 3–4 hours, or until apples are as soft as you like them.

3. Serve warm, or refrigerate and serve chilled. Serve sauce as a side dish during main course. Or have it for dessert, topping pound cake or ice cream.

Makes 6 servings

Caramel Apples

LUCY O'CONNELL • GOSHEN, MA

Prep Time: 10 minutes • Cooking Time: 2–3 hours • Ideal slow cooker size: 3-qt.

4 large tart apples, cored

14-oz. jar caramel sauce

½ cup apple juice

1 tsp. apple pie spice

1. Remove peel from top inch of whole apples.

2. Place apples in slow cooker, making sure that each one is sitting flat on bottom of cooker. Fill center of each apple with one-fourth of caramel sauce.

3. Pour apple juice into bottom of cooker.

4. Sprinkle apples with apple pie spice.

5. Cover and cook on High 2–3 hours.

Makes 4 servings

Note: Cooking time will vary according to the size of the apples. Serve with vanilla ice cream or whipped cream, if you wish.

Caramel Apples on Sticks

BECKY HARDER • MONUMENT, CO / JEANETTE OBERHOLTZER • MANHEIM, PA

Prep Time: 30 minutes • Cooking Time: 1–1½ hours • Ideal slow cooker size: 2-qt.

2 14-oz. bags caramels

¼ cup water

8–10 medium-sized apples

sticks

granulated sugar

waxed paper

1. Combine caramels and water in slow cooker.

2. Cover. Cook on High 1–1½ hours, stirring every 5 minutes.

3. Wash and dry apples. Insert a stick into stem end of each apple. Turn cooker to Low. Dip apple into hot caramel, turning to coat entire surface.

4. Holding apple above cooker, scrape off excess accumulation of caramel from bottom of apple.

5. Dip bottom of caramel-coated apple in granulated sugar to keep it from sticking. Place apple on greased waxed paper to cool.

Makes 8–10 servings

Apple Dish

VERA MARTIN • EAST EARL, PA

Prep Time: 15–20 minutes • Cooking Time: 2–2½ hours • Ideal slow cooker size: 3- to 4-qt.

¾ cup sugar

3 Tbsp. flour

1½ tsp. cinnamon, optional

5 large baking apples, pared, cored, and diced into ¾" pieces

half a stick (¼ cup) butter, melted

3 Tbsp. water

1. Spray slow cooker with nonstick cooking spray.

2. In a large bowl, mix sugar and flour together, along with cinnamon, if you wish. Set aside.

3. Mix apples, butter, and water together in slow cooker. Gently stir in flour mixture until apples are well coated.

4. Cover and cook on High 1½ hours, and then on Low 30–60 minutes, or until apples are done to your liking.

5. Serve with milk poured over top.

Makes about 7 cups

Apple Dessert

BARBARA SPARKS • GLEN BURNIE, MD

Prep Time: 15 minutes • Cooking Time: 1½–3 hours • Ideal slow cooker size: 2-qt.

3 large baking apples

1 Tbsp. butter, melted

1 Tbsp. lemon juice

1½ Tbsp. brown sugar

½ tsp. cinnamon

1. Core, peel if you wish, and then cut apples in eighths. Place in slow cooker.

2. Drizzle butter and lemon juice over apples.

3. Sprinkle sugar and cinnamon on top.

4. Cover and cook on Low 3 hours, or on High 1½ hours.

5. Serve as a main-course side dish, as a dessert (warm or cold) topped with whipped cream or drizzled with evaporated milk, or as a topping for vanilla ice cream.

Makes 5 servings

Jellied Apples

PATRICIA HOWARD • GREEN VALLEY, AZ

Prep Time: 20 minutes • Cooking Time: 4–6 hours • Chilling Time: 3–4 hours • Ideal slow cooker size: 4-qt.

10 tart apples, peeled, cored, and sliced

½–1 cup sugar, depending upon how much sweetness you like

2 cups hot water

¾ cup Red Hots candy

½ cup cold water

1 envelope unflavored gelatin

juice of 1 lemon

1. Place prepared apples in slow cooker.

2. Combine sugar, hot water, and candy in a saucepan. Heat over medium heat, stirring until sugar and candy dissolve. Continue cooking, uncovered, until mixture becomes syrupy and somewhat thickened.

3. Pour syrup over apples.

4. Cover cooker. Cook on Low 4–6 hours, or until apples are tender.

5. Turn off cooker. Using a slotted spoon, remove apples, reserving syrup in cooker. Place apple slices in a deep serving dish.

6. Place cold water in a small bowl. Stir in gelatin until dissolved.

7. Add lemon juice, along with dissolved gelatin and water, to hot syrup in slow cooker. Stir well.

8. Let mixture cool. Then pour over apples.

9. Place in refrigerator until set, about 3–4 hours.

Makes 10 servings

Note: Start this recipe the day, or the night, before you want to serve it.

Baked Apples

DONNA LANTGEN • RAPID CITY, SD

Prep Time: 15 minutes • Cooking Time: 4–5 hours • Ideal slow cooker size: 3- to 4-qt.

4 baking apples, left whole, cored and unpeeled

1 tsp. cinnamon

¼ cup brown sugar

4 Tbsp. butter

1. Place apples in slow cooker, making sure each is standing on bottom of slow cooker.

2. Combine cinnamon and brown sugar. Stuff into apples.

3. Top each apple with 1 Tbsp. butter.

4. Cover. Cook on Low 4–5 hours.

5. Delicious as a side dish served warm, or as a topping for waffles, pancakes, or ice cream.

Makes 4 servings

Apple Appeal

ANNE TOWNSEND • ALBUQUERQUE, NM

Prep Time: 10 minutes • Cooking Time: 4–5 hours • Ideal slow cooker size: 3-qt.

6 baking apples, peeled, cored, and quartered

1/4 tsp. nutmeg

2 Tbsp. sugar

3/4 tsp. Asian five-spice powder

1/4 cup apple juice

1. Place prepared apples in slow cooker.

2. In a small mixing bowl, combine all remaining ingredients.

3. Pour into slow cooker, stirring gently to coat apples.

4. Cover and cook on Low 4–5 hours, or until apples are as tender as you want them.

5. Serve apples sliced or mashed and warm, cold, or at room temperature.

6. These versatile apples may be served as a side dish with ham, scalloped potatoes, green beans amandine, cornbread, pecan tarts, and as a topping for toast!

Makes 6 servings

Note: Keep nuts in the freezer so you'll have them when you need them.

Baked Stuffed Apples

MIRIAM NOLT • NEW HOLLAND, PA / RUTH HOFSTETTER • VERSAILLES, MO
SARA KINSINGER • STUARTS DRAFT, VA / BETTY DRESCHER • QUAKERTOWN, PA
DOROTHY LINGERFELT • STONYFORD, CA / KAYE TAYLOR • FLORISSANT, MO
DALE PETERSON • RAPID CITY, SD / KAREN CENEVIVA • NEW HAVEN, CT

Prep Time: 15–30 minutes • Cooking Time: 2½–5 hours • Ideal slow cooker size: 5-qt.

2 Tbsp. raisins

1/4 cup sugar

6–8 medium-sized baking apples, cored but left whole and unpeeled

1 tsp. cinnamon

2 Tbsp. butter

1/2 cup water

1. Mix raisins and sugar together in a small bowl.

2. Stand apples on bottom of slow cooker. Spoon raisin-sugar mixture into centers of apples, dividing evenly among apples.

3. Sprinkle stuffed apples with cinnamon. Dot with butter.

4. Add 1/2 cup water along edge of cooker.

5. Cover and cook on Low 3–5 hours, or on High 2½–3½ hours, or until apples are tender but not collapsing.

6. Serve warm as is, or with ice cream or frozen yogurt.

Makes 6–8 servings

Apples and Pineapple Dessert

JOAN S. EYE • HARRISONBURG, VA

Prep Time: 25–30 minutes • Cooking Time: 7–8 hours • Ideal slow cooker size: 4- to 5-qt.

5–6 baking apples, peeled and cored

2–4 Tbsp. dark brown sugar, according to your taste preference

1–2 tsp. cinnamon, according to your taste preference

½ cup canned crushed pineapple, drained but with liquid reserved

¼ cup chopped walnuts

1. Slice peeled apples into slow cooker.

2. In a separate bowl, mix together sugar, cinnamon, and pineapple, starting first with lesser amounts of sugar and cinnamon. Taste the mixture, and then add more sugar and cinnamon, if you prefer, up to full amounts suggested.

3. Add reserved juice to sugar-pineapple mixture and spoon mixture over apple slices. Stir together well.

4. Sprinkle with walnuts.

5. Cover and cook on Low 7–8 hours, or until apples are done to your liking.

Makes 5–6 servings

Pineapple Pudding

LOIS NIEBAUER • PEDRICKTOWN, NJ

Prep Time: 10 minutes • Cooking Time: 4 hours • Ideal slow cooker size: 1½-qt.

20-oz. can crushed pineapple, undrained

¼ cup water

2 eggs, beaten

2 Tbsp. cornstarch

½–¾ cup sugar, depending upon your preference for sweetness

1. Spray slow cooker with nonstick cooking spray.

2. Mix all ingredients together in slow cooker.

3. Cover and cook on High ½ hour, then on Low 3½ hours.

4. Serve warm with a scoop of vanilla ice cream or frozen yogurt, or a dollop of whipped cream on each serving, if you wish.

Makes 4–5 servings

Whole Cranberry Sauce

SHERRIL BIEBERLY • SALINA, KS

Prep Time: 5 minutes • Cooking Time: 5–6 hours • Chilling Time: 6–8 hours, or overnight • Ideal slow cooker size: 2-qt.

12-oz pkg. cranberries

2 cups sugar

1/2 cup brandy, or white grape juice, or apple juice

1/4–1/2 cup walnuts, optional

1. Place first 3 ingredients in slow cooker. Cook on Low 5–6 hours, stirring occasionally if you're home and able to do so.

2. Remove cooked cranberries to refrigerator dish and refrigerate overnight. Serve cold.

3. If you wish, chop nuts. Spread out in a single layer in a dry nonstick skillet over medium heat. Stir occasionally, heating nuts until toasted. Allow to cool, and then stir into cranberry sauce before serving.

Makes 5–6 servings

Note: You can prepare this several days ahead of serving it, and then refrigerate it until you're ready for it.

Southwest Cranberries

BERNITA BOYTS • SHAWNEE MISSION, KS

Prep Time: 5 minutes • Cooking Time: 2–3 hours • Ideal slow cooker size: 1 1/2- to 2-qt.

16-oz. can whole-berry cranberry sauce

10 1/2-oz. jar jalapeño jelly

2 Tbsp. chopped fresh cilantro

1. Combine ingredients in slow cooker.

2. Cover. Cook on Low 2–3 hours.

3. Cool. Serve at room temperature.

4. Serve these spicy cranberries as a side dish or as a marinade for poultry or pork.

Makes 8 servings

Warm Fruit Compote

RENEE BAUM • CHAMBERSBURG, PA

Prep Time: 15 minutes • Cooking Time: 2–2½ hours • Ideal slow cooker size: 5-qt.

2 29-oz. cans sliced peaches, drained

2 29-oz. cans pear halves, sliced and drained

20-oz. can pineapple chunks, drained

15¼-oz. can apricot halves, sliced and drained

21-oz. can cherry pie filling

1. In slow cooker, combine peaches, pears, pineapples, and apricots. Top with pie filling.

2. Cover and cook on High 2–2½ hours, or until hot throughout.

3. Serve hot as a side dish with the main course. Or chill and serve, also as a side dish, or as dessert. It's also good as a topping for angel food cake, vanilla ice cream, and frozen yogurt.

Makes 14–18 servings

Rhubarb-Pineapple Compote

DOROTHY VAN DEEST • MEMPHIS, TN

Prep Time: 15-20 minutes • Cooking Time: 2-6 hours • Ideal slow cooker size: 3½-qt.

1 lb. fresh rhubarb

2 cups fresh pineapple chunks

½ cup orange soda

1 Tbsp. sugar

nutmeg, optional

1. Wash rhubarb, and then cut into 1" pieces. Place in slow cooker.

2. Stir in pineapple.

3. Add soda, and then sprinkle with sugar. Stir into fruit.

4. Cover and cook on High 2 hours, or on Low 4–6 hours, or until rhubarb is tender.

5. Serve warm or chilled. If you wish, sprinkle with nutmeg before serving.

Makes 4–6 servings

Note: This is a good go-along with a platter of roasted pork or beef. Or serve as a topping for vanilla ice cream or frozen yogurt.

QUICKIE GO-ALONGS

BREADS

Apple Nut Ring

NAOMI CUNNINGHAM • ARLINGTON, KS

Prep Time: 10 minutes • Baking Time: 25–30 minutes

2 7½-oz. pkgs. refrigerated buttermilk biscuits

¼ cup butter, or margarine, melted

⅔ cup sugar

2 Tbsp. cinnamon

3–4 medium-sized apples

⅓ cup nuts, chopped

1. Separate biscuits.

2. In a saucepan, melt butter or margarine.

3. Combine sugar and cinnamon in a small bowl.

4. Dip biscuits in butter, and then roll in sugar mixture. Arrange biscuits, so that they overlap, around edge and into center of a greased 9" × 13" baking pan.

5. Peel, core, and slice apples. Cut slices in half crosswise. Place an apple slice between each biscuit and around outer edge of baking dish.

6. Mix nuts with any remaining sugar mixture. Sprinkle over top of biscuits and apples.

7. Bake at 400°F for 25–30 minutes, or until biscuits are a deep golden brown.

Makes 10 servings

Low-Fat Chocolate Muffins

TERESA MARTIN • GORDONVILLE, PA

Prep Time: 15–20 minutes • Baking Time: 15–20 minutes

1½ cups flour

¾ cup sugar

¼ cup baking cocoa

2 tsp. baking powder

1 tsp. baking soda

½ tsp. salt

⅔ cup fat-free vanilla yogurt

⅔ cup fat-free milk

½ tsp. vanilla

confectioners' sugar, optional

1. In a large mixing bowl, combine flour, sugar, baking cocoa, baking powder, baking soda, and salt.

2. In a separate bowl, stir together yogurt, milk, and vanilla until well mixed.

3. Stir wet ingredients into dry ingredients, just until moistened.

4. Fill greased muffin tins two-thirds full.

5. Bake at 400°F for 15–20 minutes, or until a toothpick inserted in centers of muffins comes out clean.

6. Cool 5 minutes before removing from pan to a wire rack.

7. Dust with confectioners' sugar, if you wish.

Makes 12 servings

Note: These muffins freeze well.

Pillow Pizza

SHARON MILLER • HOLMESVILLE, OH

Prep Time: 20 minutes • Baking Time: 20 minutes

2 tubes refrigerated biscuits
(10 biscuits per tube)

1½ lbs. ground beef

16-oz. can pizza sauce

OPTIONAL INGREDIENTS:

chopped onions

chopped peppers

canned mushrooms

pepperoni

1 lb. mozzarella cheese, shredded

1. Cut each biscuit into quarters and place in bottom of a greased 9" × 13" baking dish.

2. In a skillet, brown beef. Drain off drippings. Add sauce to beef in skillet and stir together.

3. Pour over biscuit quarters.

4. Top with any optional ingredients, as you would a pizza. Sprinkle cheese over top, if you wish.

5. Bake at 400°F for 20 minutes.

Makes 8 servings

Ham and Cheese Sticky Buns

ROSANNE WEILER • MYERSTOWN, PA

Prep Time: 10 minutes ▪ Baking Time: 20 minutes

24 party-size potato rolls

1 lb. sliced Swiss cheese

½ lb. sliced ham

2 sticks (1 cup) butter

⅓ cup brown sugar

2 Tbsp. Worcestershire sauce

2 Tbsp. prepared mustard

2 Tbsp. poppy seeds

1. Slice rolls in half and place bottoms in 9" × 13" baking pan.

2. Layer on cheese and ham, and top with roll tops.

3. Melt butter in a saucepan and add sugar, Worcestershire sauce, mustard, and poppy seeds. Bring to boil and let boil 2 minutes.

4. Immediately pour over rolls and bake at 350°F for 20 minutes.

Makes 12 servings

Note: These can be made ahead and heated when ready to serve. When I serve these as an appetizer, everyone comes back for seconds!

VEGETABLES

Green Beans Supreme

DEB MARTIN • PENNSYLVANIA

Prep Time: 15 minutes • Cooking Time: 15 minutes

4 slices bacon

¼ cup chopped onion

1 can cream of celery, or
    mushroom, soup

⅓ cup milk

1 lb. fresh green beans, or two
    9-oz. pkgs. frozen green
    beans

1. Cook bacon until crisp in a large saucepan. Remove bacon and crumble. Set aside.

2. Sauté onion in 2 Tbsp. bacon drippings until tender.

3. Blend in soup, milk, and green beans. Heat, stirring occasionally, until beans are cooked as tender as you like.

4. Top with bacon and serve.

Makes 4–6 servings

Broccoli Casserole

RUTH H. WHITE • PENNSYLVANIA

Prep Time: 30 minutes • Baking Time: 15–20 minutes

2 bunches broccoli

¼-½ lb. cheese of your choice,
    grated

1 stick (½ cup) butter

about 36 snack crackers

1. Cook broccoli until just-tender.

2. Melt cheese with butter in a saucepan.

3. Crush crackers.

4. In a greased 2-qt. casserole dish, alternate layers of broccoli, cheese sauce, and crackers.

5. Bake uncovered at 325°F for 15–20 minutes.

Makes 4–6 servings

Crustless Spinach Pie

HELENE KUSNITZ • WEST HEMPSTEAD, NY

Prep Time: 10 minutes ▪ Baking Time: 30 minutes

10-oz. pkg. frozen, chopped
    spinach

half a stick ($\frac{1}{4}$ cup) butter or
    margarine, melted

3 Tbsp. flour

3 eggs, lightly beaten

$\frac{1}{2}$ tsp. salt

$\frac{1}{8}$ tsp. pepper

8-oz. carton cottage cheese

$\frac{1}{2}$ cup grated mozzarella
    cheese

1. Thaw and drain spinach.

2. Combine all ingredients and mix well. Spoon into a greased pie plate or quiche dish.

3. Bake at 350°F for 30 minutes.

Makes 6–8 servings

Crispy Cauliflower

PAT TAYLOR • PAW PAW, WV

Prep Time: 30 minutes ▪ Cooking/Baking Time: 25 minutes

1 fresh head cauliflower

water

1 stick ($\frac{1}{2}$ cup) butter, melted

1 cup dry bread crumbs

1 tsp. Italian seasoning

1 cup shredded cheddar
    cheese

1. Separate cauliflower into florets. Place in microwavable dish. Sprinkle with 1 Tbsp. water. Cover and cook on High 3–4 minutes.

2. Drain florets and allow to cool until you can handle them.

3. Place melted butter in a shallow dish. Mix bread crumbs and seasoning together in another shallow dish.

4. Dip each floret into melted butter, and then into seasoned bread crumbs, rolling to cover well.

5. Place in greased 9" × 13" baking dish. Bake, uncovered, at 375°F for 20 minutes. Turn off oven. Sprinkle with shredded cheese and return to oven to melt.

Makes 4 servings

Stewed Tomatoes

ESTHER J. MAST • LANCASTER, PA

Prep Time: 5 minutes • Cooking Time: 10 minutes

2 Tbsp. chopped onions

2 Tbsp. freshly chopped celery leaves

2 Tbsp. butter

2 cups canned diced tomatoes, undrained

2 Tbsp. cornstarch

4 Tbsp. sugar

½ tsp. salt

⅛ tsp. cinnamon

1. In a large skillet or saucepan, sauté onions and celery leaves in butter until soft but not brown.

2. Add tomatoes and stir in well.

3. In a small bowl, combine cornstarch, sugar, salt, and cinnamon. Pour just enough tomato mixture into dry mixture to moisten. Immediately stir into remaining tomato mixture. Continue cooking and stirring until thickened.

Makes 4–5 servings

Variations: Stir in 1½ tsp. prepared mustard at Step 2. Or stir in 1 Tbsp. fresh basil, chopped, or ¾ tsp. dried basil, at Step 2.

Note: I got this recipe from the school cafeteria where I worked when our sons were in junior high school. It became a family favorite—served as a side dish to macaroni and cheese. If the mixture gets too thick, add water until the tomatoes reach the consistency you want. Also, a teaspoon or two of brown sugar in tomato dishes enhances the flavor and helps smooth out the acid.

Yam Fries

KATHY KEENER SHANTZ • LANCASTER, PA

Prep Time: 10 minutes • Baking Time: 20 minutes

2 Tbsp. olive oil

1 tsp. salt

1 tsp. pepper

1 tsp. curry

½ tsp. hot sauce

4 medium-sized yams, sliced like French fries

1. In a large mixing bowl, combine oil, salt, pepper, curry, and hot sauce.

2. Stir in sliced yams.

3. When thoroughly coated, spread on lightly greased baking sheet.

4. Bake at 375°F for 20 minutes, or until tender.

Makes 6 servings

Parmesan Baked Potatoes

EDITH GROFF • PENNSYLVANIA

Prep Time: 10 minutes • Baking Time: 40-45 minutes

6 Tbsp. butter, melted

3 Tbsp. Parmesan cheese, grated

8 medium-sized red potatoes, unpeeled and halved lengthwise

1. Pour butter into a 9" × 13" baking pan.

2. Sprinkle cheese over butter.

3. Place potatoes cut side down on top of cheese.

4. Bake uncovered at 400°F for 40–45 minutes, or until tender.

   Makes 8 servings

Baked Potato Wedges

SALLY A. PRICE • RESTON, VA

Prep Time: 15 minutes • Baking Time: 35-40 minutes

4 large baking potatoes

1 stick (½ cup) butter, or margarine, melted

¼ cup ketchup

1 tsp. prepared mustard

½ tsp. paprika

¼ tsp. salt

¼ tsp. pepper

1. Wash potatoes and pat dry. Quarter each potato. Cut each quarter crosswise into ¼"-thick slices, cutting to, but not through, bottom of potato so each piece resembles a fan.

2. Place each potato wedge, skin side down, on large baking sheet. Set aside.

3. Combine all remaining ingredients and mix well. Brush tops and sides of potatoes with mixture.

4. Bake, uncovered, at 425°F for 35–40 minutes.

   Makes 4 servings

SALADS

Dried Cherry Salad

STACY SCHMUCKER STOLTZFUS • ENOLA, PA

Prep Time: 20 minutes • Cooking Time: 10 minutes

half a head romaine lettuce, torn

half a head red leaf lettuce, torn

half a large red onion, sliced

1 cup dried cherries

1 cup feta cheese

$\frac{1}{3}$ cup sugar

1 cup pecan halves

RASPBERRY DRESSING:

4 Tbsp. raspberry vinegar

$\frac{1}{2}$ tsp. Tabasco sauce

$\frac{1}{2}$ tsp. salt

4 Tbsp. sugar

pepper to taste

1 Tbsp. chopped parsley

$\frac{1}{2}$ cup vegetable oil

1. Place lettuces in a large salad bowl. Sprinkle with onion slices, dried cherries, and feta cheese.

2. In a skillet, over medium heat, combine $\frac{1}{3}$ cup sugar and pecans. Stir constantly until sugar melts and pecans are coated. Immediately pour pecans onto waxed paper to cool.

3. Sprinkle cooled nuts over salad.

4. To make dressing, combine vinegar, Tabasco sauce, salt, 4 Tbsp. sugar, pepper, and parsley in a small mixing bowl. While whisking, slowly pour in oil until emulsified. Just before serving, pour over salad.

Makes 12 servings

Bibb Lettuce with Pecans and Oranges

BETTY K. DRESCHER • QUAKERTOWN, PA

Prep Time: 10-15 minutes

4 heads Bibb lettuce

¾ cup pecan halves, toasted

2 oranges, peeled and sliced

DRESSING:

⅓ cup vinegar

½ cup sugar

1 cup vegetable oil

½ tsp. salt

half a small onion, chopped

1 tsp. dry mustard

2 Tbsp. water

1. Place lettuce, pecans, and oranges in a salad bowl.

2. Combine dressing ingredients in blender. (You can make this ahead of time and refrigerate it.)

3. Toss dressing with salad ingredients just before serving.

   Makes 8 servings

Spinach-Strawberry Salad

PAT BECHTEL • DILLSBURG, PA / SARAH M. BALMER • MANHEIM, PA

Prep Time: 20 minutes

12 ozs. fresh spinach

1 qt. fresh strawberries, sliced

2 Tbsp. sesame seeds

1 Tbsp. poppy seeds

DRESSING:

½ cup vegetable oil

½ cup sugar

1½ tsp. grated onion

¼ tsp. Worcestershire sauce

¼ tsp. paprika

¼ cup cider vinegar

1. Layer spinach, strawberries, sesame seeds, and poppy seeds in a large salad bowl.

2. Combine dressing ingredients in a blender. Blend 2 minutes.

3. Just before serving, pour dressing over spinach and toss lightly to coat spinach and berries.

   Makes 6–8 servings

Note: This is one of our favorite salads. I make the dressing and store it in the refrigerator. Then I make the amount of salad I want and just add as much dressing as it needs.

Mozzarella/Tomato/Basil Salad

BONITA ENSENBERGER • ALBUQUERQUE, NM

Prep Time: 8 minutes

1 pt. buffalo mozzarella cheese balls, or ¼-½ lb. buffalo mozzarella cheese, sliced

2 large tomatoes, sliced and quartered

½ cup black olives, sliced

½ cup basil leaves, torn

1 Tbsp. olive oil

1 Tbsp. red wine vinegar

¼ tsp. salt

⅛ tsp. pepper

1. If mozzarella balls are in liquid, rinse and drain them. Place in a mixing bowl.

2. Add tomatoes, black olives, and basil leaves. Mix together gently.

3. Mix olive oil, vinegar, salt, and pepper together. Pour over salad ingredients and mix gently.

Makes 6 servings

Variation: Add 1 sweet Vidalia onion, sliced, to Step 2.

Crunchy Pea Salad

DOTTIE SCHMIDT • KANSAS CITY, MO

Prep Time: 20 minutes • Chilling Time: 30 minutes

10-oz. pkg. frozen peas

1 cup diced celery

1 cup chopped fresh cauliflower florets

¼ cup diced scallions

1 cup chopped cashews

¼ cup crisp-cooked and crumbled bacon

¼ cup sour cream

½ cup ranch salad dressing

¼ tsp. Dijon mustard

1 small clove garlic, minced

1. Thaw peas. Drain.

2. In a large mixing bowl, combine peas, celery, cauliflower, onions, cashews, and bacon with sour cream.

3. In a small bowl, mix together ranch dressing, mustard, and minced garlic.

4. Begin by pouring only half of dressing over salad mixture. Toss gently. Add more if needed. (Dressing amount is generous.)

5. Chill before serving.

Makes 4 servings

Easy Fruit Salad

SHIRLEY SEARS • TISKILWA, IL

Prep Time: 20–25 minutes • Chilling Time: 3–4 hours

20-oz. can pineapple chunks,
    drained and halved

11-oz. can mandarin oranges,
    drained

15-oz. can apricot halves,
    drained and quartered

15-oz. can peach slices,
    drained and quartered

2 cups fresh green grapes,
    halved

3 bananas, sliced

20-oz. can peach pie filling

½ cup pecan halves, optional

1. In a large mixing bowl, stir all drained, canned fruit together.

2. Add grapes and sliced bananas.

3. Mix in peach pie filling.

4. Refrigerate several hours before serving.

5. Garnish with pecan halves just before serving, if you wish.

Makes 12 servings

Note: Drain the fruit well. If you need a larger salad, just use larger cans or more cans of fruit. You could add marshmallows or apples, too, if you want. This is quick to make. I keep these canned ingredients on hand all the time for last-minute preparation. I only need to purchase fresh grapes and bananas. My mom introduced me to this recipe in 1968, and I've given it to others many times.

DESSERTS

Grilled Peach Melba

STACY SCHMUCKER STOLTZFUS • ENOLA, PA

Prep Time: 10 minutes • Grilling Time: 5-10 minutes

4 large, unpeeled peaches or nectarines

2 tsp. sugar

2 cups red raspberries, fresh or frozen

sugar, optional

vanilla ice cream

1. Halve and pit peaches or nectarines.

2. Press fresh or thawed raspberries through sieve. Save juice and discard seeds. Sweeten to taste with sugar, if needed.

3. Grill unpeeled peaches cut side down approximately 2 minutes. Turn peaches over. With cut side up, fill each cavity with $\frac{1}{2}$ tsp. sugar, and continue grilling until grill marks appear on skins.

4. Serve immediately with a scoop of vanilla ice cream and drizzle with raspberry sauce.

Makes 4 servings

Cherry Berry Cobbler

CAROL DINUZZO • LATHAM, NY

Prep Time: 20 minutes • Baking Time: 45 minutes

21-oz. can cherry pie filling

10-oz. pkg. frozen red raspberries, thawed and drained

1 tsp. lemon juice

$\frac{1}{2}$ cup flour

$\frac{1}{4}$ cup sugar

$\frac{1}{8}$ tsp. salt

half a stick ($\frac{1}{4}$ cup) butter

1. In a saucepan, combine pie filling, raspberries, and lemon juice. Bring to a boil over medium heat.

2. Turn into a greased 1-qt. casserole.

3. In a bowl, mix together flour, sugar, and salt. Cut in butter until crumbly. Sprinkle over fruit.

4. Bake at 350°F for 45 minutes, or until browned and bubbly.

5. Serve warm (not hot) alone, or over ice cream.

Makes 6 servings

Butter Rum Bananas

SHARI JENSEN • FOUNTAIN, CO

Prep Time: 5 minutes • Cooking Time: 10 minutes

2 Tbsp. butter

1/2 cup sugar

2 Tbsp. water

2 Tbsp. light rum

1/2 Tbsp. lemon juice

grated peel of half a lemon

1/2 tsp. vanilla, or rum, flavoring

4 small bananas, peeled and halved

whipped cream, or ice cream

1. Melt butter in a large skillet. Add sugar and water. Stir well. Cook until reduced to heavy syrup, stirring occasionally so mixture doesn't stick to bottom of pan.

2. Add rum, lemon juice, rind, and your choice of flavoring. Cook 2 minutes, or until golden in color.

3. Remove from stove and add banana pieces. Plunge them into syrup, covering them as well as possible.

4. Serve warm, not hot, topped with a dollop of whipped cream or alongside scoops of ice cream.

Makes 4 servings

Ultimate Apple Crisp

JUDI MANOS • WEST ISLIP, NY

Prep Time: 15 minutes • Cooking/Baking Time: 25 minutes

6-8 apples (use baking apples if you can find them)

1 cup brown sugar

1 cup dry oats, quick or rolled (both work, but rolled have more texture)

1 cup flour

1 Tbsp. cinnamon

1 1/2 sticks (3/4 cup) butter, melted

half a stick (1/4 cup) butter, cut in pieces

1. Core, peel if you want, and slice apples. Place in microwave- and oven-safe baking dish (a Pyrex-type pie plate works well).

2. In a separate bowl, mix together brown sugar, oats, flour, and cinnamon. Add melted butter and mix with a fork until thoroughly mixed.

3. Place mixture on top of the apples. Microwave on High, uncovered, 10 minutes. Let stand 2 minutes.

4. Cut up the half stick of butter, and place on top of the heated apple mixture.

5. Place in oven and bake at 350°F for 15 minutes.

Makes 6-8 servings

Tapioca Pudding

MIRIAM CHRISTOPHEL • GOSHEN, IN

Prep Time: 10 minutes • Cooking Time: 5 minutes • Cooling Time: 20 minutes–2 hours

3 Tbsp. dry instant tapioca

1/3 cup sugar

1/8 tsp. salt

1 egg, beaten

3 cups milk

3/4 tsp. vanilla

1. In a 2-qt. saucepan, combine all ingredients except vanilla. Let stand 5 minutes.

2. Bring ingredients to a boil, stirring constantly. Boil 1 minute.

3. Remove from heat. Stir in vanilla.

4. Stir once after cooling 20 minutes.

5. Serve warm or cold.

Makes 5 servings

Note: This is good just as it is, or with a sliced banana and some whipped cream stirred in. It is our kids' favorite dessert. I like it because it isn't as sweet as some puddings are.

Sunny Spice Cake

KARLA BAER • NORTH LIME, OH

Prep Time: 10 minutes • Baking Time: 35 minutes • Cooling Time: 30–60 minutes

18 1/4 oz. pkg. dry spice cake mix

3.4-oz. pkg. butterscotch instant pudding

2 cups milk

2 eggs

peach halves, drained

frozen whipped topping, thawed

1. In a mixing bowl, blend together cake mix, pudding mix, milk, and eggs.

2. Pour into a greased 9" × 13" baking pan. Bake at 350°F for 35 minutes.

3. Cool.

4. When ready to serve, cut into serving-size pieces. Place a peach half on each serving of cake. Top each with a dollop of whipped topping.

Makes 15–20 servings

Entertaining

Hickory Smoked Brisket

JANET ROGGIE • LOWVILLE, NY

Prep Time: 5 minutes • Cooking Time: 8–12 hours • Ideal slow cooker size: 5-qt.

3-4-lb. beef brisket

¼ cup liquid smoke

½ tsp. celery salt

½ tsp. garlic salt

½ tsp. onion powder

1. Place beef on a piece of foil.

2. Sprinkle with remaining ingredients. Wrap foil securely around beef. Place in slow cooker.

3. Cover. Cook on Low 8–12 hours.

4. Serve warm with juice ladled over each slice.

   Makes 12–14 servings

Salsa Chuck Roast

HAZEL L. PROPST • OXFORD, PA

Prep Time: 15 minutes • Cooking Time: 7-8 hours • Ideal slow cooker size: 5-qt.

3-4-lb. chuck or round roast

1 Tbsp. oil

1 pkg. dry onion soup mix

2 cups water

1 cup salsa

1. Brown meat in a skillet in oil on both sides. Place in slow cooker.

2. Add remaining ingredients to drippings in pan. Simmer 2–3 minutes. Add to slow cooker.

3. Cover. Cook on Low 7–8 hours.

4. Serve with broth over noodles or rice.

   Makes 6 servings

There's-No-Easier Roast Beef

SUE PENNINGTON • BRIDGEWATER, VA

Prep Time: 5 minutes • Cooking Time: 6–8 hours • Ideal slow cooker size: 4-qt.

12-oz. bottle barbecue sauce

3–4-lb. beef roast

1. Pour half of barbecue sauce into bottom of slow cooker.

2. Add roast. Top with remaining barbecue sauce.

3. Cover. Cook on Low 6–8 hours.

4. Slice roast and serve with sauce.

Makes 6–8 servings

Note: Use an 18-oz. bottle of barbecue sauce if you prefer a juicier outcome.

Beef Roast in Beer

EVELYN PAGE • RIVERTON, WY

Prep Time: 5 minutes • Marinating Time: 8 hours • Cooking Time: 6–8 hours • Ideal slow cooker size: 3-qt.

2–3-lb. beef roast

1 can beer

1 onion, sliced

1. Place roast in slow cooker. Poke all over surface with fork.

2. Pour beer over roast. Cover. Refrigerate 8 hours.

3. Add sliced onion to slow cooker.

4. Cover. Cook on Low 6–8 hours.

Makes 5–6 servings

Variations: Brown roast in oil in a skillet on top and bottom before placing in cooker. Or mix together 1 cup cider vinegar and 2 Tbsp. Worcestershire sauce. Marinate roast in mixture in refrigerator for 2-4 hours. Either discard marinade when placing roast in cooker, or add it to the cooker.

Note: To thicken broth, mix together $\frac{1}{4}$ cup flour and 1 cup water until smooth. Twenty minutes before end of cooking time, remove roast from cooker. Stir flour paste into beef broth until smooth. Return roast to cooker and continue cooking. When finished, cut roast into chunks and serve with gravy.

Swiss Steak

JUDI MANOS • WEST ISLIP, NY

Prep Time: 15 minutes • Cooking Time: 6½–7½ hours • Ideal slow cooker size: 4-qt.

1½ lbs. boneless beef round steak

1 tsp. peppered seasoning salt

6-8 potatoes, cubed

1½ cups baby carrots

1 medium-sized onion, sliced

14½-oz. can diced tomatoes with basil, garlic, oregano

12-oz. jar home-style beef gravy

chopped fresh parsley

1. Cut beef into 6 pieces. Sprinkle with seasoning salt. Brown in skillet for about 8 minutes.

2. Layer potatoes, carrots, onion, and beef in slow cooker.

3. Combine tomatoes and gravy. Pour over beef and vegetables.

4. Cover. Cook on Low 7–9 hours.

5. Sprinkle with parsley.

Makes 6 servings

Variation: For more flavor, add ½ tsp. dried basil, ½ tsp. dried oregano, and 2 minced garlic cloves to the tomatoes and gravy in Step 3.

Pot-Roast Complete

NAOMI E. FAST • HESSTON, KS

Prep Time: 20 minutes • Cooking Time: 6–7½ hours • Ideal slow cooker size: 5-qt.

3-3½-lb. arm roast, boneless

2 large onions, sliced

½ cup brown sugar

⅓ cup soy sauce

⅓ cup cider vinegar

2 bay leaves

2-3 cloves garlic, minced

1 tsp. grated fresh ginger

1 cup julienned carrots, matchstick size

2 cups sliced button mushrooms

2-3 cups fresh spinach leaves, or 2 10-oz. pkgs. frozen spinach, drained

2 Tbsp. cornstarch

1. Place meat, topped with onions, in slow cooker.

2. Combine brown sugar, soy sauce, and vinegar. Pour over beef.

3. Add bay leaves, garlic, and ginger.

4. Cover. Cook on High 6–7 hours.

5. Spread carrots, mushrooms, and spinach over beef.

6. Cover. Cook on High 20 minutes.

7. Mix cornstarch with ½ cup broth from slow cooker. Return to slow cooker.

8. Cover. Cook 10 minutes more.

9. Serve over rice.

Makes 6-8 servings

Country-Style Ribs and Sauerkraut

RHONDA BURGOON • COLLINGSWOOD, NJ

Prep Time: 15 minutes • Cooking Time: 8-10 hours • Ideal slow cooker size: 5-qt.

16-oz. bag sauerkraut, rinsed
  and drained

1 onion, diced

1 red-skinned apple, chopped

2-3 lbs. country-style pork ribs

1 cup beer

1. Combine sauerkraut, onion, and apple in bottom of slow cooker.

2. Layer ribs over sauerkraut.

3. Pour beer over ribs just before turning on cooker.

4. Cover. Cook on Low 8–10 hours.

5. Serve with homemade cornbread and mashed potatoes, or serve deboned on a kaiser roll as a sandwich.

Makes 4–6 servings

Holiday Meatballs

JEAN ROBINSON • CINNAMINSON, NJ

Prep Time: 10 minutes • Cooking Time: 3-6 hours • Ideal slow cooker size: 5-qt.

2 15-oz. bottles hot ketchup

2 cups blackberry wine

2 12-oz. jars apple jelly

2 lbs. frozen, precooked
  meatballs, or your own
  favorite meatballs, cooked

1. Heat ketchup, wine, and jelly in slow cooker on High.

2. Add frozen meatballs.

3. Cover. Cook on High 4–6 hours. (If the meatballs are not frozen, cook on High 3–4 hours.)

Makes 20 servings

Variations: For those who like it hotter and spicier, put a bottle of XXXtra hot sauce on the table for them to add to their individual servings. If you prefer a less wine-y flavor, use 1 cup water and only 1 cup wine.

Pork Roast

LUCILLE AMOS • GREENSBORO, NC

Prep Time: 5 minutes • Cooking Time: 8–10 hours • Ideal slow cooker size: 5-qt.

1 Boston butt roast

1 cup Worcestershire sauce

1 cup brown sugar

1. Place roast in greased slow cooker.

2. Pour Worcestershire sauce over roast.

3. Pat brown sugar on roast.

4. Cover. Cook on High 1 hour. Reduce heat and cook on Low 8–10 hours.

5. Slice and serve topped with broth and drippings from cooker.

Makes 6–8 servings

Ham in Foil

JEANETTE OBERHOLTZER • MANHEIM, PA / VICKI DINKEL • SHARON SPRINGS, KS
JANET ROGGIE • LOWVILLE, NY

Prep Time: 5 minutes • Cooking Time: 7 hours • Ideal slow cooker size: 5-qt.

½ cup water

3-4-lb. precooked ham

liquid smoke

1. Pour water into slow cooker.

2. Sprinkle ham with liquid smoke. Wrap in foil. Place in slow cooker.

3. Cover. Cook on High 1 hour, and then on Low 6 hours.

4. Cut into thick chunks or ½" slices and serve.

Makes 8 servings

Super-Bowl Little Smokies

MARY SOMMERFELD • LANCASTER, PA / ALICIA DENLINGER • LANCASTER, PA

Prep Time: 5 minutes • Cooking Time: 2 hours • Ideal slow cooker size: 4-qt.

3 1-lb. pkgs. Little Smokies

8-oz. bottle Catalina dressing

splash of liquid smoke

1. Combine all ingredients in slow cooker.

2. Cover. Cook on Low 2 hours.

3. Use toothpicks to serve.

Makes 9–10 main-dish servings, or 15–20 appetizer servings

Aloha Chicken Cosmopolitan

DIANNA MILHIZER • BRIGHTON, MI

Prep Time: 10–15 minutes • Cooking Time: 6 hours • Ideal slow cooker size: 5-qt.

5 lbs. boneless, skinless chicken breasts, cut into strips or cubed

dash of salt

1 cup frozen orange juice

1 cup coconut milk

1 cup soy sauce

¼ cup sesame oil

1. Lightly salt chicken and then refrigerate 30 minutes.

2. Drain chicken of any juices that have gathered, then combine with other ingredients in slow cooker.

3. Cover. Cook on Low 6 hours.

4. Serve with white rice.

   Makes 12 servings

Saucy Apricot Chicken

ANNA STOLTZFUS • HONEY BROOK, PA

Prep Time: 5–10 minutes • Cooking Time: 4–5 hours • Ideal slow cooker size: 4-qt.

6 boneless, skinless chicken breast halves

2 12-oz. jars apricot preserves

1 pkg. dry onion soup mix

1. Place chicken in slow cooker.

2. Combine preserves and onion soup mix in separate bowl. Spoon over chicken.

3. Cover. Cook on Low 4–5 hours.

4. Serve over rice.

   Makes 6 servings

Chicken Alfredo

DAWN M. PROPST • LEVITTOWN, PA

Prep Time: 20 minutes • Cooking Time: 8 hours • Ideal slow cooker size: 4-qt.

16-oz. jar Alfredo sauce

4–6 boneless, skinless chicken breast halves

8 ozs. dry noodles, cooked

4-oz. can mushroom pieces and stems, drained

1 cup shredded mozzarella cheese, or ½ cup grated Parmesan cheese

1. Pour about one-third of Alfredo sauce in bottom of slow cooker.

2. Add chicken and cover with remaining sauce.

3. Cover. Cook on Low 8 hours.

4. Fifteen minutes before serving, add noodles and mushrooms, mixing well. Sprinkle top with cheese. Dish is ready to serve when cheese is melted.

5. Serve with green salad and Italian bread.

Makes 4–6 servings

Asian Chicken Cashew Dish

DOROTHY HORST • TISKILWA, IL

Prep Time: 15 minutes • Cooking Time: 2–9 hours • Ideal slow cooker size: 3-qt.

14-oz. can bean sprouts, drained

3 Tbsp. butter or margarine, melted

4 scallions, chopped

4-oz. can mushroom pieces

10¾-oz. can cream of mushroom soup

1 cup sliced celery

12½-oz. can chunk chicken breast, or 1 cup cooked chicken, cubed

1 Tbsp. soy sauce

1 cup cashew nuts

1. Combine all ingredients except nuts in slow cooker.

2. Cover. Cook on Low 4–9 hours, or on High 2–3 hours.

3. Stir in cashew nuts before serving.

4. Serve over rice.

Makes 6 servings

Levi's Sesame Chicken Wings

SHIRLEY UNTERNAHRER HINH • WAYLAND, IA

Prep Time: 35–40 minutes • Cooking Time: 2½–5 hours • Ideal slow cooker size: 4-qt.

3 lbs. chicken wings

salt to taste

pepper to taste

1¾ cups honey

1 cup soy sauce

½ cup ketchup

2 Tbsp. canola oil

2 Tbsp. sesame oil

2 cloves garlic, minced

toasted sesame seeds

1. Rinse wings. Cut at joint. Sprinkle with salt and pepper. Place on a broiler pan.

2. Broil 5" from top, 10 minutes on each side. Place chicken in slow cooker.

3. Combine remaining ingredients except sesame seeds. Pour over chicken.

4. Cover. Cook on Low 5 hours, or on High 2½ hours.

5. Sprinkle sesame seeds over top just before serving.

6. Serve as appetizer, or with white or brown rice and shredded lettuce to turn this appetizer into a meal.

Makes 16 appetizer servings, or 6–8 main-dish servings

Turkey Breast with Orange Sauce

JEAN BUTZER • BATAVIA, NY

Prep Time: 15–20 minutes • Cooking Time: 6–8 hours • Ideal slow cooker size: 5- to 6-qt.

1 large onion, chopped

3 cloves garlic, minced

1 tsp. dried rosemary

½ tsp. pepper

2-3-lb. boneless, skinless turkey breast

1½ cups orange juice

1. Place onion in slow cooker.

2. Combine garlic, rosemary, and pepper.

3. Make gashes in turkey, about three-quarters of way through, at 2" intervals. Stuff with herb mixture. Place turkey in slow cooker.

4. Pour juice over turkey.

5. Cover. Cook on Low 6–8 hours, or until turkey is no longer pink in center.

Makes 4–6 servings

Note: This very easy, impressive-looking and -tasting recipe is perfect for company.

Blessing Soup

ALIX NANCY BOTSFORD • SEMINOLE, OK

Prep Time: 20 minutes • Cooking Time: 4–12 hours • Ideal slow cooker size: 4- to 5-qt.

2 cups mixed dried beans
(10–18 different kinds)

2–2$\frac{1}{2}$ qts. water

1 cup diced ham

1 large onion, chopped

1 clove garlic, minced

juice of 1 lemon

14$\frac{1}{2}$-oz. can Italian tomatoes,
chopped

$\frac{1}{2}$ cup chopped sweet red
pepper

$\frac{1}{2}$ cup chopped celery

2 carrots, thinly sliced

1 tsp. salt

1 tsp. pepper

1. Sort and wash beans. Cover with water and soak several hours or overnight. Drain.

2. Place beans in cooker and add 2–2$\frac{1}{2}$ quarts water. Cook on High 2 hours.

3. Combine all ingredients with beans in slow cooker.

4. Add more water so that everything is just covered.

5. Cover. Cook on High 4–6 hours, or on Low 8–12 hours.

   Makes 8–10 servings

Crockpot Macaroni

LISA F. GOOD • HARRISONBURG, VA

Prep Time: 10 minutes • Cooking Time: 3–4 hours • Ideal slow cooker size: 4-qt.

1$\frac{1}{2}$ cups dry macaroni

3 Tbsp. butter

1 tsp. salt

$\frac{1}{2}$ lb. Velveeta cheese, sliced

1 qt. milk

1. Combine macaroni, butter, and salt in slow cooker.

2. Layer cheese over top.

3. Pour in milk.

4. Cover. Cook on High 3–4 hours, or until macaroni is soft.

   Makes 6 servings

Easy Wheatberries

ELAINE VIGODA • ROCHESTER, NY

Prep Time: 10 minutes • Cooking Time: 2 hours • Ideal slow cooker size: 4-qt.

1 cup wheatberries

1 cup couscous, or small
    pastalike orzo

14½-oz. can broth

½–1 broth can water

½ cup dried cranberries

1. Cover wheatberries with water and soak 2 hours before cooking. Drain. Spoon wheatberries into slow cooker.

2. Combine with remaining ingredients in slow cooker.

3. Cover. Cook on Low until liquid is absorbed and berries are soft, about 2 hours.

Makes 4–6 servings

Note: If dried cranberries are unavailable, use raisins. This is a satisfying vegetarian main dish, if you use vegetable broth.

Green Bean Casserole

BRENDA S. BURKHOLDER • PORT REPUBLIC, VA

Prep Time: 10–15 minutes • Cooking Time: 3–4 hours • Ideal slow cooker size: 3-qt.

1 qt. cooked green beans

½ tsp. sugar

10¾-oz. can cream of
    mushroom soup

¾ cup grated cheddar cheese

1. Combine ingredients in slow cooker.

2. Cover. Cook on Low 3–4 hours.

Makes 6–8 servings

Super Creamed Corn

RUTH ANN PENNER • HILLSBORO, KS / ALIX NANCY BOTSFORD • SEMINOLE, OK

Prep Time: 5–10 minutes • Cooking Time: 4 hours • Ideal slow cooker size: 3- to 4-qt.

2–3 lbs. frozen corn

8-oz. pkg. cream cheese,
    cubed

¼ cup butter or margarine,
    melted

2–3 Tbsp. sugar or honey

2–3 Tbsp. water, optional

1. Combine ingredients in slow cooker.

2. Cover. Cook on Low 4 hours.

3. Serve with meat loaf, turkey, or hamburgers.

Makes 8–12 servings

Glazed Sweet Potatoes

MARTHA HERSHEY • RONKS, PA

Prep Time: 20 minutes • Cooking Time: 3–4 hours • Ideal slow cooker size: 2-qt.

10 medium-sized sweet
  potatoes

1 stick (½ cup) butter, melted

¼ cup brown sugar

½ cup orange juice

½ tsp. salt

1. Cook sweet potatoes until just soft. Peel and cut in half.

2. Combine remaining ingredients. Pour over potatoes in slow cooker.

3. Cover. Cook on High 2½–3 hours, or until tender but not mushy.

Makes 8 servings

Note: The sweet potatoes can be cooked and peeled ahead of time, and frozen in a single layer. Defrost before putting in slow cooker.

Potatoes Perfect

NAOMI RESSLER • HARRISONBURG, VA

Prep Time: 20 minutes • Cooking Time: 3–10 hours • Ideal slow cooker size: 5-qt.

¼ lb. bacon, diced and
  browned until crisp

2 medium-sized onions, thinly
  sliced

6–8 medium-sized potatoes,
  thinly sliced

½ lb. cheddar cheese, thinly
  sliced

salt to taste

pepper to taste

2–4 Tbsp. butter or margarine

1. Layer half of bacon, onions, potatoes, and cheese in greased slow cooker. Season to taste.

2. Dot with butter. Repeat layers.

3. Cover. Cook on Low 8–10 hours, or on High 3–4 hours, or until potatoes are soft.

Makes 4–6 servings

Chocolate-Covered Pretzels

BETH MAURER • HARRISONBURG, VA

Prep Time: 10 minutes • Cooking Time: ½–1 hour • Ideal slow cooker size: 2-qt.

1 lb. white chocolate bark
  coating

2 blocks chocolate bark
  coating

1 bag pretzel rods

1. Chop white chocolate into small chunks. Place in slow cooker.

2. Cover. Heat at Low setting, stirring occasionally, until melted. Turn off cooker.

3. Using a spoon, coat three-quarters of each pretzel rod with chocolate. Place on waxed paper to cool.

4. Chop chocolate bark into small chunks. Microwave on High 1½ minutes. Stir. Microwave on High 1 minute. Stir. Microwave on High in 30-second intervals until chocolate is smooth when stirred. (Do not allow chocolate to get too hot or it will scorch.)

5. Put melted chocolate in small bag. Snip off corner of bag. Drizzle chocolate over white chocolate–covered pretzels.

Makes 10–12 servings

Note: These are easy to make; they taste wonderful and are good holiday gifts when placed in small gift bags!

Assumptions about Ingredients in *Fix-It and Forget-It 5-Ingredient Favorites*

flour = unbleached or white, and all-purpose

oatmeal or oats = dry, quick or rolled (old-fashioned), unless specified

pepper = black, finely ground

rice = regular, long-grain (not minute or instant unless specified)

salt = table salt

shortening = solid, not liquid

sugar = granulated sugar (not brown and not confectioners')

Three Hints

1. If you'd like to cook more at home—without being in a frenzy—go off by yourself with your cookbook some evening and make a week of menus. Then make a grocery list from that. Shop from your grocery list.

2. Thaw frozen food in a bowl in the fridge (not on the countertop). If you forget to stick the food in the fridge, put it in a microwave-safe bowl and defrost it in the microwave just before you're ready to use it.

3. Let roasted meat, as well as pasta dishes with cheese, rest 10 to 20 minutes before you slice or dish them. That will allow the juices to redistribute themselves throughout the cooked food. You'll have juicier meat, and a better presentation of your pasta dish.

Equivalent Measurements

dash = little less than $\frac{1}{8}$ tsp.

3 tsp. = 1 Tbsp.

2 Tbsp. = 1 oz.

4 Tbsp. = $\frac{1}{4}$ cup

5 Tbsp. plus 1 tsp. = $\frac{1}{3}$ cup

8 Tbsp. = $\frac{1}{2}$ cup

12 Tbsp. = $\frac{3}{4}$ cup

16 Tbsp. = 1 cup

1 cup = 8 ozs. liquid

2 cups = 1 pt.

4 cups = 1 qt.

4 qts. = 1 gal.

1 stick butter = $\frac{1}{4}$ lb.

1 stick butter = $\frac{1}{2}$ cup

1 stick butter = 8 Tbsp.

Beans, 1 lb. dried = 2–2$\frac{1}{2}$ cups cooked (depending upon the size of the beans)

Bell peppers, 1 large = 1 cup chopped

Cheese, hard (for example, cheddar, Swiss, Monterey Jack, mozzarella), 1 lb. grated = 4 cups

Cheese, cottage, 1 lb. = 2 cups

Chocolate chips, 6-oz. pkg. = 1 scant cup

Crackers (butter, saltines, snack), 20 single crackers = 1 cup crumbs

Herbs, 1 Tbsp. fresh = 1 tsp. dried

Lemon, 1 medium-sized = 2–3 Tbsp. juice

Lemon, 1 medium-sized = 2–3 tsp. grated rind

Mustard, 1 Tbsp. prepared = 1 tsp. dry or ground mustard

Oatmeal, 1 lb. dry = about 5 cups dry

Onion, 1 medium-sized = $\frac{1}{2}$ cup chopped

Pasta

Macaroni, penne, and other small or tubular shapes, 1 lb. dry = 4 cups uncooked

Noodles, 1 lb. dry = 6 cups uncooked

Spaghetti, linguine, fettucine, 1 lb. dry = 6 cups uncooked

Potatoes, white, 1 lb. = 3 medium-sized potatoes = 2 cups mashed

Potatoes, sweet, 1 lb. = 3 medium-sized potatoes = 2 cups mashed

Rice, 1 lb. dry = 2 cups uncooked

Sugar, confectioners', 1 lb. = 3$\frac{1}{2}$ cups sifted

Whipping cream, 1 cup unwhipped = 2 cups whipped

Whipped topping, 8-oz. container = 3 cups

Yeast, dry, 1 envelope ($\frac{1}{4}$ oz.) = 1 Tbsp.

Substitute Ingredients—
For When You're in a Pinch

For 1 cup **buttermilk**—use 1 cup plain yogurt; or pour 1⅓ Tbsp. lemon juice or vinegar into a 1-cup measure. Fill the cup with milk. Stir and let stand 5 minutes. Stir again before using.

For 1 oz. **unsweetened baking chocolate**—stir together 3 Tbsp. unsweetened cocoa powder and 1 Tbsp. butter, softened.

For 1 Tbsp. **cornstarch**—use 2 Tbsp. all-purpose flour; or 4 tsp. minute tapioca.

For 1 **garlic clove**—use ¼ tsp. garlic salt (reduce salt in recipe by ⅛ tsp.); or ⅛ tsp. garlic powder.

For 1 Tbsp. **fresh herbs**—use 1 tsp. dried herbs.

For ½ lb. **fresh mushrooms**—use 1 6-oz. can mushrooms, drained.

For 1 Tbsp. **prepared mustard**—use 1 tsp. dry or ground mustard.

For 1 medium-sized **fresh onion**—use 2 Tbsp. minced dried onion; or 2 tsp. onion salt (reduce salt in recipe by 1 tsp.); or 1 tsp. onion powder. *Note:* These substitutions will work for meatballs and meat loaf, but not for sautéing.

For 1 cup **sour milk**—use 1 cup plain yogurt; or pour 1 Tbsp. lemon juice or vinegar into a 1-cup measure. Fill with milk. Stir and then let stand 5 minutes. Stir again before using.

For 2 Tbsp. **tapioca**—use 3 Tbsp. all-purpose flour.

For 1 cup **canned tomatoes**—use 1⅓ cups diced fresh tomatoes, cooked gently for 10 minutes.

For 1 Tbsp. **tomato paste**—use 1 Tbsp. ketchup.

For 1 Tbsp. **vinegar**—use 1 Tbsp. lemon juice.

For 1 cup **heavy cream**—add ⅓ cup melted butter to ¾ cup milk. *Note:* This will work for baking and cooking, but not for whipping.

For 1 cup **whipping cream**—chill thoroughly ⅔ cup evaporated milk, plus the bowl and beaters, then whip; or use 2 cups purchased whipped topping.

For ½ cup **wine**—pour 2 Tbsp. wine vinegar into a ½-cup measure. Fill with broth (chicken, beef, or vegetable). Stir and then let stand 5 minutes. Stir again before using.

Kitchen Tools and Equipment You May Have Overlooked

1. Make sure you have a little electric vegetable chopper, the size that will handle 1 cup of ingredients at a time.

2. Don't try to cook without a good paring knife that's sharp (and holds its edge) and fits in your hand.

3. Almost as important—a good chef's knife (we always called it a "butcher" knife) with a wide, sharp blade that's about 8 inches long, good for making strong cuts through meats.

4. You really ought to have a good serrated knife with a long blade, perfect for slicing bread.

5. Invest in at least one broad, flexible, heat-resistant spatula. And also a narrow one.

6. You ought to have a minimum of two wooden spoons, each with a 10- to 12-inch-long handle. They're perfect for stirring without scratching.

7. Get a washable cutting board. You'll still need it, even though you have an electric vegetable chopper (#1 above).

8. A medium-sized whisk takes care of persistent lumps in batters, gravies, and sauces when there aren't supposed to be any.

9. Get yourself a salad spinner.

Index

An asterisk (*) indicates that photos are shown in the insert pages.